The Poems of George Meredith

Volume 2

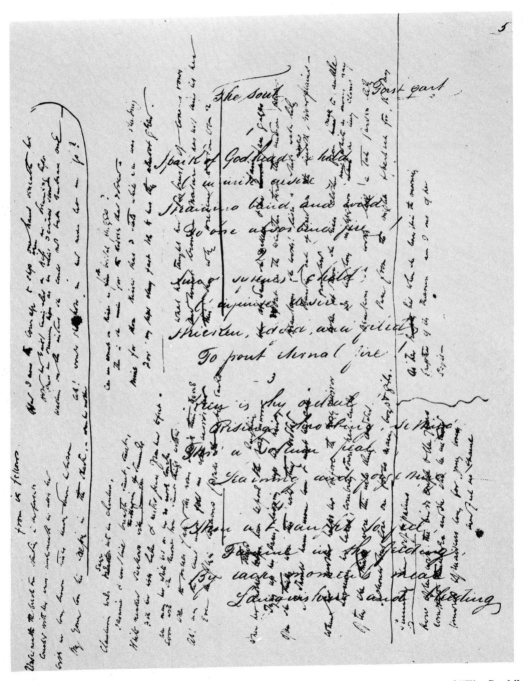

Facsimile of the first draft of "Love in the Valley" written across the first four stanzas of "The Soul."
From an early Meredith notebook in Beinecke Library, Yale University.

The Poems of George Meredith

EDITED BY

Phyllis B. Bartlett

VOLUME 2

New Haven and London, Yale University Press

1978

Designed by Helen Buzyna and John O. C. McCrillis
and set in Times New Roman type.
Printed in the United States of America by
The Murray Printing Co., Westford, Massachusetts.

Published in Great Britain, Europe, Africa, and
Asia (except Japan) by Yale University Press, Ltd., London.
Distributed in Latin America by Kaiman & Polon,
Inc., New York City; in Australia and New Zealand
by Book & Film Services, Artarmon, N.S.W., Australia;
and in Japan by Harper & Row, Publishers,
Tokyo Office.

The decorative device used on the binding
is from the title page of George Meredith,
Poems (London: Constable and Company Ltd., 1910).

Contents

VOLUME 2

PART II

POEMS PUBLISHED BUT NOT COLLECTED BY MEREDITH

PART III

POSTHUMOUSLY PUBLISHED POEMS AND TRIVIA

PART IV

UNPUBLISHED POEMS AND FRAGMENTS

Part II
Poems Published but Not Collected by Meredith

Chillianwallah

One of the last battles of the Sikh Wars was that of Chillianwalla, fought at considerable loss to the British on January 13, 1849.

Chillianwallah, Chillianwallah!
　　Where our brothers fought and bled!
Oh thy name is natural music,
　　And a dirge above the dead!
Though we have not been defeated,
　　Though we can't be overcome,
Still, whene'er thou art repeated,
　　I would fain that grief were dumb.

Chillianwallah, Chillianwallah!
　　'Tis a name so sad and strange,　　　　　　　　10
Like a breeze through midnight harpstrings
　　Ringing many a mournful change;
But the wildness and the sorrow
　　Having a meaning of their own—
Oh, whereof no glad to-morrow
　　Can relieve the dismal tone!

Copy-text: Chambers's Edinburgh Journal. *Previously printed in* Chambers's Edinburgh Journal, *n.s. 288 (7 July 1849);* Elmer Bailey, The Novels of George Meredith (*New York: Scribner, 1907); a brochure (1909)* [*MBF #49*]*;* Poems Written in Early Youth (*1909); Edition de Luxe 4 (posth.);* The Contributions of George Meredith to the "Monthly Observer," January–July 1849, *edited Maurice Buxton Forman (Edinburgh: printed for private circulation, 1928); and Robert E. Sencourt, "Unpublished Poems of Meredith,"* Commonweal 10 *(22 May 1929). MS:* "The Monthly Observer," *April 1849, subtitle:* On the recent battle on the banks of Jhelum.

6 can't be overcome] cannot be o'ercome *MS*
8 that grief were] be deaf or *MS*
15 O, whereof] Whereof *MS*
16 *MS:* Can ever change the tone,

Chillianwallah, Chillianwallah!
    'Tis a village dark and low,
By the bloody Jhelum River,
    Bridged by the foreboding foe;   20
And across the wintry water
    He is ready to retreat,
When the carnage and the slaughter
    Shall have paid for his defeat.

Chillianwallah, Chillianwallah!
    'Tis a wild and dreary plain,
Strewn with plots of thickest jungle,
    Matted with the gory stain.
There the murder-mouthed artillery,
    In the deadly ambuscade,   30
Wrought the thunder of its treachery
    On the skeleton brigade.

Chillianwallah, Chillianwallah!
    When the night set in with rain,
Came the savage plundering devils
    To their work among the slain;
And the wounded and the dying
    In cold blood did share the doom
Of their comrades round them lying,
    Stiff in the dead skyless gloom.   40

Between lines 16 and 17 MS:

Chillianwallah, Chillianwallah!
    Thou should'st be victorious ground,
Since the days of Alexander
    Thou hast been a spot renowned,
Thou art wreathed from distant ages
    In the Laurel of his Fame,
But alas! in future pages
    Can our England write the same?—

20 foreboding] providing *MS*
28 stain] slain *MS*
29 murder-mouthed] covertclose *MS*
30 deadly] gaping *MS*
31 *MS:* Wrote its death blank hand of treachery,   Wrok *misp. Chambers*

Chillianwallah, Chillianwallah!
    Thou wilt be a doleful chord,
And a mystic note of mourning
    That will need no chiming word;
And that heart will leap with anguish
    Who may understand thee best;
But the hearts of all will languish
    Till thy memory is at rest.

New Year's Eve

New Year! New Year! come over the snow,
    A thousand songs call to thee!
A thousand circles wait thee now,
    A thousand firesides woo thee!
The night is listening for the bells,
The doors are wide where the poor man dwells,
The cottage glows, the mansion gleams,
And dusky red o'er the deep snow streams.
Old Time sits mute in his silent place,
They watch his motions, they mark his face,   10
He starts! he calls! and a merry, merry din
Of voices and bells brings the New Year in.

      Happy New Year! Happy New Year!
      Give us all things kind and dear,
      And when thou art laid in earth—
      May thy death be as blithe as thy birth.

CHILLIANWALLAH

45 that] the *MS*
46 Who] That *MS*
47 But] And *MS*   hearts] hopes *MS, Chambers and thereafter, corr. GM letter,*
June 12, 1849

NEW YEAR'S EVE

Copy-text: Household Words 2 *(28 December 1850). Also printed in* TP.

Old Year! Old Year! sink down in thy vaults,
  All nature doth eschew thee—
Lie buried with all thy meeds and faults,
  For nothing can renew thee!   20
Light are the feet that dance thee dead!
Merry the music that rolls o'er thy head!
Die with thy last, loving glance on them,
Whose joyance is thy requiem.
Farewell, farewell, all good or ill
That thou hast sown, will thy son fulfil;
Give him a last word now, to heed
The good and shun the evil seed.

      Farewell, Old Year! Farewell, Old Year!
      Many a bright eye owes thee a tear!   30
      Thou wilt never again have birth;
      Hush thee calm in the bosom of earth.

New Year! New Year! come sit at the feast,
  A thousand hands prepare thee!
This night shall all men call thee guest,
  This night may all men share thee;
Soon may we know thee tried and true;
Give to the student his wreath in view!
Give to the lover his yearning bride!
Soon may we know thee true and tried—   40
Make free the slave, and make the free
Learn all the duties of charity;
Let pride die off, let love increase,
And prosper all the ways of peace!

      Happy New Year! Happy New Year!
      Give us all things kind and dear,
      And when thou art laid in earth—
      May thy death be as blithe as thy birth.

24 requiem] *TP* regimen *misp. HW*

The Congress of Nations

These verses herald the opening on May 1, 1851, of the Great Exhibition at the Crystal Palace in Hyde Park.

A mighty dome is rear'd in solemn state,
    To hold the produce of the World's invention;
The spacious palace of the labouring Great,
    Whose bloodless triumphs history loves to mention.

From every land which Man has made his home,
    Where arts and science with due culture flourish,
O'er trackless wastes and billows crown'd with foam,
    They come, the ardent Mind with food to nourish.

The trophies of the Past fade into gloom,
    Which conquerors planted on the field of battle;   10
Where breathing armies sank before their doom,
    And shouts of glory drown'd the low death-rattle.

These things were once, while yet the World was young;
    Ere it drank wisdom from the fount of reason;
Now, let a curtain o'er such scenes be hung—
    War's winter fled, we hail a softer season.

The sunder'd children of the human race,
    Crossing their bounds to mingle with each other,
In foreign nations kindred features trace,
    And learn that every mortal is their brother.   20

The love of Art engenders love to Man,
    And this, in turn, the love of his Creator;
'Tis Ignorance that mars Heaven's gracious plan,
    And rears in blood the murderer and man-hater.

Copy-text: Household Words 2 (*8 March 1851*). *Also printed in* TP.

A glorious epoch brightens history's page,
   Shedding upon the Future dazzling lustre;
How proud the thought that England is the stage,
   Which shall re-echo with the Nation's muster!

Infancy and Age

GM sent this poem, along with *Sorrows and Joys* and *The Two Black-birds*, to publisher John W. Parker on December 12, 1850, for inclusion in his first volume of poems, saying that the three poems were selected from "those published in 'Household Words.'" But, inasmuch as *Infancy and Age* was not published until April 19, 1851, GM could only have meant that Dickens had accepted it for *Household Words*. The poem did not appear in *Poems* (1851).

Sweet is the light of infancy, and sweet
The glimmering halo round the brows of age!
But mystic more than beautiful are both!—
Mystic with angels' smiles and far-shed gleams

INFANCY AND AGE

Copy-text: Household Words 3 (*19 April 1851*). *Also printed in* TP. *MS:* NB B, [*p.* 6].
Dr. 1, title del.: "*Infancy and Age*"; *dr. 2, no title, with two frags. All in faint pencil.*
1–13 *not in dr. 1, instead:*

    'Tis strange [the world *del.*] that men should banish gentle thoughts
    And sentiments of beauty, such as make their brain
    The whole wide world one family of love—
    Thoughts that the simplest heart conceives, believes
    And cherishes—thoughts that the soul of man
    Puts forth by nature as earth throws up flowers
    And but the bitter wind the [hanging *del.*] murky blight
    That hides the sky & weighs the dancing air
    Fall on them, they would bud & breathe & clothe
    Creation in the loveliest hues & show   10
    The Arcady for which mankind was made—

    For do but look on that which all men shun—
    Death and the ghosts of Dust, with such an eye,
    And lo! with what a *or* in how much calm complacent wisdom
    With what a genuine sweetness o'er the soul
    Sinks that delightful sense of quiet sleep—
    Mother of ever young eternity!
    From which with freshened vigour we shall rise

Of something much diviner than the full
Meridian,—something strange with wondrous grace!
And both are kin. The faint horizon round
Which travels the dim globe from West to East
And binds in a ring of tender amethyst
The dying splendour with the dawning rose,   10
Is but the effluence of that which crowns
Their passage thro' the world; consummate day!
From angels' arms they come, to angels' arms
They go; young eyes that greet the growing beams,
And weary lids that watch them wink and fade,
Behold the same soft twilight of the sky;
The difference is but of morn and eve.
Fresh morn and fading eve! twin mothers dear,
Whose bosoms give the milk of mortal hours
To one and to the other, evermore—   20
Eternity, nursing them both as babes!
And both are babes!—one rock'd in the lap of life
And one in the lap of death!

> Timeless and tireless!—[on del.] to the brows of age
> What mysteries of reverence belong!   20
> To infancy with its first feeble cry
> What adoration and delicious hope!
> To both what grateful & inspiring sense
> Of wonder, kindling wonder through the years!

2 The glimmering halo] The light that glimmers *frags. A, B*
3 *frag. A:* And both are beauteous in the angels smiles   *frag. B:* And both are sacred, for the loving smiles
4 *frag. A:* For angels give the one & angels take   *frag. B:* Of angels are upon them shed] off *dr. 2*
6 wondrous] awful *dr. 2*
8 the dim globe] around the world *dr. 2*
11 crowns] crown'd *dr. 2*
13 angels'] angel *dr. 2*   angels'] angel *dr. 2*
14 *dr. 1:* The child just smiling on the growing light
15 *dr. 1:* The old man sighing farewell as it fades
16 Behold] Look on *dr. 1*   sky] skies *dr. 1*
18–21 *not in dr. 1, instead:*
> From Angels arms comes one & in the arms   [*Cf. line 13*]
> Of angels sinks the other, this the sun
> Awaits & that *or* one [?] the other robed [?] with stars
20 the other] another *dr. 2*
23 *dr. 1:* And one in the lap of Death—snow crested, both.

Time

The heart may live a lifetime in an hour,
    And well embrace
A lifetime's energy, and strength, and power,
    Within that space.

We do it wrong, Time by one rule to reckon;
    For by our state—
As our stern fears deter, or fond hopes beckon—
    Should it bear date.

A minute's agony appears a day:
    Years of delight   10
Seem, traced by memory, having passed away,
    Transient as light.

With Love Time flies, Hate makes it linger;
    Says Youth, "Be past!"
Age, pointing to its sands with eager finger,
    Murmurs, "Too fast!"

Force and His Master

GM may have taken his first title for this poem, "The Labouring Giant," from Tennyson's *In Memoriam*, published on June 1, 1850. In lyric 118 Tennyson describes the "work of Time" as "The giant labouring in his youth." Tennyson hoped that what science was learning of the history of man would inspire him to reach for an ever "higher race," in order to work "out the beast" in him.

For a much later comment on force, see *Alsace-Lorraine*, IX. 45–52 (p. 606).

TIME

Copy-text: Household Words *3 (24 May 1851). Also printed in* TP.

FORCE AND HIS MASTER

Copy-text: Household Words *3 (13 September 1851). Also printed in* TP. *MSS:* NB A. *MS 1, [pp. 12–13], working draft, title: "The Labouring Giant"; MS 2, [p. 11], fair copy of lines 1–32.*

With sleepless toil on land and wave,
    A Giant served a Master wise;
This Giant seem'd a simple slave,
    But was a Genie in disguise.

His voice was power, his breath was speed;
    He gathered distance in his hands;
And in his track Time sow'd his seed
    With double hours and swifter sands.

The Elements with whom he fought
    And wrestled in his youthful wars,   10
Began, beholding all he wrought,
    To feel a mightier will than theirs.

A mightier will, and one more firm
    Of purpose, never turned aside;
With gentleness to spare the worm,
    And strength to pluck the roots of pride.

The hearth, that was his place of birth,
    With tenderness he loved, and coursed
The boundaries of the love-link'd earth
    To do the missions it enforced.   20

And over oceans, rocks, and straits,
    He flew; and in his arms he closed
The nations; till their warring fates
    On one united faith reposed.

4 Genie] Genii *MSS 1, 2*
Between 8–9, lines 17–20 appear in MS 1
10 wars] cares *MS 1*
Between 12–13, MS 1 del.:

        In solemn conclave then they met,
        And full of instance argued thus;
        Behold! our chieftain he shall sit,
        For surely he is born of us.

16 pluck] crush *del. MS 1*
21–24 *not in MS 1*

Well pleased the Master then beheld
    A work that made him feel divine;
With majesty his bosom swell'd,
    And thence he mused a dark design.

"Am I not guide where'er he goes?
    The ship hangs on the helmsman's skill;   30
From me the pilot impulse flows;
    The Giant shall obey my will."

He in the Giant's youth had fear'd
    The wild rebounding of his might;
And oft he trembled as he steer'd
    To meet the terrors of his sight.

But now that use has conquered dread,
    His tyrant spirits grow awake,—
So, on a day, he hail'd, and led
    The Giant to his throne, and spake:—   40

"Thou see'st a region at thy feet;
    'Tis threatened by each hostile wind
That blows from lands with foes replete,
    And these are children of my kind.

"Thou, therefore, go, I charge thee, forth,
    And gathering in thy forces all,
Disperse thyself, till South and North
    And East and West before me fall.

25 then beheld] did behold *MS 1*
27 *MS 1:* And richer than a realm of gold;
28 And thence] He took *or* And thence *MS 1*   mused] nursed *MS 1*
31 *MS 1:* For haven joy is shipwreck woes;—*or* From me the guiding impulse flows
32 *MS 1:* He must [shall *MS 2*] obey whate'er I will.
33 He] For *MS 1*   had] he *MS 1*
35 oft] still *del. MS 1*
38 grow] all *MS 1*
39 So] And *or* So *MS 1*
43 replete] complete *MS 1*

"In ways and means I know thee strong,
　　For thou art Force, and therefore hast　　　　50
Dominion over Right and Wrong,
　　And over all things—but the Past.

"Go!" but the Giant stirr'd no step;
　　His dark eyes flash'd, and trembling light
Electric ran across his lip,
　　And o'er his forehead hung with night.

White clouds wrapt round his rising form,
　　Where lightnings shot like veins of fire;
And with a voice like coming storm,
　　He answer'd from his smoke-wreath'd spire.　　　60

"O Master! as thy Slave I serve,
　　And work thy will in love and awe,
And from thy will I cannot swerve,
　　While thou obey'st thy higher Law.

"But know that, when thou fail'st to heed
　　That Law which is the Lord of thee,
And turnest to revenge and greed,
　　Thou art no longer Lord of me.

"It is my mission to create;
　　A mission I fulfil with joy:　　　　70
Yet blackly am I arm'd by fate
　　With equal powers to destroy.

49 *MS 1 del.:* I know thee strong in ways & means
57 White] Dark *del. MS 1*
58 shot] ran *MS 1*
60 answered from] call'd aloud *del. MS 1*
62 love] fear *del. MS 1*

Between 64–65, MS 1 del.: For thou art servant to a Lord

66 which] that *del. MS 1*
70 I fulfil] that I work *MS 1*
72 equal] greater *MS 1*

"Creation and Destruction, now
    Are wrestling for the regal world;
And one must conquer, one must bow,
    Which side soever I am hurl'd.

"Behold! I wait upon thy breath
    To make thee blest, or most accurst;
But should'st thou bid me reap for Death
    His victims—*Thou* wilt be the first."   80

The Gentleness of Death

Who that can feel the gentleness of Death,
    Sees not the loveliness of Life? and who,
Breathing content his natural joyous breath,
    Could fail to feel that Death is Nature, too?
And not the alien foe his fears dictated,
A viewless terror, heard but to be hated.

One died that was beloved of all around;
    And, dying, grasped a flower of early spring,
To hold beside her in the quiet ground,
    While every season shook its varied wing.   10
The pale flower died with her; but soon rose others,
Not planted by her sisters or her brothers.

FORCE AND HIS MASTER

75 And one must] And each will *or* And one must *MS 1*
77–78 *MS 1 del.:*

                Behold! the choice is thine—the die
                To be most bless'd or most accurst,

78 blest, or most] blessed or *MS 1*
79 bid me reap] choose me gather *or* [bid] me reap *MS 1*
80 His *or* More *MS 1*

THE GENTLENESS OF DEATH

Copy-text: Household Words *4 (4 October 1851). Also printed in* TP.

Her sisters and her brothers came each day,
    And wondered to behold the young fresh flowers,
Like that she held before she pass'd away—
    Warm'd by the sun and cherished by the showers:
And they would not believe the sweet bird's sowing
Had brought the flowers about her gravestone growing.

They said—These flowers are offspring of the same
    That lies beside our sister underneath;   20
And unto us as messengers they came
    From her, and we will bind them in a wreath,
To hang amid the dews that glisten purely,
And every spring will say, "she liveth surely."

So thus Death grew to them most holy sweet;
    A bringer and a taker of all love:
The link to that which lay beneath their feet,
    The bond of all they looked for from above.
His gentleness was on them, and His duty
Gave all their future life redoubled beauty.   30

A Word from the Cannon's Mouth

Tremble no more to hear my voice!
    For not in thunders, as of old,
When the far-echoing deadly noise,
    That over hill and hollow roll'd,
Was follow'd by the wild death-shriek,—
But harmless as a child, I speak.

Tremble no more! Not charged am I,
    As in those days, with iron shot,
And smoke that blacken'd the blue sky,
    And made the earth one reeking blot;   10
My mission ends its mortal lease,
And I would speak before I cease.

A WORD FROM THE CANNON'S MOUTH

Copy-text: Household Words *4 (25 October 1851). Also printed in* TP.

For I have play'd a mighty part
    In human change, and have, therefore,
A right my burthen to impart,
    Ere I become a thing of yore:
A monster in the calendar
And annals of red-written war.

Have I not built imperial thrones,
    And batter'd old foundations down?   20
Old warfare was a strife of crones
    Before I rose on field, and town,
And heaving deck,—a creature strange,—
And utter'd the great voice of Change!

A voice that I must hear in turn,
    And feel to be a thing of doom;—
A voice that, day by day, I yearn
    To hear, as now, with gradual boom,
It rises in acclaiming notes
From myriads of united throats.   30

The cry is "Peace!" and, at the word,
    I feel as though my time were come,—
The time when I shall not be heard;
    For I am dead when I am dumb.
The earth may claim a parting roar,
And I shall shake its fields no more.

'Tis well! I came when I was call'd;
    I go before a growing good:
May that fair seed be not forestall'd
    By Tyranny's last struggling brood,—   40
A deeper curse—a fiercer ill—
Than war, or perverse human will.

I go. Ambition cannot now
    Abuse me or its purpose vile;
Nor Avarice claim the peaceful plough

By my curst aid and light the while.
The crimes of monarchs and of states
Henceforth I leave unto the Fates.

Or do I dream?—who thus so long
    Have stood upon this bastion'd height,   50
Uncall'd to mediate with Wrong,
    In its perpetual strife with Right:—
Is it a dream—that I have done,
And see the setting of my sun?

Queen Zuleima

The play *Zapolya*, by Coleridge (published 1817), inspired this dramatic
monologue.

Not less a Queen, because I wear
No crown upon my weeping hair!

Not less a Mother, that my breast
Is childless, and a rifled nest!

Not less a Woman, for the oath
I swore—to be avenged for both!

O youth! thou hast a comely grace;
Strange sympathy is in thy face.

QUEEN ZULEIMA

Copy-text: Household Words 4 (*1 November 1851*). *Also printed in* TP. *MSS:* NB A,
[*p. 4*]; Berg, *between pp. 20 and 21.*

1 wear *or* brow *NB A*
2 weeping *or* wandering *NB A*

Between 2 and 3 NB A: No golden circlet honors now.

8 sympathy] tenderness *B*

And hast thou heard of mine and me,
In that old City by the sea?   10

Give me thy hand, and let me feel
What one soft pressure may reveal.

I read by hands; 'twas thus I tried
My husband, when I was a bride.

'Tis well! but that it throbs too much,
As if it felt its mother's touch.

Thy mother? Tell me, is she far?
And art thou, youth, her wand'ring star?

It trembles! Dost thou fear a Queen
Discrowned, and seen as I am seen?   20

Nay! kneel not, kneel not! Wherefore thus
Is this wild trembling come on us?

Two strangers! Did I tremble then
Before the hosts of eager men:

That sea of savage lips and eyes,
Clamouring murder to the skies?

They threw my husband from his throne.
They mock'd me as I sat alone.

---

12 may] can *NB A*
After 12, NB A: lines 15 and 16
After 14: for a long passage in B, see Supplementary Textual Notes.
After 18 NB A:
          No mother as I have no son
          Misfortune therefore[?] made us one.
19 Dost thou fear a Queen] Thou art stalwart firm *del. NB A*
20 *NB A:* Thou wouldst not spurn a woman[?] *or* Discrown'd & seen as I am seen.
21 kneel not, kneel not] kneel not. Listen! *or* Kneel not *NB A*
24 eager] murderous *NB A*

I sat in state, and let them mock:
Mad waves against the regal rock! 30

Robed and crown'd I calmly smiled,
And lifted up my little child.

"Your future King!" I cried aloud;
And many of the people bow'd.

But as I held it, strode a man—
A stern, black-bearded ruffian—

He strode, and snatched my child away,
Albeit I left my throne to pray.

I clung about his knotty knees,
And wept and shriek'd my agonies. 40

I came again to conscious breath;
I heard the anguish worse than death.

No handmaid near, but one old nurse,
Whose face flashed like a living curse;

And yet her wrinkled woman's heart
Fell faltering on the bitterest part.

She could not speak it—woe is me!
Made human by my misery.

But thou art changed! Rise from the spot;
Still at my feet? I say, kneel not! 50

Thou claspest me! What word?—what word?—
Mother?—is't "Mother" that I heard?

Mother, and Queen?—O, hungry breast,
Feed on his beauty!—Rest, rest, rest!

Believe, it, O true heart! now trace
Thy trembling when thou saw'st his face;

And weep, that thrones should dawn again,
To give our pleasure pomp—and pain.

Weep, weep, to see him standing there,
With his proud father's noble air.

60

Joy, Joy! but weep that there should be
So proud a thing as majesty.

I fear it, now it is re-won;
We will arise and go, my son!

Britain

My faith is in my native land;
    Her maids are pure, her sons are brave;
And Liberty sails from her strand,
    That free-born men may free the slave.
Her courage is the fear of God:
    From Him she gathers strength complete,
To tread the path that One hath trod,
    And One, alone, with naked feet.

QUEEN ZULEIMA
For insertion probably between 56 and 57 margin B:
    And is it so? 'tis so indeed!
    I do believe it in my need.
    Nay, can I doubt, with that twin-fleck
    That was upon my young child's neck!
    And must I call that man our friend,
    Who snatcht my child, and made me bend?
    He waits my will, my will; to fight
    The battle of our bleeding right?
    He saved you and has rear'd you—he!
    The woman thanks him meagrely.

57 And] Yet *B*
59–60 *not in B*
BRITAIN
Copy-text: Household Words *4 (22 November 1851). Also printed in* TP.

She is not what she yet may be;
    And, therefore, till her work is done,   10
I know she marches onward free,
    On to the setting of her sun.
Great splendour will the world behold;
    The West will shine with wondrous light,
And she, on clouds of crumbling gold,
    Will sink to her immortal night.

A welcome hand she reaches out
    To modern friend, or ancient foe;
Nor can her grasp give birth to doubt
    Of honest faith, or friendship slow.   20
In forward steps her sons are bold,
    But to her system firm and true,
They know the value of the Old,
    They feel the virtue of the New.

Her may the Arts for evermore
    Ennoble for their nourriture!
Her may the distant sheening shore
    Enrich; and may her temples pure
To all men preach the living truth!
    But never let her missions roam   30
Unblest abroad, while age and youth
    Are pining to be taught at home.

Her mighty names can never die;
    The Fountain-spring baptised their years:
She is the foremost in the eye
    Of Destiny, through them and theirs;
And while her sons remain sincere,
    And what they feel speak freely forth,
The moving world may never fear
    The icy fetters of the North.   40

Familiar Things

There is a truth that travel brings,
    A truth of homely birth;
We dwell among familiar things,
    And little know their worth.
The emigrant in distant lands,
    The sailor on the sea,
For all that, round us, silent stands,
    Have deeper hearts than we.

We dwell among familiar things;
    And daily, with dull sight,   10
We touch a thousand secret springs
    Of sorrow and delight:
Delight and reverential bliss
    To those who, exiled far,
Stretch dreaming arms to clasp and kiss
    Each little household star.

We dwell among familiar things;
    We know them by their use;
And, by their many minist'rings,
    Their value we deduce: 20
Forgetful each has had an eye,
    And each can speak, though dumb;
And, of the ghostly days gone by,
    Strange witness might become.

We dwell among familiar things;
    But should it be our lot
To sever all the binding-strings
    That form the household knot;

Copy-text: Household Words *4 (6 December 1851). Also printed in* TP.

To wander upon alien mould,
    And cross the restless foam;—   30
Now clearly should we then behold
    The Deities of Home!

A Child's Prayer

The day is gone, the night is come,
    The night for quiet rest:
And every little bird has flown
    Home to its downy nest.

The robin was the last to go,
    Upon the leafless bough
He sang his evening hymn to God,
    And he is silent now.

The bee is hushed within the hive,
    Shut is the daisy's eye;   10
The stars alone are peeping forth
    From out the darkened sky.

No, not the stars alone; for God
    Has heard what I have said:
His eye looks on His little child,
    Kneeling beside its bed.

He kindly hears me thank him now
    For all that he has given,
For friends, and books, and clothes, and food;
    But most of all for Heaven,   20

Where I shall go when I am dead,
    If truly I do right;
Where I shall meet all those I love,
    As Angels pure and bright.

A CHILD'S PRAYER

Copy-text: Household Words 4 *(13 December 1851). Also printed in* TP.

The Glastonbury Thorn

The poem appeared in *Household Words* with the following note: "There is an old legend that Joseph of Arimathea came to Glastonbury, and planted there a *thorn*, which grew and flourished, and blossomed every Christmas-day."

For the disciple of Jesus, Joseph of Arimathea, see Matt. 27:59. GM might have added that the thorn was supposed to be from the true crown of thorns.

There grew, within a favour'd vale,
As old traditions tell the tale,
A famous, flowering, Eastern thorn,
Which blossom'd every Christmas morn.

No lowly hearth, no lordly hall,
New dress'd for the yearly festival,
But gathered it, as the gift of May,
To honour the auspicious day.

And brightly mid the Christmas green
It shines, in the fire-light's ruddy sheen,   10
Mix'd with hard berries that gleam and glow
From holly and from mistletoe.

That tree is like the Tree of Life,
Which buds when the season of joy is rife,
And flowers when the bright dawn wakes above
The day that Religion gave birth to Love.

And, as Time the eternal morn resumes,
Humanity's grateful joy o'erblooms
The naked sight of the bleeding thorn,
Which Love on his brows for man hath worn.   20

O! let us still through love unite
To celebrate the holy rite;
That all the thorns of life may show
Nought but sweet flowers above the snow!

Copy-text: Household Words *4 (20 December 1851). Also printed in* TP.

To Alex. Smith, the 'Glasgow Poet,' on His Sonnet to 'Fame'

The sonnet written by the lace-pattern designer, Alexander Smith (1830–67), had appeared in a long review-article about Smith's "Life— Fragment" in the *Critic*, an annual, in 1851. The sonnet concluded that it is as foolish for the poet to "seek the look of Fame" as for a desert wanderer to "gain the notice of the Sphynx."

Not vainly doth the earnest voice of man
Call for the thing that is his pure desire!
Fame is the birthright of the living lyre!
To noble impulse Nature puts no ban.
Nor vainly to the Sphinx thy voice was raised!
Tho' all thy great emotions like a sea,
Against her stony immortality,
Shatter themselves unheeded and amazed.
Time moves behind her in a blind eclipse:
Yet if in her cold eyes the end of all   10
Be visible, as on her large closed lips
Hangs dumb the awful riddle of the earth;—
She sees, and she might speak, since that wild call,
The mighty warning of a Poet's birth.

Copy-text: Leader, 20 December 1851. Also printed in the Edition de Luxe 4 (posth.); and in Mem. Ed. MSS: NB B, [p. 11], title: "To Alex Smith on Sonnet" (Sphinx); frag. A, lines 10–12; frag. B, lines 9–14.

2 Call] Cry *MS*
8 Shatter] Shattered *MS*
9 moves behind] stands beside *or* moves behind *MS*; stands beside *frag. B*
10 *frag. A:* [*blank*] cold immortality of stone,
11 Be visible, as on] Who holdeth dumb upon *frag. A*
12 *MS, frags. A, B:* The mighty [fretted *MS*] secret *or* riddle [riddle *frag. A*] of the moving earth
13 *frag. B·* Hangs dumb, she sees since that wild wondrous call
14 mighty warning] joyous advent *frag. B*; advent *or* warning *MS*

Blue Is the Sky

Blue is the sky, blue is thine eye,—
    Which shall I call heaven?
Star is there, and soul is here,—
    Tell me which is heaven.
I cannot know unless thou say,
So kin are both in orb and ray,
    So full of heavenly feature;
The fall of dews, the flush of hues,
The tenderness of soften'd views,
Lovely alike by night and day,   10
    And both of heavenly nature.

Blue is the sky, blue is thine eye,—
    Both would image heaven;
Light is there, and love is here,—
    Each the child of heaven.
Oh, might it be, and may it be,
That I who worship heaven in thee,
    May so fulfil thy mission,
That light and love from heaven above,
And star and soul, my bridal dove,   20
May blend and open heaven to me,
    Through thy celestial vision!

A Wassail for the New Year

In December of 1851 GM grants or withholds his cheers according to
the political status of the countries he mentions.

Bring in the steaming bowl, my lads,
    Bring in the piping bowl!
And apples in a shoal, my lads,

BLUE IS THE SKY
Copy-text: The Book of English Songs: From the Sixteenth to the Nineteenth Century,
edited by Charles Mackay (London: National Illustrated Library, 1851), p. 80.
A WASSAIL FOR THE NEW YEAR
Copy-text: Household Words 4 (*3 January 1852*). *Also printed in* TP.

All hissing hot and whole!
The jolly yule-log is flaming its last,
    For the Year hath reach'd his goal.

The bright keen stars they gaze below,
All eager to see the ghostly show;
How the New Year will come and the Old Year go
O'er the wolds so white with the glimmering snow;   10
    And there's need of wood and coal, my lads,
      There's need of wood and coal!

O, the bright keen stars they throng so low!
And the winds are hush'd, and breathe with woe;
    For they hear a Death-bell knoll, my lads,
      They hear a Death-bell knoll!
O, the winds right soon with joy shall blow,
When the New Year peals, and the cock doth crow
    The news from pole to pole, my lads,
      The news from pole to pole!   20

The vanguard of advancing men—
    We English pitch our tents to-night!
And reach to all our brethren
    A loving hand and a guiding light,
    And a harbour free of toll, my lads,
      A harbour free of toll!

A hand whose grasp makes all men free!
And a guiding light, that they may see
    Our flag of care is furl'd!
And do as we, where'er they be,   30
And hear us drink, with three times three,
    A wassail to the world!
         Wassail!

Good barley-wine and honest brew,
    Right worthy drink, I wot.
Aye! and the world shall hear us too,

In every silent spot:
        Wassail!
    Wassail to every soul, my lads,
        Wassail to every soul!

Wassail to Her whose crown is now
    The quiet star of hope and peace;   40
The blessings on her royal brow
    Are many! may her joys increase!
        Swiftly the moments roll, my lads,
        Swiftly the moments roll!

Wassail to those whose household smiles
    Have given the hearth a double glow!
Wassail to all the sister Isles,
    For ever one in weal and woe!
        Pass round the piping bowl, my lads,
        Pass round the piping bowl.   50

Wassail to France! and may she draw
    This night a worthy King and Queen,
Or virgin-pure Republic; Law
    The guardian of her spotless sheen.
        I hear a Death-bell knoll, my lads,
        I hear a Death-bell knoll!

High wassail to the Sultan! he,
    To whom we owe a nation's debt;
Who dared to set the Patriot free,
    And let the carrion-eagles fret!   60
        Pass round the piping bowl, my lads,
        Pass round the piping bowl!

Wassail to Austria?—No, good faith!
    So little can our hopes agree;
But rather waft, with genial breath,
    Wassail to noble Hungary!
        I hear a funeral dole, my lads,
        I hear a funeral dole.

Wassail to Prussia? she, whose chance
    It was to have been the German star: 70
But on a Gorgon's countenance
    She gazed, whom Europe calls the Czar:
        Wassail to Polish hopes, my lads,
           Pass round the foaming bowl.

Wassail to proud Italia! hail
    And wassail! not in vain she clanks
Her cruel chains, and shrieks her wail
    Above her children's shatter'd ranks;
        Swiftly the moments roll, my lads,
           Swiftly the moments roll! 80

Wassail to those free men o' the West,
    Whose land is by the setting sun;
The yearning of a mother's breast
    Unites us, and our hopes are one.
        Wassail to every soul, my lads,
           Wassail to every soul!

The Linnet-Hawker

I met, in a close City square,
    A linnet-hawker, hawking loud;
And, though small melody was there
    To draw a member from the crowd,
A mournful thought went with his song,
    That secretly attracted me:
So, fixed I stood, and brooded long,
    While thus he chimed in rudest key:—
        Linnets, linnets, full-song linnets, O!

THE LINNET-HAWKER

Copy-text: Household Words 4 (10 January 1852). Also printed in TP.

The fledgling bliss, the wavy flight,   10
    The feathery ecstasies that flow
From freedom in the airy light,
    The little captives may not know.
Of their own birthright robb'd, alas!
    What voice of anguish might they lift
In music for the time that was—
    Betrayed by so divine a gift!
        Linnets, linnets, full-song linnets, O!

Far from their woodland joys are they!
    Far, far from the forsaken nest,   20
And from their parents far away!
    Who sit and brood with vacant breast
Amid the sunlight on the leaves,
    Where now a fitful song they sing
Of sorrow that more inly grieves,
    And will not hope in anything:
        Linnets, linnets, full-song linnets, O!

But now—since evil has its good—
    A latent truth the soul knows well;
What mission have the stolen brood   30
    In this great City's depths to dwell?
It is to cheer the sick at heart
    With Eden songs of country days;
Of grass, and balm for every smart;
    Of freshness, flowers, and woodland ways.
        Linnets, linnets, full-song linnets, O!

And, through their little throats, a stream
    Of sweet impulsive song will flow;
To some—a yearning and a dream;
    To all—a sweet relief from woe.   40
Heard, spirit-like, the tide to stem
    Of toiling men, who muse and moan
To breathe the woods again!—for them,
    Old Linnet-hawker, still sing on:
        Linnets, linnets, full-song linnets, O!

War

I

Two Mothers lifting prayers unto one God,
In alien language, and on hostile sod.

Two Maidens wailing in a different tongue,
The gory mass of silent men among.

Two Monarchs couch'd in indolent repose,
Reaping Ambition by their subjects' throes.

Foes, that have never done each other ill:
Friends, whose sole union is the aim to kill.

Banners clutch'd fierce—the death-grasp of the brave—
A tatter'd rag that glorifies the grave.   10

Far-rolling smoke above a vulture plain;
Artillery piled on ramparts of the slain.

Nature swathed round in one close crimson shroud;
Black speechlessness of the low thunder-cloud.

The fields untill'd, the rich Heavens raining dearth;
Weeds in the garden; weeping by the hearth.

II

Now, in the Land of Shades two Mothers meet,
Mourning, embracing,—with ensanguined feet.

Two Maidens clasp one urn that doth enclose
The ashes of their lovers, who were foes.

Copy-text: Household Words *4 (21 February 1852). Also printed in* TP.

Two Kings in silence meet—in silence part—
They find, too late, they have a human heart.

Nations of slain, whose armies won and lost,
Mingle their shades: Death holds no hostile ghost.

Their records shall instruct, with heartfelt moan,
Their sons to combat with life's ills alone.   10

Nations, who strove to waste each other's lands,
Turn swords to ploughshares for their common hands.

Oh, misery! before that day can come,
War-fiends may thrust their fangs in many a home.

The First-Born

The First-born is a Fairy child,
    A wondrous emanation!
A tameless creature, fond and wild—
    A moving exultation!
Beside the hearth, upon the stair,
    Its footstep laughs with lightness:
And cradled, all its features fair
    Are touched with mystic brightness.

First pledge of their betrothed love—
    O, happy they that claim it!   10
First gift direct from Heav'n above—
    O, happy they that name it!
It tunes the household with its voice,
    And, with quick laughter ringing,
Makes the inanimate rooms rejoice,
    A hidden rapture bringing.

THE FIRST-BORN

Copy-text: Household Words 5 (*10 July 1852*). *Also printed in* TP.

Its beauty all the beauteous things
By kindred light resembles;
But, evermore with fluttering wings,
On fairy confines trembles.   20
So much of those that gave it birth,
Of Father and of Mother:
So much of this world built on earth,
And so much of another!

Translations from Austrian and Hungarian Poets

A letter dated March 18, 1851, from GM to John W. Parker, Jr., publisher of GM's *Poems* (1851) and editor of *Fraser's*, establishes GM as the author of the fairly well known, unsigned article, "Austrian Poets," in *Fraser's*, August 1852. (See David Bonnell Green, "George Meredith's 'Austrian Poets': A Newly Identified Review Essay with Translations," *Modern Language Review* 54 [July 1959].) In the letter, now in the Roberts Collection, Haverford College, GM offered to write for *Fraser's* twelve or fewer articles on the "Austrian Poets," naming especially Grillparzer and Lenau. Parker settled for the one article, which included references to collections of Austrian poets published in London and on the continent. The order of GM's translations in the present edition follows the order of their appearance in the article.

Vogl: To an Old Gipsy

GM calls Johann N. Vogl (1802–66), "one of the healthiest of the Austrian poets," who, since he is "half Hungarian," is alert to the charms of wandering Hungarian, fiddling gipsies. GM gives only the beginning of Vogl's poem.

Seize the bow, old swarthy fiddler!
Newly strung with black horse-hair:
Seize the bow, and seize the fiddle:
Play some old familiar air!

VOGL: TO AN OLD GIPSY

Copy-text: Fraser's *46 (August 1852)*.

Dream, with thy strange wailing music,
    Back the golden time again,
When throughout the world thou wandered'st,
    Poor as now, but without pain.

Dream thyself in those black forests,
    By the tent-fire's dying light,   10
Where, with thy brown sunburnt sweetheart,
    Sinless was thy sleep, by night.

Dream thee in the darken'd wine-room,
    'Mong the robbers rough and rude;
Where they clash'd the sounding cymbals
    To thy bass so swiftly bow'd.

Dream thyself in that far desert,
    Where, in tears, her grave was made:
Where, in the true gipsy fashion,
    Died she, far from human aid. . . .   20

Lenau: The Three Gipsies

Nikolaus Lenau (1802–50) was a Hungarian poet who, according to GM, wrote of the Zigeuners, the gipsies, "no less lovingly" than Vogl. Later in his article GM mentions with sorrow Lenau's melancholy death in a Viennese madhouse.

Once as my carriage wearily dragg'd
    Over heath and sandy mound,
I saw three gipsies lying alone,
    On a slope of pasture ground.

The first in his hands a fiddle clasp'd,
    All to himself he play'd;
Play'd to himself a fiery tune,
    In the glow that the sunset made.

LENAU: THE THREE GIPSIES

Copy-text: Fraser's 46 (August 1852).

The second held his pipe in his mouth,
 Follow'd the smoke with his eyes;   10
Happy as tho' from the whole round earth
 His wants naught more did prize!

Pleasantly lay the third asleep,
 His cymbal hung on a bough;
Over it softly the breezes ran,
 A dream went over his brow.

Tatters and patches, many-hued,
 Bore on their clothes all three;
But they snapt their fingers at fortune and fate,
 And laugh'd at misery!   20

Threefold unto me they proved,
 When life its scourge applies,
How we fiddle it, smoke it, and sleep it,
 And it thrice despise.

After the gipsies long I looked,
 As slowly we did fare:
After the dark-brown faces flush'd,
 The coal-black locks of hair.

Vogl: The Sweetheart of the Csikos

GM explains that the Csikos is a "Hungarian horseman of the plains, a rider from his birth, who helps to form that great feature in the Austrian army, the unrivalled hussar. . . ."

Without saddle, without stirrup,
 See, how swift the Csikos flashes!
Has he wings, my little courser,
 That with such mad speed he dashes?

VOGL: THE SWEETHEART OF THE CSIKOS

Copy-text: Fraser's *46 (August 1852).*

Far around my whip's sharp cracking
    Echoes! and the wolf in haste
Leaves in peace his mangled booty,
    For he scents a fearful guest.

Clouds are racing high in heaven,
    Swift as they my merry steed!   10
Who would be so bold to wager
    Which goes at the greatest speed?

Deep in the wood, where, in a tavern,
    Dark with smoke, guitars are play'd,
Lives a girl I think of blithely,
    She who waits as servant maid.

Up and down the stair she dances,
    And the jugs and mugs hands she;
And like her there's none so lively,
    In the whole of Hungary.   20

Drési, Drési, merry lassie,
    Hear'st thou not the cracking whip?
Stroke the hair back from thy forehead,
    Leave the guest with thirsty lip.

Hark! through the wood he bursts, and flying,
    Flying comes—thy János, thine!
Huzza, Gipsies! bow like wild-fire!
    Dance, and bright Hungarian wine!

Beck: The Hungarian Horse-Herd

GM notes the "wild energy and descriptive force" of this poem by Karl Beck (1817–79) but gives only a part of it. Beck and most contemporary poets writing in the German language take a rap from GM for their lack of rhythm: "They require to be chastised by an Alexander Pope. . . ." GM retaliates by translating Beck's poem without rhyme.

BECK: THE HUNGARIAN HORSE-HERD

Copy-text: Fraser's 46 (August 1852).

Out, out, away! my blood boils up!
Away; out, out! my spirit mounts!
All anxiously the hamlet waits,
The untamed creature runs on the plains.
The manes are tossing, the hoofs are thundering,
Sharp sounds the whip to the wild huzza!
I near him now—my right hand slings
Over his head the cunning lasso;
The lads they exult, and the girls mutter prayer!
Twelve steps backward at once I tread,   10
And pitch myself, stretch myself flat to the ground,
And with mighty effort I pull the rope
Round his proud neck,
And give the swing to the snorting courser.

Scarce feels
The plunging, foaming horse the lasso,
But away he scours like the wings of the storm,
Rushing and storming in narrow circles,
While the rope tightens across his throat:
The whips are cracking, the dogs are barking,   20
The grass is trampled and withered,
The clouds of dust whirl up to the sky,
And the gay crowds they spring and they sing.
But I bide close, with a quick, keen eye,
On the trembling ground,
And nearer and nearer the frothing horse,—
Still holding the rope I mightily strain,—
And my hands are gall'd,
And my mouth foams white,
And ev'ry pulse is beating,   30
And the sweat rolls down in heavy drops.
O Lord God, Lord God, Lord God!
Forsake me not, forsake me not,
Let never the children laugh at me!
His breath is going—he totters—he falls—
Terribly drops the reeking beast,
And his eye weeps, and my heart how it laughs!

Grillparzer: Field-Marshal Radetzky

(JUNE, 1848)

Franz Grillparzer (1791–1872), the Austrian dramatist, remains the best known of the poets from whom GM quotes in his article. In translating Grillparzer's "celebrated address" to Field Marshal Radetzky in his campaign against King Charles Albert of Sardinia during the Austro-Sardinian War of 1848–49, GM explains that the poem obliterates any suspicions that Grillparzer might have been pro-Italian. The date that accompanies Grillparzer's poem points to Radetzky's reoccupation of Vicenza, June 9, 1848.

> Courage, my chieftain, and strike the blow,
>   Not alone for the lustre of fame;
> For in thy camp is Austria,
>   Mere instruments we to her aim.
>
> Through folly and through vanity
>   Our feuds have caused our fall;
> Of those thou leadest to battle now,
>   One spirit lives in all.
>
> No youth is there who would ever dare
>   To question thy behest: 10
> He knows truth dwells not in his dream,
>   He knows thy word is best.
>
> And thy body-guard not only awake,
>   But watchful to shelter thee right;
> Little reck they of lives to lose,
>   When the battle drums beat at night.
>
> Thy moving city's citizen,
>   This city to him is all;
> He feels, should the flames but seize it once,
>   He perishes in the fall.   20

Copy-text: Fraser's *46 (August 1852).*

And again, thy gallant officers,
    Their sharp swords glitter bright;
To discipline if need there be,
    Obedience is peace in the fight.

Men God as Slave and Magyar made,
    Words wake no strife among;
They follow, tho' German their marshal's cry,
    For 'Forwards' is also their tongue.

One common help in one common need,
    Has founded both cities and states;   30
'Tis but in death man is ever alone,
    'Tis life and endeavour that mates.

Were now an example thy mighty campaign,
    Our hands we would joyfully reach!
In the union of all is victory,
    The aim is the weal of each.

Lenau: The Postillion

GM remarks particularly on the ending of this poem, "with its thin, weird, impalpable music ringing remotely in the memory, suggesting so much, closing both the sentiment and the picture of the poem so completely. . . ."

Lovely was the night of May,
    Silvery cloudlets flying,
Seem'd like the fair spring-tide array,
    Merrily onward hieing.

Meadow and grove in slumber lay,
    Every path forsaken;
Nothing but the moon's white ray
    Upon the roads did waken.

LENAU: THE POSTILLION

Copy-text: Fraser's 46 (August 1852).

Softly and low the Zephyrs crept,
    And with foot-pause hushing,
Through sleep's silent chamber stept
    Spring's sweet children blushing.

10

The rivulet sang innerly,
    And through the open spaces,
Breathed abroad deliciously,
    The blossoming embraces.

But of far rougher stuff my Postillion was born,
    He crackt his whip, and blowing,
O'er hill and dale to the blast of his horn,
    I heard the echoes going.

20

And with a rattling, wild delight,
    My four swift horses bounding,
Flew through the dreamy odorous night,
    Their measured hoofs resounding.

Forest and plain in rapid flight,
    No sooner seen than banish'd;
And vision-like, with glances bright,
    The peaceful village vanish'd.

Right in the heart of the May-tide joy,
    A small church-yard was standing,
That fixt the hasty traveller's eye,
    Earnest thoughts commanding.

30

Against the mountain's misty gloom,
    The pallid walls were leaning;
Christ's crucifix rose up in dumb
    Pathetic anguish sheening.

Silent my companion rode,
    Sadder, and more slowly;
Check'd the swift steed he bestrode,
    Gazed at the picture holy.

40

'Here must I halt, wheel and horse,
    Have no cause to fear me;
Yonder lies my old comrade's corse,
    In the cool earth so near me.

'O such a jolly fellow!—Sir,
    'Tis an eternal pity!
None blew the horn with such a stir,
    Or rang so clear a ditty.

'Here do I rest each time I pass,
    His favourite tune repeating,   50
Who sleeps so calm beneath the grass,
    And give him trusty greeting.'

And to the white churchyard he sent
    Songs of the merry wayfaring,
That in the peace of the grave they went,
    To his old friend repairing.

And the far echo's thin, clear tone
    Came from the mountains ringing,
As though the dead Postillion
    With his loved songs were singing.   60

Full gallop, then, we sped away,
    By fields and leaping fountains;
Long within my ears still lay,
    That echo from the mountains.

Vogl: Love of the Woods

One "strong feature in" Vogl "is his passionate love of woodland life,"
but **GM** objects that he raves about it "violently and unendingly."

VOGL: LOVE OF THE WOODS

Copy-text: Fraser's 46 (*August 1852*).

Away, through bramble, bush, and trees,
Ere the wingèd joyance fly
Drain the cup unto the lees
Nature gives with loving eye.

Drink with thirsty spirit, drink
The breathing spring; the winds that pass;
Sink with joy delicious, sink,
Deep in moss and dewy grass.

Happy as the sounding horn,
Through the waking woods I'd sweep;   10
Flattering the fair vales at morn,
Echoing through the cloven steep.

Like the early sunrise bright,
Full of love's divinest sheen,
Would I bathe, O rare delight!
In the rich and youthful green.

Even as the wild uproarious storm,
Rapture-driven, O woods! I'd haste,
Revelling, flying, rushing warm,
Fling myself upon thy breast.   20

Vogl: The Recognition

A roving boy comes, staff in hand,
Home again from a foreign land.

His face it is burnt, and there's dust in his hair,
Who will remember the boy so fair?

Thro' the ancient gate of the town steps he,
At the bar leans the toll-keeper lazily.

VOGL: THE RECOGNITION
Copy-text: Fraser's 46 (August 1852).

The toll-keeper was his friend beloved,
Often had they clash'd cups, well proved.

But, behold! his friend forgets all trace,
So fiercely the sun has burnt his face!   10

After short greeting, the boy goes on,
Shaking the dust from his feet anon.

When from a window his treasure he spies,
"Hail, blooming maiden! to those bright eyes."

But, behold! the girl has forgotten all trace,
So fiercely the sun has burnt his face!

Further his way thro' the street he seeks,
A stealthy tear on his sunburnt cheeks.

His mother comes tottering from the church door,
'God greets thee!' he says, and nothing more.   20

But, behold! his mother sobs for joy,
'My son!' and falls on the breast of her boy.

Tho' fiercely the sun has burnt his face,
The mother's eye lights up each trace.

Seidl: To the High-Flyers

GM classes Johann Gabriel Seidl (1804–75) together with Vogl as "healthy, joyous men," but feels that they are too prolific, and therefore fatiguing, in their records of "pleasant impressions."

SEIDL: TO THE HIGH-FLYERS

Copy-text: Fraser's 46 (*August 1852*).

Keep ever on your eagle flight,
    You spirits swift and strong;
This quiet vale is my delight,
    Nor more requires my song.

You circle in the dizzy height,
    And gaze in haughty mood;
A cleft—the vale is in your sight,
    A timber heap—the wood.

The beauteous trees, the silver stream,
    That winds with reach and creek,   10
Through meadows in the ample gleam
    Is mapp'd to you—a streak.

The little bird who sits and sings,
    Right to man's deepest joys,
Before into the clouds he springs,
    Is but a tuneless noise.

What matters it that you neighbours be
    To morn and even-glow?
Around doth silence, as a sea,
    Make life like death to show.   20

So will I praise my quiet vale,
    With all that peace provides;
Where lovingly and warmly, all
    Bows to me, and confides.

There have I in a little space,
    All that a man can have;
The world looks friendly in my face,
    And that which looks doth live.

Seidl: Hans Euler

'Hark, Martha! some one knocks without; go, let him in, I pray!
'Tis a poor weary pilgrim, who, may-be, has lost his way.
Right welcome, honest warrior! Take place at table, here,
The bread is white and pure, and the drink is fresh and clear.'

'I come not here to eat or drink, I come not here for food,
But if you be Hans Euler, I come to have your blood!
Know that for months I've sought you out, your sworn and deadly
    foe;
I had a brother once, that brother fell beneath your blow.

'And as he weltered on the ground, and took his dying breath,
I swore to him that, late or soon, I would avenge his death.'   10
'And if that I have slain him, in equal fight he fared;
And come you to revenge him? Right well, I am prepared!

'But not beneath this roof fight I—not between wall and door,
In the face of those belovéd ones for whom I fought before!
My sword, good Martha! that with which I slew him—give it me:
And should I not return, Tyrōl is large enough for thee.'

Together to the nearest jutting mountain-rock they pace,
The golden gates of rising morn made bright each silent face;
Hans led the way, the stranger follow'd, striding quick and close;
And higher, ever, over both the sweet sunshine arose.   20

Now on the peak they stand—below, the Alpine world they see,
The vast and wondrous valley, with its gleaming scenery;
Low, floating mist reveal'd the vales in all their joyance drest,
The cottages within their arms, the herds upon their breast.

Copy-text: Fraser's *46 (August 1852).*

Bright waterfalls between, and thence ravines descending fair;
Dark hanging woods on either side, above the free blue air:
And surely felt, albeit unseen, in heart and smoking cot,
The true old spirit breathed, and God's peace was on the spot.

This scene they both behold—the stranger drops his hand,
But Hans points proudly down on the beloved Father-land;   30
'For that it was I battled, that your brother had betrayed,
For that it was I fought, and for that I struck him dead.'

The stranger looks below—looks again in Hans' calm face,
To raise his arm he seeks, his arm he does not raise.
'And if that you have slain him, your cause it was the right,
And if you will forgive me, Hans, come grasp me strong and
     tight.'

Holidays

They come to us but once in life,
     The holidays of Yule;
When, wild as captives from the cage,
     We bounded home from school.
Unshackled by the dreary task—
     All lessons put away;
The world a bright revolving mask
     Of pantomime and play.

What welcome shall we ever have
     Till this long journey ends,   10
Like that which marked the merry time
     From sisters and from friends?
When presents given and received,
     Brought heart to heart in view,
And every day was golden-leaved,
     With wonders rich and new!

HOLIDAYS

Copy-text: Household Words *8* (*24 December 1853*). *Also printed in* TP.

The Christmas sights, the Christmas lights,
    The Christmas nights, how grand
To us who walked the glittering lanes
    Of boyhood's fairyland!   20
Remote among its spangled bowers
    Old memories parade,
And watch the gorgeous bubbling hours
    All rise, and burst, and fade.

We will not sigh to see them pass—
    To know them was enough;
Nay, Father, let us joy that we
    Were made of sterner stuff.
Who then enjoyed the Yule Log's blaze
    In retrospect enjoys: 30
So, welcome to your holidays,
    My merry girls and boys!

Be blissful in the time of bliss,
    Unloosed from toil and school:
They come to you but once in life,
    These holidays of Yule.
For us, among the world's dark ways,
    Our eyes are on one star,
Beyond which shine our holidays,
    Though dim, and distant far.   40

Motley

Before a world of tremulous green baize,
    Whose slightest motion made us leap and start,
And nudge with elbows eloquent (in ways
    That boys drive expectation to the heart;

MOTLEY

Copy-text: Household Words 8 *(4 February 1854). Also printed in* TP.

Unlike the etiquette of later days
　　Which misses oft its aim from too much art,)
Each other's aching ribs, in pleasure's search
We sat, three youngsters fresh from school and birch.

The curtain of the mysteries before us
　　Hung with a solemn sense of all it knew;   10
The gallery gods and chandelier flamed o'er us,
　　Like an Olympus glorious to the view.
We heard the frequent nectar pop, and chorus
　　Shrilling aloud, impatient for its due.
Time and the fiddlers, in dumb concert playing,
Seemed for our special wretchedness delaying.

Sudden the tinkling of a mystic bell
　　Proclaimed the preparations were complete,
And through the green baize sent a shuddering spell
　　That took us for the time half off our feet;   20
The curtain curled, and with a gradual swell
　　Rose. Ah! who shall say what sight did greet,
As orchestra and gallery ceased their wrangles,
To gaze on glory, gorgeousness, and spangles?

A glittering lady with a silver wand,
　　Which, (oh, how gracefully!) she softly sway'd
To music, with the smallest whitest hand,
　　Stood in the opening of an emerald glade.
Behind her, brightly grouped, a fairy band,
　　Each inclination of her arm obey'd,   30
And like a gliding lustre forth did flow,
Or like a wizard top spun on tiptoe.

Her mortal enemy, a mighty dragon,
　　Too base his beastly entrance to announce,
Surprised her. In one claw he clutched a flagon,
　　The other held her tightly by the flounce

37 on,] *om. HW*

(Threatening to leave her soon without a rag on,
  In spite of our low-muttered wrath and frowns),
Then drew her quickly to his loathsome cavern,
Stored grim with evil spirits like a tavern.   40

But her good genius rising on a shell
  As Aphrodite rose (yet far more fair),
Dissolved the power of the magician fell,
  And sent him shivering down to sulphurous air.
Then all those ladies, issuing from the bell
  Of many a drooping flower, enring'd her there,
Like human leaves round some angelic rose,
They linked their arms and quivered on their toes.

She gazed, and gazed direct upon us three,
  With worlds of unintelligible meaning;   50
Above them like a silver-seen birch tree
  (Horrible simile!), in beauty leaning—
Leaning towards us wistfully, while we,
  All bashfulness from boyish ardour weaning,
Shadowed the pit in answer, clapping red,
Till the masks entered, and her figure fled.

Oh wondrous length of nose! Oh breadth of cheek
  Whose bloom all mortal rivalry defies!
Capacity of mouth, and body sleek!
  Oh hugeous head, and monstrous goggle eyes! 60
The tickle of late laughter sure is weak
  To that which your appearance first bids rise.
Lord! how we laughed! Meantime, demeanour
   solemn
Marked the great pate upon the puny column.

Fair Rosamond, embowered by royal Harry,
  Upon the balcony her flower-pots waters.
A broad Scotch colonel, intent to marry,
  (Whose claymore each unseen opponent
   slaughters),

Fired with impatient love, no more can tarry,
    But hopes to take by force this worst of
        daughters.   70
He scales her window stealthily on the sea-side;
Sagacious Harry wooing her on the side.

She seizes, most alert, the colonel's ladder,
    And flings him off to court the willing billow,
Whereon he falls; and, like some briny bladder,
    Floats, the while his men set up a hillo!
And drag him up the friendly beach, a sadder
    If not a wiser Gael. Down like a willow
Hangs his proud plaid. He, with a monstrous spoon,
Snuffs his wide nose, and sneezes to the moon.   80

Great Harry, underneath her balcony,
    Lutes to her softly a sweet serenade;
When, lo! the flower-pot that she waters free,
    Falls from its perch and fixes on his head!
A right reward of naughty majesty
    Caught in its trap. But what more need be said?
Clown, Harlequin, and Pantaloon in station,
Startle us all by wondrous transformation.

Ah, Clown! with what a welcome wert thou greeted,
    Hailed like a hero to some lighted city.   90
And Pantaloon, old fool! for ever treated
    Horribly ill, and looking not for pity.
Diamond-cut Harlequin, with magic heated,
    Least loved, yet luckiest, as in committee
We three acknowledged when the play was over,
For he was Columbine's accepted lover.

Shall Clown for ever rest unsung of bard?
    His notable profundity of pocket,
At once a garden and a poultry-yard;
    Stored secretly with cracker, squib, and rocket;   100

Still yawning in abysm wide-barr'd,
    Enough to make all tradesmen strike their
        docket.
For every kind of bibible and edible,
With a digestion perfectly incredible.

Choice son of Mercury, whose cool mendacity
    Delighted us, delights us in perspective,
The laws are not for one of thy capacity;
    Thou bidd'st defiance to the 'cute detective,
So indiscriminate in thy voracity,
    Save when to grumblers giving sharp corrective,   110
Thy face of brass our golden age brings back again,
And sends us wandering in that dreamy track again.

Thou art not flesh and bone; no wife hast thou
    Who watches shudderingly the magic leap,
With hands clasped close, and anxious furrowed
        brow,
    Gasping to think that life should be so cheap.
No little ones sleep in thy homestead now,
    Whose daily bread thy nightly risks do reap;
Else art thou such a fighter in our battle
As seldom yet heard arms and harness rattle.   120

In vain of thee they write the grave biography,
    Telling us thou wert mortal and knew pain;
Thou livest in a world remote from geography,
    Somewhere between our earth and the inane—
To the blithe adolescent's mixed cosmography
    Familiar: o'er thy grave no starry wain,
When midnight whispers soft its bright wheel rolls,
Oh vernal presence to our passing souls!

So laugh, and have our love! Be'st thou, indeed,
    Mortal as we, Oh whither shall we turn,   130
When the young flowers of life are choked with weed,
    For one thing faithful in our ashy urn?

The gayest piper on our human reed,
  Of him the saddest lesson must we learn?
Alas! that he should e'er belie his paint!
Humanity seems in him almost a taint.

Boyhood and Manhood have their separate clown,
  And hard we find it from the first to part;
Yet tenderly to the latter, when well known,
  We cling, for he is of us, and the heart   140
Is not beguiled by fancy. Cheer the town
  For many a week, old favourite as thou art.
We owe thee much; ungrateful would not be;
And will remember thy humanity.

Fireside Reverie

These verses were written to accompany a portrait of GM's wife, Mary,
by Henry Wallis, who later became her lover. Lionel Stevenson copied
them from the *Catalogue of the Royal Academy* (1855), where they appear
under the heading:
              H. Wallis, 8, Gray's Inn Square.
              1150. Fireside Reverie
Neither Stevenson nor I have succeeded in our efforts to find the painting.

Is she the star of one that is away?
She that by the fire so gravely dreams,
In Evening's lulling stillness, while the ray
Tints her soft cheek like Sunset on fair streams.

But folded in herself she sits, and low
The fire may fall, white ashes strew the grate.
The Past is pictured there, its joy, its woe,
She reads the Future's yet unveiled Fate.

FIRESIDE REVERIE
*Copy-text: MS, The Wallis Estate, courtesy of Professor Diane Johnson. Previously
printed: the first stanza in the* Catalogue of the Royal Academy (1855).
First stanza canceled:
2 by the fire so gravely dreams] that dreams so gravely by the fading fire
4 *incomplete*
8 The Future & its yet unvision'd *or* She reads the Future's yet unveiled

Rhine-Land

This poem recalls the wedding trip of Mary Peacock Nicolls and GM in the late summer and early autumn of 1849.

We lean'd beneath the purple vine,
  In Andernach, the hoary;
And at our elbows ran the Rhine
  In rosy twilight glory.

Athwart the Seven-hills far seen
  The sun had fail'd to broaden;
Above us stream'd in fading sheen
  The highway he had trodden.

His farewell crimson kiss he left
  On clouds suffused with blushes: 10
One star beam'd down the dewberry-cleft
  Across the mirror'd flushes.

From cliffs of slate the vintage call'd
  In muffled leafage dusky:
And down the river grandly wall'd,
  The grape reel'd ripe and husky.

Copy-text: Household Words *14 (19 July 1856). Also printed in* TP. *MSS:* NB B, [*pp. 21–22*], *lines 1–4, 9–12, 17–24 + five lines;* Berg, *lines 1–4, 9–12, 17–24 + one stanza, between pp. 80 and 81.*

3 *NB B:* Red at our feet the ripe old Rhine *or* By your dear elbow flow'd the Rhine *B del.:* Red at our feet the ripe old Rhine
4 *NB B:* Was flowing in his glory *or* In [ruddy *del.*] rosy evening's glory   *B:* Was flowing in his glory. *del.* In ruddy twilight glory.
9 *NB B, B:* The sun had kiss'd the hills, and left
10 *NB B, B:* A violet flush to grace us:
11 beam'd] shone *NB B, B*
12 *NB B, B:* That o'er the stream did face us.
Between 12 and 17, B stanza [*3*]:

> We cared not the darkness came
>   With its bright crescent headed:
> 'Twas Summer with our mingling flame,
>   We two were Summer-wedded.

We reach'd entwining hands to seize
  The clusters round us glowing:
Our locks were fondled by the breeze
  From southern sandhills blowing.   20

The long-neck'd flask was not unbent,
  The globed green glass unemptied;
The god of honest pleasure lent
  Young Love his powers, untempted.

Home-friends we pledged; our bridal-maids;
  Sweet wishes gaily squander'd:
We wander'd far in faëry glades,
  Up golden heights we wander'd.

Like King and Queen in royal bliss,
  We paced a realm enchanted,   30
A realm rose-vista'd, rich from this,
  Tho' not from this transplanted.

For this Rome's frontier foot endear'd,
  Her armèd heel made holy;
And Ages grey as Time's own beard,
  Wreathed it with melancholy.

Old days it has that live in gleams
  Of suns for ever setting:
A moth-wing'd splendour, faint as dreams,
  That keeps the fancy fretting.   40

17 entwining hands] our arms the fruit *NB B*; our hands the grape *B*
18 *NB B:* On either lip bestowing: *or* In drooping clusters glowing   *B:* In drooping clusters glowing:
19 Our locks were fondled by] And gratefully we felt *NB B, B*
20 southern] inland *NB B*; inland *or* southern *B*
Between lines 20–21, NB B:
            We cared not that the darkness came
              With its young crescent headed:
            'Twas Autumn with our mingling flame,
              We two were Summer-wedded.
            We two had learn'd in love to bask
23 honest] Lovers' *NB B*

A gorgeous tracing dash'd with gloom,
    And delicately dusted:
To grasp it is to spoil its bloom;
    'Twas ours because we trusted.

No longer severing our embrace
    Was Night a sword between us;
But richest mystery robed in grace
    To lock us close, and screen us.

She droopt in stars; she whisper'd fair;
    The wooded crags grew dimmer;   50
The arrow in the lassie's hair
    Glanced by a silver glimmer.

The ruin-rock renew'd its frown,
    With terror less transparent,
Tho' all its ghosts are hunted down,
    And all its knights are errant.

The island in the grey expanse,
    We watch'd with colour'd longing:
The mighty river's old romance
    Thro' many channels thronging.   60

Ah, then, what voice was that which stirred
    A breathless scene before us:
We heard it, knowing not we heard;
    It rose around and o'er us.

It rose around, it thrill'd with life,
    And did infuse a spirit
To misty shapes of ancient strife:
    Again I seem to hear it!

The voice is clear, the song is wild,
    And has a quaint transition;   70
The voice is of a careless child
    Who sings an old tradition.

He sings it witless of his power;
 Beside the rushing eddies,
His singing plants the tall white tower
 Mid shades of knights and ladies.

Against the glooming of the west
 The grey hawk-ruins darken,
And hand in hand, half breast to breast,
 Two lovers gaze and hearken.   80

Monmouth

In an effort to seize the English throne on the accession of James II in 1685, James Scott, Duke of Monmouth, collected his undisciplined army at Taunton in Somerset, June 18–20, and marched from there on June 25. Decisively defeated at Sedgemoor on July 5, he was beheaded on July 15.

The windows flash in Taunton town
 With hurrying lights and muffled lamps,
And torches wander up and down
 The streets, alive like scattered camps:
Far goes the word o'er field and fen,—
Monmouth is here with all his men!

Follow the Duke! and fife and drum
 Startle the nightmared country round.
Hither in flocks the lads are come,
 The gallant lads so staunch and sound;   10
Hither in troops they march all night,
And wives and mothers mourn their flight.

MONMOUTH

Copy-text: Household Words *14 (1 November 1856) Also printed in* TP; *and in the Edition de Luxe 36 (1911).* MSS: NB B, [*pp. 17–18*]; Berg, *between pp. 34 and* [35].
1 flash] flame *NB B*
2 muffled] swinging *NB B, B*
5 Far] Swift *del. NB B*
7 Follow the Duke] Monmouth is here *NB B, B*
8 nightmared] low dark *NB B, B*
11 troops] flocks *NB B*

The whisper warns that close on dawn,
      Before the village cock crows thrice,
He leads his merry people on,
      And bravely flings the battle dice.
Look to your arms, lads; temper them well.
Lest that the unflesh'd steel rebel!

Auburn heads and grey are here,
      Who grasp the pike from door to door;   20
Their sires who followed Oliver,
      And work'd at Worcester, and the Moor.
Again the cheering of the town
They hear denounce a faithless crown.

They hear again the admiral's name
      With his great master's coupled high,
And drink, in brown October, shame
      To Papists, till the cup is dry.
March, merry men! and shoulder blithe
Pike and musket, bill and scythe.   30

Over the main street floats a flag,
      The toil of twenty noble maids;
Soon will it stream a blushing rag,
      But now 'tis bright with symbol'd braids;
And as the young men march beneath,
Its long folds wave and flattering breathe.

Swings the banner from the hall
      Where Monmouth holds his night carouse,
And views his eager followers fall

13 *NB A, B:* Monmouth is here: and in the dawn,
14 village] ruddy *NB B, B*
16 bravely flings] throws in fate *del. NB B*
18 the] your *or* the *NB B*
Lines 19–30 not in NB B, B
33 will it stream] doom'd to *del.* will it be *NB B*; will it be *B*
34 But now] Now *or* But now *NB B*   symbol'd] cunning *or* many woven *del.* virgin
NB B; virgin *B*
36 long] wide *NB B, B*   flattering] *NB B, B*; flatterers *HW, de L*
37 Swings the banner] The broad red banner hangs *NB B, B*
39 views his eager] sees his [faithful *del.*] crowding *NB B*

On bended knee, with loyal vows.   40
Sweet women blossom in the throng,
And pledge success in cup and song.

They pledge him deep, and to reply
    He rises from his cushion'd chair;
The monarch's joy is in his eye;
    He bows and drains the goblet there.
The kingly wine that crowns his brain
Runs royally through every vein.

He feels the purple warmth, the weight
    Of golden glory on him shed: 50
He wins the battle lost by Fate,
    He mounts the height that claims his head;
He mounts the height so many moan
Who find a scaffold for a throne.

"To horse!—to horse!" The war-steeds prance;
    High vaults he with a chieftain's grace,
And many a lovely lady's glance
    Dwells fondly on his fated face.
With warmer red their red cheeks bloom
While he waves round his princely plume.   60

---

42 success] him deep *NB B, B*

Lines associated with 42–43, NB A, [*p. 5*]:

    Aloud they make the pledge of faith
    And loyalty to him alone

47 *NB A*, [*p. 5*]: The royal life is in his veins,
49 warmth] robes *or* warmth *NB B*
50 golden] springing *del. NB B*   him shed] his head *del. NB B*
52 claims] dooms *del. NB B*
54 find] found *or* find *NB B*; found *del.* find *B*
55 to horse] he cries *NB B*; he cries *del.* to horse *B*
56 High vaults he with] He sits *del.* leaps *del.* vaults with all *NB B*; He vaults with all *del.* High vaults he with *B*
58 fated] handsome *NB B*; handsome *del.* fated *B*
59 warmer] deeper *NB B*
60 *NB B, B:* The while he waves his proud white plume.   proud white *del.* princely *B*

And tears and sighs, and wild adieus,
    Bubble beneath his bounding bliss;
Sad dreams of the past night refuse
    Consoling by the soldier's kiss.
The mother and the bosom wife
Have dreamt dark issue to the strife.

The cheerless wife, the mother, clings
    To him she loves, and will not part.
The young son up the stirrup springs,
    To feel once more his father's heart.   70
The townsmen mount the grey church-tower,
All glorious in the morning hour.

"God speed to Monmouth! Speed and aid!"
    They shout, as through the gate defiles
The gallant, glistening cavalcade;
    And round the fresh-eyed pasture smiles,
Among the shining streams and shaws,—
"God speed to Monmouth and his cause!"

"Speed!" And the mimic echoes run
    From hill to hill, and wail the word: 80
Over his head to greet the sun

63 the past] yester *del. NB B*
65 bosom] little *or* bosom *NB B*
66 dark] the *del. NB B*   to] of *del. NB B*
67 cheerless wife, the] bosom wife and *NB B, B*
68 him she loves] them they love *del. NB B*
69 young son] children *del. NB B*
70 his] their *del. NB B*
71 mount] climb *NB B*
72 glorious] shining *del. NB B*
76 fresh-eyed pasture] landscape *del.* dewy pasture *NB B*
77 streams] woods *NB B*; woods *or* streams *B*
79 mimic] mocking *or* ready *NB B*   run] take *NB B*
80–82 *NB B:*

        With mimic tongues the human cry,
        Which from the gray mist-hidden brake
        Wide o'er the land they multiply—

81 Over his head] With quivering wings *del.* Above their heads *B*   greet] meet *B*

Quivers the ever-cheerful bird.
The people shout, the clear chimes ring,
And the calm heavens receive their king.

Grandly to take what none contest
    He rises, by all earth desired;
And the liege-limits of the west
    With his effulgent eye are fired.
Duke Monmouth to his saddle-bow
Baring his lustrous head, bows low.   90

Low to the rising sun he bends,
    And at the sight all heads are bare:
"Victorious we shall be, my friends!"
    The host put up a hasty prayer.
"Speed the good youth," sigh distant dames,
"And rid the land of Papist James."

Again Duke Monmouth waves on high
    His bonnet, to the Orient arch:
"See, gentlemen, our augury!"
    And with fresh heart the men all march.   100
Loud, loud, the exulting music plays,
As broader spread the mounting rays.

And cries are yell'd, and caps are flung,
    And up the ranks gay pass-words skim;
And oaths are sworn, and songs are sung,

Lines possibly associated with 83, NB B, [p. 18]:

The lads toss up their caps & bonnets
The exulting music

82 *NB B MS ends here.* Quivers] Upsoars *del. B*
84 calm] blue *or* great *B*
87 *B:* Mountains, and clouds that [line *del.* climb *del.*] scale the West, *or* And [woods *del.*]
heights & clouds that scale the West
94 hasty] mutter'd *B*
95 youth] cause *B*   sigh distant dames] for pure our aims *or* sigh distant dames *B*
101 exulting] *B;* exalting *HW*
102 mounting] ambitious *del. B*
103 caps are flung] songs are sung *del. B*

And stories told in praise of him:
The darling son of English home!
The Cavalier of Christendom!

So lithe of limb, so fleet of foot,
    'Tis he can throw, and leap, and laugh;   110
What marksman with his aim can shoot,
    Or play the steel, or ply the staff?
And some have sisters whom he dower'd;
On all his kindly smiles have shower'd.

For luck, for luck, the boy was born;
    He claims, and he shall have, his own!
And, hopeful as the springing morn,
    They glisten down the curves of Tone.
That he'll be king, his life one stakes:
When he is king, a wife one takes.   120

107 son of] of each *B*
109 lithe of limb] strong of arm *or* lithe of limb *B*
110 leap] fight *del. B*
112 steel] sword *del. B*
115 boy] lad *del. B*
116 *B del.:* Defeat he never yet has known
117 springing] glistening *B*
118 glisten down the curves of] flashing *del.* flash into the quiet *B*
Lines 121–56 not in B; instead:

    King! and what a king he'll be
        For harvest and the merry May!
    [Stout *del.*] Firm as old hall to [sweep? *del.*] the sea;
        Gentle as Charley, and as gay.
    Lord, how the girls will love him then!
    They love him now as much as the men.
    And hot with Feversham to clash
        And buffet with stout English blows,
    They spur the lagging line, and rash
        Cheer to the eye that counts their foes: 130
    Never by numbers known they'll be
    To Englishmen or Victory!
    Still seen, from Taunton town, long seen
        From Taunton tower, the lagging line
    Among the light and dusky green,
        Creeps with its gleaming serpentine;
    There, Monmouth reins to greet the array,—
    Yon, caracoles ill-omen'd ray.
    [Long *del.*] Still seen from Taunton tower, seen long
Berg MS ends here.

King?—It is night, the dream is done,
    And darkness snatches back the crown
That, golden, rose with morning's sun,
    And dropp'd in blood o'er Taunton town.
King of a day, said tidings quick,
While expectation falters sick!

Rumour, with omens in her train,
    Rustles and hums from hedge to hedge:
The battle's fought!—they lose! they gain!
    Alas! delay, that dulls the edge   130
Of keenest blades! Nay, here rides one
To tell us if 't be lost or won.

And one rides in as one rides out;
    And, when the wretched truth is told
At Taunton gates, who does not doubt,
    And in the teeth of fate grow bold,
As if he held, to aid his chief,
A citadel in unbelief?

Drop down the veil on blood and tears,
    Muffle the ear from women's wail;   140
Courage still sits with worthiest peers,
    However basely fortune fail:
But cowards, in the battle's heat,
Carry in their own hearts defeat.

And he that rode Ambition's chace,
    To shine with Europe's highest prize,
Now the most abject of his race,
    Fawns to the hands that most despise.
He hath a love: in her embrace
To live, the man can bear disgrace.   150

And, though they bleed in Taunton town,
    And round the Blood Assize crouch pale;
On no man's forehead comes a frown,

Nor women's curses when they wail,
Point the betrayer out for blame,
At mention of Duke Monmouth's name!

Over the Hills

The old hound wags his shaggy tail,
    And I know what he would say:
It's over the hills we'll bound, old hound,
    Over the hills, and away.

There's nought for us here save to count the clock,
    And hang the head all day:
But over the hills we'll bound, old hound,
    Over the hills and away.

Here among men we're like the deer
    That yonder is our prey: 10
So, over the hills we'll bound, old hound,
    Over the hills and away.

The hypocrite is master here,
    But he's the cock of clay:
So, over the hills we'll bound, old hound,
    Over the hills and away.

The women, they shall sigh and smile,
    And madden whom they may:
It's over the hills we'll bound, old hound,
    Over the hills and away.   20

Let silly lads in couples run
    To pleasure, a wicked fay:
'Tis ours on the heather to bound, old hound,
    Over the hills and away.

OVER THE HILLS

Copy-text: Once a Week *1 (20 August 1859). Also printed in the Edition de Luxe 4
(posth.), and in Mem. Ed.*

The torrent glints under the rowan red,
　　And shakes the bracken spray:
What joy on the heather to bound, old hound,
　　Over the hills and away.

The sun bursts broad, and the heathery bed
　　Is purple, and orange, and gray: 30
Away, and away, we'll bound, old hound,
　　Over the hills and away.

The Story of Sir Arnulph

(Matt. xxii 37–39.—"Thou shalt love the Lord thy God with all thy heart, and with all thy soul, and with all thy mind. This is the first and great commandment. And the second is like unto it, Thou shalt love thy neighbour as thyself.")

I

An earnest man, in long-forgotten years,
Relieved the maladies and stanched the tears
Of pining multitudes, who sought his aid
When death their homesteads threatened to invade.

II

Blest with one only son (a gentle youth,
Trained in the fear of God, and love of Truth,)
He fondly hoped that Arnulph might aspire
Disease and death to baffle, like his sire.

III

But the boy, musing gloomily apart,
Avowed at length the impulse of his heart:
"To some calm cloister, father, I would go,
And there serve God." His father answered, "No."

THE STORY OF SIR ARNULPH

Copy-text: corrected proof for the Edition de Luxe. Previously printed in Once a Week *10 (23 January 1864). MSS: Yale. Corrected TS; corrected proof for "Scattered Poems," Edition de Luxe. Not included in Edition de Luxe.*

IV

"Thou doest well to wish to serve the Lord,
By thine whole life imperfectly adored;
But choose thy work amid the world, and then
Thou canst serve God, and bless thy fellow-men."

V

The boy, still yearning to achieve his plan,
Spake,—"It were better to serve God than man."
"Pray God for help," the father said, "and He
Will solve the riddle of thy doubt to thee."

VI

So Arnulph to his chamber went, and prayed,
That in his doubts the Lord would send him aid;
And, in a vision of the silent night,
A phantom stood before him, clothed in white:
A form for earth too beautiful and grand,
With crimson roses blooming in each hand.

VII

And Arnulph asked the Angel, "Are these flowers
Fresh culled from Eden's amaranthine bowers?"
He answered, "Nay: these offerings are from all
Whom God the doers of His will doth call."
"And can I offer nothing?" sighed the boy;
"May I not also serve the Lord with joy?"
"Surely thou may'st," replied that Spirit fair,
"In my left hand, behold, thy gift I bear."

VIII

Then Arnulph said, "I pray thee, tell me why,
In thy left hand the flowers all scentless lie,
But in the right they breathe a gracious smell,
And do my soul to covet them compel?"

VII.7 Spirit] Seraph *OaW; corr. GM proof for de L*
VIII.3 *OaW:* Which long within the haunted sense doth dwell? *Corr. GM proof for de L*

IX

The Angel answered, with no chiding tone,
"In my left hand I bear the gifts alone
Of those who worship God, the Sire above,
But for His children testify no love;
While *these* sweet roses, that shall ne'er grow wan,
Come from the lovers of both God and man."

X

The vision faded, Arnulph cried, "Alas!
My soul was blind!" And so it came to pass,
That the changed boy a cloister entered not,
But with God's working-men took part and lot.

In the Woods

For the history of this poem, see headnote to *Foresight and Patience*, page 685 and MBF, page 194. The idea may have germinated from a note made as early as 1850 in NB A, [p. 17]:

Dusk of Eve
Night
Midnight
Dusk of Dawn

In the original *Fortnightly* version, section VIII was the present section VI; IV was *Whimper of Sympathy* (see p. 342); VII was *Woodland Peace* (see p. 423); and a final section IX was *Dirge in Woods* (see p. 427).

I

Hill-sides are dark,
And hill-tops reach the star,
And down is the lark,
And I from my mark
Am far.

THE STORY OF SIR ARNULPH

IX.1 no chiding] pathetic *OaW*; entrancing *TS; corr. GM proof for de L*
IX.5 that] which *OaW; corr. GM proof for de L*

IN THE WOODS

Copy-text: the Fortnightly *14 (1 August 1870). Also printed by GMT, pp. 342–46.*

Unlighted I foot the ways.
I know that a dawn is before me,
And behind me many days;
    Not what is o'er me.

II

I am in deep woods,
    Between the two twilights.

Whatsoever I am and may be,
Write it down to the light in me;
I am I, and it is my deed;
For I know that paths are dark
    Between the two twilights:

My foot on the nodding weed,
My hand on the wrinkled bark,
I have made my choice to proceed   10
By the light I have within;
And the issue rests with me,
Who might sleep in a chrysalis,
In the fold of a simple prayer,
    Between the two twilights:

Flying safe from even to morn:
Not stumbling abroad in air
That shudders to touch and to kiss,
And is unfraternal and thin:
Self-hunted in it, forlorn,   20
Unloved, unresting, bare,
    Between the two twilights:

Having nought but the light in me,
Which I take for my soul in arms,
Resolved to go unto the wells
For water, rejecting spells,
And mouthings of magic for charms,
And the cup that does not flow.

I am in deep woods
        Between the two twilights: 30

Over valley and hill
I hear the woodland wave,
Like the voice of Time, as slow,
The voice of Life, as grave,
The voice of Death, as still.

III

Take up thy song from woods and fields
Whilst thou hast heart, and living yields
        Delight: let that expire—
Let thy delight in living die,
Take thou thy song from star and sky,
        And join the silent quire.

IV

With the butterfly roaming abroad
        On the sunny March day,
The pine-cones opened and blew
Winged seeds, and aloft they flew
Butterfly-like in the ray,
        And hung to the breeze:
Spinning they fell to the sod.
        Ask you my rhyme
        Which shall be trees?
        They have had their time.   10

V

I know that since the hour of birth,
        Rooted in earth,
        I have looked above,
        In joy and in grief,
        With eyes of belief,
            For love.

A mother trains us so.
But the love I saw was a fitful thing;
   I looked on the sun
     That clouds or is blinding aglow: 10
  And the love around had more of wing
Than substance, and of spirit none.

Then looked I on the green earth we are rooted in,
     Whereof we grow,
    And nothing of love it said,
    But gave me warnings of sin,
    And lessons of patience let fall,
    And told how pain was bred,
    And wherefore I was weak,
    And of good and evil at strife,   20
    And the struggle upward of all,
And my choice of the glory of life:
     Was love farther to seek?

VI

The lover of life holds life in his hand,
   Like a ring for the bride.
The lover of life is free of dread:
The lover of life holds life in his hand,
   As the hills hold the day.

But lust after life waves life like a brand,
   For an ensign of pride.
The lust after life is life half-dead:
Yea, lust after life hugs life like a brand,
   Dreading air and the ray.   10

    For the sake of life,
    For that life is dear,
    The lust after life
    Clings to it fast.

For the sake of life,
For that life is fair,
The lover of life
Flings it broadcast.

The lover of life knows his labour divine,
And therein is at peace.   20
The lust after life craves a touch and a sign
That the life shall increase.

The lust after life in the chills of its lust
Claims a passport of death.
The lover of life sees the flame in our dust
And a gift in our breath.

The Labourer

This poem was GM's second effort to support Gladstone's fight for
Irish Home Rule, the first having been a short article in the *Pall Mall
Gazette*, 9 July 1886 (see *Miscellaneous Prose*, Mem. Ed., 23:143–45).
    For GM's memorial sonnet to Gladstone, see *Hawarden* on page 675.

For a Heracles in his fighting ire there is never the
        glory that follows,
    When ashen he lies and the poets arise as flames
        from the work he has done.
But to vision alive under shallows of sight, lo, the
        Labourer's crown is Apollo's,
    While stands he yet in the grime and sweat of his
        wrestle for fruits of the Sun.

THE LABOURER

Copy-text: Westminster Gazette, *6 February 1893. Also printed in* LP *and in the Edition
de Luxe 4 (posth.).*

MSS: BM *39, 927. Fair copy; corrected proof for WG; letter to E. T. Cook, 10 February
1893.*
1 a Heracles] Herackles *corr. proof*
2 as flames from] to sing of *fair copy, WG, LP, corr. GM letter to Cook*
4 *fair copy:* While, many beset, in his grime & sweat, he toils for the fruits of the Sun
While] White *misp.* WG, LP, *de L*   the grime and sweat of his] in his grime and
sweat— to *WG, LP, corr. GM letter to Cook*

Can an enemy wither his cheer? Not you, ye fair
    yellow-flowering ladies,
  Who join with your lords to jar the chords of a
    bosom heroic, and clog.
'Tis the faltering friend, an inanimate land, may
    drag a great soul to their Hades,
And plunge him far from a beam of star till he hears
    the deep bay of the Dog.

Apparition is then of a monster-task, in a policy
    carving new fashions:
  The winninger course than the rule of force, and
    the springs lured to run in a stream: 10
He would bend tough oak, he would stiffen the reed,
    point Reason to swallow the passions,
  Bid Britons awake two steps to take where one
    is a trouble extreme!

Not the less is he nerved with the Labourer's resolute
    hope: that by him shall be written,
  To honour his race, this deed of grace, for the
    weak from the strong made just:
That her sons over seas in a rally of praise may
    behold a thrice vitalised Britain,
Ashine with the light of the doing of right: at the
    gates of the Future in trust.

The Warning

On its publication in the *Daily Chronicle* (6 July 1896), *The Warning* was dated "July 4th, 1896."

This sonnet and the next warn the British against colonial aggression. On June 15, 1896, Leander Starr Jameson was committed for trial in connection with his famous, unauthorized raid into the Transvaal at the end of December 1895. Moreover, Lord Kitchener was at that time leading the Egyptian Army in a bloody expedition to recover Mahdist-controlled Sudan.

THE WARNING
Copy-text: Daily Chronicle, *6 July 1896. Also printed in* LP *and in the Edition de Luxe 4 (posth.).*

We have seen mighty men ballooning high,
And in another moment bump the ground.
He falls; and in his measurement is found
To count some inches o'er the common fry.
'Twas not enough to send him climbing sky,
Yet 'twas enough above his fellows crowned,
Had he less panted. Let his faithful hound
Bark at detractors. He may walk or lie.
Concerns it most ourselves, who with our gas—
This little Isle's insatiable greed　　　　　　　　　10
For Continents—filled to inflation burst.
So do ripe nations into squalor pass,
When, driven as herds by their old pirate thirst,
They scorn the brain's wild search for virtuous light.

Outside the Crowd

See headnote to *The Warning* above.

To sit on History in an easy chair,
Still rivalling the wild hordes by whom 'twas writ!
Sure, this beseems a race of laggard wit,
Unwarned by those plain letters scrawled on air.
If more than hands' and armsful be our share,
Snatch we for substance we see vapours flit.
Have we not heard derision infinite
When old men play the youth to chase the snare?
Let us be belted athletes, matched for foes,
Or stand aloof, the great Benevolent,　　　　　　　10
The Lord of Lands no Robber-birds annex,
Where Justice holds the scales with pure intent;
Armed to support her sword;—lest we compose
That Chapter for the historic word on Wrecks.

THE WARNING
11 to] the *misp. DC*
13 pirate] private *DC, LP, de L; corr. errata, de L 1911*
OUTSIDE THE CROWD
Copy-text: National Review 28 *(September 1896). Also printed in* LP *and in the Edition de Luxe 4 (posth.).*

Trafalgar Day

GM also wrote a poem for the centenary of the Battle of Trafalgar;
see *October 21, 1905* on page 788.

I

He leads: we hear our Seaman's call
    In the roll of battles won;
For he is Britain's Admiral
    Till setting of her sun.

When Britain's life was in her ships,
    He kept the sea as his own right;
And saved us from more fell eclipse
    Than drops on day from blackest night.
Again his battle spat the flame!
    Again his victory flag men saw!
At sound of Nelson's chieftain name,
    A deeper breath did Freedom draw.

II

Each trusty captain knew his part:
    They served as men, not marshalled kine:
The pulses they of his great heart,
    With heads to work his main design.
Their Nelson's word, to beat the foe,
    And spare the fall'n, before them shone.
Good was the hour of blow for blow,
    And clear their course while they fought on.

Copy-text: Daily Chronicle, *21 October 1896. Also printed in* LP *and in the Edition de Luxe 4 (posth.)*

III

Behold the Envied vanward sweep!—
    A day in mourning weeds adored!
Then Victory was wrought to weep;
    Then sorrow crowned with laurel soared.
A breezeless flag above a shroud,
    All Britain was when wind and wave,
To make her, passing human, proud,
    Brought his last gift from o'er the grave!

IV

Uprose the soul of him a star
    On that brave day of Ocean days:
It rolled the smoke from Trafalgár
    To darken Austerlitz ablaze.
Are we the men of old, its light
    Will point us under every sky
The path he took; and must we fight,
    Our Nelson be our battle-cry!

He leads: we hear our Seaman's call
    In the roll of battles won;
For he is Britain's Admiral
    Till setting of her sun.

At the Funeral

FEBRUARY 2, 1901

    Queen Victoria had died on January 22, 1901, and on January 28 GM sent these verses to his son with directions to have them printed "in large type and spaced," preferably in the *Morning Post*, "the day before the Funeral." These instructions were followed, and the poem was framed in black.

AT THE FUNERAL

Copy-text: The Morning Post, *1 February 1901. Also printed in* LP *and in the Edition de Luxe 4 (posth.).*

Her sacred body bear: the tenement
   Of that strong soul now ranked with God's Elect.
Her heart upon her people's heart she spent;
   Hence is she Royalty's lodestar to direct.

The peace is hers, of whom all lands have praised
   Majestic virtues ere her day unseen.
Aloft the name of Womanhood she raised,
   And gave new readings to the Title, Queen.

'Atkins'

Thomas or Tommy Atkins, a familiar name for the typical private soldier in the British Army, arose from the casual use of this name in the specimen forms of the official regulations, 1815. It was popularized by Rudyard Kipling's ballad "*Tommy*," in *Barrack Room Ballads* (1893).

Yonder's the man with his life in his hand,
Legs on the march for whatever the land,
   Or to the slaughter, or to the maiming,
      Getting the dole of a dog for pay.
Laurels he clasps in the words 'duty done,'
England his heart under every sun:—
   Exquisite humour! that gives him a naming
      Base to the ear as an ass's bray.

These verses, dated March 5, 1901, were written for the album of Mrs. Clement K. Shorter, wife of the editor of the *Illustrated London News*. Shorter told Maurice Buxton Forman that she had made six pulls of them on her hand press (MBF, pp. 135–36).

'ATKINS'

Copy-text: Westminster Gazette, *18 February 1901. Also printed in* LP *and in the Edition de Luxe 4 (posth.).*

BLEST IS THE SWORD

Copy-text: BM Ashley MS 3638. *Also printed in* Ashley Catalogue *3, no. 137, and in MBF, p. 135.*

Blest is the sword that leaps from sheath
    To break in guarding righteous laws.
There is a heaven shall drop its wreath
    On those who fail in such a cause.

They fall, whose blood is seed beneath
    The victor's tread, a tiger's paws.
Await the day, and swords from sheath
    In thousands leap for such a cause.

The Voyage of the 'Ophir'

The Duke and Duchess of York (later to become King George V and
Queen Mary) sailed in the *Ophir* on March 16, 1901, for a round-the-world
tour of the colonies. The plan had been made before the death of Queen
Victoria on January 22, 1901, and was confirmed by King Edward VII.
    The ship was named after a place often mentioned in the Old Testament
that has never been accurately located and from which Solomon regularly
fetched gold and other precious cargo.

Men of our race, we send you one
Round whom Victoria's holy name
Is halo from the sunken sun
Of her grand Summer's day aflame.
The heart of your loved Motherland,
To them she loves as her own blood,
This Flower of Ocean bears in hand,
    Assured of gift as good.

Forth for our Southern shores the fleet
Which crowns a nation's wisdom steams,   10
That there may Briton Briton greet,
And stamp as fact Imperial dreams.

THE VOYAGE OF THE 'OPHIR'

Copy-text: Pall Mall Magazine 24 (*May 1901*). *Also printed in* LP *and in the Edition de
Luxe 4 (posth.).*

Across the globe, from sea to sea,
The long smoke-pennon trails above,
Writes over sky how wise will be
    The Power that trusts to love.

A love that springs from heart and brain
In union gives for ripest fruit
The concord Kings and States in vain
Have sought, who played the lofty brute,   20
And fondly deeming they possessed,
On force relied, and found it break:
That truth once scored on Britain's breast,
    Now keeps her mind awake.

Australian, Canadian,
To tone old veins with streams of youth,
Our trust be on the best in man
Henceforth, and we shall prove that truth.
Prove to a world of brows down-bent
That in the Britain thus endowed,   30
Imperial means beneficent,
    And strength to service vowed.

GM sent this couplet to Frank Harris, founder and editor of the *Candid Friend*. Harris found the advice "Unacceptable. From my schooldays I have believed that the man who 'struck because he loved' was usually a hypocrite, and invariably a prig" (the *Candid Friend* 1); nevertheless he printed the couplet.

The phrase stems from a quatrain by George Canning in the *New Morality*, 1823:

Give me the avowed, erect and manly foe;
Firm I can meet, perhaps return the blow;
But of all plagues, good Heaven, thy wrath can send,
Save me, oh, save me, from the candid friend.

THE CANDID FRIEND

Copy-text: the Candid Friend *1 (18 May 1901), with facsimile.*

Quoted by Robert Peel in a parliamentary debate, 1845, Canning's words were turned against him in a triumphant rebuttal by Disraeli (Robert Blake, *Disraeli* [New York: St. Martin's, 1967], p. 185).

> The Candid Friend who strikes because he loves,
> Should curb his muscles when he plies the gloves.

The Crisis

Spirit of Russia, now has come
The day when thou canst not be dumb.
Around thee foams the torrent tide,
Above thee its fell fountain, Pride.
The senseless rock awaits thy word
To crumble; shall it be unheard?
Already, like a tempest-sun,
That shoots the flare and shuts to dun,
Thy land 'twixt flame and darkness heaves,
Showing the blade wherewith Fate cleaves,   10
If mortals in high courage fail
At the one breath before the gale.
Those rulers in all forms of lust,
Who trod thy children down to dust
On the red Sunday, know right well
What word for them thy voice would spell,
What quick perdition for them weave,
Did they in such a voice believe.

THE CRISIS

Copy-text: Times, *23 March 1905. Also printed in* LP *and in the Edition de Luxe 4 (posth.).* *MS: Yale. Variants are from this MS.*

3 torrent] downward
6 To fall, & still it is unheard
8 flare] gleam
16 would spell] will tell
17–18 *not in MS*

Not thine to raise the avenger's shriek,
Nor turn to them a Tolstoi cheek;   20
Nor menace him, the waverer still,
Man of much heart and little will,
The criminal of his high seat,
Whose plea of Guiltless judges it.
For him thy voice shall bring to hand
Salvation, and to thy torn land,
Seen on the breakers. Now has come
The day when thou canst not be dumb,
Spirit of Russia:—those who bind
Thy limbs and iron-cap thy mind,   30
Take thee for quaking flesh, misdoubt
That thou art of the rabble rout
Which cries and flees, with whimpering lip,
From reckless gun and brutal whip;
But he who has at heart the deeds
Of thy heroic offspring reads
In them a soul; not given to shrink
From peril on the abyss's brink;
With never dread of murderous power;
With view beyond the crimson hour;   40
Neither an instinct-driven might,
Nor visionary erudite;
A soul; that art thou. It remains
For thee to stay thy children's veins,
The countertides of hate arrest,
Give to thy sons a breathing breast,
And Him resembling, in His sight,
Say to thy land, Let there be Light.

19 Not thine to raise] As little heeds [?] *or* Not thine to raise
20 Nor] As *or* Nor
Between 20 and 21 del.: The tyrants glower, the goaded rave
22 Man of] Who has *del.*
26 to thy torn] for thy wrecked
34 reckless] stolid
36 offspring] children
40 view] views
46 sons] land *del.*

October 21, 1905

The hundred years have passed, and he
Whose name appeased a nation's fears,
As with a hand laid over sea;
To thunder through the foeman's ears
Defeat before his blast of fire;
Lives in the immortality
That poets dream and noblest souls desire.

Never did nation's need evoke
Hero like him for aid, the while
A Continent was cannon-smoke   10
Or peace in slavery: this one Isle
Reflecting Nature: this one man
Her sea-hound and her mortal stroke,
With war-worn body aye in battle's van.

And do we love him well, as well
As he his country, we may greet,
With hand on steel, our passing bell
Nigh on the swing, for prelude sweet
To the music heard when his last breath
Hung on its ebb beside the knell,   20
And VICTORY in his ear sang gracious Death.

Ah, day of glory! day of tears!
Day of a people bowed as one!
Behold across those hundred years
The lion flash of gun at gun:

Copy-text: Outlook in Politics, Life, Letters, and the Arts *16 (21 October 1905), title:*
October 21; *reprinted in the* Observer, *23 May 1909, with facsimile of stanzas 2 and 3. Also
printed in* LP *and in the Edition de Luxe 4 (posth.). MSS: The Fales Collection, New York
University. Stanzas 1–3, 5 numbered IV; uncorrected TS of the same stanzas.*

2 a nation's] his country's *MS, TS*
5 blast] burst *MS, TS*
12 Nature] heaven *del. MS*
17 on] to *MS, TS*   steel] gun *del. MS;* gun *Observer facsimile*   our] the *del. MS*
20 on] at *MS*   beside] above *MS*
Stanza 4 not in MS or TS, 5 numbered IV
22 tears] fears *misp.* Outlook

Our bitter pride; our love bereaved;
What pall of cloud o'ercame our sun
That day, to bear his wreath, the end achieved.

Joy that no more with murder's frown
The ancient rivals bark apart.   30
Now Nelson to brave France is shown
A hero after her own heart:
And he now scanning that quick race,
To whom through life his glove was thrown,
Would know a sister spirit to embrace.

Angela Burdett-Coutts

GM sent this "epigram," as he called it, in a letter to the Editor of
the *Times* on January 4, 1907, saying that he was "uncertain of anything
but the good intention" and that he preferred the simpler name to "The
Baroness Burdett Coutts." The Baroness had died on December 30, 1906,
and was buried in Westminster Abbey on January 5, the day these lines
appeared in the *Times*.

Angela Georgina Burdett-Coutts (born 1814) enjoyed a vast fortune and
was the most renowned female philanthropist of her day. Queen Victoria
had made her a peeress in 1871. She is now chiefly remembered for the
letters that Charles Dickens wrote to her.

OCTOBER 21, 1905

29 Joy that no more] No longer now *del*. But now no more *or* Joy that no more *MS*;
But now no more *TS*
30 rivals bark] foemen stand *del. MS*
31 Now Nelson to brave] In Nelson's life would *del*. Our *del*. Nelson to fair *MS*
33 *MS*: And sure wd he in that [brave race *del*.] proud face *del*. And wd not he in that
proud face *del*. And her now scanning that quick race   *TS*: And sure would he in that
proud face
34 through life] throughout *MS, TS*
35 Would know] Havst seen *or* Would see *or* Behold *or* To whom *or* Wd know *MS*;
Behold *TS*
Stanza 5 [IV] TS:

But now no more, with Murder's frown,
    The ancient rivals bark apart
Now Nelson to fair France is shown
A hero after her own heart.
And sure would he in that proud face,
To whom throughout his glove was thrown,
    Behold a spirit sister to embrace.

ANGELA BURDETT-COUTTS

Copy-text: Times, *5 January 1907. Also printed in* LP *and in the Edition de Luxe 4 (posth.).*
MS: Texas.

Long with us, now she leaves us; she has rest
    Beneath our sacred sod:
A woman vowed to Good, whom all attest,
    The daylight gift of God.

The Centenary of Garibaldi

We who have seen Italia in the throes,
Half risen but to be hurled to ground, and now
Like a ripe field of wheat where once drove plough,
All bounteous as she is fair, we think of those
Who blew the breath of life into her frame:
Cavour, Mazzini, Garibaldi: Three:
Her Brain, her Soul, her Sword; and set her free
From ruinous discords, with one lustrous aim.

That aim, albeit they were of minds diverse,
Conjoined them, hot to strive without surcease;   10
For them could be no babblement of peace
While lay their country under Slavery's curse.

The set of torn Italia's glorious day
Was ever sunrise in each filial breast.
Of eagle beaks by righteousness unblest
They felt her pulsing body made the prey.

Wherefore they struck, and had to count their dead.
With bitter smile of resolution nerved
To try new issues, holding faith unswerved,
Promise they gathered from the rich blood shed.   20

THE CENTENARY OF GARIBALDI

Copy-text: Yale, *two TSS corrected by GM. Also printed in the* Times, *1 July 1907; in* LP;
and in the Edition de Luxe 4 (posth.).

9–12 *not in Times*
10 hot] not *del. TSS;* not *misp. LP, de L*

In them Italia, visible to us then
As living, rose; for proof that huge brute Force
Has never being from celestial source,
And is the lord of cravens, not of men.

Now breaking-up the crust of temporal strife,
Who reads their acts enshrined in History, sees
That Tyrants were the Revolutionaries,
The Rebels men heart-vowed to hallowed life.

Pure as the Archangel's cleaving Darkness thro',
The Sword he sees, the keen unwearied Sword,   30
A single blade against a circling horde,
And aye for Freedom and the trampled few.

The cry of Liberty from dungeon cell,
From exile, was his God's command to smite.
As for a swim in sea he joined the fight,
With radiant face, full sure that he did well.

Behold a warrior dealing mortal strokes,
Whose nature was a child's: begirt by foes
A wary trickster: at the battle's close,
No gentler friend this leopard dashed with fox.   40

Down the long roll of History will run
The story of those deeds, and speed his race
Beneath defeat more hotly to embrace
The noble cause and trust to another sun.

And lo, that sun is in Italia's skies
This day, by grace of his good sword in part.
It beckons her to keep a warrior heart
For guard of beauty, all too sweet a prize.

38 begirt by] amid his *del. TSS*; amid his *LP, de L*
39 battle's] *TSS*; warfare's *Times*
42 those] *Times;* these *del. TSS;* these *LP, de L; corr. errata, de L 1911*

Earth gave him: blessèd be the Earth that gave.
Earth's Master crowned his honest work on earth: 50
Proudly Italia names his place of birth:
The bosom of Humanity his grave.

The Wild Rose

This poem, written in GM's elderly, shaky hand, is his ultimate celebration of a lifetime favorite. See *The Wild Rose and the Snowdrop*, in *Poems* (1851):

The Wild Rose blooms, all summer for her dower,
Nature's most beautiful and perfect flower.

High climbs June's wild rose,
Her bush all blooms in a swarm;
And swift from the bud she blows,
In a day when the wooer is warm;
Frank to receive and give,
Her bosom is open to bee and sun:
Pride she has none,
Nor shame she knows;
Happy to live.

Unlike those of the garden nigh,   10
Her queenly sisters enthroned by art;
Loosening petals one by one
To the fiery pursuer's dart
Superbly shy.
For them in some glory of hair,
Or nest of the heaving mounds to lie,
Or path of the bride bestrew.

THE WILD ROSE

Copy-text: Scribner's *42 (December 1907). Also printed in* LP *and in the Edition de Luxe* 4 *(posth.).* MS: *Yale, lines 10–38.*

13 pursuer's] Passion's *LP*
16 lie] die *MS*
17 path] the path *MS*

Ever are they the theme for song.
But nought of that is her share.
Hardly from wayfarers tramping along,   20
A glance they care not to renew.

And she at a word of the claims of kin,
Shrinks to the level of roads and meads:
She is only a plain princess of the weeds,
As an outcast witless of sin:
Much disregarded, save by the few
Who love her, that has not a spot of deceit,
No promise of sweet beyond sweet,
Often descending to sour.
On any fair breast she would die in an hour.   30
Praises she scarce could bear,
Were any wild poet to praise.
Her aim is to rise into light and air.
One of the darlings of Earth, no more,
And little it seems in the dusty ways,
Unless to the grasses nodding beneath;
The bird clapping wings to soar,
The clouds of an evetide's wreath.

18 Ever are they] And ever are they *or* these *del.* And they are *MS*
19 But nought] Nothing *del. MS*
20 Hardly] Only *MS*
22 And] But *del. MS*
24 only] barely *MS*
25 *MS*: As a Magdalen [without *del.*] witless of sin
27 spot] trace *MS*
29 descending to] resulting in *MS*
30 die in] fade ere *MS*

Il y a Cent Ans

I

That march of the funereal Past behold;
    How Glory sat on Bondage for its throne;
How men, like dazzled insects, through the mould
    Still worked their way, and bled to keep their own.

II

We know them, as they strove and wrought and
      yearned;
    Their hopes, their fears; what page of Life they
      wist:
At whiles their vision upon us was turned,
    Baffled by shapes limned loosely on thick mist.

III

Beneath the fortress bulk of Power they bent
    Blunt heads, adoring or in shackled hate;
All save the rebel hymned him; and it meant
    A world submitting to incarnate Fate.

IV

From this he drew fresh appetite for sway,
    And of it fell: whereat was chorus raised,
How surely shall a mad ambition pay
    Dues to Humanity, erewhile amazed.

Copy-text: Pierpont Morgan Library, *proof corrected by GM. Also printed in* The Flag: The Book of the Union Jack Club, *edited by H. F. Trippel* (*London: The London Daily Mail, May 1908*); *and in* LP. *MSS:* The Pierpont Morgan Library, *fair copy 11 stanzas; corrected proof with additional MS stanzas IX and X; revise;* Yale, *proof corrected by GM 11 stanzas.*

III.1 bulk] birth *corr. proof* Y

V

'Twas dreamed by some the deluge would ensue,
    So trembling was the tension long constrained;
A spirt of faith was in the chirping few,
    That steps to the millennium had been gained.

VI

But mainly the rich business of the hour,
    Their sight, made blind by urgency of blood,
Embraced; and facts, the passing sweet or sour,
    To them were solid things that nought withstood.

VII

Their facts are going headlong on the tides,
    Like commas on a line of History's page;
Nor that which once they took for Truth abides,
    Save in the form of youth enlarged from age.

VIII

Meantime give ear to woodland notes around,
    Look on our Earth full-breasted to our sun:
So was it when their poets heard the sound,
    Beheld the scene: in them our days are one.

IX

Will there be rise of fountains long repressed,
    To swell with affluents the forward stream?
Will men perceive the virtues in unrest,
    Till life stands prouder near the poets' dream?

V.1 dreamed] deemed *MS*
V.3 spirt] spirit *corr. proof Y*   chirping] chosen *MS, corr. proof Y, LP*
VI.3 the passing] however *MS, corr. proof Y*
VIII.2 to our] to the *del. MS*
IX–X *insert in Morgan proof, not in LP*

X

Our hopes, in battling acts embodied, dare
  Proclaim that we have paved a way for feet
Now stumbling; air less cavernous, and air
  That feeds the soul, we breathe; for more entreat.

XI

What figures will be shown the century hence?
  What lands intact? We do but know that Power
From piety divorced, though seen immense,
  Shall sink on envy of a wayside flower.

XII

Our cry for cradled Peace, while men are still
  The three-parts brute which smothers the divine,
Heaven answers: Guard it with forethoughtful will,
  Or buy it; all your gains from War resign.

XIII

A land, not indefensibly alarmed,
  May see, unwarned by hint of friendly gods,
Between a hermit crab at all points armed,
  And one without a shell, decisive odds.

The Call

On June 25, 1908, GM asked his son to send copies of the *Oxford and Cambridge Review*, in which *The Call* appeared, to The Hon. A. Deakin, Prime Minister of Australia, and to The Lady Edward Cecil.

In a letter to H. M. Hyndman, January 5, 1909, GM referred to *The Call* as a poem that cried for a national army. "One may fear that a landing of foreign artillery on our shores alone will arouse the mercantile class. Doubtless, also, there is an apprehension as to the prudence of schooling the toilers in the use of arms. We are not yet a people."

IL Y A CENT ANS
X.4 That] Of *del. MS*
XI.4 a wayside] the humblest *MS, LP*
XIII.2 see] view *del. MS* hint] signs *del. MS*
THE CALL

Copy-text: Oxford and Cambridge Review 4 (*Midsummer 1908*). *Also printed in* LP *and in the Edition de Luxe 4* (*posth.*).

Under what spell are we debased
    By fears for our inviolate Isle,
Whose record is of dangers faced
    And flung to heel with even smile?
Is it a vaster force, a subtler guile?

They say Exercitus designs
    To match the famed Salsipotent
Where on her sceptre she reclines;
    Awake: but were a slumber sent
By guilty gods, more fell his foul intent.   10

The subtler web, the vaster foe,
    Well may we meet when drilled for deeds:
But in these days of wealth at flow,
    A word of breezy warning breeds
The pained responses seen in lakeside reeds.

We fain would stand contemplative,
    All innocent as meadow grass;
In human goodness fain believe,
    Believe a cloud is formed to pass;
Its shadows chase with draughts of hippocras.   20

Others have gone; the way they went
    Sweet sunny now, and safe our nest.
Humanity, enlightenment,
    Against the warning hum protest:
Let the world hear that we know what is best.

So do the beatific speak;
    Yet have they ears, and eyes as well;
And if not with a paler cheek,
    They feel the shivers in them dwell,
That something of a dubious future tell.   30

For huge possessions render slack
    The power we need to hold them fast;
Save when a quickened heart shall make
    Our people one, to meet what blast
May blow from temporal heavens overcast.

Our people one! Nor they with strength
        Dependent on a single arm:
Alert, and braced the whole land's length,
        Rejoicing in their manhood's charm
For friend or foe; to succour, not to harm.   40

Has ever weakness won esteem?
        Or counts it as a prized ally?
They who have read in History deem
        It ranks among the slavish fry,
Whose claim to live justiciary Fates deny.

It can not be declared we are
        A nation till from end to end
The land can show such front to war
        As bids a crouching foe expend
His ire in air, and preferably be friend.   50

We dreading him, we do him wrong;
        For fears discolour, fears invite.
Like him, our task is to be strong;
        Unlike him, claiming not by might
To snatch an envied treasure as a right.

So may a stouter brotherhood
        At home be signalled over sea
For righteous, and be understood,
        Nay, welcomed, when 'tis shown that we
All duties have embraced in being free.   60

This Britain slumbering, she is rich;
        Lies placid as a cradled child;
At times with an uneasy twitch,
        That tells of dreams unduly wild.
Shall she be with a foreign drug defiled?

The grandeur of her deeds recall;
        Look on her face so kindly fair:
This Britain! and were she to fall,
        Mankind would breathe a harsher air,
The nations miss a light of leading rare.   70

Youth in Age

Once I was part of the music I heard
  On the boughs or sweet between earth and sky,
  For joy of the beating of wings on high
My heart shot into the breast of the bird.

I hear it now and I see it fly
  And a life in wrinkles again is stirred,
  My heart shoots into the breast of the bird,
As it will for sheer love till the last long sigh.

On Como

GM first saw Lake Como in the summer of 1861 when, with his young
son Arthur and his friend Bonaparte Wyse, he traveled there to visit
Wyse's mother, the Princess Letitia, at her home the Villa Ciani. On this
trip they had walked through the Swiss, Austrian, and Italian Alps, and
GM was overwhelmed by them. They became a symbol of aspiration for
the attractive characters in nearly all of his subsequent novels. Diana, in
Diana of the Crossways (1885), at one point settles down to do her writing
at Bellagio on Lake Como (chap. 15). *On Como* is possibly a revision of a
poem written in 1861 or shortly thereafter.

A rainless darkness drew o'er the lake
As we lay in our boat with oars unshipped.
It seemed neither cloud nor water awake,
And forth of the low black curtain slipped

YOUTH IN AGE

Copy-text: Country Home *1 (May–October 1908). Also printed in* LP *and in the Edition de Luxe 4 (posth.).* MS: *Yale.*

1.2 between] beneath *del. MS*

ON COMO

Copy-text: Scribner's *44 (December 1908). Also printed in* LP *and in the Edition de Luxe 4 (posth.).*

Thunderless lightning. Scoff no more
At angels imagined in downward flight
For the daughters of earth as fabled of yore:
Here was beauty might well invite
Dark heavens to gleam with the fire of a sun
Resurgent; here the exchanged embrace   10
Worthy of heaven and earth made one.

And witness it, ye of the privileged space,
Said the flash; and the mountains, as from an abyss
For quivering seconds leaped up to attest
That given, received, renewed was the kiss;
The lips to lips and the breast to breast;
All in a glory of ecstasy, swift
As an eagle at prey, and pure as the prayer
Of an infant bidden joined hands uplift
To be guarded through darkness by spirits of air,   20
Ere setting the sails of sleep till day.
Slowly the low cloud swung, and far
It panted along its mirrored way;
Above loose threads one sanctioning star,
The wonder of what had been witnessed, sealed,
And with me still as in crystal glassed
Are the depths alight, the heavens revealed,
Where on to the Alps the muteness passed.

Milton

DECEMBER 9, 1608: DECEMBER 9, 1908

These lines were written at the request of Professor Israel Gollancz,
then Secretary of the British Academy, who read them at the Tercentenary
Commemoration at Burlington House on December 8, 1908, the eve of
Milton's birthday. GM had written Gollancz on October 26 that he was

MILTON
Copy-text: The British Academy, The Tercentenary of Milton's Birth, Inaugural
Meeting. At the Theatre, Burlington Gardens, Tuesday, December 8, 1908. *Also printed
in the* Times, *9 December 1908; in* LP; *and in the Edition de Luxe 4 (posth.). MSS:* Yale.
Fair copy; fragment lines 41–46; facsimile lines 38–46 in Mem. Ed., Poems 3, *facing p. 250.*

highly complimented by the request and had written "some lines" that
he would have set in type and sent on to him but that he would not mind
if they were "dismissed" and "would much rather have the task placed in
other hands." Gollancz told Maurice Forman (MBF, p. 141) that the
lines were in most of the newspapers the next day.

In private conversation GM was not so adulatory of Milton as in this
poem. He had told Edward Clodd on October 28, 1899, that "Milton has
masses of fine passages amid wastes of blank verse; he has echoed so much
of current theology. Was there ever a more clumsy set of fables made the
fundamentals of a 'revealed' religion?" He agreed with Leslie Stephen
that Milton was the supreme master of blank verse and that Book 1 was
the best book of *Paradise Lost* but of course was unsympathetic with the
theology: "Some of the conceptions are provocative of humour, material
for which will sadly decrease as dogma decays" (*TLS-II*; Clodd, p. 152).

What splendour of imperial station man,
The Tree of Life, may reach when, rooted fast,
His branching stem points way to upper air
And skyward still aspires, we see in him
Who sang for us the Archangelical host,
Made Morning, by old Darkness urged to the abyss;
A voice that down three centuries onward rolls;
Onward will roll while lives our English tongue,
In the devout of music unsurpassed
Since Piety won Heaven's ear on Israel's harp.   10

The face of Earth, the soul of Earth, her charm,
Her dread austerity; the quavering fate
Of mortals with blind hope by passion swayed,
His mind embraced, the while on trodden soil,
Defender of the Commonwealth, he joined
Our temporal fray, whereof is vital fruit,
And, choosing armoury of the Scholar, stood
Beside his peers to raise the voice for Freedom:
Nor has fair Liberty a champion armed
To meet on heights or plains the Sophister   20
Throughout the ages, equal to this man,
Whose spirit breathed high Heaven, and drew thence
The ethereal sword to smite.

6 urged] called *del. MS*
18 voice] note *MS*

                Were England sunk
Beneath the shifting tides, her heart, her brain,
The smile she wears, the faith she holds, her best,
Would live full-toned in the grand delivery
Of his cathedral speech: an utterance
Almost divine, and such as Hellespont,
Crashing its breakers under Ida's frown,
Inspired: yet worthier he, whose instrument   30
Was by comparison the coarse reed-pipe;
Whereof have come the marvellous harmonies,
Which, with his lofty theme, of infinite range,
Abash, entrance, exalt.

                We need him now,
This latest Age in repetition cries:
For Belial, the adroit, is in our midst;
Mammon, more swoln to squeeze the slavish sweat
From hopeless toil: and overshadowingly
(Aggrandized, monstrous in his grinning mask
Of hypocritical Peace,) inveterate Moloch   40
Remains the great example.
                    Homage to him
His debtor band, innumerable as waves
Running all golden from an eastern sun,
Joyfully render, in deep reverence
Subscribe, and as they speak their Milton's name,
Rays of his glory on their foreheads bear.

32 have] has *MS*
35 This latest] A later *del. MS*   cries] sings *MS*
41 *frag.:*

                Abash, entrance, exalt. Homage to him,
                The pure of aim, trilustral in his robe
                Of poet, patriot & citizen;

42 *frag.:* His debtors now innumerable as the waves
43 Running] Leaping *frag.*   an] an *or* their *frag.*
44 in deep reverence] reverentially *MS*
46 bear] wear *MS*

Part III
Posthumously Published Poems and Trivia

These posthumously published poems and trivia are arranged in the probable order of their composition.

St. Therèse

Saint Theresa (1515–82) was the famous mystic of Avila, who reformed the Carmelite order. The versification and sentiment of the poem are obvious imitations of Tennyson's *St Agnes' Eve* (1837, 1842).

1

With holy earnest eyes enshrined
　　She bendeth on her knees
Her voice is heard above the wind
　　Shrill from the northern seas:
The sisters stoop on either hand
　　She smileth mild on each
And in the wind a choral band
　　Comes singing to her speech.

2

Her hands are tested palm to palm
　　Then folded as in rest
Beneath her dawning eyelids calm
　　Upon her snow white breast
Her snowy garments rustle clear
　　As snowflakes rise or mix
And to her neck there presseth near
　　A silver Crucifix—

Copy-text: "*The Monthly Observer.*" *Previously printed in* The Contributions of George Meredith to the "Monthly Observer," January–July 1849, *ed. Maurice Buxton Forman* (*Edinburgh: printed for private circulation, 1928); and in Robert E. Sencourt, "Unpublished Poems of Meredith,*" Commonweal 10 (22 May 1929). MSS: "*The Monthly Observer,*" *January 1849;* NB A, [*p. 5*], *stanzas 3 and 4.*

3

Around her gloried form the air
   Is starr'd with falling snows
That cover all the convent bare
   With symboll'd pure repose
Above her haloed head the sky
   Is studded thick with spheres
All swimming to one blissful eye
   Whose beam is bright with tears—

4

She knoweth that the time will come,
   And in the deepened night
Discerneth well her Heaven home
   The morning and the light
And thro' the shadow of her pain
   A seraph sister voice:—
But now she kneeleth once again
   That others may rejoice

Brotherhood

1

The Land is rich where'er we go
   With Flowers and Fruits in clusters,
No little spot so poor and low
   But some sweet tribute musters;
Abundance blesses—all things show
   We should bless one another;
"Take"—says the Lord—but man says "No"
   —But these are mine—my Brother—

BROTHERHOOD

Copy-text: "The Monthly Observer." Previously printed in Forman, Contributions;
Sencourt, "Unpublished Poems of Meredith"; and Jack Lindsay, George Meredith: His
Life and Work (London: Bodley Head, 1956), p. 35. MS: "The Monthly Observer,"
March 1849.

2

Strange is the difference which breeds
 Dissension among creatures,
Which binds the slave for slavish greeds
 And brands his godlike Features—
One Family are we, and Oh
 The children of one mother!—
"Live"—says the Lord but man says "No"
 Thy Life is mine—my Brother—

3

The treasures of the Earth how vast
 Exhaustless and unnumbered!
Stored with the hivings of the past
 Since first old Chaos slumbered—
And is there then no thankful glow
 To knit us to each other?
Ah God when will this dreary "No"
 Melt at the name of Brother?

4

Religion is a war of sect,
 And Fatherland of Factions;
Each deems himself the sole elect
 But not thro' virtuous actions,
Not in the deeds whereby we know
 The light no clay can smother—
Alas! to all things man says "No"
 And still denies his Brother.

Sonnet

Hateful are those false themes of speculation
Goading the wise and harrassing the weak—
This world of ours—so lovely and unique
Why is it subject to such sad vexation?—
'Tis all for want of proper occupation
"PHILOSOPHERS" become so VOID and VAIN;
With birth, life, death, mind, matter, bone and brain
Can there be any doubt of our CREATION?—
And of our Spirits early information—
Intelligence and Action?—chief whereby   10
Thro' rapid glances of the inner eye
The Soul is sentient of its own salvation
And in the Faith that such a knowledge brings
Feels the great glory of its Future wings.

Translations from German Poets

GM edited the June 1, 1849, number of "The Monthly Observer" and wrote in the reviews at the end of the number: "These are almost literal translations from celebrated German lyrists among which class the illustrious Göthe ranks conspicuously. They will be continued during the term of our Editorship—" His editorship continued through July 2, 1849, after which there are no further extant numbers known. The manuscript journal may have perished at this point (Maurice Buxton Forman, *George Meredith and "The Monthly Observer"* [London: privately printed, 1911], p. 22).

HATEFUL ARE THOSE FALSE THEMES

Copy-text: "The Monthly Observer." Previously printed in Galland, p. 421; Forman, Contributions; *and in Sencourt, "Unpublished Poems of Meredith." MS: "The Monthly Observer," March 1849.*

HEINE: MY HEART

Copy-text: "The.Monthly Observer." Previously printed in Forman, Contributions; *and in Sencourt, "Unpublished Poems of Meredith." MS: "The Monthly Observer," June 1849.*

Heine: My Heart

1

Thou lovely Fishermaiden,
Steer in thy boat to Land;
Come to me and sit Thee down
We'll whisper hand in hand.

2

On my heart thy little head
Lay down and fear not me,
Thou who daily trustest
The wild, wild sea.

3

Even as the sea my heart
Has storms and ebb and flow,
And many a beauteous pearl
Lies calm in its deeps below.

von Eichendorff: Moonlight Night

Josef Freiherr von Eichendorff (1788–1857) was a Catholic poet of
Upper Silesia, and *Mondnacht* was one of his most popular lyrics.

1

It was, as if the Heaven
Had kiss'd Earth with its beam
That she in blooming glimmer
Must sweetly of it dream.

HEINE: MY HEART
1.4 We'll] And *del.*

VON EICHENDORFF: MOONLIGHT NIGHT
Copy-text: "*The Monthly Observer.*" *Previously printed in Forman,* Contributions; *and
in Sencourt,* "*Unpublished Poems of Meredith.*" *MS:* "*The Monthly Observer,*" *June
1849.*
I.4 it] him *del.*

2

The breeze went over the Fields,
The ears were waving light,
The woods were gently rustling,
So starry was the night.

3

And my whole soul outspreading
Her wings abroad to roam,
Flew thro' the sleeping Land,
As if towards its home.

Göthe: Song

Joyful
And woful,
And thankful remain;
Swaying
And praying
In hovering pain;
Heavenwards exulting
Deathhurl'd from above;
Happy alone
Are the souls that love!   10

Göthe: Confession

What is hard to hide? the Fire!
For by day the smoke betrays it
And the Flame by night, the monster.
Again 'tis hard our Love to hide,

GÖTHE: SONG

Copy-text: "The Monthly Observer." Previously printed in Forman, Contributions; and
in Sencourt, "Unpublished Poems of Meredith." MS: "The Monthly Observer," June
1849.

GÖTHE: CONFESSION

Copy-text: "The Monthly Observer." Previously printed in Forman, Contributions; and
in Sencourt, "Unpublished Poems of Meredith." MS: "The Monthly Observer," June
1849.

For howsoever you enclose it,
Out of the eyes it softly smites you.
But hardest 'tis to hide a Poem,
Under no bushel you'll conceal it.
Has but the Poet freshly sung it
Thereby is he quite overcome;   10
Has he just smartly dash'd it off
He wills, that the whole world shall love it.
To all he reads it glad and loud,
Whether it fret us or instruct.

Uhland: The Landlady's Daughter

Three Students went over the Rhine one day
And to a good Landlady made their way—

"Now Landlady have you good wine and beer,
"And how is your little Daughter dear"?

"My wine and beer, is fresh and clear
"On her Deathbed lays my Daughter dear."

And as they into the Chamber stept
In a black coffin they saw she slept.

The first from her face the white veil took
And look'd at her long with a sorrowful look.   10

"Ah! wer't Thou alive Thou maiden flower
"Thee should I love from this very hour."

The second he put the white veil to
And turn'd away and wept anew.

UHLAND: THE LANDLADY'S DAUGHTER

Copy-text: "*The Monthly Observer.*" *Previously printed in* Forman, Contributions; *and in* Sencourt, "*Unpublished Poems of Meredith.*" *MS:* "*The Monthly Observer,*" *July 1849.*

"Ah that thou liest on Thy Death bier
"Thee have I loved this many a year."

The third again put by the veil
And kiss'd her on the lips so pale.

"Thee loved I ever and still I love Thee
"And Thee shall I love thro' Eternity."   20

Creed

Two Brothers went a journey hand in hand—
It was the road of life with many paths,
And many feet had left a weary print
To guide them; these with thankful lips they blest—
And one built pillars where the thorns were thick,
Recording names of those that triumph'd there
For worship to the ages; bending low
The other shaped them in his inmost heart.

It was the middle of their pilgrimage;
The Flowers and Thorns were known—both Fruits of life,   10
When morning met them on an eastern hill,
And down a wide survey they saw the dawn
Brush softly on the eyelids of all men!
There stood they in the soul's serenest calm,
And watch'd the waking motions of the earth.

Then spake the Elder—He who marked old paths—
"I will build temples unto Him I praise!"
The other answered not, and he resumed;—
"I see beneath me men who labour long
"And finish their tired days with song and dance,   20

CREED

Copy-text: Yale *MS. Previously printed in* Altschul, *pp. 3–5 with 3 lines omitted and other errors. Variants are from* Yale *MS.*

16 old paths] the ways *del.*
20 song and dance] dance and song *del.*

"Instead of thanks and prayer; to them comes death—
"The unseen Presence of their joyfullest hours,
"The echo of their laughter! When it comes—
"Dust is their only offering to the earth,
"And of them nought remains but scattered dust.
"Say, shall eternal spirits be content
"Thus to be mocked by fleetingness? to see
"Their fellow creatures issuing from the husk
"Thus daily—all the symbols of their doom
"Before them—all the Drama of their Fate.   30
"And not one congregated work to show
"Their strength in this world and their faith in the next?
"Some sculptured Image of the All-present Power;—
"Some architecture of sublime design;—
"Some vast creative system of Belief;
"Set chaunts and solemn services ordained—
"These things would awe to universal Creed,
"And earth steam up with incense to the skies!
"Emotions such as seize the dying soul
"Would thrill and quicken the deep hearts of men,   40
"Thro' all their daily toil and then—O then,
"Thanksgiving like the flower of the grave
"Fresh from the heaving green would smile and bloom!
"Lo! I will raise them in the name of God
"And on the work His lineaments shall shine,
"And of the Angels who before Him kneel,
"Feathering their dazzled brows with their large wings;
"Such is the gleam of His incessant glory!
"Yea! and before this structure I design,
"The multitudes shall kneel; beholding there   50
"Impersonate, the splendour that they worship!
"And unto us His Ministers anointed—
"Us, Martyrs in divine humility,
"That splendour shall be poured, so that the people
"Gazing on us shall see poor human flesh

45 shine] stand *del.*
51 that they] they shall *del.*

"Elsewhere so frail and feeble, fill'd with Grace,
"And able to dispense the gift of God!
"O grandeur of the thought! that this great work
"Should image His Eternity and stand
"Eternal on the earth for evermore!"   60

Thereat his Brother lifting up at once
His eyes and hands towards the full blue sky—
"And will it live its days so long as that?—
"Or like yon cloudlet change when it is will'd
"And yet not pass away? Or like those hues
"Obey the sister seasons one by one,
"In beauteous evanescence of all grace?
"O can one sculptured Image ever give
"One lineament of likeness unto Him
"We reverence in the souls unfathom'd depths?   70

"Divide not men! for all will never come
"To bow within your temples—shun the thought!
"Religion should be universal love,
"And not a coop for blind Enthusiasts,
"Who cannot sympathize with natural life,
"And all the sweet desires of human being!
"This is a ruin that you meditate;—
"Weeds only can take growth from the decay;—
"But in an everduring life behold
"The flowers of nature! Quickened with a joy   80
"Unconscious and divine, they pay their debt,
"By smiling thro' the beauty of their seasons;—
"To die and to relive in deathless change!
"We? what can we? but gratefully throb thro'
"The limits of our lives? content to do
"Good deeds and learn the duties of our state!
"Making mortality worthy of the hope
"Of immortality! and gaining Faith
"In future life by reverence for the present!

"—— O Brother, Brother! 90
"To do thy duty is to act a prayer
"More earnest in the conscious eye of God,
"Than all the Formulas of earth-built Creed:
"Duty is prayer—truth to human kind
"And glad devotion unto Him who made.
"The conflicts of the soul will sink the knee—
"But not in Temples built of the cold stone!"

They parted—and those Brothers to this day,
With kindred love and one religious aim—
Are strangers to each others Heart and Home! 100

The Years Had Worn Their Seasons' Belt

Although this poem could well have been one of the "last" poems that William Maxse Meredith discovered for his hastily contrived *Last Poems* (1909), whether it is a late composition can be questioned. The idea of a cozy group of friends, for instance, "our ring" (line 17) and "On us" (line 29), echoes the *Requiem* for a maiden in *Poems* (1851), "Thou cam'st to us . . ." (p. 20). The Wordsworthian echo of line 9 is also an early influence. In "She dwelt where 'twixt low-beaten thorns" one hears "She dwelt among the untrodden ways," with a side-reference to *The Thorn*.

> The years had worn their seasons' belt,
>   From bud to rosy prime,
> Since Nellie by the larch-pole knelt
>   And helped the hop to climb.
>
> Most diligent of teachers then,
>   But now with all to learn,
> She breathed beyond a thought of men,
>   Though formed to make men burn.

THE YEARS HAD WORN

Copy-text: Scribner's 46 (*October 1909*). *Also printed in* LP.
Title and 1 seasons'] season's *LP*

She dwelt where 'twixt low-beaten thorns
    Two mill-blades, like a snail,   10
Enormous, with inquiring horns,
    Looked down on half the vale.

You know the grey of dew on grass
    Ere with the young sun fired,
And you know well the thirst one has
    For the coming and desired.

Quick in our ring she leapt, and gave
    Her hand to left, to right.
No claim on her had any, save
    To feed the joy of sight.   20

For man and maid a laughing word
    She tossed, in notes as clear
As when the February bird
    Sings out that Spring is near.

Of what befell behind that scene,
    Let none who knows reveal.
In ballad days she might have been
    A heroine rousing steel.

On us did she bestow the hour,
    And fixed it firm in thought;   30
Her spirit like a meadow flower
    That gives, and asks for nought.

She seemed to make the sunlight stay
    And show her in its pride.
O she was fair as a beech in May
    With the sun on the yonder side.

There was more life than breath can give,
    In the looks in her fair form;
For little can we say we live
    Until the heart is warm.   40

9 'twixt] twist *misp. S*
26 knows] know *S*

To R. H. H. with Daphne

For GM's relationship with Richard Henry (or Hengist) Horne, see
Introduction, page xxx. *Daphne* was included in *Poems* (1851); see page 33.

That you will take the meaning of this verse
I know, deep-hearted friend and earnest man,
Poet! and thro' the simple picture see
The winged fancy rising from the flower!
Too delicate for me to touch, or do
Aught but suggest; send forth as Nature sends
The unfettered insects fluttering with delight
Thro' the long warm blue summer's day and folded
At eve behind some rainy leaf, while the woods
Sing wet with Tempest—On its wings alone   10
Let it depend when once the warm-fingered sun
Has touched it into life—Enough for me
To paint the flower in all its natural hues
And plant it; this done, its fate is with the sky.
But you will know how in these after days,
First love still follows the fair fleeting shape!
From the flush'd morning wave and woodland valley
Urging its wild pursuit, while still in vain
Swift Nature lends her forces, still in vain
The old prophetic trees wave overhead—   20
Ah! happy he whose last inspired desire
Conquering its anguish shall have power to pluck
The never-fading laurel! Round his brows
Sweet Beauty hovers and a dawning gleam
Wakes ever on the leaves, for they are steep'd

Copy-text: NB WW, *scrap of white paper pasted therein; above the title:* "Not fit."
Previously printed in WMM, pp. 5–7; and in Cline, Letter 9.

7 insects] insect *MS*
18 while still *MS* while *om. WMM*
24 a] the *del. MS*

I' the springs of day, and therefore do we mark
This strange foreshadowed crown of poet love,
The crown of poet passion. Thus to you
I dedicate, and in your hands I place
Daphne, the darling of my own first love.   30
So take her, part in friendship, but indeed
Chiefly a tribute to the noble lyre
Which sang of the giant bright whose starry limbs
Still scale the midnight Heavens and plant aloft
Heroic footsteps up untravelled space!—
Live long and wear that constellated wreath.

Ode to H.I.M. Napoleon 3d

GM sent these opening lines of an ode [September 20, 1854] to his first
publisher, John Parker, Jr., saying that he would finish it, evidently for
the September 1854 issue of *Fraser's*. He was writing from Dover, "in
view of Calais cliffs." The ode did not appear in *Fraser's*.

Imperial by the People's will,
And swaying with such sovereign skill
Power that is a gorgeous pyre
        To Sceptre's slaves of Ire—
Thou &c &c

TO R.H.H.

26 do we mark] scans it why *del. MS*
28 you] thee *del. MS*
29 your] thy *del. MS*
33 giant bright] bright giant *del. MS*

ODE TO H.I.M. NAPOLEON 3D

Copy-text: Yale *MS. Previously printed in Cline, Letter 28.*

Song of Ruark to Bhanavar the Beautiful

Inasmuch as I count 733 lines of verse in *The Shaving of Shagpat*, I would not willingly have dissevered any of them from their parent body, but these two poems (Mem. Ed., pp. 43, 294) were included in GMT, and students of GM may expect to find them in this edition.

Bhanavar the Beautiful is the type of a fated vampire woman, and Ruark, a tribal chief, is her victim. Noorna first appears as an old crone who promises the barber hero Shibli Bagarag magical powers if he kisses her. He does so, and, like Gawain's bride, she turns into a beautiful young woman who aids him in his difficult task. His goal is to shave Shagpat, a pretentious tailor who holds dominion over a city because of the power that lies in his immense hairiness.

> Shall I counsel the moon in her ascending?
> Stay under that tall palm-tree through the night;
> Rest on the mountain-slope
> By the couching antelope,
> O thou enthroned supremacy of light!

> And for ever the lustre thou art lending,
> Lean on the fair long brook that leaps and leaps,—
> Silvery leaps and falls.
> Hang by the mountain walls,
> Moon! and arise no more to crown the steeps,   10
> For a danger and dolour is thy wending!

The Teaching of the Blows of Fortune

> Ye that nourish hopes of fame!
> Ye who would be known in song!
> Ponder old history, and duly frame
> Your souls to meek acceptance of the thong.

SONG OF RUARK TO BHANAVAR

Copy-text: GMT, pp. 575–76.

THE TEACHING OF THE BLOWS OF FORTUNE

Copy-text: GMT, p. 576.

Lo! of hundreds who aspire,
Eighties perish—nineties tire!
They who bear up, in spite of wrecks and wracks,
Were season'd by celestial hail of thwacks.

Fortune in this mortal race
Builds on thwackings for its base;   10
Thus the All-Wise doth make a flail a staff,
And separates his heavenly corn from chaff.

Think ye, had he never known
Noorna a belabouring crone,
Shibli Bagarag would have shaved Shagpát?
The unthwack'd lives in chronicle a rat!

'Tis the thwacking in this den
Maketh lions of true men!
So are we nerved to break the clinging mesh
Which tames the noblest efforts of poor flesh.   20

Although William Maxse Meredith, in WMM (p. 18), reported that these verses were given to Miss Janet Duff Gordon in 1859 or 1860, I believe that they were written in the winter of 1856–57 when GM was living at Seaford on the English Channel and his wife, Mary, was spending most of her time in London. The verses may have been given to Janet to help explain how GM had felt on the brink of his wife's desertion. The first stanza is echoed in the last two lines of *Modern Love*.

The waves are pressing up with force,
Along the screaming shore;
Like Phantom hosts of warrior horse,
They charge, beneath the roar.

THE WAVES ARE PRESSING UP

Copy-text: WMM, p. 18.

And each darts out a foamy tongue
   As prone he falls, and dies:
The dirge of many a soul is sung
   Beneath yon stormy skies.

And may it be my dirge of dust,
   If she who has my plight,   10
If she I love shall wreck my trust,
   And wrap my soul in night.

Hungarian Air

Remember'st thou
The golden hours
I pluck'd the flowers
To wreathe your brow?—
     Ah, not as now!

Remember'st thou
The kiss witheld,—
Thy tremours quell'd;
The double vow?
     Ah, not as now!—   10

Lied von Castelli

WMM (p. 19) printed *Lied von Rastrelli*, a name that I have pursued in vain. Deducing that he transcribed carelessly, as he often did, I propose Ignaz Franz Castelli (1781–1862), a member of the Viennese "Posse" school. "The humour of the 'Posse' was a humour of situation and local allusions, a favourite comic effect being to transfer the ordinary citizen of Vienna to the incongruous surroundings of fairyland" (J. G. Robertson, *A History of German Literature*, 4th ed. [Edinburgh: Blackwood, 1962], p. 450). Castelli and Eduard von Bauerfeld are named by GM in his unsigned review article, "The Austrian Poets" (see headnote on p. 741) as "humorous writers . . . great favourites with the Viennese."

HUNGARIAN AIR

Copy-text: Yale *MS. Previously printed in MBF, p. 223, from* Mr William Brown's Catalogue of Books and Autographs, *no. 231 (1918).*

Deep, deep, under the sea,
Pearls throw their soft lights uselessly:
Hear the wave wander,
Hither and yonder:
Deep, deep, under the sea.

High, high, thro' the bright spheres,
Music there is no mortal hears:
Love's divine chorus,
Passes dead o'er us:
High, high, thro' the bright spheres.   10

Dark, dark, here in my breast
Treasures and harpstrings idly rest:
All my life lingers
Dumb for thy fingers:
Dark, dark, here in my breast.

⟨⟩

This poem and those following, through "We sat beneath the humming pines," were written for Janet Duff Gordon (later Ross). WMM (p. 19) added the preceding translation, *Lied von Rastrelli* [Castelli], but it is not among the Janet Ross papers at Yale.

For the story of GM's relationship with this charming young woman after he had settled with his son Arthur at Copsham Cottage, Esher, in 1859, see LS, chapter 4, and Janet Ross's own account in *The Fourth Generation*. In her book Mrs. Ross recalled the meetings with "my poet" by the Black Pool: "I made him write down some of the verses he improvised as we sat among the heather, and still have the faded scraps of paper with his characteristic writing in the well-known blue ink." Janet, at sixteen, dictated to GM what the heroine of *Evan Harrington* (1860) would or would not say. "*Evan Harrington* (which was first called *He would be a Gentleman*) was *my* novel, because Rose Jocelyn was myself" (p. 50).

LIED VON CASTELLI

Copy-text: WMM, pp. 19–20.
7 *or* Harps of the Angels thrill heavenly ears:

SING ALOUD THAT SHE IS MINE

Copy-text: Yale MS. Previously printed in Altschul, p. 36.

Sing aloud that she is mine,
O hills, that morn discover!
Of her love I have the sign—
Too sweet to declare.

But know you a maiden's manner
Of revealing to her lover
That 't is he whom she doth favour
The first of them there?

Sing aloud that she is mine,
O hills, that morn discover! &c

The chambers of my heart are many, dear:
You must not know in which you sit enthroned:
Where lies its central seat must not be own'd,
Nor whether inmate it has any, dear.

Night walks the earth with silver feet:
The upper sky shines cold as steel.
I would I were with you, my sweet,
To tell you what I feel.

'Tis midnight in the skies, my dear.
'Tis night o'er fowl and fish!
I am not very wise, my dear,
In wishing such a wish:

THE CHAMBERS OF MY HEART
Copy-text: Yale *MS. Previously printed in* Altschul, *p. 36.*
NIGHT WALKS THE EARTH
Copy-text: Yale *MS. Previously printed in* Altschul, *p. 36.*
'TIS MIDNIGHT IN THE SKIES
Copy-text: Yale *MS. Previously printed in* Altschul, *pp. 36–37.*

Yet still methinks could I lie by
While you are soft asleep,
'T were sweet to hear your equal sigh,
To mark your dream—how deep!

But what is this? Ah, thought of dread!
Ah! thought of rage and shame!   10
That—lower when I lean my head—
I hear—the CURATE'S NAME!

Think not, should your husband swear
Furious love and frantic zeal,
He will shave a single hair,
Though, petitioning, you kneel.

Think not, though his eye surveys
Now, your ample girth—his Queen!
He will ever speak with praise
Of that breadth of crinoline.

Now, the happy lover scorns
Gastronomical excess: 10
You might tread upon his corns,
He your little foot would bless.

Soon the jolly husband sits
Gloating o'er recherché fare:
Ah! where then have gone his wits?
And his taste has gone—Oh, where?

THINK NOT, SHOULD YOUR HUSBAND SWEAR

Copy-text: Yale *MS. Previously printed in* Altschul, *p. 37.*

Schubert's "Farewell"

FOR JANET

Janet Ross wrote: "My Poet was very fond of music, and his favourite song was Schubert's *Addio*. I complained about the commonplace German words, so he wrote for me the following verses, which have brought tears to many eyes" (p. 52). This gift was probably given late in 1860 after Janet had announced her engagement to Henry James Ross. Shortly thereafter the Hardmans (see headnote on p. 829) wished to see his words, and GM wrote Janet on February 15, 1862, asking whether, if she had no objection, she would send the poem to him. But she did object on the grounds that the verses were written for her alone.

The pines are darkly swaying:
The skies are ashen-gray:
I mock my soul, delaying
The word I have to say.
    As if above it thundered
    That we, who are one heart,
    Must now for aye be sundered,
    My passion bids me part:
I dare not basely languish,
Nor press your lips to mine;   10
But with one cry of anguish,
My darling I resign.

Our dreams we two must smother:
The bitter truth is here:
This hand is for another,
Which I have held so dear!
    To pray that, at the altar,
    You may be bless'd above:–
    Ah, help me, if I falter,
    And keep me true to love!   20

Copy-text: Yale *MS. Previously printed in WMM, pp. 12–13; and in Ross, p. 53.*
7 Must] Should *WMM*
15 This] The *WMM*

But once, but once, look kindly–
Once clasp me with your spell:
Let joy and pain meet blindly,
And throb our dumb Farewell!

While Janet eyes the Lanthorn's Magic,
Lo her poet stays composing:
Now, his mood is wild & tragic,
Now, 't is naught but spoony prosing.

Schubert's song the wretch has written,
And (the feeling to ensure it)
He has striven to be smitten
With the ardours of the Curate.

Is he deep? pathetic? touching?
(Heaven! how thou a freak avengest!)   10
He himself feels something clutching
At his heart, like what he penn'd just.

Crown him, crown him, and for laurel,
Use a nightcap! else how soon he
May betray his folly!—
                    Moral:
Ape the Spoon, you *must* be spoony!

SCHUBERT'S "FAREWELL"

22 your] thy *del. MS*
24 dumb] life's *del. MS*

WHILE JANET EYES

Copy-text: Yale *MS. Previously printed in* Altschul, *pp. 37–38.*

13 and for] quick[?] with *del. MS*
16 you] you'll *del. MS*

⌒∿∿⌒

We sat beneath the humming pines:
　　We knew that we must part,
I might not even speak by signs
　　The motions of my heart:

And as I took your hand, and gazed
　　Subdued into your eyes,
I saw the arm of Fate upraised,—
　　And still'd the inward cries:

I saw that this could never be
　　Which I had dared to pray: 10
And in the tear that fell from me,
　　There fell my life that day!

⌒∿∿⌒

This set of verses and the two following were addressed to GM's friend
Bonaparte Wyse in the spring of 1861. Only the second is dated: "Copsham,
May 3rd, 4th, or 5th" (Ellis, p. 118). In Avignon Wyse, having fallen under
the spell of Provençal poetry, especially that of Mistral whom GM also
admired (see p. 705 and headnote), wrote poems in the dialect.
　"It's many a penny" parodies Poe's *Annabel Lee.*

It's many a penny you'll pay to go
　　To a town beneath the skies,
Where a gentleman dwells whom you may know
　　By the name of Bonaparte Wyse.

WE SAT BENEATH THE HUMMING PINES

Copy-text: Yale *MS. Previously printed in WMM, p. 17.*

Associated with line 1, NB B, [p. 12]: Beneath the swarming whispers of a pine

3 might] dared *del. MS*
7 arm] hand *del. MS*
9 could] might *del. MS*

IT'S MANY A PENNY

Copy-text: Cline, Letter 93. Previously printed in Ellis, p. 117. MS: University of
California, Los Angeles.

I was a pote, and *he* was a pote,
　　In this town of merchandize:
And we laughed at jests profane to quote,
　　I and my Bonaparte Wyse,
We cracked our joke improper to quote,
　　I and my Bonaparte Wyse.　　　　　　　　　10

　　Chorus—Tol-loddi, tol-loddi;
　　　　Tol-le-loddi—tolloddi—tollieo.

The unfulfilled engagement was for a walk in the Vale of Mickleham.

　　I look'd for my poet—he came not!
　　　　He came not, though much I expected him.
　　His breach of agreement I blame not,
　　　　But Faith has forever rejected him!

　　　　(*Chorus*—Through Eternity, "Forever," etc.)

Yes, tho' the weather be December O!
　　Is this a fair excuse, my Bonaparte,
For Friar's Omelettes kill'd in embryo,
　　And breakfasts spoilt, or eaten on'y part?

Lo, the sweet sunshine to shame thee!
　　'Tis the weather for poets to forage in.　　　　10
In the clouds I reproachfully name thee,
And they say—Here his promise has origin!
Of us, and in us, see his origin!
His misty, remarkable origin!

I LOOK'D FOR MY POET

Copy-text: Cline, Letter 94. Previously printed in Ellis, p. 118.

In facetious imitation of Christopher Marlowe's most famous lyric,
"Come live with me and be my love."

> Yes, we'll pic-nic in the woods,
> And touch on the diviner moods,
> We will forget that we are clay,
> And live the fulness of our day.
> On ladders of pure Niersteiner,
> On Burgundy or simple Claret,
> (Than which on Earth there's nothing finer,
> When waiters stand not by to mar it),
> We'll mount diviner and diviner,
> Until at last on men we glance   10
> Olympian-like, electively,
> And 'gin to laugh, and shout, and dance,
> And get locked up, effectively.

Madrigal

"Tuck" was William Hardman, a barrister whom GM met at Esher in
the summer of 1861. They were great walking and laughing companions,
and adopted nicknames for each other from the legend of Robin Hood:
GM being Robin, Hardman being Friar Tuck. Hardman was the model
for the politically conservative Blackburn Tuckham in *Beauchamp's
Career* (1875). He was a busy man-about-town in London and sent a
monthly journal, of which he kept copies, to a friend of his Cambridge
days who had emigrated to Australia. This journal, *The Hardman Papers*,
is a source of primary importance to an understanding of the life and
character of GM.

GM's letters to Hardman are now in the Garrick Club and have been
published by C. L. Cline. The first of these verse letters was sent [May 5,
1862] from Copsham, which was the name of the cottage near Esher
where GM lived from 1859 until his second marriage in 1864. "The
Mound" was a conspicuous hill near by.

Cline dates this Madrigal [May 5, 1862] and adds that it was inspired
by Hardman's cancellation of a visit on the weekend.

YES, WE'LL PIC-NIC

Copy-text: Cline, Letter 100. Previously printed in Ellis, p. 120. MS: Yale.

Since Tuck is faithless found, no more
        I'll trust to man or maid;
I'll sit me down, a hermit hoar,
        Alone in Copsham shade.
The sight of all I shun
        Far-spying from the mound:
I'll be at home to none
        Since Tuck
        Since Tu-a tua tua
taiaaia tuuuoa Tuck   10
        is faithless found.

⧸⧹

"Tuck! Tuck!" was sent from Copsham the day after the *Madrigal*.
Ripley, like Esher, is a village in Surrey. GM noted that the verses were to
be sung to the tune of "Johnny's too late for the fair."

Tuck! Tuck! Once you would flatter me,
Saying that I in due season should fatter be,
Here is Asparagus—what can the matter be?
        Why don't you join in the fare?

Ripley's the place with the jolly old Talbot Inn,
Once we two passed there, you know, and were all but in.
Rhyme now commands me to throw here a small 'but' in.
        Why don't you join in the fare?

SINCE TUCK IS FAITHLESS FOUND
Copy-text: Cline, Letter 158. Previously printed in MVP, *pp. 126–27; and in* WMM, *p. 69.*
7 to none] no more *WMM*

TUCK! TUCK! ONCE YOU WOULD FLATTER ME
Copy-text: Cline, Letter 159. Previously printed in MVP, *p. 127; and in* WMM, *p. 70.*
4 fare] Fair *MVP, WMM*
8 fare] Fair *MVP, WMM*

⌒〜〜⌒

These stanzas are part of a letter written to William Hardman from Ryde Pier Hotel [August 16, 1862], in which GM asked Hardman to write his weekly *Ipswich Journal* article for him so that he could sail with friends as far as the Channel Islands. GM added that the ditty was to be sung to a "Popular London air, commonly chanted by Tuck and Robin," and Hardman noted that this was a "melody of the nigger character" (*MVP*, p. 177).

> To-morrow I am going
>   —I cannot tell you where
> The wind is stoutly blowing
>   The ladies'—
> (word of 2 syllables à discretion)
>   bare
> And now for a toast!
>   (To Tuck the toast shall be)
> I'm off along the coast,
>   I would he were with me.

[Asks William Hardman to do this week's article for the *Ipswich Journal*.]

> For I'll be in a cabin,
>   Just 3 feet long, 4° square;
> Just ponder on your Robin,
>   The figure of him there.
>   I don't give a dam,
>   etc. etc.

⌒〜〜⌒

The reference to Black Foakes' Day that leads into "Willy-nilly" is again to the *Ipswich Journal*, in a letter to Hardman dated George Inn, Great Marlow [September 7, 1862]. The black day was the Thursday of each week that GM had to spend in the London office of Thomas Eyre Foakes, owner of the *Ipswich Journal*.

TOMORROW I AM GOING

Copy-text: Cline, Letter 171. Previously printed in MVP, *p. 177, first stanza; and in* WMM, *pp. 77, 78, second and third stanzas.* MVP *quotes from memory;* WMM *omits first stanza.*

I say, that but for black Foakes'-day, known to no calendar save
mine—alas! I would,

> Willy-nilly,
> be off with you a jolly dance
> To Falmouth, Torquay, Penzance,
> or Scilly.

⌒〰⌒

This quatrain was part of a letter to Frank Burnand, in late September
of 1862. Francis Cowley Burnand (1836–1917) was at that time on the
staff of *Fun*, a newly founded magazine in imitation of *Punch*. In 1880 he
became editor of *Punch*, a position that he held for twenty-six years.

> As often in a bun,
> The currants you surprise,
> Behind the mask of Fun
> I catch my Franco's eyes.

⌒〰⌒

GM subscribed these verses to Hardman: "Madrigal written in St.
John's Col[lege], Cambridge, Saturday, October 4, 1862."

> Tuck, sweet charmer, tell me why
> I'm at ease when you are by?
> Have you had a 'round' with Care,
> Left him smoshen, stript him bare,
> That he never more can try
> Falls with me when you are by?

WILLY-NILLY

Copy-text: Cline, Letter 172. Previously printed in WMM, p. 80.

AS OFTEN IN A BUN

Copy-text: Cline, Letter 178. Previously printed in WMM, p. 83.

TUCK, SWEET CHARMER

Copy-text: Cline, Letter 180. Previously printed in MVP, p. 187; and in WMM, p. 84.
Previous texts faulty and incomplete.

Ah, but when from me you're screened
Atrabiliar glows the Fiend:
Fire is wet and water dry:
Candles burn cocked hats awry: 10
Hope her diamond portal shuts,
Grim Dyspepsia haunts my—ahem!

※

A verse letter to Mrs. Augustus Jessopp, November 4, 1862. Arthur
Meredith, aged nine, had been accepted by her husband into Edward VI
Grammar School at Norwich, but GM had neglected to provide for the
boarder's equipment.
   The letter is headed: "Tune: '*Lady Geraldine*' Burden, '*Chatter,
chatter*' *ad inf.*" The allusion is to Elizabeth Barrett Browning's poem,
Lady Geraldine's Courtship, a poem that begins, "Dear my friend and
fellow-student."

Dear, my friend & honour'd madam! of hard facts I'm not a
      hoarder,
And that you will quite forgive me my forgetfulness, I beg!
It had pass'd me what was requisite to stock the little boarder,
But dream we of its feathers when the chick has burst the egg?

Oh! the happy close of Norwich, with its towering Cathedral!
Its boys that shout at Prisoner's Base, the envy of a man!
Oh, the happy 'harping' hours when of Confederate & Federal,
We talked, what time of Partridge full & eke of Parmesan!

Methinks, to let the days slip by, it was not noble, Madam,
While my infant was deficient in such necessary things;   10
Compell'd to rest on charity, or else to sleep like Adam
Without a tow'l to wipe his face, a spoon to oil his springs.

DEAR, MY FRIEND
Copy-text: Yale *MS. Previously printed in Ellis, p. 176; in* Altschul, *pp. 41–42; and in*
Cline, *Letter 186.*

Ha! you scorn us? is it not so? I am led to think it, certes;
But so terrible a poet's wrath, I pardon ere I blame.
I see the little fellow who so lovely in his shirt is,
And I swear an oath that this day week the sheets shall own his
    name.

The pillow-cases likewise, towels six, & silver fourchette;
The tea-spoon & dessert-spoon (For I have it all by rote):
I will send them in a jiffy—But, pray, tell me (with the door shut);
Do you find him such a darling 't is no wonder that I dote?   20

Oh! had I but a passion now, to tear it all to tatters,
And storm as doth the limp young man who frightened Geraldine!
I have chatter'd as that weedy, woman's-tender-ruffian chatters—
May it give you satisfaction!—which remaineth to be seen.

Oh, Lady of the Three Black Cats! farewell, & let me hope a
Meeting we may compass, ere in effigy you stand,
In Norwich's Cathedral, our illustrious St. Jessopa,
A scroll to tell a Boarder's needs in Heaven, in your hand!

The Jolly Young Carpenter

Hardman introduced these verses from a letter of November 10, 1862, by saying that GM had taken "to felling trees and sawing up logs of wood, as a healthy exercise, to promote the circulation and improve his digestion" (*MVP*, pp. 206–7). The meter is that of the popular song, "The Jolly Young Waterman" (1774) by Charles Dibdin, and Hardman commented that the manufactured rhyme "*Sarpenter*" is appropriate if given "the Yankee pronunciation" (p. 207).

> Oh! did you ne'er hear of a jolly young Carpenter,
>   Sawing his logs, with the song of the lark:
> In tripping the lasses there ne'er was a *Sarpenter*,
>   Didn't they think his voice sweet after dark!

THE JOLLY YOUNG CARPENTER

Copy-text: Cline, Letter 188; excerpts previously printed in MVP, *p. 207. Lines 6 and 8 omitted in* MVP.

To give his opinions and thoughts in extenso,
   I can't, so, to say they were moral, will do:
His Bible he stuck to, in spite of Colenso,
   And taught the girls Genesis while the cock crew.
      Ahem!——

⌒⌥⌒

This was an apology to Hardman for breaking a dinner engagement
[December 3, 1862].

   O shrive me Friar, my ghostly Friar!
      Quick, shrive me now, he cried.
   For I have kiss'd a mortal maid,
      And something more, beside.

   The Friar he frown'd, his belt he hitched,
      In accents stern spake he.
   The thing that in my day I did,
      Was never meant for thee!
      Etc., etc.

⌒⌥⌒

The day that GM was to dine with Cotter Morison (see p. xxxiii) was
December 10, 1862.

   Tuck, my treasure! Tuck, my pleasure!
   Lucas won't have a meet at the 'Cheshire
   Cheese' till after Christmas—truly,
   He's a bore and I'm yours, duly,
                Robin!
P.S.
   And if you love me, write and say so.
   Quaequae cupit, sperat—sings Ovidius Naso:

O SHRIVE ME FRIAR
Copy-text: Cline, Letter 191. MS: Garrick Club.
TUCK, MY TREASURE
Copy-text: Cline, Letter 192. Previously printed in WMM, p. 90; lines 3–6 in MVP, p. 216.

To-day, you know, I dine with Morison.
Is there a dinner with Tuck in the horizon?
I'm expecting, of course to behold Mrs. Hamilton,   10
First subject of Bonny (which to mention were
      dam'ill ton).

These verses appear in a letter to Hardman, December 13, [1862],
breaking an engagement because GM's son Arthur was arriving in
London from school.

Adieu, adieu, my Friar, he cried;
    My lusty Friar, adieu!
O, much I trust that they have lied,
    Who tell these things of you:

That when you go forth to tell your beads,
    That waggling paunch behind,—
You do but count the maidenheads
    You've ta'en from maids too kind:

And therefore in a jealous fit,
    Damn every mother's son,   10
Who fain would have a taste of it,
    By humbly taking *one*.

GM reported [December 13, 1862] that he had to take Arthur down to
play amid the furze on Copsham Common. His regular nickname for
Arthur was "Sons" in the plural. The reference to Hardman's pronuncia-
tion of "Thursday" is to his Lancashire accent.

And tho' my friar's mandate is severe,
The wishes of the Son of Sons are dear.
    I really fear
I must bring home my little man on Thursday;
(As you would rhyme) that he may in the furze play.

ADIEU, ADIEU
*Copy-text: Cline, Letter 194. Previously printed, in garbled form, stanza 1, in WMM, p. 91.
MS: Garrick Club.*
AND THO' MY FRIAR'S MANDATE
*Copy-text: Cline, Letter 195. Previously printed in WMM, p. 90; and in MVP, p. 225 n.
MS: Garrick Club.*
4 home my little man] my little man home *MVP*

The *Irene* had just been bought by Cotter Morison, who injudiciously invited a party of friends on a winter cruise. These verses were sent to Hardman from Esher [January 6, 1863], a few days before the expedition.

> The *Irene* ducks and runs amuck
> At all she meets on ocean bobbin':
> Hard to the taffrail clutches Tuck:
> There's little of the 'cock' in Robin'!
> Below, discussing pipes and beer,
> And all that may and all that mayn't be,
> St. Bernard says that he feels queer,
> And queerer still feels Mrs. St. B.
> James Parthenon of tempest tells,
> Five jolly yachtsmen once were lost in: 10
> Pales the red cheek of Tuck, as swells,
> With Ocean's wrath, the gorge of Austin.
> 'Now, do you think, you Argue-nots,'
> St. Bernard asks, 'sea-sick was Jason?'
> The jolly yachtsmen eye their cots:
> Austin cries 'Oh!'—and Tuck 'A bason!'
> St Bernard hurries on the deck;
> Not long his chattering teeth have kept tune,
> To waves that threat the *Irene*'s wreck,
> When one bears off his pipe to Neptune!   20
> Then Tuck, half doubting he's afloat,
> Rolls up, with eyes all greeny-sheeny:
> Clutches St. Bernard by the throat:—
> 'Tell me! did Cubitt build the *Irene*?'
> —Five jolly yachtsmen! Yachtsmen five!
> And have you seen five jolly yachtsmen?
> If they're not dead, why, they're alive:—

Copy-text: Cline, Letter 202. Previously printed in WMM, *pp. 96–97; and in* MVP, *pp. 243–44. MS: Garrick Club.*

16 Oh] Ho *WMM*
19 To] At *MVP*

They're sprawling mid the pipes and pots, men!
A ghostly yacht at night you'll see
Come sailing up the British Channel   30
A poet and a Friar there be
On board: the latter frock'd in flannel.
Like Lucifers with Lobsters dash'd,
The hue upon their cheeks and noses.
The Friar cries loud: 'Our fate we've hash'd,
Why sail'd we not i' the time of Roses?
There was a place called Gordon Street,
'A planet known as Francatelli:'

On the cruise of the *Irene*, anticipatorily described by GM in the
preceding verses, GM composed this limerick "about Swinburne, a wild,
red-haired poet, who lives with Rossetti" (*MVP*, p. 245).

There was a young poet of Chelsea
Who never was able to spell 'sea.'
    With 'C.' he . . .
    But it always came . . .
'That'll do!' said the poet of Chelsea.

These three stanzas are contained in a letter to William Hardman from
Copsham [February 1, 1863]. GM was inviting "Tuck" to dinner, and
somewhat to his surprise, Hardman accepted.

Friar uxorious!
Ain't it notorious
You have no joy a-
-way from Detroïa?

29 A] The *WMM*   at night] which now *WMM*
30 Come] Go *WMM*
31 there] there'll *WMM*
36 i'] in *MVP*
THERE WAS A YOUNG POET
Copy-text: MVP, *p. 245. Also printed by Maurice Buxton Forman in* Meredithiana
(*Bibliographical Society, 1924*), *p. 304.*

Write me no pretty note
Puling excuses.
Scorn'd by the Muses,
Who's tied to a petticoat!

No, he *wouldn't* leave his wife,
And he *shouldn't* leave his wife   10
 He didn't come to Copsham, cos,
He COULDN'T leave his wife!

A verse letter to Hardman [March 25, 1863].

 O have you seen my Tuck? my bonny bonny
  Tuck!
 O have you seen my Tuck? my darling and my
  dear!
 He carries of his paunch like a ship about to
  launch,
(Bis) With his body-guard of Bass's bitter beer!

(Chorus) He carries etc.

Tupperian Chorus. He carries a million times etc.

 O I have seen your Tuck! your bonny bonny
  Tuck!
 O I have seen your Tuck! your darling and
  your dear!
 He followed of his paunch like a mighty
  avalanche,
(Bis) With his body-guard of Bass's bitter beer!

FRIAR UXORIOUS!
Copy-text: Cline, Letter 208, three separated stanzas. Previously printed in part and inaccurately in WMM, pp. 100–01. MS: Garrick Club.

O HAVE YOU SEEN MY TUCK?
Copy-text: Cline, Letter 217. MS: Garrick Club.

Little Martin Tupper
Sang for his supper   10
In such pretty verses,
Praised the Northern Lass,
Deep from Tuck the curses
Came from Beer of Bass.

The verses about crossing the *T* of Tuck and the following couplet
("At the first ball") are included in a letter to Hardman [July 4, 1863].
GM writes that the third quatrain was interrupted by a sneezing fit and
asks Hardman to finish it.

The world is full of different fates,
Of good and evil luck:
Happy is he who at Love's gates,
May cross the T of Tuck!

My friends in smiles of Fortune bask,
The flowers of Fortune pluck:
I envy not: I only ask
To cross the T of Tuck.

Survey man's race: the few in front,
The many in the ruck!   10

See above headnote. The couplet alludes to a cricket match at the
Curragh, Ireland, in which the Prince of Wales, later Edward VII, had
been bowled out.

At the first ball his wicket fell, and sins
No more has batted your illustrious Prins.

THE WORLD IS FULL OF DIFFERENT FATES
Copy-text: Cline, Letter 234. Also printed in The Letters and Memoirs of Sir William
Hardman, *edited by S. M. Ellis (London: Constable, 1928), p. 47. MS: Garrick Club.*
AT THE FIRST BALL
Copy-text: Cline, Letter 234. Also printed in WMM, p. 108; and in Hardman, *as for
preceding verses, p. 48. MS: Garrick Club.*

[Verses by GM and Lionel Robinson]

Lionel Robinson (1839–1923) worked many years in the accounting departments of Somerset House. He lived next door to the Hardmans in Bloomsbury (see Cline, Letter 234, n.1). Taking an immediate liking to him, GM nicknamed him *poco curante*, soon shortened to Poco.

This letter, in prose and verse, was written to William Hardman by GM and Lionel Robinson. R = Robin, GM; P = Poco, Lionel Robinson (Cline, Letter 239).

R.—   Tuck, Demitroïa,
           Ariadne, and Froyja;
           The loveliest quartette
           To give a man joy-a!—

R.—   But, O my Tuck, go not before me!
           A lonely sun is shining o'er me.
           Think of your Robin, 'tis no joke, O,
           Left in the grasp of demon Poco!

P.   —Believe him not; no sun, nor moon
           Afford the faintest light—
           But only candles such as made
           Of patent composite.

R.—   Even as some little doggie
           Whom his mistress will not see,
           Quasi-squatted by the wayside
           One leg lifted; fixed on three.

P.   —My verses run (by rail at least)
           Though *some* may say they hobble
           What matter's that?—for well it's known:

Copy-text: Cline, Letter 239. Twelve lines printed at random by WMM, p. 114. MS: Garrick Club.

Two poets always squabble ⎫ utrum horum mavis
We're starting for Grenoble ⎭ accipe—

R.—   Tell me where he wanders,
        Gentle breezes, pray!
        If in peace he saunters (qy, spelling?)
        Regular each day.—

[R.]   —A poet by the wayside went.
        He met a monk, a holy man.
        'O shrive me, friar', he said and bent
        His head. 'Confess', the monk began.

        'O one of thine I've loved too well.
        Too well I've loved that friar so fat.
        The muses blew into a shell
        Whene'er he laughed, and sweet his chat!'

        'No more', the dark Confessor said.
        'I know him: one of many, thou!   10
        He when thy heart is won, has fled:
        For ages he has done as now.

        'There is no hope: thou canst not rest:
        Obedient to his wanton whim,
        Yea, North and East and South and West,
        Forever must thou follow him.

        'Young Cupid was he call'd of old;
        With Will o'Wisp incorporate:—

R.   'Tuck is he named, a reveler bold
        To follow him is ay thy fate.

        'He hath thee in a golden mesh
        And thee will have forevermore.
        He is the Genius of the Flesh,'
        —Yet still, my Tuck, I thee adore.

[R.]   —Pity the sorrows of a *poor young man*
        Who vainly seeks a rhyme

[P.]   Of rhythm he's not over much
        But compensates in *time*.

In a letter to Hardman, August 1, [1863]. In order to improve his circulation and digestion, GM was tossing the beetle, an instrument with a heavy head and a handle for driving wedges and for ramming (Cline, Letter 199, n.2).

The beetle soars, the beetle spins,
The beetle is up in the air, Tuck;
'Twill crack Robin's crown as a stamp for his sins,
Or make him defy old care, Tuck.

These verses, as well as the preceding ones about the beetle, are in Cline, Letter 241.

My jolly friar,
Now lift thy cowl,
And send me a laugh
Like a revelling owl.
Were I lying and groaning
In pits of fire,
Thy laughter like water
Would fall, my friar!

THE BEETLE SOARS

Copy-text: Cline, Letter 241. Previously printed inaccurately in WMM, p. 117; and in Ellis, p. 189.

MY JOLLY FRIAR

Copy-text: Cline, Letter 241. Previously printed inaccurately in WMM, p. 117; and in Ellis, p. 189.

❧

Hardman, in his journal-letter of October 1865, chatting about Fenianism even reaching occasionally into the ranks of the British Army, added that a "*young lady*, aye a lady, has actually joined a Volunteer regiment as a Vivandiere! Meredith describes her dress to me in doggerel verse as follows" (*The Hardman Papers, 1865–1868*, p. 61).

> Her trousers are red; she wears a coatee;
> Behind, like a bustle, a barrel you see;
> She swings it in front, and carries it handy,
> This barrel contained nothing other than brandy.

Hatton's 'God of War'

These are the opening lines of an unpublished poem "Described as 'comprising 28 lines and dated from Esher, 6th March, 1864.' Accompanied by an autograph letter to 'Dear Lewis' referring to the poem, and in which Meredith says—'Will this do? I think it beats t'other.' The piece is stated to be a 'War Song in support of Denmark in her war with Germany of 1863—4.'" During this year intervention on behalf of Denmark against her Prussian and Austrian invaders was a popular cause in England, but it had been thwarted by Palmerston in the interest of the Queen whose late husband's origin made her pro-German. The "Lewis" addressed in this untraced letter is undoubtedly Arthur Lewis, conductor of a choir, with whom GM had dined on March 3, 1864 (Cline, Letter 267, n.2). The popular composer, John Liptrot Hatton (1809–86) had evidently contributed a tune to Lewis with the rhythm of "God save the Queen," and Lewis wanted words for it. Since GM sent the poem just three days after dining with Lewis, it seems likely that "t'other" poem which he refers to in his covering note had been written by someone else.

> Come with the cannon-wheel,
> Banner, and naked steel,
> God of our last appeal,
> Come to our aid!

HER TROUSERS ARE RED

Copy-text: William Hardman, The Hardman Papers: A Further Selection (1865–1868), *edited by S. M. Ellis (London: Constable, 1930), p. 61.*

HATTON'S 'GOD OF WAR'

Copy-text: MBF, p. 222, from Maggs's Catalogue, no. 346 (1916).

Shine on us in the fray;
Justice is scoffed away;
Rights must be held this day
    By the stout blade.

Here a small host we stand,
Fronting that mighty band   10
Which the fair Danish Land
    Dares to invade! Etc.

Cleopatra

From as early as 1851–52 GM had contemplated a poem on Cleopatra.
A quatrain appears in Berg between pages 110 and [111]:

In the great passion of her eye
    All midnight stars wax dim.
The burning Heavens come from their sky
    And round her throb & swim.

But the poem did not crystallize until his honeymoon with his second wife,
Marie Vulliamy, in Ploverfield, Bursledon, Southampton. He wrote to
William Hardman, October 18, 1864: "I am working mightily. Last night
I awoke, and at 3 o'clock struck a light and wrote a poem on 'Cleopatra'
for the *Cornhill*, to suit Sandys' illustration." The following month, from
the same place, he wrote to the Reverend Augustus Jessopp: "The
'Cleopatra' to Sandys' illustration is done. 'Lines' merely! Not of much
value, but containing fire as well as wind." When Frederick Sandys's
drawing of Cleopatra appeared in the *Cornhill*, September 1866, the poem
accompanying it was by Swinburne.
    The Egyptian coin with the head of Cleopatra may well have been a
gift from Janet Ross (for whose stay in Egypt, see Ross, pp. 133–54).
Although she did not mention the fact in her reminiscences, she was again
in England at the time of GM's marriage to Marie and attended the
wedding on September 20, 1864 (Galland, p. 277), so that the coin may
have been a very recent gift.

CLEOPATRA
Copy-text: Yale *MS, in Marie Vulliamy Meredith's script. Previously printed in Phyllis
Bartlett,* "George Meredith's Lost Cleopatra," *Yale University Library Gazette 33
(October 1958): 57–62.*

My friend hands me a coin of ancient stamp
As one that has passed current on the Nile.
'Tis slippery, as from Egyptian thumbs:
Green from fierce proving of the elements
Fire, air, & water: & from long lying there
In the unhealèd earth; green as the slime
Of salt sea-rivers. Just so green a spot
The Crocodile must carry near his eye
In some dry corner. Egypt had a mint
Of Crocodiles. 'Twas she who coin'd their Queen.   10

  Purged of its sin of devil-service now,
It lies within my hand, & I behold,
In marvelous distinctness, features traced,
Which no Egyptian thumbs could rub away,
Nor proving of the elements, water, air,
Fire, nor long lying in the unhealèd earth.
For of Time's daughters this is verily one
That walks beside him, will not be at rest;
Laughs at pale ashes, keeps her blood & life
While there are poets in the land: (when they   20
Depart, mankind may put a nightcap on.)
Drunken she sent the sun to bed, & shrieked
In chorus with her women as he rose:
Earth danced beneath her, & has since been dull.
This crown'd Bacchante had the soul that's struck
Twixt sunlight & the grape: she had the heat
Of vestals madden'd by their sickly flame.
She had the ecstasy of those who hear
The interminable harmonies aloft.
A sister to the Poets, wonder not   30
They sing of her; rejoice in her;—she had
The sensual divination of delight,
Imperious will for pleasure, flushing zeal,
And appetite unquenchable—a force
Of full vitality radiant in her breast,
As beams the silver shield upon a star.

Spit at her, O philosopher! but own
That she had mastered of the Mystery
A measureless portion when she did display
The faith of animals in life bestowed;   40
Their joy of limb & eyesight, without which
Our groping senses are but worms in dust,
Dust in a coloured sheet!
                    But, was she lovely?
One scarce can meditate upon this coin
With any clearness; for the woman's name
Is buzz'd about by rhapsodists; her name—
It is an Epoch when the stars hung low
And were a robe about the naked world.
And torchfire in the darkness of the time
Was her small woman's hand. But, if we let   50
Our instinct for realities see day,
Though there is disenchantment, there's reward.
We dwarf humanity by miracles:
Impoverish it by making human Gods.
The Antiquarian Sentimentalist
Unto his counter would nail down this coin,
Proclaiming it a scandal on the Queen
And pointing to her history, how she sway'd
The blood of men: a moon of their life's heaven,
And therefore beautiful. Does he know men?   60
Beauty is a month's mistress;—hence a moon.
Could Beauty net the Julius who raged
In midnight Rome? Or Antonies compel
To homage to the death? We clutch her wings
And she no more is Beauty. Queen of boys
Not men, is this serene ascendant Light.
She has her faithful regiments in the boys.
Men ask for other qualities. Howl aloud,
You antiquarian sentimentalists!
Philosophy declares it;—and by my life!   70
No sooner is the fact revealed to me
Than the green coin shows vivid lineaments.

The features are half-hawkish: deep the eyes;
Not small, but deep: communicative to Brows
Long, very clearly marked; level & long.
She was no babbler, say those eyes; she flashed
Them,—living—when the spark illumined her
In gaieties of revel; & she read
More than she uttered. Likewise tell the lips.
They are close lips. She could look like a hag!   80
She had her hag-like moments when she breathed
Bitterness, scorching ear & sight, to melt
In softness when she would:—when politic.
Was Pleasure her hypocriscy? Oh, no!
But Policy was its twin-sister. Thus
She was divided & against herself
Before mankind: and thus she ruled one man.
Know you how these divisions counteract?
Throw for the large & win the little stake?

   The nose is ravenous. It must have worn   90
Small majesty at Actium: spite & hate
And malice were its characters in flight:—
'If one of us must die, why, thou for me:'
The nose says that much. But, when Fortune shone,
It was a Royal feature & no more
The draggled eagle; a still mounting bird
Nearer & nearer to the blazing beams!
Dispenser of huge bounties, making wealth
Seem poverty; she grasped to give, & gave
That she might grasp. My antiquarian says   100
Her nose was Grecian—yea, Athenè's nose!
My physiologist maintains it turn'd
Rich, Coptic nostrils to the sun, & was
A nose to which the French have given a name,
It being partly national, & which I
Would call a wren-tail nose. I cannot read
The historic writing by that sign.
       Her neck?—

It thrusts the head forth like a serpent's head.
Reality & poetry unite,
That nervous neck once seen. Tis fair & smooth   110
But underneath the smoothness you perceive
A fulness of the veins. Her passions' quick
To pump up torrents of blood, obscuring brain
And drowning conscience—all, save Policy,
Which swims & gasps until the Deluge sinks.
And when it sinks, her heart is tenderly full
Sweetly regretful: of which mood she makes
Both vocal loveliness, & visible.
An actress, not an hypocrite. She feels
The moment: then she mints it.
                       Pray you, mark   120
Again the eyes; could such be slaves of love?
The slaves of love put arms about our breasts
But hang on us no chains. These are rare eyes,
That will look at you luminous, nor lose
A little of their meaning in their light.
They tell you Love's a Science, & she knows it,
She hath command of this fine Science, Love!
'My Chosen, come, adore me Antony,
'Come, as came Caesar. Others are more fair,
'Others are suppler. I alone fire men.'   130
Think of those eyes at midnight at the feast!
She can give lightnings from those eyes, as were't
The dead sun flickering still. You might believe
A legend of her flying to the sun,
To drink his dying blood when out he lay
Scarlet along the desert's edge; too faint
To shake from off his breast the vampire bat.

Could Beauty reap such harvest if she sow'd?
There's more than Beauty in this possible hag.
—You call her Cleopatra? asks my friend.   140
No, not the Cleopatra of the Poets:
And yet the daughter of the Ptolemies.

'Tis she who in Life's goblet of Delight
Cast her strong soul, & drank it straightway off
And felt herself no loser. This is she.

To P. A. Labouchère Esqre

A. Koszul copied this sonnet from the manuscript in the Municipal
Library of Nantes. Pierre-Antoine Labouchère (1807–73) was a painter
whose daughters Emilie and Marie married Edouard and Justin, brothers
of GM's wife, Marie Vulliamy. The sonnet was sent from The Old House,
Mickleham, the home of the Vulliamys in Surrey, on Friday 29, 1865,
with no month noted.

Oft have I looked on France with envy vain,
Not of her vines, nor of her sunny land,
Nor of her glory; but of that bright band,
The Wits by whom huge Dulness has been slain;
Who seem'd another Saturn in his reign,
And with his Titans dared a moral hand
To find his headpiece vulnerably plann'd:—
Transfix'd is he by arrows of the brain!

Of these keen archers, Molière and Montaigne
To me are dearest: for these two combine   10
Wisdom and laughter: these I am full fain
To call most precious countrymen of mine:
They bridge the Channel waters once again,
And add a proof that Genius is divine.

CLEOPATRA

Lines associated with 143–44 *NB B,* [*p. 55*]:
Cleopatra, Egypt's ruler, the Queen divine
Who melted her life into the wine-cup of love *or* in Love's
    goblet of wine

TO P. A. LABOUCHÈRE

Copy-text: A. Koszul, "An Unpublished Sonnet by George Meredith to P. A. Labouchère
Esqre," Nineteenth Century and After 647 (1931): 1–3; The Living Age 340 (1931):
98–99.

Tuck, thou graceless sinner!—
Not till thou'st done thy dinner,—
But having done it, then go
And pass th' abode of Bengo!—

'Tis the terrible stench of slain horses decaying,
On whose carcases myriads of blue flies are preying
The little boys run with their noses clutch'd tightly.
Your Robin goes groaning and retching unsightly;
    Yawns whitely;
Reels, and is haunted by whinnyings and neighing.   10

The stoutest man 'twould flummox:
It sounds the gong in our stomachs.
To Hades, say, shall men go
Because of Tuck and Bengo?

'Levius fit patentia
Quidquid corrigere est nefas—'

[Vittoria Concluding the Opera of "Camilla"]

CAMILLA, *supported by* CAMILLO

If this is death, it is not hard to bear.
Your handkerchief drinks up my blood so fast
It seems to love it. Threads of my own hair
Are woven in it. 'Tis the one I cast
That midnight from my window, when you stood
Alone, and heaven seemed to love you so!
I did not think to wet it with my blood
When next I tossed it to my love below.

TUCK, THOU GRACELESS SINNER!
Copy-text: Cline, Letter 337. MS: Garrick Club.
[VITTORIA CONCLUDING THE OPERA OF "CAMILLA"]
Copy-text: GMT, p. 576.

CAMILLO (*cherishing her*)

Camilla, pity! say you will not die.
Your voice is like a soul lost in the sky.   10

CAMILLA

I know not if my soul has flown; I know
My body is a weight I cannot raise:
My voice between them issues, and I go
Upon a journey of uncounted days.
Forgetfulness is like a closing sea;
But you are very bright above me still.
My life I give as it was given to me:
I enter on a darkness wide and chill.

CAMILLO

O noble heart! a million fires consume
The hateful hand that sends you to your doom.   20

CAMILLA

There is an end to joy: there is no end
To striving; therefore ever let us strive
In purity that shall the toil befriend,
And keep our poor mortality alive.
I hang upon the boundaries like light
Along the hills when downward goes the day;
I feel the silent creeping up of night.
For you, my husband, lies a flaming way.

CAMILLO

I lose your eyes: I lose your voice: 'tis faint.
Ah, Christ! see the fallen eyelids of a saint.   30

CAMILLA

Our life is but a little holding, lent
To do a mighty labour: we are one

With heaven and the stars when it is spent
To serve God's aim: else die we with the sun.

[Vittoria's *Italia* Song]

1

I cannot count the years,
    That you will drink, like me,
The cup of blood and tears,
Ere she to you appears:—
Italia, Italia shall be free!

2

You dedicate your lives
    To her, and you will be
The food on which she thrives,
Till her great day arrives:—
Italia, Italia shall be free!

3

She asks you but for faith!
    Your faith in her takes she
As draughts of heaven's breath,
Amid defeat and death:—
Italia, Italia shall be free!

4

I enter the black boat
    Upon the wide grey sea,
Where all her set suns float;
Thence hear my voice remote:—
Italia, Italia shall be free!

[VITTORIA'S "ITALIA" SONG]

Copy-text: GMT, p. 578.

These verses are dated April 25, 1867. A note by Canon Anthony Deane accompanying the facsimile in the *Bookman* states that they were found among his mother's papers and were probably a wedding present to her.

> Fresh Spring has come with flower and leaf to warn
> All men that they with leaf and flower enfold
> Their hearts' desires, and in her fruitless gold
> And fruitful rains stand wistful of the corn
> That by and by shall greet a golden morn
> In waves of wealth. Take courage, hearts a-cold,
> For living with the Seasons, you grow old
> No more than they, nor ever are forlorn.

Opening of a letter to Hardman, July 6, 1870. For GM's verses to William Hardman, see headnote on page 829.

> Sweet Justice of Norbiton, neighbour of Jones,
>   Have you paid in the £15 cheque?
> The account at my banker's has recently grown's
>   Fat as the Princess of Teck.
>
> But 'tis sweating already, it dwindles apace:
>   So I pray you (and here's to your luck)
> Don't give to the matter a minute more grace,
>   And adieu, Serenissimo Tuck!

FRESH SPRING HAS COME

Copy-text: facsimile, The Bookman (*London, April 1923*), *opposite p. 19. Also printed in* Forman, Meredithiana, *p. 302. MS:* Yale.

7 For living with the seasons, you grow old] For he who with the Seasons lives, grows old *or* (For living with the Seasons, you grow old) [*sic*]
8 are] is *or* (are)

SWEET JUSTICE OF NORBITON

Copy-text: Cline, Letter 452. Previously printed in WMM, p. 206; first stanza, Ellis, p. 216; first stanza, The Hardman Papers, *p. 152 n. MS:* Berg.

Written [ca. July 19, 1870] in the context of the Franco-Prussian War, this is the opening of a poem in a letter to John Morley.

Friend, when the thundercloud is low,
And in the expectancy and throe,
Field, hill, and wave of forest grow
   The hue that edges black on fair,
   No voice is heard, and not a sound,
   Though listen all the hollow ground;
But swift I have known a white dove thread the air.

   So now these lines to you, between
   The loaded darkness and dead green,

In a letter to Hardman, February 15, [1871]. Ellis (p. 261) explained that after having held a number of civic posts, including Justice of the Peace, Hardman had become Mayor of Kingston. GM adds to his verses: "But I say, tell me you're not going to wear the robes. I can't stand it. . . ."

Cool you proceed at speed
   From station unto station,
While I but in giving heed
   Shed drops of perspiration!

FRIEND WHEN THE THUNDERCLOUD

Copy-text: WMM, pp. 209–10. Also printed in Cline, Letter 454.

COOL YOU PROCEED

Copy-text: Cline, Letter 468. Previously printed in Ellis, p. 261.

Millicent Maxse!

These verses were included in a letter to Frederick A. Maxse (see p. xxxii) on March 21, [1872]. After them GM wrote, "It won't do. It's horrid. It dances on the *m's* hoydenly."

Miss Millicent Maxse was fond of her Ma,
And chanted her aristocratic tra-la
In contempt of her stern democratic Papa,
And to spite him she married a Markis—ha! ha!

To Carlyle

WMM records John Dennis telling him how GM composed this sonnet at the Garrick Club in the early morning hours of Carlyle's eightieth birthday, July 17, 1875 (p. 260). The manuscript in the National Library of Scotland is endorsed: "written and presented to me by Meredith at the Club J D. [*sic*]." Dennis did not date the presentation.

This eightieth year of thine sits crowned in light
To lift our England from her fleshly mire:
Two generations view thee as a fire
Whence they have drawn what burns in them most bright:
For thou hast bared the roots of life with sight
Piercing; in language stronger than the lyre:
And thou hast shown the way must man aspire,
Is through the old sweat and anguish Adamite,
As at the first. Unsweet might seem his fate.
Sole with a spade between the stars & earth!—   10
Giving much labour for his little mirth,
And soldier-service till he fail to strike:
But such thine was, & thine to contemplate
Shall quicken young ambition for the like.

MILLICENT MAXSE!
Copy-text: Cline, Letter 497. Previously printed in WMM, p. 235.
TO CARLYLE
Copy-text: MS, National Library of Scotland. Previously printed in WMM, p. 206.
7 And thou hast shown the way must] Hast shown the way whereby must *del. MS*
10 &] of *WMM*

[Rosalind]

In this verse letter dated February 11, 1876, GM accepted an invitation to read the part of Orlando in *As You Like It*. A distinguished group of friends was meeting at the home of Mr. and Mrs. E. L. Brandreth in Elvaston Place, London, for Shakespeare readings. Their young daughter Alice read well, but her strict mother "would not allow me to dress up, or have any scenery, and, moreover, she absolutely declined to let me read any part with a young man as my lover." GM himself would mark the passages that the young people in the group must not read. Alice (Lady Butcher by her second marriage), added after her transcription of these verses that the mathematical scholar, Professor James Joseph Sylvester, who participated in the readings, "printed three hundred odd lines to rhyme with Rosalind." After receiving them, GM wrote to Mrs. Brandreth a final rhyme:

> Now so richly *Sylvestrined*
> Here's the last word to Rosalind.

These events are the subject of Lady Butcher's second chapter in her *Memories of George Meredith, O.M.*

Samuel Johnson had made the same play on single rhymes in "To Mrs. Thrale, on Completing her Thirty-fifth Year."

> Wife being absent, I could find
> Nought to say to Rosalind.
> She returns, and swift as wind
> Now I write to Rosalind.
> —Young Orlando, reared as hind,
> Was fit mate for Rosalind,
> (When his manners were refined).
> He had youth like Rosalind.
>
> —Shall a man in grey declined,
> Seem the same for Rosalind?
> Yea, though merely aged in rind,
> Is he worthy Rosalind?

10

Copy-text: Cline, Letter 555. Previously printed with inaccuracies in WMM, pp. 260–61; and in Butcher, pp. 23–24.

This in grave debate should bind
Parliaments and Rosalind.
—Still, if, captious, wayward, blind,
And the rest of 't, Rosalind
Should insist:—if to her mind
(If she have one) Rosalind
Thinks me (if to thought inclined
Ever): I with Rosalind   20
(And I say it, having dined,
Slept and dreamed of Rosalind)
I will do my best; and kind
Prove our audience, Rosalind!
Take these words for treaty signed
—No Orlando, Rosalind!
But a man with wrinkles lined,
Vows to read with Rosalind.

                                        G.M.

These verses were sent to Alice Brandreth on February 28, 1877. For
Alice, see headnote to [*Rosalind*] above. Jim Gordon was her cousin,
an electrical engineer whose pastime was hunting.

Gordon, Jim,
Life and Limb
Risking, 'cause it is his whim,
Hounds to foller,
Breaks his collar-
Bone while giving a view-holler.
Ain't this news?
What's more it's true,
Then in bed the poor lad stews;

GORDON, JIM
*Copy-text: Cline, Letter 582. Previously printed in WMM, pp. 271–72; and in Butcher,
p. 54.*
3 'cause] cos *Butcher*
4 foller] follow *Butcher*
9 Then] There *Butcher*

His neck twirling
Mr. Curling
Straight has set like surgeon sterling.

Mentor and Pupils

This poem was enclosed in a letter to John Morley on April 5, 1877. GM wrote that it was somewhat in Goethe's manner but a poor return to Morley for his gift of *Das Göttliche*, a "Hymn for men."

The first two lines of Goethe's famous poem are so often quoted that they have become a cliché:

Edel sei der Mensch
Hilfreich und gut!

The theme of *Das Göttliche* is that man alone of Nature's creatures can choose between good and evil.

Mentor

Be warned of steps retrieved in pain.

Pupils

We have strength, we have blood, we are young,

Mentor

Youth sows the links, man wears the chain.

Pupils

Shall a sweet lyric cease to be sung?

Mentor

The song is short, the travail long.

GORDON, JIM
11 sterling] stirling *WMM*

MENTOR AND PUPILS
Copy-text: Cline, enclosure in Letter 594. Previously printed in WMM, pp. 275–77. MS: Yale, early draft. The title in the MS is "Mentor & Disciples," and the speakers are, accordingly, "Mentor" and "Disciples."
2 strength] health   blood] strength *MS*
3 links] limbs [?] *MS*
5 the travail] The silence *MS*

Pupils

Shall the morning brood over her grave?

Mentor

Forge weapons now to meet the throng.

Pupils

There's a bird flying white o'er the wave.

Mentor

The torrent of the blood control.

Pupils

'Tis a steed bounding whither we will.   10

Mentor

In more than name discern the soul.

Pupils

There is Love like a light on the hill.

Mentor

That light of Love is fleeting fire.

Pupils

In the deep sea of Love let us dive.

6–8

> *Disciples*
> There's a bird flying white o'er the wave
> Mentor
> Forge weapons now to meet the throng [for fights to come *del.*]
> Shall the morning brood over her grave? *MS*

Between lines 8 and 9: Your blood is as a *del. MS*
Lines 9 through the end are all spoken by Mentor in the MS
9 the blood] your blood *MS*
11 soul] Soul *MS*
12 Love] love *Cline*
13 That] The   fleeting] earthly *del. MS*
14 In the sea of deep ['Tis divine to the *del.*] Love let us dive. *MS*

Mentor

The test of Love is in the lyre.

Pupils

Give us Love, and the lyre is alive.

Mentor

The chords are snapped by passion's touch.

Pupils

She is there, by the tall laurel-rose.

Mentor

You sway the staff—you grasp the crutch.

Pupils

She is beckoning: who shall oppose?   20

Mentor

Behold a giant in his prime.

Pupils

On her breasts are the beams of the day.

Mentor

A cripple he, surprised by Time!

Pupils

She has loosened her girdle: give way!

16 lyre] god *MS*
17 touch] hand *del. MS*
22 beams] beam *MS*

GM sent this poem to Alice Brandreth in the name of himself and his wife, April 11, 1878, on the occasion of her marriage with James Edward Henry Gordon, the young man who had broken his collar-bone in the verses beginning "Gordon, Jim" (see page 858).

> Now dawns all waxen to your seal of life
> This day which names you bride to make you wife.
> Time shows the solid stamp; then see, dear maid,
> Round those joined hands our prayers for you inlaid.

Echoing Sir Walter Scott in *The Lay of the Last Minstrel*, canto 6, GM protests to the men on a picnic on Box Hill in the summer of 1878 while they all, himself included, allow Alice Brandreth Gordon to remove the kettle for tea (Butcher, p. 59).

> Lives there a man with such base mettle
> To let a lady lift a boiling kettle?

Some time after 1880 Jim Gordon had provided GM's younger son with a job in his electrical works at Greenwich (Butcher, p. 64).

> When Will was at home in his palace of zinc,
> He had no room to move; but plenty to think!

NOW DAWNS ALL WAXEN

Copy-text: Butcher, p. 56. Also previously printed in WMM, p. 289; and in Cline, Letter 614.

LIVES THERE A MAN

Copy-text: Butcher, p. 59.

WHEN WILL WAS AT HOME

Copy-text: Butcher, p. 64.

CRWAD

These verses followed a comment to Cotter Morison on March 28, 1881, that the *Pall Mall Gazette* was flourishing under the editorship of John Morley while the *St. James's Gazette* was languishing under that of Frederick Greenwood.

> The day is going, now 'tis noon,
> Greenwood 'gins baying the Gladstone moon,
> While temperate Morley with assuaging voice
> Bids England in her bigger G. rejoice.

CRWAD

GM is asking on May 17, 1881, for free tickets that his wife wants from Arthur Cecil Blunt to any theatrical performance that would amuse her and her nieces.

> There was a fair footman of Torrington Square
> Desired to a Theatre Royal to repair,
> With her nieces three, purple as Scotia's thistle,
> And enjoy the rich humours of great Mr. Cecil,
> Who of the Comic Muse questionless mate is,
> And this they were anxious for perfectly gratis.

Epitaph
on the Tombstone of
James Christopher Wilson

(d. APRIL 11 1884)
IN HEADLEY CHURCHYARD, SURREY

James Christopher Wilson and his wife had been former neighbors of GM. Wilson bought Ashurst (part of Mickleham Manor, Surrey) in 1872 and sold it in 1882. After his death, GM wrote a number of letters to his widow.

THE DAY IS GOING
Copy-text: Cline, Letter 691. Previously printed in WMM, p. 312.
THERE WAS A FAIR FOOTMAN
Copy-text: Cline, Letter 694. Previously printed in WMM, p. 314.
EPITAPH: JAMES CHRISTOPHER WILSON
Copy-text: LP.

Thou our beloved and light of Earth hast crossed
The sea of darkness to the yonder shore.
There dost thou shine a light transferred, not lost,
Through love to kindle in our souls the more.

～∞～

Palgrave, grave pal of mine, the pall, the grave,
Do suit thy sombre hue, the bounding wave
Thy temperament; and thou dost aye recall
Eternal Youth; therewith the grave, the pall.

～∞～

These lines, described by GM as "poor stuff," were delivered to Miss Louisa Lawrence on December 31, 1885, for some unspecified use. For the Lawrence sisters see headnote to *Hernani*, page 344.

Dost thou behold some woeful soul
    With bitter weeping blighted,
Thy tears that rise do not control,
    But let them flow united.
A gentle word, a true caress,
    The darkest woe has tided:
Then join in prayer; all grief is less
    When tenderly divided. } Alternative:
    Full half when 'tis divided. } both absurd
But should it be an eye in beams
    Of Love's own rosy sparkles,   10
Arrest thy step, keep thy dreams
    Where thy own yearning darkles.
For Love is to itself enough,
    And in itself lives only:
Divided Love is less than Love.
    Then must thy prayer be lonely.

PALGRAVE
Copy-text: Cline, Letter 2435, n.1. MS: Texas.
DOST THOU BEHOLD
Copy-text: Cline, Letter 957. MS: the Lawrence family, by kind permission.

From "Notes of a Lonely Papa" sent to his daughter Marie on August 10, 1886.

O 'tis my delight
In the dead of the night
To rush to the Lucifer match,
And allume all the room
For a sight of the bite
That has cloven my slumbers to fill me with spite,
And indulge in a desperate scratch!

Hilda's Morning and Evening Dose of Rhyme

For Hilda de Longueuil see the headnote to *The Sage Enamoured and the Honest Lady* on page 463. This verse letter is dated February 28, [1887], and GM adds the prescription: "To be taken, two verses, with consideration of the accents on the words and the right meaning of them: total repression (*pro tem:*) of sighs; face to the East," etc.

Can another love be born
In heart that love has left outworn;
Appearing dead to sweet desire
Its mouths of earth once mounts of fire?

Question first, if thou would'st know,
This wilful love that wasted so;
And ask one heart that wildly went
To ashes, why the flames are spent.

O 'TIS MY DELIGHT

Copy-text: WMM, p. 384. Also printed in Cline, Letter 996.

HILDA'S MORNING AND EVENING DOSE

Copy-text: Cline, Letter 1039. Previously printed in R. E. Gordon George (Robert Esmonde Sencourt, "Unpublished Letters of George Meredith," Nineteenth Century 103 (February 1928).

Was it to our heavens bared
Reflectively when forth it fared?   10
And knew it when it took the leap
Of whether shallow, whether deep?

Loved she an angel of the light?
All meaner forms must woman slight.
Or was the Prince of Darkness he,
Her wreck is out in deepest sea.

But less than either, bids the mind
Right measure of the man to find;
From wider knowledge, keener thought,
To fathom how the spell was wrought.   20

And has he borne his manhood high,
For whom she cast that gambler's die,
Her heart? And doth her spirit through
The senses read, and love renew?

Ah, that first love! It comes to prove
How creatures of the senses love;
Before the brain has gained control
To show how they may love in soul.

Give life to Life; in turn it gives.
Believe thy heart alive; it lives.   30
Know Love more heavenly than of old
Revealed, and Love will not be cold.

The Past is dust: thy heart is blood;
It bears thy fate upon its flood,
Set it on nobleness, and soon
A nobler love will crown thy noon.

It was apparently in 1889 that GM called this couplet after "Mr. Arthur Blunt (Arthur Cecil, the actor)" when he said that he must catch a train in order to pick up a light meal before a performance (Butcher, p. 83).

> The Bumble Bee—the Bumble Bee,
> He *had* to get home to his early tea.

This quatrain is part of a letter written to Mrs. Leslie Stephen on June 17, 1889. On June 13 GM had concluded a letter, "We send our love to the stout angel. . . ." The angel, therefore, must be Mrs. Stephen, and Cline, in a note to Letter 1206, suggests that the appellation may allude to Coventry Patmore's *The Angel in the House.*

> An Angel, be ye ne'er in doubt,
> Though lean below, above is stout;
> And let her wax all eyes t' appal,
> It proves her more angelical.

These two stanzas enclose a prose note to Mrs. George Stevenson of Glasgow and are dated by Cline as ? July, 1891. GM had visited Lochearnhead, Perthshire, the Stevensons' home in July–August 1890. Thereafter, his nickname for Mrs. Stevenson was "Callandria," from her birthplace, Callander. Prior to these verses sent to Mrs. Stevenson he had written in a letter to her husband, June 16, 1891: "I see the loch [Lochearn] as I write, and our good Callandria perhaps on the Glenogle burn's banks."

THE BUMBLE BEE

Copy-text: Butcher, p. 83.

AN ANGEL

Copy-text: WMM, p. 428. Also printed in Cline, Letter 1209.

Remember what a night of storm
Roused ancient battle up the braes,
Sons of the cloud and mount, a swarm
We saw descend the zig-zag ways,
Athwart where drenching vapour sailed,
And Scotia bled and Ossian wailed!

What song has now Glenogle's burn,
Callandria? Does he leap his run
To swell the waters of Lochearn,
That silver oval under sun?   10
And shed you with the Highland rose,
Your shadow on him as he goes?

A letter to the poet's daughter Marie, July 10, 1891.

She scarce has a word for Papa,
    To tell how she carolled and sported O!
So, with just, How d' ye do and Ta-ta,
    She runs from her pen to be courted O!

To write were a foolish endeavour,
    But, to show that her humour is still in her,
And flourishing fatter than ever,
    She sends him the
        Bill of her Milliner.

REMEMBER WHAT A NIGHT OF STORM

Copy-text: WMM, p. 423, dated 1889. Cline believes this date to be wrong, because there were no such hostile reviews as GM mentions in the letter to Mrs. George Stevenson, whereas in 1891 there were hostile reviews of One of Our Conquerors (*Letter 1342, n.1*).

SHE SCARCE HAS A WORD FOR PAPA

Copy-text: WMM, p. 439.

Sent on September 28, 1894. "Queen Jean" was GM's name for the wife of Walter Palmer of the biscuit company, a generous and attractive hostess in the late years when the poet could still manage to visit London.

There stood in her street a poor exile of Queen Je'n,
He sang a long ballad devoid of all point;
And the sole thing made clear by this broken down engine,
Was 'Harry has put my old nose out of joint.'

Sent on November 1, 1894. See headnote above.

I would I were with Jean,
Atripping on the green,
And she to call me her true knight,
And I to crown her queen.

The ordering of her set,
We'd leave to sweet Riette,
And Walter he should pipe our dance,
Upon the flageolet.

In a letter to Frank C. Burnand, May 10, 1895, inviting him to Box Hill. For Burnand, see headnote on page 832. Claremont was the name of the private park near Esher where GM lived from 1859 to 1864.

THERE STOOD IN HER STREET

Copy-text: WMM, p. 470.

I WOULD I WERE WITH JEAN

Copy-text: WMM, p. 472.

In Claremont woods we wandered once
(Alas, that seasons won't endure,)
Ere you were Editor of Punc',
And I was Britain's great obscure.

Nature and Man

Edward Clodd (see headnote on p. 874) said in his *Memories* (p. 139) that GM wrote this poem in his copy of *Poems and Lyrics of the Joy of Earth* when visiting him in Aldeburgh in 1891, but the notes on his conversations with GM clearly date this event as June 1895 (*TLS-I*).

Where all is black,
Love is the light for creatures looking in
Behind her red rose blush and lily skin;
A lamp that yet we lack.

[Parody of Alfred Austin]

Alfred Austin (1835–1913), who was appointed Poet Laureate on the New Year list of 1896, was dubbed by GM "Alfred the Little." On October 26 or 27, 1895, GM told Clodd that Austin's "'Three cheers for Winter, that makes the timber splinter,' is in the good old Beef School. The regulation rhyme style" (*TLS-II*). As a run of GM's letters to Austin (now at Yale) shows, however, they were on cordial terms personally.

Three cheers for lusty winter
That blows the hunter's horn,
And makes the branches splinter,
And threshes out the corn.

IN CLAREMONT WOODS
Copy-text: Cline, Letter 1617.
NATURE AND MAN
Copy-text: Clodd, p. 139.
[PARODY OF ALFRED AUSTIN]
Copy-text: Clodd, p. 149.

The violets for Madeline Meynell were accompanied by a note to her
mother Alice, including the verses, on March 24, 1896.

Dearest Dimpling, we believe
We of violets are the last:
But for this we do not grieve
If on Dimpling's lap we're cast.
They that follow, they will be
Prouder flowers of maiden state,
Good perhaps to decorate—
Not so one with her as we.

Shall I again have Lilac week?
The coming days of sequence seven
I view, and see an aspect bleak
Beside that flash of quiet heaven
Your presence gave; till I can think
An angel in one flitted wink
Was with me; and because I yearn
I needs must doubt, almost despair,
Of such kind season's chance return:—

'Tis but a moment's gasp for air.   10
A moment more and I behold
Your Lobby in her bonnet white
Among the grasses' blue and gold
So sagely gathering; near in sight

DEAREST DIMPLING

Copy-text: The Letters of George Meredith to Alice Meynell (*London: Nonesuch, 1923*),
p. 12.

SHALL I AGAIN HAVE LILAC WEEK?

Copy-text: Letters to Alice Meynell, *p. 23.*

Her tutelary Monica;
And near, their pencilling Mama:—
The mother with the ready smile,
Who wages warrior fight the while.

To A. M.

Enclosed in a letter to Alice Meynell, June 26, 1896. This is the only
surviving sonnet of a series that GM proposed should be addressed to her
with the title, "The Lady of the Time" (*Letters of George Meredith to
Alice Meynell* [London: Nonesuch, 1923], p. 32). The flower named after
her was a blue iris.

A stately flower in my garden grows,
Whose colour is the dawn-sky's maiden blue;
The loveliest to my Lady's thinking too.
And when the Lord of June bids her disclose
Her very heart, all bashfully she throws
An inner petal o'er the orange hue,
As one last plea; submitting to his view,
Yet virginally majestic while he glows.
For reasons known to us we give the name
Alicia Caerulea to that flower,   10
Sweet as the Sea-born borne on the sea-wave:
That Innocent in shame where is no shame;
That proud Reluctant; that fair slave of power,
Who conquers most when she is most the slave.

These verses and the "reply" following were sent to Mrs. Walter
Palmer on February 24, 1897. For Mrs. Palmer, see headnote to "There
stood in her street," on page 869.

TO A. M.

Copy-text: Cline, Letter 1704. Previously printed in Letters to Alice Meynell, *p. 33.*

'Twas yesterday such a black-dye-day
as never will be or has been!
For she vowed to come hither on Friday;
she vowed, she deceived us, our Queen!
and I who had called the day *my* day,
embraced an intangible Jean.
For her Duke 'twas a sweet apple-pie-day.
Her Poet he fed on a bean!

Reply of the County of Surrey
to the Poet's Pathetic Address
in Dispraise of Jean

—Yes, that was a Sunless bad Friday,
    Denied apparition of Jean!
Though she vowed; and thy cottage was taidy,
    Thyself in the happiest mien.
It was an accursed suici'day,
    Now wailing in Hades, we ween.
But beware of Jean's promise of *thy* day,
    Some day when no Duke fills the scene.
For O she's a volatile Laidy,
    Her poet a reed of the bean!   10

'TWAS YESTERDAY

Copy-text: Yale *MS. Previously printed in Cline, Letter 1751.*

REPLY OF THE COUNTY OF SURREY

Copy-text: Cline, Letter 1752. MS: Lady Halsey.

Edward Clodd (1840–1930), "who earned his living as Secretary of the
London Joint Stock Bank but found his real career in writing books to
popularize evolutionary and agnostic theories" (LS, p. 266), met GM in
May 1884. After the summer of 1895 GM called him "Sir Reynard,"
because Clodd, as President of the Omar Khayyám Club, had played him
a foxy trick in persuading him to come in after a dinner of the Club at the
Burford Bridge Hotel. GM had stipulated that he would not speak, but
after encomiums from Thomas Hardy and George Gissing he could
not do otherwise. That GM enjoyed the companionship of Clodd is
abundantly evident in his letters.

> 'Tis good to keep hinderward eyes
> For the lessons in paths we have trod;
> 'Tis good to be wary & wise,
> —Why linger so long on the way?
> All that is no more than to say—
>   'Tis good to be Clodd!

> The Buddha, with head like the crown
> Of an infant or pea in a pod,
> Immersed in the study hued brown;
> Uprises at length on a start,   10
> Nirvana rejects from his heart—
>   'I'd rather be Clodd!'

This poem was included in a letter to Mrs. Seymour Trower, July 11,
1899, declining an invitation to visit the Trowers at Weybridge on the river
Wey. Although Trower was associated with the Navy League, he could be
counted on to take them for a peaceful boating.

> There is for me no sweeter holiday
> Than in this radiant season of the year
> When by the Wey sits Lady BytheWey,
> And League becomes pacific Gondolier.

'TIS GOOD TO KEEP HINDERWARD EYES
Copy-text: BM MS Ashley 3637. *Previously printed in* Letters from George Meredith to
Edward Clodd and Clement K. Shorter (*London: printed for private circulation, 1913*),
p. 6. Facsimile and transcription, Ashley Catalogue *10, pp. 150–51; and in Cline, Letter
1854.*
THERE IS FOR ME NO SWEETER HOLIDAY
Copy-text: WMM, p. 505. *Also printed in Cline, Letter 1896.*

GWWC

A verse letter to Edward Clodd, August 3, 1899.

Thou pirate nested over Alde!
Stern wrecker of the Established Faith!
From whom the parson shrinks appalled;
In whom the mariner sees his wraith;
Attracts thee in the gassy glare
Of evening some fishmonger's slab?
And still dost mix for supper fare,
The shelly with poetic Crabbe?
Or else, while sinks the enlarging star,
Of night libidinous the herald,   10
Thou drink'st of ebrious Omar
From the gold goblet named FitzGerald?
Then into Nature's entrails peer'st,
Not finding there the Christian God;
Or on the surface pioneer'st
A beacon to thy fellows, Clodd?
Hither, I pray thee, be't addressed
(Besides the crab and following pill),
Thy news, and when thou quitt'st the nest,
And when the visit to Box Hill.   20

GWWC

Dr. H. G. Plimmer, a bacteriologist and Fellow of the Royal Society, shared musical interests with his wife, whom GM called "Verandah," and with her son, whom he called "Cello." GM was difficult about accepting gifts, and Sencourt records that "Mrs. Plimmer had the knack of giving things to him, and his letters to her are full of joking gratitude" (p. 270). Sencourt does not date this thank-you note.

THOU PIRATE NESTED OVER ALDE!

Copy-text: Cline, Letter 1900. Also printed in WMM, pp. 506–07.

11 of ebrious] to glorious WMM
12 gold goblet] goblet WMM
16 beacon] bearer WMM

To Plimmer, Verandah and Cello,
Who shine as the green of the land,
The thanks of a crippled old fellow.
Though why one so lost in the yellow
Is noticed, he can't understand.

⁂

Although the fragment "This love of nature" was printed in the
Morning Post (20 September 1909) and *LP* as the last of four fragments,
the handwriting is somewhat earlier than that of "Open horizons round,"
"A wilding little stubble flower," and "From labours through the night."

This love of nature, that allures to take
Irregularity for harmony
Of larger scope than our hard measures make,
Cherish it as thy school for when on thee
The ills of life descend.

⁂

Dated April 18, 1901, and sent to Lady Ulrica Duncombe, daughter of
the Earl of Feversham. LS briefly sketches Lady Ulrica as one who
"proved to resemble the ideal heroines of his novels, combining beauty
and social distinction with the serious interests that had been fostered
when she was an undergraduate at Girton" (p. 336). GM continued to
further her higher education by learned correspondence.

We violets white and blue,
From off the vernal banks,
In homage come to you,
And shun the word of 'Thanks'.

TO PLIMMER
Copy-text: Sencourt, pp. 269–70.

THIS LOVE OF NATURE
Copy-text: Yale *MS. Previously printed in the* Morning Post, *20 September 1909; and in*
LP.
MS, lines associated with This love of nature:
to Him,
Whose reign is in the boundless Now,
Above the tides, beyond decay.

WE VIOLETS WHITE AND BLUE
Copy-text: Cline, Letter 1992. MS: Mrs. G. B. Foster.

Our joy is unsurpassed
By those among the Blest,
May we but breathe our last
Beside Ulrica's breast.

The thief was Theodore Watts-Dunton, to whom GM wrote this protest on June 6, 1901. In a note to the letter, Cline explains that Oronte in line 4 is "A fop in Molière's *Le Misanthrope* who is called 'l'homme au sonnet.'"

Au voleur, au voleur, au voleur!—
All day I've been thinking upon it,
And cannot devise what to say:
Oronte comes to me with sonnet,
And carries my penknife away!

In a letter to Lady Ulrica Duncombe, April 19, 1902.

My Lady has Diana's brows,
Diana's deer-like step is hers;
A Goddess she by every sign;
Then wherefore is she not divine?
She has no ears for lovers' vows,
For lovers' vows she has no ears.

AU VOLEUR

Copy-text: Cline, Letter 2203. MS: Yale.

MY LADY HAS DIANA'S BROWS

Copy-text: Cline, Letter 2076. MS: Mrs. G. B. Foster. Also printed in WMM, p. 533.

Ireland

I

Fire in her ashes Ireland feels
    And in her veins a glow of heat.
To her the lost old time appeals
    For resurrection, good to greet:
Not as a shape with spectral eyes,
    But humanly maternal, young
In all that quickens pride, and wise
    To speed the best her bards have sung.

II

You read her as a land distraught,
    Where bitterest rebel passions seethe.
Look with a core of heart in thought,
    For so is known the truth beneath.
She came to you a loathing bride,
    And it has been no happy bed.
Believe in her as friend, allied
    By bonds as close as those who wed.

III

Her speech is held for hatred's cry;
    Her silence tells of treason hid:
Were it her aim to burst the tie,
    She sees what iron laws forbid.
Excess of heart obscures from view

Copy-text: TS corr. by GM. Previously printed in Scribner's 46 (*July 1909*), *and in* LP.
MSS: Yale. *MS 1; MS 2, fair copy; corrected TS.*
I.2 her] *not in MS 1*
I.8 speed] *MS 1, MS 2*   speak *misp. TS; S, LP*
II.1 land] wretch *del. MS 2*
II.2 bitterest] all the *MS 1*
II.4 For so is known] So may you see *or* For so is known *MS 1*
III.1 is held] you take *del. MS 1*
III.3 aim] wish *del. MS 1*

A head as keen as yours to count.
Trust her, that she may prove her true
In links whereof is love the fount.

IV

May she not call herself her own?
That is her cry, and thence her spits
Of fury, thence her graceless tone
At justice given in bits and bits.
The limbs once raw with gnawing chains
Will fret at silken when God's beams
Of Freedom beckon o'er the plains
From mounts that show it more than dreams.

V

She, generous, craves your generous dole;
That will not rouse the crack of doom.
It ends the blundering past control
Simply to give her elbow-room.
Her offspring feel they are a race,
To be a nation is their claim;
Yet stronger bound in your embrace
Than when the tie was but a name.

VI

A nation she, and formed to charm,
With heart for heart and hands all round.
No longer England's broken arm,

III.7 that she may] & she will *MS 1*
III.8 links] bonds *MS 1*
IV.5 gnawing] iron *MS 1*
V.2 crack] clap *or* crack *MS 1*
V.3 It] What *MS 1*   past] old *MS 1*
V.4 Simply] 'Tis but *MS 1*
V.5 feel] know *MS 1*
V.6 is their] proudly *del. MS 1*
V.7 your] our *del. MS 1*
VI.3 England's] Britain's *MSS 1, 2*

Would England know where strength is found.
And strength to-day is England's need;
    To-morrow it may be for both
Salvation: heed the portents, heed
    The warning; free the mind from sloth.

VII

Too long the pair have danced in mud,
    With no advance from sun to sun.
Ah, what a bounding course of blood
    Has England with an Ireland one!
Behold yon shadow cross the downs,
    And off away to yeasty seas.
Lightly will fly old rancour's frowns
    When solid with high heart stand these.

This fragment and the two that follow appeared in the *Morning Post* (20 September 1909) under the title: "The Last Poems of George Meredith," with the note: "The following poems (hitherto unpublished) were written by Mr. Meredith shortly before his death." The extreme shakiness of the handwriting is corroborative.

Added to these three was a fourth fragment, "This love of Nature" (see p. 876), but because the handwriting of this fragment is less shaky, I have placed it slightly earlier.

Open horizons round,
O mounting mind, to scenes unsung,
Wherein shall walk a lusty Time:

IRELAND
VI.4 England] Britain *MSS 1, 2*
VI.5 England's] Britain's *MSS 1, 2*
VI.8 warning] *MSS 1, 2*   warnings *misp. TS; S, LP*
Stanza VII not in MS 1
VII.4 England] Britain *MS 2*
VII.6 *MS 2 del.:* And off to yeasty seas from land
VII.7 Lightly will fly] So lightly flies *del. MS 2*   frowns] frown *MS 2, TS, S, LP*
OPEN HORIZONS ROUND
Copy-text: Edition de Luxe 4 (posth.). Previously printed in the Morning Post, *20 September 1909; and in* LP. *MSS: Yale. MS 1, title: "Ode"; MS 2.*

Our Earth is young;
Of measure without bound;
Infinite are the heights to climb,
The depths to sound.

A wilding little stubble flower
The sickle scorned which cut for wheat,
Such was our hope in that dark hour
When nought save uses held the street,
And daily pleasures, daily needs,
With barren vision, looked ahead.
And still the same result of seeds
Gave likeness twixt the live and dead.

From labours through the night, outworn,
Above the hills the front of morn
We see, whose eyes to heights are raised,
And the world's wise may deem us crazed.

OPEN HORIZONS ROUND

4 Earth] world *MS 1*
5 Of measure without] Young and of measure passing *MS 1* Of] Her *del.* young, & her *del.* young of *MS 2*

A WILDING LITTLE STUBBLE FLOWER

Copy-text: Edition de Luxe 4 (posth.). Previously printed in the Morning Post, *20 September 1909; and in* LP. *MS:* Yale.
2 scorned which] spared, that *del. MS*   wheat] corn *or* wheat *MS*; corn *LP, de L; corr. errata, de L 1911*
6 ahead] abroad *MS, MP*

FROM LABOURS THROUGH THE NIGHT

Copy-text: Edition de Luxe 4 (posth.). Previously printed in the Morning Post, *20 September 1909; and in* LP. *MSS:* Yale, *two working drafts.*
dr. 1:

Of what the morning had to tell,
I was a seeker in old days;
And though I knew her beauty well,
'Twas ever fresh *del.* Fresh did it shine *del.* It smote me fresh for
    tongue of praise.

While yet her lord lies under seas,
She takes us as the wind the tree's
Delighted leafage; all in song
We mount to her, to her belong.

Mary Barrie, an actress, was the wife of James Barrie, the dramatist.
Married in 1894, they were divorced in 1909.
This verse letter [? September 14, 1908] is signed "Congress of
Admirers (Some in mourning)."

O Mary Barrie, Mary Barrie,
You bear a witching ballad name:
In some mossed dell it seems to tarry,
Till a brave tale shall form its frame.

And Mary Barrie, Mary Barrie,
You of the lureful ballad name:
Which of us all will be the quarry
When you are huntress, swift as flame?

Del.: She took me as the wind the tree's
Del.: Delighted foliage th[*sic*]
While yet her lord lay under seas,   [*Cf. lines 5*]
She took me as the wind the tree's   [*Cf. lines 6*]
Delighted foliage; [made me wise *del.*]   [*Cf. line 7*]
Del.: Beyond my years of earth & skies.
    [made me sway *del.*]
Del.: With joyfulness from root to spray.

1 From labours through the] Forth from the skirts of *del. dr. 2*
3 see] see *or* view *dr. 2*
4 may deem] ones rank *or* may deem *dr. 2*; ones call *MP*
6 tree's] *MSS*; trees' *LP, de L*

verso of dr. 2:

The [?] now is lodged in thought
Strength is the prize that men have bought
With sweat of brow, & made bequest

O MARY BARRIE

Copy-text: Cline, Letter 2499. MS: Texas.

The name, O Mary, Mary Barrie,
There's magic in your ballad name.   10
It rings as from a realm of faery,
It puts all other tones to shame.

But Mary Barrie, Mary Barrie,
What of the woman, wild or tame?
As to her heart, opinions vary;
As to her head, there's loud acclaim.

None other plays at thrust and parry,
With such rare skill the fencing game!
Not J.M.B. himself can carry
Wit to so proud a pitch of Fame.   20

But Mary Barrie, Mary Barrie,
Woe worth the ode that ends in blame;
Your promises are visionary,
Your vows are webs, capricious dame.

Part IV

Unpublished Poems and Fragments

These previously unpublished poems and fragments are
arranged in probable order of their composition.

The Soul

1

Spark of Godhead! child
Of infinite desire,
Straining blind and wild
To one absorbing fire!

2

Sun of sy[s]tems!—child
Of infinite desire,
Stricken, edged, and filed,
To spout eternal fire!

3

Keen is thy ordeal!
Rising, throbbing, setting
Through a solemn peal
Learning and forgetting.

4

Thou art taught to feel,
Famine in thy feeding,
By each moment's meal
Languishing and bleeding.

MS: NB A, [*pp. 7, 10, 12, 13*].

SECOND PART

9

A doubtful Love distempered,—
    A fretful, fevered ache,—
A Passion stung and pampered,—
    A wrapt self hugging sake.

10

Thoroughly encompassed,
    Ocean, Earth, and sky:
Thoroughly encompassed,
    Head and heart and eye.

11

The winds about Thee voiceless
    Tell neither joy nor woe
They bear Thee onward—choiceless
    Onward Thou must go.—

THIRD PART

5

Tho' both to Thee are one—
    The emptiness of space—
Moonless, without sun—
    Formless without face—

6

Yet ever undivining—
    Thou wilt not cease to crave,
Ever, ever pining,
    From the heaving wave.

7

To the Light above Thee,
    To the Dark beneath,
Something dear to love Thee
    Be it Life or Death.

8

Wash'd Thou know'st not whither,
    In Thy bounded brain,
Hither and still thither,
    On the boundless main.

9

Heavy with Thy mission,
    Ceasing not to droop,
Till upon Thy vision,
    Dawns the darling Hope.

10

And the Picture, painted—
    Meet Thine inner eye,
Of those figures saintëd,
    Known beneath the sky.

11

Then no longer voiceless—
    Chanting winds are heard—
Thou wert never choiceless,
    Young immortal bird!!

Love

5

Kindred forgets Thee.
    I alone bear the Smart.
The small worm that frets Thee,
    Is cold at my heart.

LOVE
MS: NB A, [*p. 15*], *stanzas 5–8.*
A flourish after stanza 8 indicates the end of the poem.

6

Farewell! the world now
    Reclaims our first troth,
Claims—till this willow bough
    Droop over both.

7

Flowers are springing,
    Bright over Thy grave
Merrily singing,
    Their song as they wave.

8

Flowers are dying,
    Dim over Thy grave
Mournfully sighing,
    Their song as they wave.

Mortesto

I rose with my own human might
And cast myself headlong—great wave!
Upon thy bosom I was caught
Thy bosom rolled me to the rock
Unhurt without a single shock
Asleep or dead the people thought.

It was the Bell I heard just now—
Or the wild whooping of the wind—
They have all left me—hush!—I find,
That all things are at heart unkind   10

MORTESTO

MS: NB A, [*p. 17*].

Or I could never meet with love
Save that of Thine white wingëd Dove
And Angels only love like Thou
Who wert an Angel then as now—
Hark! the twelve peals of the midnight Bell
Are tolling slowly knell for knell
Telling the hour I knew so well
By the strange tumult of my mind
And the old horror on my brow
While the nightwind hangs dead above.   20

Six hours will bring in the day
And sing the sun from the hearing sea
But Thou must listen quietly
My Love, and hear me patiently
For that will keep me from decay.
I would that I could faint away
And melt to music of the air
I often think of that, and pray
To be with Thee as Thou with me,
They say that it is Phantasy,   30
And that it cannot, cannot be,
But Thou Beloved will help me there.

Translations from German Poets

Uhland: The Boy's Death

This is the first stanza from the original four of *Des Knaben Tod*. The
boy stumbles into a band of brigands, and while they plunder and murder
him, a beautiful virgin pities him.

"The woods are dark, tempt not its ways!
Thou youthful Boy 'twill cost thy days!"
"My God is in Heaven, my light is he
And in the dark woods he'll be with me."

UHLAND: THE BOY'S DEATH
MS: NB A, [*p. 16*].
2 days] Life *del.*

Uhland: The Good Comrade

Once I had a Comrade
A better ne'er has been
The battle drums were beating
In equal measures treading
Beside me he was seen.

There came a bullet flying—
Is it for me or Thee?
Him it strikes and dying
Before my feet he's lying,
Even as a part of me.   10

Will the hand reach to me
That I so lately knew!
My hand I cannot give Thee
To Eternal Life I leave Thee
My Comrade good and true.

Schiller: Evening, after a Picture

Descend O radiant God!—the plains are thirsting
To drink the cooling dews—and man is tir'd—
       More faintly pull the Steeds—
          Sink in thy chariot down.

Behold who from the Oceans crystal wave
Smiles lovingly and beckons! Knows her thy heart?—
       More swiftly fly the Steeds
          Thetis the Divine one beckons—

UHLAND: THE GOOD COMRADE
MS: NB B, [*p. 2*].
SCHILLER: EVENING, AFTER A PICTURE
MS: NB B, [*p. 1*].

Quick from the chariot into her arms
Springs the God Driver—Love usurps the reins   10
    Still halt the panting Steeds
       And drink the cooling flood!

With gentle steps into the heavenly arch
Rises the dewy night—her follows sweetly
    Love—Rest all and love
       Phoibos the Beloved one rests!—

Wandering Willie

Canto 1

The Last Wandering of Poor Willie

"Wandering Willie" is the most ambitious of GM's early undertakings. He probably began it in 1848 or 1849 and abandoned it some time in 1854 to write *The Shaving of Shagpat* in the hope that the latter, an Arabian fantasy, would pay his debts. Although the epigraph (see p. 934) is the first line of Robert Burns' song, "Wandering Willie," GM's meditative and spasmodic poem has no relation to that of Burns and is, rather, a domesticated offspring of Wordsworth's *The Excursion*, with Willie replacing the Wanderer and the Author. In the fragmentary remains of GM's poem the members of Willie's family are not always clear: they are Joan, his wife; Marian, their daughter and first-born child; Willie, his son; and a baby.

    Sweet summer days had past & gone,
    And now the sun of harvests shone
    In plenteous splendour on the earth,

THE LAST WANDERING OF POOR WILLIE
MS: NB A, [*pp. 29–37*], *Canto 1.*
[*p. 29*] *top margin right:*
        Mountains rearing night & day
        The visage of the sky
3 plenteous] golden *or* plenteous

And ripeness fill'd men's hearts with mirth.
Sweet summer days had past, & now
Poor Willie fruitless from the plough
That he had put to different soil,
Must tread again the path of toil.
The path that needs the spirit of spring,
And happy birds that o'er us sing,   10
And flowering greens that under thrive,
To keep the wakeful hope alive.
The labouring hope that thro' the gloom
Should see the wealth of Autumn bloom
The golden sheaves, the yellow sky
Or in the furrow it will die.
Poor Willie with his darling wife—
Fair Joan in the merry days—
The [?] courting days, when rife
With bachelor pride, he sang her praise;   20
Daring the world with boasting much,
To bring or show another such:
Another with such laughing eyes,
So blue, & with such lightning fire,
Another of so dear a size,
Fill'd with all sweets heart could require.
Fair Joan still! with eyes still blue!
Blue eyes alas! poor Willie saw
With something closely kin to awe,
A distant Heaven in their hue.   30

13–14 top margin right:

      That needs to see
      With *or* The golden wealth of autumn gloom

13 labouring] wakeful *or* labouring
15 yellow] golden *del.*
18 merry] happy *del.*
19 courting] bridal *del.*
21 Daring] And dared *del.*

Between 25 and 26, del.:

      Soft hushed, frolic, with a foot
      That never yet was known to tire

26 sweets] peace *del.*

And she was fair; with such a look
As saints have in some holy book.
For suffering, & hopeless thought,
And insufficient food, had wrought
A marvel in the shining face,
That gave the old Maytime half its grace,—
Ah! when to love restored, her last
Maternal anguish well was past,
And to her husband's fond embrace
All tenderly she turn'd again;   40
Telling him that for him to bear
The burden that is woman's share,
Was all that she would ask in prayer—
Poor Willie's heart died in him there.
He sobb'd aside—his choking breath
Grew thick,—such woe he never dream'd
Thro' all the watchful hours—it seemed
As if an Angel spake thro' Death.

And in her arms that latest born
Was lying, and before her lay,   50
Shouting at the small sisters play,
The first pledge of their nuptial morn.

He shouted, free from any care;
The manhood of his father's heart
Was in him, and that other part—
His mother's blushing days were there.
A beauteous boy was he
To him a roofless house was naught.
And chilly nights, & days of rain,

35 the] that *del.*
37 *Del.:* And when, from pain relieved, her last
38 well was] had been *del.*
40 All tenderly] She turn'd *del.*
41 Telling] And told *del.*
45 He sobb'd aside] Poor Willie turn'd *del.*   sobb'd] turn'd *del.*
51 the] his *del.*

Were all the sadness that it brought—   60
This child had not been born in vain,
And often with a prophet's power
Aye thus that in him like a flower
Grew natural to the place—had sent
Swift counsels of serene content.

So thus with three to feed, the twain
Did journey on the white highway,
To where, as Willie trusted fain,
Bread he might earn & shelter gain.
And pitch his wandering tent & pray   70
In peace when daily work was done.
For now the setting of the sun
Was darkness to their souls, and night
A thing of terrors to their sight;
A fear born not of idle fright.

They rested by the green wayside;
Distant, a planet of the vale,
One little village gleam'd, & pale
The blue smoke in the sunlight died.
An avenue of lofty trees   80

---

61 born] sent *del.*
63 Aye thus] The hope *del.*
Between 65 and 66: Hint here at previous hope—life—aims—fortunes—failures
Between 71 and 72, del.:

> For now the setting of the sun
> Was something not desired & sad
> It was to see the darkness spread
> And every threshold barr'd—not one
> To welcome them with board & bed.
> Not one to call their own—their own—
> Not one to which they could be known.

75 not of] of no *del.*

Between 75 and 76: (Describe part of their journey) land—travellers, cottages, railway—
reflections.
80 margin: dead leaves of Autumn by the wayside

Unto the village inn led down;
Tall lime, and dusty elm, and brown
Burnt chesnut withering in the breeze.
A mass of shade they made below,
That hung above the thirsting pond,
Where ducks were paddling to & fro,
One weeping willow drooped beyond.
Far off, mid circling poplars, bright
The village spire was seen to point,
The sunbeams seeming to anoint   90
Its silent faith with dazzling light.
While fading far, & fed with brooks,
Where stood the kine & lapped the flocks,
Well garnered farms & fields new-reaped,
Were in the hazy splendour steeped,
With here & there a rising flight
Of starlings—here of noisy rooks—

"'Tis well that we are here" at length
Spake Willie, "while I have the strength
To put a helping hand once more   100
To gather for the great world's store;
And be the thing upon the earth
That God intended at my birth.
"Cheer up my Joan"! and full of guile—

84 A] One *del.*
87 weeping] drooping *or* weeping
88 Far off] Scarce seen *del.* Half seen *del.*
Between 91 and 92, del.:
            While far away the fields & farms
            Stretched westward fed with shining brooks,
            Where from the heat the fleecy swarms *or* new-shorn flocks
            Lapp'd peacefully
92 fading far] far away *del.* fading off *del.*
Between 93 and 94: Stretched sank
95 Were in the] Stretched, all in *del.* All in the *del.*
97 noisy] daws & *or* noisy
After 97: So long did Willie hold his gaze *del.*
Before 98: More reflections *space*
102 the thing] that thing *del.*

The guile that half itself deceives
And in its garbed lie believes,
He turned upon her with a smile
So deeply charged with sparkling joy—
The kindling light struck thro' his boy
Who straight began to shout & sing   110
And make the ambush'd echoes ring—
But Joan knew better; she indeed
Withheld not her sweet answering glance,
But all know how a heart may bleed
Beneath a smiling countenance.
She put her hand in his—"Too late
God's bounty cannot come" said she;
"And she was well content to be
God's creature & her Willie's mate."
Poor Willie! had she needed cheer,   120
He would have summoned Iron force,
And rode down fences like a horse;
But now he could not check the tear.
His quivering lips refused to speak
Three heavy drops rolled down his cheek;
Yet stronger in her strength they fell;
For faith sown in our souls by those
In whom our deepest passion grows,
Works more than magic or the spell
They utter in enchant'd land;   130
Faith is the spirit that angel like
The soul can thro' its sister strike,
And spur it, mingling, to command
With twofold force of mystic fire
The thing that is its pure desire.
And faith in Willie Joan had,

111 echoes] hollows *or* echoes
127 sown in our] in human *or* sown in our   by] from *or* by
130 utter] fable *del.*   land] tales *del.*
132 sister] fellow *del.*

With many a thing to make her sad
But greater still was Willie's trust
In Joan, & his heart was just.

Sweet Joan! in his glimmering eye   140
She trembled, like a trembling star,
That, stedfast in the rosy sky
Trembles thro' dews to us afar.
And ever in the swelling tear
More starlike she became,
Till like a flash of lightning flame
It dropt; & he beheld her clear:
With clasping arms that knew her near,
And lips that said she was the same.
His own! for Willie worshipped her.   150
And to his mind all image proved
Of angel beauty did appear

139 his heart] the thing *del.*
After 139 [*pp. 32, 31*] *abandoned but not del.:*
            One kiss could Willie not resist;
            With one long kiss her mouth he kiss'd;
            And looking deep into her eyes
            His own [*were del.*] grew dim with happy mist,
            Like stars before the sweet moonrise.
            His eyes grew dim, her angel face
            In all its Eden innocence,
            Swam to him full of bashful grace,
            Swam sinking into his embrace
            And fill'd him with its love intense.   10
            And O so lovely were they both!
            Ne'er since the day that seal'd their troth
            Did each to each together press
            With such a wistful tenderness—
            Nor ever had their mutual thought,
            Beneath their God in Heaven above
            With such electric passion sought
            That Eden[?] sight[?] of wedded love.
140–210 [*p. 32*]: After "the thing was just"—sunset—golden eagle—the children play-
ing—the sweet twilight emotion of the two—[*p. 32*]: After / And his heart was just
[*line 139*]
141 like a trembling] with a lustrous *del.*
145 starlike] distant *del.*
151 proved] seen *del.*

True likeness to the one beloved;
And often with a chidlike fear
He prayed she might not be removed
For one of God's own angels! she
So full of angel purity,
Humility and charity!
His senses by each outward sign,
Declared his darling wife divine: 160
His soul by all his soul desired,
Trembled to her as one inspired.
Ye whose souls have felt the same
Or yearn to feel so purely fired
Know that to kneel at such a shrine
A manly love can feel no shame.
But this was Willie's vestal light
That did not burn to prying[?] sight;
Like other gentlemen was he
In kindness & in courtesy.   170
Together did their thoughts resort
To give each other good support
While now their evening meal was shared,—
Hard bread & water from the well!
To wend along they all prepared.

The sun was melting down the sky
Broad amber, and the childrens cry
Lovelier in its clearness toned,

163 Ye whose] And all *del.*
Between 163 and 164 del.:
                    Will know to feel so pure a flame
                    Will know such passion free from blame
166 A] That *del.*   can] need *del.*
Between 167 and 168: more description pastoral
167 But this was Willie's] And everburning *del.*
Lines associated with 170 [p. 37]:
                    For Gentleness and Courtesy
                    Repays us still like Gawains bride

As on they moved with weary feet
And weary thoughts that never moan'd,   180
But still had force to feel love sweet;
On Joan's breast the babe still lying,
Unconscious of the woe within;
Its little life was folded in;
Cradled asleep with secret sighing.
In Willie's arms the little girl
Droop'd wan & tired; the one great curl
That roll'd on her cheek to the morning breeze
Hung tinted like the Autumn trees,
(She was, indeed, an autumn bud:—)   190
Over his shoulder dreamingly.
But Willie strode on sturdily;
Half angered when his boy began
Less dauntily & vauntily
In the rich racing of his blood,
To emulate the pace of man.

And lovelier the children's cry
Rang from the village, & the sky
More wonderful in glory grew;
The clouds in robes of purple flew   200
To close the falling orb, which threw
A blinding brightness up their edges;
Shooting down the mossy ledges
Colours ne'er caught by mortal woof.
The west was one deep sheeted view,
The blue sky yellowing aloof.
And now the sun pierced keenly thro';
Severing apart the cloudy roof
And looking, with great wings outspread,

Between 181 and 182 del.: Young love in all his strength complete:
188 morning] playful del.
193 when] that del.
205 deep] bright del.   view] hue del.
208 Del.: And touched the clouds with smouldering [?]
209 And looking, with great] Looking, with mighty del.

An eagle with a golden head,   210
An eagle darkening for a flight
To the dim east thro' the dark night.

Upon the wanderers as they went
The amber beams fell tranquilly,
Infusing half their mild content.
But aimless thought, & weariness,
And hope athirst now objectless,
Like nature sick for nourishment,
Before a desert pageantry
Are things that will not easily   220
Attune themselves to pictured calm,
The heart hath need of peace and balm
Within itself, ere it receives

After 212 [p. 34] abandoned passage; cf. lines 301–14. GM's several attempts at the passage have here been conflated, with variants indicated. Lines 4–9 originally appeared in the order 8, 9, 6, [7], 4, 5.

     [1]   And now the clouds again [closed *del.*] close o'er,
     [2]   And leaning on the western hills
     [3]   Draw down the day for evermore:
     [4]   The swallow tweets, the skylark trills;
     [5]   The pale leaf eddies from the tree;
     [6]   Cold [bleating *del.*] huddled fleeces in [*or* from] the fold
     [7]   Bleat in the stillness piteously;
     [8]   The robin's evening carol fills
     [9]   The quiet air in lane & lea;
    [10]   Moist smells rise from the dewy mould,
    [11]   And chilly mist burns [distant *del.*] western red;
After [11] del.:
        The one large twilight star is out
        And waters shine in placid

        The day that with one piercing gleam
        Dazzles the eye &c—
    [12]   The day is dead, the day is dead.
213 wanderers] travellers *or* wanderers
214 amber] setting *or* amber
215 mild] calm *del.* strange *del.*
218 Like] And *del.*   sick for] void of *del.*
221 pictured calm] symboll'd peace *del.*
223 itself, ere it] it ere it can *del.*

Those lavish treasures that the eye   ,
From every aspect spread on high
So subtly grasps, so richly gives.
For what is home to homeless men?
Home to the housed is Heaven on earth,
But to the homeless 'tis a dearth
More dreary than this darkling fen.   230

To Willie in his youthful time,
This would have been a glorious show;
And mortal weakness, mortal woe,
Have faded from the scene sublime.
But now 'twas alien imagery
Now 'twas almost a mockery!
He felt he did not now belong
To it, nor it, alas! to him—
The lark who sings where sight is dim—
Would he not sing a different song,   240
If, dropping to his nest, he found
No nest on the unhappy ground?
Ah! circling ever round & round
The one sole spot & rifled mound;
What anguish would the little thing
Shake from his wild low fluttering wing!
Even so with Willie; sadly shines
The glory, & his soul repines
To feel the old joyance of his breast,—

---

225 spread on high] of the sky *del.*
231 youthful time] time of youth *del.*
234 scene] sight *del.*
239 *Del.:*

      The lark, whose song is nature's *or* morning's glee,
      Who sings & sings where sight is dim,

Between 240 and 241 del.: A different song if song at all
Between 246 and 247 del.:

      To feel the joyance of his breast
      Had caused disaster to the nest.   *[Cf. lines 249, 252]*

The spirit of song that bore him up,   250
Has pledged him such a bitter cup
And caused disaster to the nest,
Made sacred now for Joan's sake
And those that, on their way, they take;—
New-comers! strangers! strangely dear!
"O wherefore, wherefore, are they here?"

More sadly than his mind conceives,
Our Willie doubts & disbelieves
In the one Power that raises dust;
His great ambition was his bane;   260

252 And] Has *del.*   the] his *del.*
253 sacred] dearer *del.*
Between 256 and 257 del.:
    No voice [replied *del.*] replies; not even the voice
    That ever [to the Christian *del.*] from affection preaches,
    And in their *or* all depth of suffering teaches
    Gentle natures to rejoice.
    No voice! alas, the voice that would
    Reply to such a questioning
    Must come from the contented mood
    That knows the false & feels the good.
    No voice! alas! the emptiness
    Of heart, that, for its deep distress,   10
    Rejects sweet natures symboll'd joys
    [Could *del.*] Would starve, or drown so [sweet *del.*] true
        a voice—
    Moreover should the answer spring
    'Twould check [it in *del.* at once *del.*] i' the bud the
        questioning—
    And "wherefore, wherefore are they here?   [*Cf. lines 255–56*]
    These [?] beings so strangely dear"
    Would have for answer in the air,
    "That question is thy black despair."
    Forgets the sacred [joy *del.*] pride he felt
    To be a father & the bliss
260 great] own *del.*

Cold disappointment's hardening crust
Of dark endurance works in vain
To cherish hope or deaden pain.

Frolic and down of heart by turns,
His patience squanders all it earns—
He has not learnt, with all his love,
That Heavenward soaring wings must soar—
Only to rise has been his aim,—
And he has fallen! give gentle blame!

Not so with Joan—mother's faith,   270
And mothers strength in all she saith,
And all she doth; her sufferings even
Remain unnoticed & unspoken,
Albeit her health is almost broken;
And faints at many a warning token.
She seems a blessed saint of Heaven!
As noble mothers truly are.
She walks beside him like a star
Unto a child of darkness sent,
Shorn of immortal strength, but still   280
Dowered with a mission to instil
Its own divine encouragement.

261–63

      [And *del.*] Wedded to that he frets in vain
      In disappointments hardened crust. *or* And
          disappointment, deadening pain,

263

        or It does but serve to deaden pain
        By murdering hope

Between 265 and 266 del.:

        Forbearing with his wayward fate
        The crown of patience comes to[o] late
        For which he only seeks to bear
        To conquer he can have no care
        His heart is atheist to his hope

266–67 *Del.:*

        Oh! ye who soar to seek the Heavens   *[Cf. line 267]*
        As every soaring wing must seek

She walks beside him on the road
That darkens under elm & hedge,
And on by waters fringed with sedge,
That wind to reaches smooth & broad.
She walks where purple brambles catch
Remorselessly her tattered gown,
By cottages thick-roofed with thatch
And fields where autumn seeds are sown.   290
On to the often-uttered town
She walks, tho' that is far away—
Far distant over dale & down,
And will not cheer the dying day—

Her foot is on the flinty track,
The dusty way, the stony path—
She bears the scourge upon her back
With all the courage that she hath.
Complaining not; her Faith is great;—
Her patience stronger than her fate.   300

283–85 *two drafts:*

        She walks where [mellow *del.*] vistas look
        With mellow eye & mournful gaze
        By doors where in some ingle nook
        The little gamesome kitten plays.

        She walks where languid *or* supple grasses lean
        And plants wherein the blights are set,
        By sleeping cock with eyes of jet
        And spreading boughs of couching green.

287 purple] crawling *or* purple
288 tattered] single *del.*

Between 294 and 295 del.:

        She passes many a [quiet *del.*] little church
        With clustered graves and quiet air;
        Dark ivy creeping [round *del.*] up the porch
        And round the windows, gleaming fair.
        She passes many a merry home
        With gardens where the [*blank*]
        Is [closing in *del.*] shrinking from the gradual gloom

After 300 del.:

        Religious reverence fills her mind
        With meekness—and for all mankind
        She has more strong compassion left
        Than for herself of home bereft—
        This want in Willie she supplied

And now the clouds again close o'er,
And, leaning on the western hills,
Draw down the day for evermore.
The swallow tweets, the skylark trills;
The robin's vesper carol fills
The quiet air in lane & lea;
The pale leaf eddies from the tree;
Cold huddled fleeces in the fold
Bleat in the stillness piteously;
The travellers darken on the wold;   310
The stars brighten overhead
Moist smells rise from the dewy mould,
And chilly mist burns western red;
The day is dead, the day is dead

          End of Canto 1st

Canto 2

The Inspiration of the Great West Wind

Against the unlighted lids of morn,
A full West Wind was blowing hard,
When Willie wakened—hapless bard!
And threw his dreams away with scorn.

THE LAST WANDERING OF POOR WILLIE
Prose note NB A, [p. 36]:
Introduce mention of his Town life
Anecdote
307 pale] dead *del.*
311 burn *or* brighten
Prose note NB A, [p. 37]: Conclude the first part with close of day—Second part
commencing with the morning & the wanderers sleeping in the tenantless house
THE INSPIRATION OF THE GREAT WEST WIND
MS: NB A, [*pp. 39–57*], *Canto 2.*
1 unlighted lids] cold gray eye *del.*
Between 1 and 2 del.:
          Half opening on the sea wave *or* misty spawn
          Of darkness & his[?] fading cars
2 A full] The south *del.*

He flung them in among the spheres
Which brought them, charged with wistful tears,
That made the barren daylight swim;—
Too often had they play'd on him.
And now, thus harshly out of tune,
The touch of dreamland brought no boon: 10
He flung his haunting dreams away
Like ghosts before the scaring day—
And looking round him as he rose
From Joan's side, remembered how
The bright-eyed midnight guided them
To this sole refuge for repose
Of weary life & weary limb.

4–5 *Del.:* And left his dreams among the stars.
6 Which brought] That brought *or* Which bore *del.*
7 barren daylight swim] laughing daylight dim *del.*   barren] stern *del.*
9 thus harshly] that he was *or* thus harshly *del.*
After 9 del.:

'Twas bitter music! let it play
When stars shine on the heartless day.
Loud, jarring, and lifelessly almost—
The sighing of a new born ghost
(Who would not sink with discontent,
From Harmonist to Instrument!)
'Twas doleful discord; notes & keys *or* bars
Trembled in jarring *or* together in dismal jars.
All keys confounded—gay, & sad,
And glad, & melancholy mad.   10
Our Willie when his [time *or* youth *del.*] youth was ripe
To every key could pitch his pipe,
And weave most [sweetly every *or* cunningly each *del.*]
     cunningly each tone
That Nature [harbours *or* doth own *del.*] to herself alone
Doth sing, where wood-lands shine with dew
And valleys circle to the blue,
Or where the salt sea waters dash
Or where the torrents fall & flash.
Even discord to delightful sound
He wedded, & in wedlock bound;   20
Where, all her lonely moods denied,
She proved a wondrous, wealthy bride.

12 scaring] staring *or* scaring
13 looking] gazing *del.*

And better could the Fates allow?

It was a ruined House that stood
Upon the borders of a wood,   20
And lean'd upon a rivers brink,
In which it peer'd thro' many a chink,
With vacant eye; the battered door,
The scatter'd tiles, & windows bare,
The plaister damp, and dusty floor,
Where sleep was shielding Joan from care;
Spake mutely in their nakedness
Of desolation, & distress,
Far distant, but appealing still
Here was some hidden human ill,   30
Unburied, tho' without record:
But Willie felt a grateful gush
Of thanks to feel it could afford
Such shelter to the outcast, such
Deep lesson to him in his need
Of inward power & strength indeed.

22 peer'd] gazed *del.*
After 22 abandoned but not del.:
        In truth, his *or* For, *or* And, he, whose passion did consist
        In being Nature's harmonist;
        But who would *or* How could he sink with calm content *or*
        Who would not sink with discontent;
        From harmonist to instrument?
30 Here was] Against *del.*
31 tho'] & *del.*
35 Deep] A *or* Deep
36 inward power] power divine *del.*
Alternative for 37–40 del.:
        Misfortune is, and ever was
        A daughter of the [Gods *del.*] Heaven's; divine
        As they, and where her foot shall pass
        Is counsel, comfort—and the wine
        Of wisdom from God's vineyard press—
        Her path is [strewn *del.*] hedged with Holiness,
        Her person sacred for the woes
        Her children bring *or* She bears about where'er she goes.

He felt misfortune cannot be
So outcast in its misery
To fail, beneath its scourging fate,
In sheltering the desolate.   40
Self-pitying pride ran thro' him then,
And peace towards his fellowmen.
High-pitch'd to every influence
Was Willie, as he knelt
In prayer, this sacredness he felt
Diffuse itself thro' every sense—
The inviolate feeling clothed him warm
Ran thro' his blood and shaped his form.
Among the rafters over-head,
He glanced; where now the spider swung,   50
Or where, above its shining thread,
The hereditary cobweb hung,—
Close to the driving cloud—he gazed
Upon the old fireside's empty grate;—
The brooding spirit there he praised,
And blessings did reciprocate.

His waking wife, no taunting dream
Disturb'd; she laid their scanty meal
And washed her children in the stream,
Without a look that might reveal   60
Oblivious of her work to do;—
Nor grief that daylight shd renew
The burden. Differently the two
Did travel to the common end;—

43 High-pitch'd] Open *or* High-pitch'd
44 as] and before
47 and made him warm *or* form
53 driving] flying *del.*
Between 54 and 55 del.: Where once the happy circle sate.
After 56 abandoned: For there a crouching spirit sate
59 washed her] dipt the *del.*
64 common end] self-same *or* common end

For she by instinct straight did wend.
He wandered in a zig-zag maze,
And wildering labyrinth of ways—
But caught from Nature's visage sights
That saved him from his impish lights.

And now upon their path they haste   70
Once more, of other roofs unknowing—
"Farewell to this" and may they taste
As true a welcome where they're going.
Deserted nature offers aye
That welcoming which men deny.
"Here, where the nettle now is growing"
Cries Willie, "here with fond regret,
"Will we look back, & not forget,
"When roses in our porch are glowing."

Aloud the full West Wind is blowing!   80
And with a voice of carnage bends
The trees whose tawny robes 'tis strowing.
With a fierce ruthless hand he rends
The leafage, o'er the fields, bestowing
The whirling groups of summer day—

After 69 del.:
                Swift, sudden glances of her wild,
                Strange mother's beauty—when she smiled
                And brought him to her flying face—
                In many a wild [*blank*]
Before 70: (As they say farewell to their place of shelter a gentler feeling comes over
him, forgetfulness of misfortune, belief in the beneficence of creation and a feeling of
openness to nature which is exaggerated by the tumult of the wind [Describe])
70 path] way *or* path   haste] speed *del.*
79 porch] ground *del.*
82 tawny robes 'tis] leaves his breath is *del.*   tawny] yellow *or* fevered *del.*
83 With a fierce ruthless hand] Amain & ruthlessly *or* With a fierce ruthless hand
84 o'er the fields, bestowing] & the bowing heads *del.*
85 day] dead *del.*

Elms are struggling, beeches shrieking—
Aloft the cowering clouds are streaking
Their folds with flying blue & gray—
The poplars swing, the pine-trees sway
Like tossing fleets with mast to mast   90
Heaved on a black tempestuous ocean—
The lime trees hold their leaves to the last;
The oaks are battling in the blast,
Like warriors set with wild commotion.
The dark death circle fi[e]rcely mowing
The willows weep with wild emotion.

Aloud the full West Wind is blowing!
And o'er the waters slowly flowing
Breathes shady ripples & tiny waves:
The forest roars, the thicket raves.—   100
On one great ceaseless organ swell
Of sound, the rushing wind doth dwell.
And "hark", cries Willie, smiling arch,
"What mighty music plays our march!
"Few warriors in the great campaign
"Of life e'er tramp'd to such a strain.

Between 86 and 87 del.:

       The birks their golden foliage shed—   *[Cf. line 94]*
       And every barren bough is creaking
       Harsh as a death shout in the fray;
       Associated frag., NB A, [p. 37]: the birch
       Its showers of golden foliage shows
       Associated frag., NB A, [p. 41]:
       Fair birks their golden foliage shed,
       Wide the maples wave their banners red.
87 cowering] sweeping *del.*
88 flying] shifting *del.*
90 tossing] scattered *del.*
91 black] dark *del.*
99 shady] running *or* shady
101 On] With *del.*
105 warriors] soldiers *or* warriors
106 tramp'd] march'd *del.*

"And could they, think you Joan, fail
"Beneath their leader's eye, to gain
"That victory which, not in vain—
"Is promised in the trumpet gale,   110
"With ear to hear, and heart to feel,
"And will to follow, come woe or weal!"
A fiery look of expectation
He flash'd on her: his moods she knew;
She did not share his inspiration,
But shared his heart with fervour true;
A feeling fraught with reverence too;
To see him throw, with spirit single,
His burdened heart abroad, & mingle
With nature like an angel new.   120
She loved this weakling of the world
So strong wherein the world is weak.
Loved him; & her deep love impearl'd
With tender tears each faulty freak
His ardour offered to temptation;—
Her love bow'd into veneration
When she beheld the deep & strange
Prophetic insight he could draw
From every object that he saw,
And all the elements in their range;—   130
Which in that prayerful breast of hers,
She knew to be God's ministers.

110 promised] whispered *del.*   trumpet] impelling *del.*
112 will] strength *del.*
Lines probably to follow 112 [p. 45]:
              But while the forehead reads the skies
              Divining, with all beauteous eyes
              [*blank*] let the foot be firm
              And sure of its earth as the shrinking worm
              Let foot & eye go well together
              And they'll defy foul wind or weather.
114 flash'd] turn'd *or* flash'd
123 Loved] She loved *del.*
126 bow'd] soar'd *del.*
127 the deep &] with what deep, *del.*
128 insight] impulse *or* insight
131 breast] heart *del.*

Scarce to his heart her answer sank;
For he was wild, & wd not brook
Low tones, but from her gentle look
A moment's glance of love he drank
That might have fill'd a man for ever.

Too wise was she to wish to sever
Her Willie from the invisible link
That bound him to an outward being,   140
That buoy'd him up; nor let him sink;
This child at heart so old in sorrow!
That buoy'd him up all unforeseeing—
Blind to the changes of the morrow!
Too well she knew that to restrain,
Would tighten the mysterious chain—
Or break it, and his life would be
Either too fettered or too free.
So thus from wisdom's deepest source,
A loving breast, she steer'd her course.   150

And Oh! what strength this noble soul
Possest, who thus could think & speak,
And all her natural thoughts controul.
While on her baby's tinted cheek
She gazed, & on her boy's so pale.
What promise in the trumpet gale
Felt she? little, or none perchance!
Or if she felt a meaning there,
'Tis that which makes the dead leaves dance
Their frenzied dance of dead despair;   160

135 gentle] friendly *or* gentle
137 fill'd] daz'd[?] *or* fill'd

Between 140 and 141, line 143 del.

146 mysterious] uncounted *or* mysterious
150 breast] heart *del.*
151 this] that *del.*
155 And on her boy's she gazed *del.*
160 frenzied] fevered *or* frenzied

Beneath the pallid autumn glare.
Dance, & eddy, and whirl, & rise,
Mingled together, all hues & kinds;
Yellow & purple & scarlet dyes,
Heap'd by the eight great piping winds.
But hers was not a strength that waits
The spur of elements or fates.
Or from the changing season knows
The dawn of hope, the dread of woes.
This strength lives not in women: nor   170
This weakness, and their striving war.

Aloud the full West Wind is blowing!
And round him & against him blows,
As though some winged seed 'twere sowing,
That in a soil of promise grows,
And throws up instant flowers & fruit:
Now, sounding like a mellow lute
Over some smooth, deep twilight water
Now rising to a noise of slaughter,
When rival clans & hostile hordes   180
Shriek in a clash of shields & swords.

165 Heap'd] Pluck'd *del.* Torn *del.*   eight] four *del.*
167 spur] voice *or* spur
169 dawn] birth *del.*
After 171 del.:

And morn in midday vanish'd soon
And midday fell away to noon
And noon [*blank*]

After 171 inserted later: Whether 'tis better that so it be

177 mellow] golden *or* mellow
179 noise] cry *or* noise
181 Shriek in] Meet with *or* Shriek in
After 181 del.:

Meantime from the abating West
A milder spirit blew, & bared
The peeping Heavens, & dispossessed
The folded clouds that, scattering, shared
Warm hues of sun & sky, and paved
The sun's descending path & drew
His glory down the golden blue,
Where now a loving welcome waved.

Scarce to his heart her answer sank;
But never yet had warrior knight,
Or legendary squire of rank,
Or soldier lad in feud, or fight,
Or foray, such a comrade sure
As Willie felt with Joan secure
In his campaign and battle of life:
So staunch & steady in the strife,
So valorous in adversity,   190
So full of all resource was she!
In strength & patience so complete
To build up victory o'er defeat.
He knew it, and even while he shouted,
Felt that on him would fall the blame,
The pointing finger and the shame,
If he in this great fight were routed.
But triumph was a thing undoubted
Now, with all his blood a-flame,
His brain fermenting, and his Muse   200
Ready to flood the earth, and flying
Light as a lark o'er morning dews,
Or echo to the hills, replying.
"Courage"! he cries, his brows down-bent,
As if to charge a thousand shot
From some advancing regiment,—
With Death before it like a blot,
And a concentered deadly eye;—
"Courage! for thou who bravely die,
"Are conquerors by divinest right,   210
"And only those who turn to flight
"Are conquered; never such was I.
"Valour is more than men or might.

184 legendary squire of] squire of high, or humble *del.*
186 sure] true *del.*
187 felt with Joan] in his wife *or* felt with Joan
191 all resource] help & aid *del.*
204 cries] cried *del.*   his] with *del.*
208 concentered] united *or* concentered
213 Valour] Courage *del.*

"Have courage! Forward to the van!
"And living, thou shalt gain the crown
"Of victory & the great renown,—
"Or dying, vanquish more than man.

"And pipe aloud, O Wind o' the West"
Sings Willie; "pipe! & sightless, hueless,
"Take the whole world within thy viewless   220
"Vast embrace! Pervade, invest,
"And nerve with thy voice all living Creatures,
"And all the cold Autumnal features
"Change with thy warmth, O Wind o' the West
"And over copse & pasture hoary,
"Pour with thy great invisible glory;
"Where'er thou comest a welcome guest!
"Pipe, pipe aloud O Wind o' the West!
"Aloud! and with the shrill hallooing
"When the fox drags his brush, renewing   230
"The outcry of the wild unrest
"Pipe—pipe aloud O Wind o' the West!
"Aloud! and thro' the weeping branches
"Fall with the force of avalanches,—
"Where the thick snows are hoarded best.
"Pipe, pipe aloud O Wind o' the West!
"Pipe with thy deep melodious changes,
"Pipe with thy grand orchestral ranges—
"Forest & woodland wait thy test.
"Pipe, pipe aloud O Wind o' the West!   240
"Tune to thy varied alternations
"Trees & seas and mountain stations,
"Clouds and rocky torrent crest.

219 Sings] Cries *del.*
222 nerve] fill *del.*   voice] force *del.* power *del.*
224 O Wind o'the West] & every breast *del.*
229 with] like *del.*
230 the fox] Renard *del.*
231 outcry] rapture *or* outcry
235 "Where the thick snows join to [?]
239 test] hest *del.*
243 Clouds] Trees, seas *del.*   torrent] mountain *del.*

"Pipe, pipe aloud O Wind o' the West!
"Lo! the wild storm in leash thou holdest!
"The thunder in thy arms thou foldest
"The lightning lodges in thy breast.
"Pipe, full of power O Wind o' the West!
"Come from the mouth of God! who breathing
"Sends thee abroad, his missions wreathing;   250
"Charged with His Presence and behest!
"Call with His Voice O Wind o' the West!"

And Joan with three quick kisses seal'd
This sudden faith her mate reveal'd
That God was with them everywhere:
A thing she fear'd he did not care
To feel, or fancy, turning swift
She caught him, & her lips did lift,
Sweet lips in that small face so fair!
And thrice she kiss'd him, then & there!   260

251 His Presence] his presence *del.*
Lines possibly associated with 254–57:
> [*p. 42*]: First principles of faith & creed
> [*p. 43*]: Faith is never sown in vain
>   In any soil
>   As joy will softly tremble[?] thro
>   As in lush grasses gray with dew,
>   The little eyebrights nestling blue
257 turning swift] happier she *del.*
After 260 [p. 47] del.:
> But dewdrops in the [drinking *del.*] thirsty rose,—
> The young sun's wine-cup,—disappear
> Less swiftly than those tribute kisses
> Vanished before the viewless blisses,
> The full-voiced spirits that, round, & near,
> And o'er him hovered, singing clear;
> And clung about him warm & close.
> The one great joy that in him glows
> Drinks with its golden desert lip
> Each [verdurous *del.*] green-hued spring that thro' him flows, 10
> Dry, and [all *del.*] the [dark *del.* light *del.*] clouds that drip,
> Or drench on passing *or* flying wings.—His cheek
> Flush'd for a moment, & to speak
> His mouth began;—but more than speech
> Was in him, and his face resumed
> The stronger light with which it bloom'd,

Then pipe aloud O Wind o' the West!
And meet them as they mount the hill,
And linger by the rain-swoln rill,
Or in the valley urge their quest
For work to help them on; and pipe
The pastoral joy into their ear;
The joy of seeing all things ripe
And reap'd; the thankful harvest cheer.
And blow against them where they go
Unhappy with their sad rebuff;   270
Their utter helplessness of woe;
Against them blow with greeting rough.
Follow them when from thee they turn,
And whirl the dead leaves round & round.
Follow them thro' the dead red fern
And thro' the silent pine wood ground,
Where solemnly thy voice is heard
And answered—thro' the oak wood follow,
Where yet 'tis green in every hollow,—
And hush the cricket & the bird   280

And like the smooth [moist *del.*] sands on the beach.
[That suck the white wreaths *del.*] Sucking the showers
      of briny spray,
[Answered in smiles then *del.*] In bright, still moisture pass'd
      away:
[The *del.*] To starry light *or* beams of tears unwept;—   20
[That *del.*] [They *del.*] Thus sank to the heart again & slept.
271 *Del.*: The desolation of their woe;
Lines associated with 275 [p. 44]:
            Reap music from the thorny bushes,
            From the sere reeds & bending *or* soughing rushes
            Whirl the dead leaves all wildly showering,
            Drive the dark clouds like ouzels cowering
            Low on their wings from brake to nest.
            Pipe, pipe aloud, O Wind o' the West
280 hush] drown *or* hush

With loftier sound, and pipe aloud
And bear aloft the streaming cloud!
And meet them in the green recess,
Where moss is soft & thick & deep,
And gray firs toss their ancient dress
And gold-hued birch shrubs wane & weep.
Clothe them close with warmth & balm,
And circle them with holy calm.
And follow them thro' the forest ways
Where the branch roofing swings & sways   290
Beneath thy sweeping fingers fierce,
And Autumn sheds her wildest tears.
And meet them on the outcast moors
Where like to them thou travellest lone,
And on the great heath's purple floors
Where wildest wings have wildly flown.

Between 282 and 283 del.:

      And meet them in the green recess   *[line 283]*
      Where they sink down with weariness
      And circle them with holy calm, *or* And   *[line 288]*
          clothe them close with warmth & balm,   *[line 287]*
      Where mo[*blank*]

284 thick] sweet *del.*
284—96 *margin:* heath, moor, forest, copse, gorse—
285 toss] hold *del.*
290 *Del.:* Where Autumn chaunts her dirge & fades *Del.:* Where Autumn sings her loudest dirge,   Where [Autumn *del.*]
294 to them] themselves *or* to them
295 great] wide *or* great
Top of [*p. 41*]:

      Across the great heath's lifted lines
      Of heaving purple

296 wildest] thy wild   wings have wildly] flapping wings are *del.*
After 296 del.:

      And urge them, urge them when they tire,
      And aid them, aid them if they sink;
      For iron Patience must expire
      Thus push'd on Desolation's *or* upon Destruction's brink!

After 296 abandoned but not del. [*p. 46*]:

      Destruction? [O just Heaven! contrast *del.*]
         in so rich a land?
      [Thy meaning *del.*] No warding fate, no helping hand?
      Nor any want of Willie's aid
      To any handicraft or trade?

O light of heart & limb! as one
Who breathes the thinner mountain breath,
High up among the Heavens, was he!
And not a shadow from his glee   300
Fell with its finger pointing death;
For Joy was his meridian sun.

His large blue eyes still fiercely flashing
As when the exulting sea is dashing
With power, weak mortals read for wrath,—
Proclaimed the passage & the path
On which his soul had taken wings—
Among the wild wind-wakened things,
All streaming from the West, & shrill
With Western music, piping still.   310
He walked with feathered feet; he clapt
His boy upon the back, and rapt
A barbarous tatoo, and sang
Blithe snatches of old songs, and sprang
As if to reach a dropping sphere;
And dandled his little daughter dear.

The lyric impulse of delight
He shared with every thing in sight;
Whether the gray-lined hills that, dim

Then wherefore is he here and why
Should dark destruction linger by
With open jaws so long; nor snatch
The meal for which he lays in watch?
Patience! there is a stronger Will
Than mortal woe; then trust it still

298 breath] air *del.*
301 pointing death] cold & bare *del.*
303 fiercely] wildly *del.*
304 exulting] joyous *or* exulting
314 Blithe] Half *del.*
317–38 *two drafts; copy-text: dr. 2*
Between 318 and 319 dr. 2 del.:

And shot a kindling glance on all
That stood [spread *dr. 1*] around him, great or small—
Nor to his mind was aught [Nor could there be a thing *del.* Nor
  could an object be *dr. 1*] too mean

Along the distance seem'd to swim;   320
The clouds that from their ragged sides
Threatened to pour Autumnal tides;—
Whether the green-bank'd brook, whose voice
Made the lush herbs and weeds rejoice;
The roadway with its shading eaves,
And eddying rings of yellow leaves;—
The white geese on the windy green,
The hewn logs by the cottage clean,
The sheep among the scattered furze,
The grazing ass with lazy ears;   330
Or the moss-spotted old farm wall,
All brown & gray, where ivies crawl,
And wallflower roots in stonecrop hide,
And yellow weeds wave thick and wide.
He shared with every thing in sight
The lyric impulse of delight,
And imaged it, as doth a river
Mirroring all it meets, for ever.

For ministering joy, once seen. [He rush'd not to embrace when
    seen. *del.* To check his swift embrace, once seen *dr. 1*]
[And *dr. 1 del.*] He warm'd it with the warmth he held,
Till into subtler life it swell'd.
320 distance] horizon *dr. 1*
323–28 *not in dr. 1*
323–26 *another draft del.:*
324 lush] green
325–26
        The winding road whose dusty whirls
        Rose up in column'd wreaths & curls—
328 hewn logs] sand heap *dr. 1*
329 scattered] common *dr. 1 del.*
Between 329 and 330 dr. 1 del.: The little rambling villagers,
334 *dr. 1:* Or the rook-haunting elm, not wide.
335 every thing] all that came *dr. 1 del.*
337 it] all *dr. 1*
After 338 marginal note: Natural riches, stores & wealth of the world
After 338 del. [p. 48]:
        All that Earth on her bosom bears
        And all for which [dear Nature *del.*] she fondly cares
        And holds up as an offering

"And O green bounteous earth!" he cries—
"Bacchante beauteous! drinking deep   340
"Of spirit wines that, from the steep
"Where the high gods hold revelries,
"Spilt over! spilt from Hebe's hand!
"And meant alone to quench the drouth
"Of those who feel and understand
"The yearnings of immortal youth—
"Great joyous Mother! on the skies
"Gazing for aye; with amorous eyes;
"Distended innocent & bare

In every round horizon ring
Sing to the sky her mate divine
All that thou see'st is mine & thine.

After 338 abandoned but not del. [p. 48]:

Shivering thro' his veins he felt
The strange emotion run, and melt
His coarser crust [*blank*]
Shivering through his veins he felt
The strange emotion rushing warm,
Shivering thro' each startled vein,
Up from his body to his brain,
As thro' the fibred foliage stealt
The [?] of [*blank*]

The strange emotion shivers thro his veins

After 338 del. [p. 50]:

Shivering thro his veins, he felt
The strange emotion rushing warm,
Shivering thro' each tense-strung vein
Up from his body to his brain:
Shivering thro' his veins, he felt
[The *del.*] Quick preludes of poetic storm.

The marvels of the world, the store
Of still revivifying wealth;
The wondrous germinating stealth,
The lavish beauty to adore;
The mystery shrouded at the core,
The deep munificence it bore
Which the great hour proclaimed aloud.
The [ghost of *del.*] blessings in the bursting cloud;
Its rain of flowers, and budding speech
With April groves of birch & beech.
Its whisper with the yellow grain.

339 green bounteous] wild rapturous *del.*

"To the old Eden of the air   350
"Mother! with fruitful breasts up-swelling,
"As in their nuptial adoration;—
"Shout! shout! and join, from waste & dwelling,
"The loud tumultuous agitation!
"Never can I see desolation,
"Never can I read sad decay
"In this lush season's manifestation,
"While thus I hear thy voice & say
"'Earth knows her circle meets the verge,—
"'She sings aloud her lamentation,   360
"'But soon the sigh that breathed a dirge,
"'Becomes a joyous acclamation!
"'Prophetic of the years to be;
"'Like the wild western war-chief sinking
"'Down to the death he views unblinking,—
"'Her dirge swells to a jubilee!
"'He for his happy hunting fields
"'Forgets the muttered chaunt, and yields
"'His ebbing life to exultation:—
"'In the proud anticipation   370
"'Shouting the glories of his nation;
"'Shouting the grandeur of his race;
"'Shouting his own great deeds of daring:—
"'And when at last death grasps his face,
"'And on the grass he lies in peace,
"'With all his painted terrors glaring,—

---

349 *Del.:* Breathes Eden. Innocent & bare!   innocent & bare] while the naked Eden
del.
354 agitation] acclamation *del.*
355 see] read *del.*
358 hear] hark *del.*
359 her circle meets] that she is on *del.*
Lines associated with 360–62:
                    Not long can she continue sad,
                    With such an impulse to be glad.
Between 363 and 364 line 366 del.
366 swells to] becomes *del.*
374 grasps] sets *del.*

"'His tribes know well he leaves the place,
"'To [*leaf torn*] father's in the chase.
"'And thou who makest the dead leaf soar,
"'And these sere startling hues to shake,   380
"'And shoutest with a sounding roar:—
"'Thy faith is firm, and well awake!
"'Thou can'st never be forlorn,
"'Mother of young Spring unborn.
"'But to a time thy steps do tend,
"'When that fair child will not be given:—
"'Remember then, all human end,
"'Is but the deathless dawn of Heaven.
"'Then like the princely savage, sum
"'The glory of thy deeds, & shout   390
"'Thy greatness to the great To-come,
"'And meet its hush without a doubt!—
"'Then, with thy loftiest voice arise,
"'And sing, as thou art singing now,
"'With inspiration in thine eyes,
"'And God's white hand upon thy brow!'"

And Joan again his arm did press,
And smiled assenting tenderness;
Half wondering in her mind, how he
From his first Pagan imagery,   400
And heathen impulses, should drop
On so correct a faith & hope,
And put it forth with such deep feeling,

377 well he leaves] he has left *del.*
378 To] And *del.*
380 these] this   sere] wild *del.*
381 with a] till the *del.*
387 all human] what has an *or* all human
388 Is but the deathless dawn of] Of human, also has a *or* Is but a deathless dawn of *del.*

And with such firm assurance name it,
And even as one inspired proclaim it;
The thing she trusted, nightly kneeling.

She press'd his arm, but spake no word;
One darkening dimple like a bird
Of twilight when the swallows twit,
Across her quiet face did flit   410
And flew away. Still loudly blowing
Sweeps the strong Wind with shock on shock,
Like to the sea against a rock,
When the close waves, their white peaks showing,
Mount each on each, & darkly dash
In the red tempest's pausing flash.

Between 406 and 407 del.:
          The dear one knew not that, to love
          Our earth is the chief requisite
          For learning that which lives above;
          Del.: An ever brooding, blessing Dove:
          All channels for true love are fit;
          Del.: The means can never hinder it;
          Nor can it be by forms represt:
          And so it was with Willie's wit,
          Who, loving best, did learn the best.
          For love, the sole thing that can solve
          All mysteries that here revolve,
          And test the central truth at sight.   10
          This love which is one great birthright,—
          As every mortal born of woman
          Is child of love divine & human—
          The talisman whose touch is gold,
          We banish like a houseless ghost!
          Wisest is he who loveth most!
          A truth well sung by bards of old.
          Ah! do we wonder, Joan, wonder
          We know so little of each other;
          Of this strange world which hides another,   20
          And what is over, [& *del.*] what is under?
          Variants from deleted passages:
                    [8] And truly love, alone, can solve
                    [12] As] For
                    [14–15] But love goes like a houseless ghost
                              [While *del.*] The while his false name *or*
                                   Where'er his name is bought & sold.
                              And they who dig the cynic mould,
                              And make the grave of all mankind,

Aloud the full West Wind is a blowing!
Rushing, & wrestling, and overthrowing
The many arms of oak & lime
That catch him in his streaming course,   420
Seeking, in vain, to tame & time
His fury of resistless force.

Aloud the full West Wind is blowing!
And a deep warning voice he yields,
Dark & strange as the midnight lowing
Heard from glimmering starless fields
By those who in the gulfs of sleep
Awake and know not why they weep.

"And pipe aloud! and sealike heave
"Thy swelling gusts," sings Willie, "pour   430
"Thy healthfulness for evermore
"Upon us! pipe, and pour, and cleave
"Unto us! ever grandly calling,
"And like a foamy cataract falling
"Rapidly, with a volumed roar.
"Stream on, and swell the fleets of cloud
"Up the gray Heavens! stream on, and shroud
"With darker hosts the sun behind.

May well declare they cannot find
The talisman whose touch is gold.
[17] sung by] sung [of old *del.*] by
412 *Del.:* Swept *or* Sweeps the strong [great *del.*] Wind, and with its shock
413 Like to] Beats like *del.* Sounds like *del.*
414 close] great *del.*
415 dash] flash *del.* dashing *del.*
424 deep] strange *deleted passage 423–28* [*p. 54*]
424–28 [*p. 48*]:

And a strange oaring sound it yields,
Mysterious! as *or* with the midnight lowing,
Heard from [the *del.*] glimmering starless fields,
By dreamers waking—
427 in] from *del.*   gulfs] depths *del.*
429 aloud] and pour *del.*
433 ever grandly] still forever *del.*
435 volumed] lengthened *del.*

"Breathe bare the soft pale yellow spaces
"In the far sky; breathe bare, half blind,   440
"The little breaks of blue whose traces
"Tint the cloud chasms remote; unwind
"The western gleams with crimson lined;
"And paint the ambient vaulted roof
"With colours varying as the woof
"Of wavering silks that, quivering, tremble
"With the quick lustres they dissemble.

"Pipe, pipe aloud! and pour, and stream,
"Bearing aloft the shifting gleam,
"And the low rolling splendour, bearing   450
"The wondrous mantle day is wearing;
"And such as never king of yore,
"From nation-shaking shoulders wore,
"Where on high festivals of state
"He strode like a robed & royal Fate.

"Pipe, pipe aloud, all earth enthroning!
"Lo! as a voice of measured moaning
"Haunting the mouths of cavernous mines
"Where precious darkness broods and pines,—
"Such mystery loads the distant droning   460
"Heard in the west, like mounting seas
"When hurricanes the waves upbraid;
"And loud as when the ear is laid
"Close to the buzz of vengeful bees.

441 breaks] peeps *del.*
450 And the low] The *del.*
452 of yore] before *del.*
455 a robed & royal] an anointed *del.*
457ff [*p. 54*] *del.:*
       "Yea! like that measured moaning voice
       "[That haunts *del.*] Haunting the mouths of precious mines,
       "Thy words would say 'rejoice,' rejoice"
       "To those who know thy mystic signs;—
       "'Rejoice, I bear the treasure health,
       I sing of the world's exhaustless wealth.'"
458 Haunting] Heard in *del.*

"Pipe, pipe aloud! and give thy mission
"Word to man!—to me, to me!
"Give to my eyes the mighty vision
"Of thy vast Eternity!
"Sing in my ears the secret meaning
"Of thy voice the soul divines!   470
"Teach me to read the splendour shining
"In thy track! the mystic signs
"That speak to more than eye or ear:
"Dumb language traced in lustrous lines!
"The pageantries that roll revolving
"Each over each, far off & near:
"The presences they symbol clear,
"Unsolved themselves, all mystery solving!

"Take me, and make me even of those
"That are thy instruments! uniting   480
"With thy loud harmony that glows
"Out of thee! and in all delighting.

"O the great joy! to be a harp
"To every mood of Nature's mind!
"To feel her fingers thrilling sharp,
"Vibrate thro' all my being, and bind
"My spirit up in one sensation,
"Such as the tree thus takes the wind
"In tempestuous animation!
"Such as the sea in white vexation!   490
"Thou blindest the sun that he may pour
"His yellow floods on the western rim;

471 splendour] mystic *del.* lustrous *del.*
481 loud] great *del.*
482 Out of] about *del.*   around *del.*
486 Vibrate thro' all my being] Sweep all the chords of life *del.*
489 Loud *del.*
492 yellow] glory *del.*

"Picturing the realms that know not him,
"The rich-veined depths of orbless ore;
"Where miser spirits rave and roam
"To bury their gold from the grovelling gnome.

"Thou paintest the colours of Romance
"In those long lines of dying light
"That gaze with such a mournful glance
"And into distance lead the sight;   500
"Lead it away thro' oblivious space,
"Into the lands of love and grace.

"But Thou! thy works reveal thee not:
"O Wind! thy works but serve to hide.
"Constant to all and to no spot,
"Meek, and yet of tameless pride.
"Urgent as some near[?] torrent tide;
"Gentle as love-breath, music-fraught.

"A Stranger & an Intimate
"A Friend, a Foe, a Chance, a Fate.   510

"If with a will thy works are done,
"All senses must thou have, or none.

496 To] And *del.*
497 colours of] hues of old *del.*
Before 503 del.:

         "And O wild wind" he murmurs low
         Faint from the

         "And deeper than the source of tears
         Is that which stirs within me! yea,
         The living spirit of this day
         Has sown the parent seed of years.

Between 508 and 509 del.:

         Thou! whether Slave, or mighty Lord,
         Whether thy mission is thine own—
         Beloved, abjured, invoked, abhorr'd,
         When most present most unknown.
         Match'd with the world, yet all alone:
         Strange power of tongues—without a word.

"Thou art without; in all thy din
"Great as the mystery within.

"Time cannot touch thee, but sublime,
"Thou singest the Requiem of Time."

He paused, as if his heart were eased;
And fixed his eyes on Joan: but swift
As clouds are scattered into drift,
Again he felt his being seized,   520
Crying—
            "O world! such shouts & sounds
"Such clash and roar, such grand acclaim,
"Await, when from thy crumbling grounds
"Thou fallest, and thy shaken frame
"Fades from the banded seraphs singing
"Music of love! with pipe, and cymbal,
"Timbrel and harp! great rapture bringing!
"Compassed with clouds & lightnings nimble:
"Lightnings that coil like serpents tame,
"And quicken round the gloomy glory!   530
"Thunder, the crash of planets hoary,
"Gnashing together, until One Name,
"One name is heard! then soft & mellow,
"Mellow with subtle sweetness stealing
"O'er the still strings of buried feeling,
"Life will awake, and golden-yellow
"The Dawn will break, and golden-mute,
"More thrilling-strange than flute or lute,
"Green radiance on each dreaming grave
"Will fall, and each from its calm hollow,   540
"Rising, will call unto its fellow,

522 grand] great *del.*
535 still] deep *del.*   buried] mortal *or* buried
539 Green] Rich *del.*
540 calm] deep *del.*

"And all will roll as one broad wave,
"Before the wind, towards the Throne,
"In homage to the Saviour Son,
"The eternal fount, the promised One!"

Again he paused: the listening tears
Were bright on Joan's brimming lid,
Where shone the buried hope of years;
And all for lack of language hid,
And one to summon it from its sleep: 550
An eye drown'd in religious bliss,
Like the moon in a smooth-rolling deep,
Gazed on him; and a trembling kiss
Fluttered across his mouth, as flees
A rose-leaf on the summer breeze.

This was her constant faith, in woe!
That souls unhappy here below,
And like to part—should meet again
Never to part, or suffer pain,
Childlike unto Christ, her look   560
Appealing dear the Lord who took
The little children to his knee,
Comforted her in her misery.

Fragments and notes associated with Willie's apostrophe to the wind [p. 55]:
> Whose yearless youth shall match with thine

> What can Creation match with thee
> For yearless immortality?

> Creation cannot match with thee
> Her boasted youth of land & sea.

> This wind met Adam when he first
> Turn'd from the bright *or* blind forbidden gates
> And in his ear with [?] & moan
> Sounded like memory of old joy.

> This eternity[?] will unite to that time

> The inspiration of the world never dead

548 buried] unspoken *del.*
556 in woe] poor dear *del.*
557 *Del.:* That they who were unhappy here,
561 Appealing] She lifted and *del.*

Often had Willie sung like this,
And fallen as oft from what he sung!
His faith was just a chrysalis,
That by impulsive life is sprung,
To gaudy wings, which seek straightway
What blossoms and what buds are out
By meadow trench or garden gay,   570
And while it finds them, cannot doubt
That Heaven a crowning world decreed;—
But when they bloom not, doubts indeed!

She knew the frequent strange confusion
In his mind; when, full of scoff,
The faith from which he'd fallen off,
He treated as a poor delusion:
Knew his weakness & his want;
For like a wreck he wandered here,
Nor anchor to hold, nor helm to steer,   580
His flag still flapping an idle taunt.

But none the less her love admired
These passionate bursts wherewith inspired,
He spake her trust, as dumb it knelt:—
More than she knew, yet all she felt!

568 *Del.:* And breaks to gaudy wings, which seek
570 *Del.:* By garden walks & meadow creek
573 they bloom not] they're hidden *del.*
578 want] wants *del.*
579 wreck] ship *del.*
581 His flag still flapping] While his flag still flapp'd *del.*
584–85 *Abandoned but not del.:*

> He woke her wordless trust and spelt
> More than she knew yet all she felt

> He spake her trust as dumb it kneels:—
> More than she knew, yet all she feels.

Fragments for "The Harvest Home" and "The Doe"

"Here awa, there awa, Wandering Willie"
Robert Burns

[FRAGMENT 1]

Full loud & fresh crows Chaunticlere!
The Orient like an opening rose
Warm'd in a bridal bosom, glows
Before the sunrise breathing near,
And mounting in its golden gear.

Full loud and fresh crows Chaunticlere,
For in the van of dawn he crows;
And as a full-plumed general may,
He marshals in the pomp of day.

High on his sovereign 'steaming heap'   10
He springs & plants his scornful spurs:
Crowing as he would kill meek sleep;
Till all the drowsy farmyard stirs,
And bustles round him and about him;
Like brisk courtiers met together:
And laggards warm i' the downy feather,
Heartily wish the world without him!

See how he crows, and swells his throat,
And shakes his comb, & lifts his head!
Pride o' the morn! unwelcome note   20
To all who love to lie in bed
And slumber in the arms of sloth:
Loathe to leave it, & leave it loth;
Or else forlorn and lingering stay,
Feeling fast bounden to obey,

MS: NB WW.

Albeit they'd give a peck of barley
Just for one more smooth-dozing parley.

See how he crows, & crests his head!
As tho' the ruddy daylight from it
Down on the world he shook & shed!   30
As tho' 'twere some red-tethered comet
Caught as a crown for him, as it sped
One dawnward night thro' the streaming air,
Henceforth men from all sleep to scare.

See how he crows, and claps his plumes
So glossy grand, as tho' 'twere he
From whom the panting East resumes
Its gradual broadening pageantry
Each morn, while in the breezy front
He struts in his ancestral wont.   40
As tho' 'twere he who led that light
So subtle-soft & stealing-bright,
Thro' each slowly quickening bar
Of sleepy cloud; and thence invaded
All the wide arch of dawn, which lay
A rainbow's span, and mixt array:
Drenching the quivering morning star,
That like a fair sweet bather waded
Up to the throat in lucent colour:
Flinging aside each dewy tress   50
To show its Angel nakedness
More smilingly; till fading duller,
Deep in the Heavens it receded,
Lessening distant, dim, and gray,
And beckoning upward, pass'd away,
By many of this earth unheeded.

And crow! and with the thought sublime,
Flatter thy soul, O Chaunticlere!

34 all sleep] that land *del.*

Prince of the vigour-breathing prime,
And lord of morning's pearly ear.   60
Crow while the woods & coverts wake,
And with a dewy rustling coolness,
Breathe moist breath, & while the lake
Mirrors the Orient in its fulness.
Shadowing in the brushing breeze
So timid-chill, its chill blue eye,
That holds, & to the dawning sky
The bird of dawn ascending sees.

Crow, while the lush-leaved forest sighing,
Whispers in its dream remote!   70
And in its depths far echoes crying,
Faintly renew each morning note:
Running tiptoe from dell to dell
Hand to mouth: & in the well
Where Summer's green, & Autumn's gold,
Dances its shadow refreshfully,
The maiden light to bathe is bold,
And the blithe dawning dips with glee.
And while long forest vistas gaze
Less darkly thro' their natural haze,   80
Down on the dewy glistening valleys
Where with dim shapes old Memory dallies.
And while quick forest creatures start
To pasture, and the stately hart,
Leaving his thick green couching dingles,
His antlers with the morning mingles.

And crow, and warm'd with adulation,
Crown with thy plumes the glowing prime!
Crow from thy day-dispensing station,
And on each topping crow still climb   90
With loftier crow! while over range
Of farm, & holt, and weedy grange,

Cock answers cock throughout the nation.
Cock answers cock with shrill alarms,
Calling all England up to arms.

Who can resist? It is resistless!
Lads and lasses gay & listless;
Busy women & brawny men
Up they leap & out they pour;
Out with the robin & the wren   100
From the wide-swinging cottage door.
And down the rosy orchards some,
And some along the fields & roads,
And some to neighbour friends' abodes,
Hurry, & all the breezes come
With grey-chin gossip, and bursting jest,
And pranks of yesternight confest,
So tricksily play'd: and following after,
Bubbling rounds of ringing laughter.

Vain is the pillowy debate   110
Now held 'twixt farmer's wife & farmer;
Who every moment waxing warmer,
Curse that cock as a cruel Fate:
That cock, the Sultan of such hens
As never before hatcht chicks by tens:
Confound him as a red-capt Fury
Worse than half the plagues of Jewry.

Vain is the prayer in anguish prest
From every sad & balmless breast

After line 95 del.:

> And up, my little Island, up!
> To arms, for there is work to do.
> A morning health, & a pledging cup,
> And each man to his task in view.
> Up! & with the bees about:
> The hiving of each to the hive of all:
> Merrily up, & merrily out,
> And follow the mighty captain's call.

108 tricksily] slily *or* tricksily

Awaking with a start, to what   120
It numbly feels, but has forgot,
For further peacefulness, that fleeing,
Buoys no more the weight of being.

Vainly the silken dame would hold
Soft dalliance with her dreams, & mould
Creation to her dainty pleasure
In the close-curtain'd lifeless leisure.
The voice that cudgels ghosts, can pierce
Keen as the light her fortrest shutter:
And in her ear full loud & fierce,   130
Its dreaded disenchantment utter.
Giving each foolish phantom chase,
And making what seem'd fond & fair,
Fade off chapfall'n, shamed, & bare,
With long-drawn dolorous grimace.

Sir Chaunticlere in his martial ire
Forgets that oily unctuous gloze
Such dames and damosels require
In dealings with the world: he crows
Regardless of all womankind;   140
And to the amorous yawn is blind,
And to the pretty pout of anger,
The warm voluptuous rose-lipt langour.
Fine-gentleman is he; refined,
And mighty in appreciation;
But both his manners & his mind
Are Eastern, East his education.
And thus, albeit he may admire
Her charms, & flush with flattering fire,
A woman's will to him is null   150
As much as to the Great Mogul.

What! tho' a thousand perfumed sighs
Reproach him, & old Time, the traitor,
Feigns to forsake him, half defies

And veering, loiters, loiters later,
In those rich-cushion'd roseate rooms,
Where beauty so divinely blooms.
What! tho' ten thousand magic tips
Of fair pink fingers coax & wheedle,
And plead with the twin-budding lips: 160
Each finger a magnetic needle,
Stretching his progress to detain,
And of its own attractions vain.

It matters not: he hath a mission,
This Chaunticlere! and Beauty spares not:
Mindful of that old tradition
Which is his knighthood's stain, he cares not
Even tho' in his zeal, he vexes
The Cream & Lover of the Sexes.

For he, the sluggard, 'twas—no other—   170
Who first made Love of light ashamed,
And of Himself, what time his Mother
Blusht till the eyes of gods were tamed,
And in that Crimsoning distress,
Saw nothing but her loveliness!

He who; winking at his post,
Betray'd the Secret to the sun:—
Alas! why scares he now the roost
Ere half the enamour'd night is done?
Faithless still to Love he seems,   180
In both his treacherous extremes.

157 beauty so divinely] loveliness so warmly *or* beauty so divinely
178 scares he now] doth he scare *or* scares he now
179 enamour'd] hasty *or* enamour'd
Lines associated with 180–83 del. [*p. 206*]:
                    Faithful to every clockwork scheme
                    Of single & of double-dealing:
                    Faithless to every fluttering dream
                    Of fiction hovering over feeling.

Faithless to Love! as if avenging
The hour of his corporeal changing.
False to young lovers at the least;
In warning thus the jealous East—
To trouble the consenting moon,
And wither her fair fond face so soon!

Ah! cock; grey cock! on what a sea
Thou callest us to embark each morrow,
Grey cock! with what a little key   190
Thou openest worlds of joy and sorrow!

It matters not! he hath a mission!
And thrice himself that mission makes him.
And terrible will be Time's contrition
When he in evil hour forsakes him.

After line 187 del. [*p. 205–06*]:
        False to young lovers! faithful only,
        To the grim miser clutching lonely,
        Slippery hoards that shine like snakes
        Thro' his skinny hands, until he wakes,
        Hearing thee; joy & anguish mixt;
        And sees his treasure lockt & fixt.

        False to young lovers! false to Love!
        Calling down all the powers above,
        To part them, and their plight espy:
        Calling the Sun to peer & pry!   10
        Severing young lovers ere the kiss *or* them ere the bashful kiss
        Of meeting has been closed in bliss *or* [*nigh del.*] grown bold in bliss.

        Faithful, indeed, to those who count
        Foregone all time but their one hour:
        Wedded to measures paramount,
        Not moments: who forego the flower
        To pluck the fruit far less alluring,
        Frequent, or sweet: but more enduring.

        Eagles upon the cliffs are they;
        Their eyries taste the stormy spray: 20
        Their vision seizes every height;
        And ravenous is their instant flight:
        But much they lose when they despise
        The privilege of butterflies.
188 on] *to del.*

Lured, it may be, awhile to linger
Above a lovely lip or finger.
Limp as a reed, with abject chin,
He on his scythe will loll & lean:
While to the clarion morning rolls   200
Her Ocean of immortal Souls
Beyond him in that Isle of sands
Where, sinking and alone, he stands;
Feeling himself, in quaking awe,
One meal for young Oblivion's maw.

"And crow," cries Willie, from his pillow
Rising with wide-waking lids,
As if from sleep's pale-ebbing billow
Heaved: crow on, creation bids!
Nor ever rearward let me lag.   210

Thus rich in metaphors, he rises.
What is it all his soul surprises
When in the garden walk he hears
From one not rich in metaphors,
A fair—"Good morning, Willie mine!
"Awake yet?" and his boy comes running
Out of the wood that skirts the meadow,
The meadow sweet with couching kine:
And when he sees dear Joan sunning
The baby in her arms, her shadow   220
Broad on the peach-wall, & her gown
Tuckt up to shun the gray dawn-dews
That shine upon her tripping shoes
Fresh from the meadow-grass unmown?

She laughs; & little Willie musters
Pocketsful of reproachful clusters,
No visionary kernels in them:
Boasting the work he had to win them,
With toiling up & toppling down,
From the brookside hazels brown.   230

And looking like a young barbarian
Glowering with haste & heat,
While in the lap of little Marian,
He tumbles the whole tawny treat,
Gathered chiefly to provide her;
And sprawls with pleasure close beside her;
And thro' the open window plies
Hot skirmish with the shells he shies,
While, ever and anon, he cries
"Up, Father, up! rise, Father, rise!"   240

And soon comes Willie to his call:
And on sly Joan's mouth he sets
A kiss to dam the laughter jets
That toss him like a fountain ball.
A kiss he gives her with good will,
And draws her to him close, but still,
Like water thro' a moonlight weir,
Through her white teeth the laughter clear,
The streaming chimes of laughter fall.
"—What, Willie? You!" and Willie hums   250
Deaf tunes, and on the bloomy plums
Dilates a wealthy eye, till fairly
Vanquisht, he joins her loud & rarely;
Laughs from his heart, & thus securely,
With her own weapons foils her surely.

Down the old garden wall they go:
By nectarine trees, and apricots,
And plums and peaches rail'd in row:
And strawberry beds with the freckled spots
Of Autumn on their leaves; and apples   260
That the gay dancing sunlight dapples,
And with its kiss the dew doth wipe
From every cheek so rosily ripe,

259 strawberry beds] strawberries or strawberry beds
261 That] Which or That
262 kiss] lips or kiss

Or ripely yellow. Down the wall
Patcht with old moss, and at the top
Weed-grown, they go: bent pear-trees tall,
Invite them, and the ruddy crop
Sweet-smelling from the orchard, becks
As floats the gust in gleaming specks.

Tenderly round her little waist   270
One arm he folds, and timidly
As Egypt's sacred priests displaced
The veil of a panting mystery,
He lifts her shawl where, huddled warm,
Lay the sleepy dimpled form:—
Gazing until the child had sent
On all his face its infancy
Of peace: and ever tenderly,
And with soft fingers reverent,
Further aside the shawl he pusht,   280
And on the one breast heaving bare
And shrinking from the guilty air,
Gazed; and with such a blush she blusht,
While sheltering with the pearl she bore him,
It brought their bridal days before him,
Vividly sweet, albeit the fruit
                    [*Passage incomplete*]

                          [FRAGMENT 2]

"—But, Joan, where is Bessy?"—"She
"In younger wood has walked with me,
"And Marian & her brother too,
"He left her there to look for you,
"All haste, for taking bags of nuts."

FRAGMENT 1

266 bent] rich *or* bent
269 As floats the] With every *or* As floats the
275 sleepy] little *or* sleepy

And looking where the river cuts
The meadow like a shining sickle,
Hard by the wood in winding curve—
He saw her coming, & each nerve
[?] tingled to think how fickle   10
The peopled haunts of childhood were
To stricken hearts: the fair Romance
Whose life is aye a flying glance.
A vista's glimpse: how rich they were
When Nature in her motherly truth
Paid homage to the strength of youth!
Fallen from them, not they from her,
Was this poor child; and he could see
That like all frail inconstancy
When others fail from stedfastness,   20
They had not spared reproach:—
                              To press
Upon her shrinking cheek at meeting,
The privilege of a brother's greeting,
Was Willie's instant act, and Joan
Put in her arms the fondling pet:
No kinder thing could she have done:
And Marian at her side did fret
For kisses; & little Willie gently
Took her by one cradling hand
And lookt into her eyes intently.   30
Language he could not understand,
He read there; and, unconsciously,
The sweetness of a mystery
His young imagination fann'd.
For, to a fervent boy, is nought
So fascinating as the grief
Of woman: fresh unbudding thought
May gaze upon the blighted leaf
And nothing see but wondrous hues:

13 aye] still *del.*

And in her eyes, with no bright dews   40
Compassionate, the boy beheld
And loved her for it, sorrow unprobed;
      [Passage incomplete]

[FRAGMENT 3]

"Poor things! we know not what they suffer;"
Mused the old man:—"I meant not wrong:
"Poor child! I had forgiven her long:
"We are less tempted and much tougher.
"Yes, yes! Your words seem true, but you—
"Could you remember, as I do,
"The little girl I used to kiss
"At night—and it has come to this!"

He falter'd: idle aspens shake
Unheeded: but when sorrows wake   10
The oak to sighs, there is no leaf
But shudders with foreboding grief.

"May she in her household labours
"Be at peace from babbling neighbours!
"May she be happy with me here!"
He added with returning cheer.

Quoth Willie—"Your forgiveness sums
"All medicine for her consolation:
"For with it self-forgiveness comes,
"And the calm Heaven of meditation.   20
"The village gossips—let them prate
"And give their raging virtue rein:
"The world is generous in the main,
"But not until well school'd by Fate,

"And she—once let her mind review
"The passage of her whole life thro';
"Survey it from its morning pure,
"Up to the blush she must endure;
"Observe where Love first dazzled in,
"And virtue took the woof of sin;   30
"Catch the bright gleam to Christians dear,
"And hear Christ's words in Mary's ear;—
"All will be well!—The sailor lad
"Shipwreckt upon his native Isle,
"When in the dawn his heart is sad
"To look far inland many a mile,
"And think of his brave Comrades gone
"Never to see another dawn;
"Himself alone in that strange lull:—
"To look upon the shatter'd hull   40
"Bright on the breakers, and the prow
"Drown'd in the deep—is like her now.
"Flutter the gaze of both away
"To where the full sail swept the bay,
"And going with the prosperous gale,
"The sea-line circled round the sail.
"Picture it how it danced & drew
"So gently—till the tempest grew,
"And image that mad glimpse of home
"In darkness and in fiery foam:—   50
"Then when the past with life unites,
"The strangeness of familiar sights
"Will speak to them with loving stress,
"Vision'd in natural holiness.
"Nature's reviving life will show
"How precious that with which they glow,
"And then—all mortal dangers braved—
"Their one great thought be—I am saved!

30 took the woof of] slided into *or* took the woof of

"Saved she is! if, still unsteady,
"In the new path she drags her chain,   60
"Trust in the strength of Time—already
"The blue sky breaks behind the rain."

Jerking aside the farmer shook
As with strange tingling in his feet;
Spake as in haste:—"I see't, I see't!
"Your words are like some rhyming book:
"Just such a one as Nancy read
"When she could scarcely lift her head;
"I listening; nor its meaning crost
"Till she was lost—till she was lost!   70
"To understand them, it seems needful
"Great sorrow first should make us heedful.
"It would have been mere sing-song stuff,
"Dull as the chatter of a chough.
Once—"
            —"Why, see you not the vein
You've struck," cried Willie, eyelids wide,
Neck forward, as in some dark mine
His fancy trackt a glittering line:
"—You find that grief has been your gain,
"A point beyond all mortal pride: 80
"You find that where misfortunes hit
"Is deeper heart and truer wit:
"You find that every human sting
"Is given 'neath a honey'd wing:
"You find that every woundy blow
"Makes paths through which great feelings go.
"For even if sorrow be a curse,
"It weds us with the universe;
"And they who bear it trebly bind
"Their beings up with humankind."   90

74 Dull as] Worse than *or* Dull as
87 *Although I have numbered lines 87–111 consecutively, the three passages are discretely spaced.*

And doubt not that he did, thus quicken'd:
However in past time he sicken'd;
And to another shoulder shifted
The load he should have lithely lifted.
For not unlike a dark magician
Was Willie to his inner vision;
Calling up Spirits from the deep
That else had held a life-long sleep.
Spirits that in the densest clod
Abide, tho' sturdily they lurk: 100
For all men are forecast of God,
And all are God's good handiwork.

His large gray eyes with kindness shone,
And matcht his ruddy cheeks, and matcht
The clustering ripeness round him, snatcht
A juicy light of Autumn's own,
A bounteous sparkle while he spake,
Giving our Willie's fist a shake,
"I do; and I shall not forget
"How much I owe you!—that's a debt   110
"It makes a man feel rich to pay!"

And underneath an orchard spray
That with its burden like a willow
Droopt to the dew, they saunter'd, skipping
Grave matters by degrees, and slipping
Into the genial season. Grandly
Rose the day o'er them; spreading mellow
Threatening heat: and golden-yellow
Mounted the husbanding sun, and blandly
Blew the sweet South-wind from its bed: 120
Rippled in Southern Heaven, and paved
Smooth on the sunning blue aloft,
Clouds of the South lay warm and soft.
Over the land the South-wind waved
The gorgeous Autumn banners; red,

Amber, and purple. Like a flame
Stood the great haystack: glass-like flow'd
The river: humming noises came
From neighbouring field, and lane, and road.
Hot insects rose & sank: late swallows   130
Purple-backt, swift-wing'd, white-breasted,
Skimmed, & soar'd, and never rested:
A golden haze hung round the hollows.
Perching and pecking in the shade,
The blackbird piped: to clench his prize
The spider crawl'd, as headlong flies
Paid homage to his ambuscade.

They heard, and markt; and from chance phrase
To silence fell: each on his mind
And memory gradually declined;   140
Woo'd by the wistful Autumn rays.
And of the doe, from lapse to lapse,
Mused Willie, and how human-dear,
How humanized by love, how near
Our life she was; and what mishaps
Might chance to her; and the farmer's saying
That in the world to come, he pray'd
To meet her. Likewise the old man sway'd
Thoughtfully to & fro, and swaying,
On Willie's fortunes toucht; his mate   150
So true, & his improvident state:
Thence to his own poor child, and thence,
By no self-scarr'd benevolence,
To Willie's children.

152–54 *Prose note possibly associated with these lines,* NB A, [*p. 37*]: Love of parents &
children They who had so much to give and it so much to gain.

Sudden—and momently hurrying nigher—
Rose a piteous exclamation:—
Each started, as at cry of fire
To one who dreams of conflagration.
Seeking confirming looks askance
From either's questioning countenance.   160

Then Willie—"Tis for the doe!" "Nay run!"
The farmer cried: "here comes your son;
"He is alone: they have been straying
"On the deep river-banks, and playing:
"I hear him shouting out for help!
"And listen now!—no, no! you're right,
"He thinks my Nancy's in some plight."
And listening they caught the querulous yelp
And ravenous-joyful bark of dogs
Closing upon the quarry:—
                              "—O, Sir!   170
"I saw her stumble on some logs:
"She's lost! there's no one to deter
"Her enemies from killing her! Sir!
"Hasten with me! O, do you not hear?—"

Twas little Willie, breathless, eager;
Anguish in all his face & figure.

"Ay, ay! my boy!" the farmer laught.
"We'll see who gains her first; quick, quick!"
"And while the boy flew like a shaft,
"He whisper'd smiling:—"Tis her trick,   180
"The cunning thing! and I can't cure her:
"When she is fresh, and they are flagging,
"Sometimes limping, sometimes lagging,
"But getting eye and footing surer,
"Marking well their distance from her,
"Instantly down she'll drop, and stretch
"Her flanks, loll out her tongue, and watch
"With her sharp ears the nearest comer.

"But have no fear! she'll take no hurt!
"She'll keep a space between them still: 190
"She knows the ground; what woods to skirt:
"The windward of the windy hill.
"I've seen her while the pack all torn
"Tugg'd hard thro' the tough brakes of thorn,
"Quietly couch till her scent they drew
"Fresh down the pasture—when off she flew.
"Lord, such a sight! and look, look, look!
"I see her! she leads the pack in line,
"And now, she bounds across the brook,
"Now, doubles round the lonely pine: 200
"Winds by the hazel copse, & wends
"Riverward like a flinging colt,
"As if preparing the final bolt
"That brings her safe among her friends.
"See you?—but no! she takes the height,
"She turns—and so she'll sweep in sight,
"Vain winsome creature! giving them slip
"Just where those oaks the pasture clip.
"See you? and what a way she has
"Of lilting along the long lush grass;   210
"Why, she's as fresh as fire! fore Heaven!
"What a fine run the girl has given!"

Loudly he chuckled; sweeping proudly
His arm across the chase, as were't
A princedom of his own; and loudly
To see their favorite free from hurt,
The children laught, and jumpt, and call'd her
Pretty pet names; and Willie sent
A rapturous look, as on she went

194 Tugg'd hard thro' the tough] Were tugging thro' the *or* Tugg'd hard thro' the
195 her scent they drew] they caught her scent *or* her scent they drew
196 flew] went *or* flew

Beside the river's fringing alder,   220
Up the dark stubble, down the mead,
With undeteriorated speed.

Dashing along with forward chest
And queenly head, and neck of pride,
And noble pleasure manifest
In every limb, she circled wide
Before them, and her shape, descried
A moment on the bounding knolls,
And in between the sloping boles,
Was taken by the gazing tide   230
In tremulous ripples: tremulously
The fever-flushing foliage threw
Quivering lights as on she flew
In glancing swiftness fairily,
From field to field, and fallow slant,
And over brook, and over brake,
The steaming hounds still in her wake,
Straining their lengths, and long & gaunt,
As up the Heavens the Morning glow'd,
Their shadows racing by them, strode.   240

Fairily into view & fairily
Out of sight she flew; and airily
Up the high banks she bounded, clearing
Leaps that the huntsmen love, and leering
Round on her foes, as though to taunt
Their tardiness with triumphant vaunt.

223–40 *On the page that carries lines 241–70 is pasted at the top a torn-out scrap of matching paper with an earlier draft of these lines.*
229 sloping] knotty *draft*
233 Quivering lights] Shadow & shine *draft*
Between 234 and 236 draft:
> Beside the wood that skirts the sweep
> Of greensward to the greeny deep,
> Across the fallow slope that crowns
> The village opening toward the downs,
After 238 draft: Their shadows from the sunlight slant.

And—"look, and look" the farmer urged
Whenever from covert her shape emerged:
"She leads them o'er hurdle, & hedge, & stile,
"With playful manner so like a smile."   250

Fairily into view, & fairily
Out of sight she flew; and charily
Husbanding strength, and re-appearing,
She brought the dull tramp of the chase in hearing;
Mingled with many a shrill halloo
The ambushing echoes fail'd not to renew.

And—"Sing to her hooves, green hills, that gloom
"With the old Romance that you entomb!
"Sing to her hooves," cried Willie, "she flies
"With a golden wake from the wistful skies."   260

Fairily into view, and fairily
Out of sight she flew; & warily
Clipping the pasture, & quickly nearing,
Haunches tightening, head up-rearing,
Full on them all with her foes compact,
She pour'd like a reinless cataract.

Between 260 and 261 draft:
     Such thro' the world is the pace & the press
     Of self-confiding Loveliness.
261–64 drafted on verso of scrap described in note to 223–40, draft ending.
Upside down on the same verso of scrap:
     Vain is the struggle to forget
     Vain
     Vainly the wretched would revive
     Forgetfulness again
     Vain is the [*blank*] thus gave
     Pale Lethe to the self-sold slave
     Whose Life spent like a fiery rocket
     Has wasted all his manly force
     And left him to blank intercourse
     Between his spirit & his pocket.   10
     Drill'd with debt & drugg'd with sin,
Cf. NB A, [p. 36], with lines 7–10:
     For life spent like a fiery rocket
     And master of its manly force,
     What leaves it, but blank intercourse
     Between the spirit & the pocket

And—"home, she's home!" together all
United in one exulting call;
As to their vision dizzily
The reeling landscape roll'd on the lea.   270

Home, with her knees beneath her bent,
And panting safely in the ring
Of lowing horns, she lay nigh spent.
Beautiful, and so confident,
Her sleek sides softly shimmering,
That of the baffled pack no reck
She show'd, but turn'd her shining neck
To meet her master's eyes, & flapt
Her flutter'd ears as Marian clapt
Joyfully both small hands to praise her.   280

"But what is this upon her flanks?"—
The farmer mutter'd, as thro' the ranks
Of herded cows they enter'd:—"Raise her!"
Willie replied—"She's hurt."—"Nay, nay!
"She is not, can't be hurt, I say!
"She knows the ground, she loves the sport;"
Came the half passionate retort.
But in his voice there was a tone
That Willie knew was not his own:
And when he spake, after a space,   290
A shadow crost his open face.

—"She is not hurt, I would she were!
"Rather than what my fears infer.
"I would she were, I would she were!
"You see above that sp[l]ash of mud,
"Those three wet streaming spirts of blood?
"That blood, man! does not come from her,
"It comes from yonder whining cur.
"I would she were! I would she were!"

Then gathering force to speak his meaning,   300
His elbow upon Nancy leaning:
"—Yes! tho' for life she had been lamed,
"I'd rather it so than have her blamed
"By him to whom those dogs belong,
"For this mischance. And he is one
"Who never can forget a wrong:
"The cud of something I have done
"To anger him, even now he chews
"And finds it very sweet, I fancy.
"Sure am I all his art he'll use   310
"To work some evil thing on Nancy.
"Ah! lift your eyes, my girl! You're safe
"While I am near, so let him chafe.
"But only yesterday he swore
"That I should pay him some old score
"And with me soon, he'd reckon, too,
"With interest doubled since 'twas due;
"His keepers tell me. Well, for that,
"My friend, I care not my old hat.
"He dreads me quite as much; and yet   320
"I cannot sleep upon his threat
"To shoot her or to have her shot
"Whenever on his grounds she's caught.
"His keepers are staunch men & true;
"A deed so base they'd never do.
"But he has moods—Ho! Mulberry, hither!
"She is the queen-cow & together
"Nancy & she are always seen:
"She fought with Clover to be queen.
"Hither, my lady! see, how sleek   320330
"She steps! & what an eye! that streak
"Of crimson 'twixt her horns tells truly
"Who gored the hound that was unruly:
"Hey, my Beauty?—"

312 You're] Your *MS*

So fond

She footed: So sweet she breathed:
Richly on her glow-purple wreathed
The splendour of the sun:
                              —"Beyond,
"If friendship could bare cast the chances,
"I think, though, you'd have spared his dances,
"As many a time you've done before:—   340
"Or meant the rascal mischief, sure?"

And with a loving hand he chid her,
Threatening that to the highest bidder
He would sell both; perversely showing
The fulness of content o'erflowing.
Calling her names that Willie feign'd
To take as earnest; interceding,
And with a full-mouthed fervour pleading
That his true feelings well sustain'd.
"—What eye could more than view the risk?   350
"What love could less than ward it brisk?—"
Till to man's level he did lift
The creature with one god-like gift:
"—Pure instinct charged with love's sole sense
"Is such divine intelligence!"

A signal from the orchard broke
This rhapsody: "Yo ho!" replied
The farmer, and with a parting stroke
To Mulberry, their speed they tried,
And up to Joan their laughing goal,   360
Came with bright cheeks that burned like coal.
Each with an unsuspicious thought,

348 a full-mouthed] an acted *or* a full-mouthed
352 Till to man's level he] And to the level of man *or* Till to man's level he
361 bright] red *or* bright   that burned like] like flameless *or* that burned like

Anxious by frolic to efface
The undevelopt dread that wrought
Remembrance of that gory trace.

"—A letter for the winner!—guess!"

"—For Farmer Gale! the seal three bees."

"—Right stamp, right claimant, right address!"

"—Tis from my son across the seas!"

"—O Willie, Willie! fie, Sir Snail!   370
"For breakfast race, or cease to boast."

"—Let mortals run! I praise the Mail,
"And ape the all-outstripping Post!"

And in its honour, trolling forth
In tripping dactyls, doggerel rhymes;
Much earnestness he fledged with mirth,
This dwarf upon the giant times!
Puffing the virtues of a penny
High as the lustrous gold tracks[?] under us;
"—For with it Love has made the Many   380
"Serve each & him with magic wondrous!"

"—Right!" chimed the farmer, and I'd rather
"This than what follows in these days:
"He's not unmindful of his father,
"And sends me 'just a sample' he says."

"—Gold!" shouted Willie, making skips,
A miser's lines about his lips.

364 undevelopt] sullen secret *or* undevelopt
373 "And sing the [glories *del.*] merits of the Post!" *or* "And ape the all-outstripping
Post!"

—"Ay! pure as if Victoria's head
"Were on't now! but, hey?—methinks
"The time has somewhat swiftly sped,   390
"As the day mounts, my stomach sinks!"

"—Great privilege of appetite
"To balance with the God of Light!
"And mine!—Less swiftly blazing wheel!
"Let not our systems variance feel!"

Fresh as the dawn, the morning meal
Awaited them; home loaves, & warm
Sweet milk that cream-like poured—pure food
The contributions of the farm.
White welcome to their hungry mood   400
And pasturing eyes, the snowy cloth
Presented with its shining knives
And burnisht plate, & all things good
That keep the spirit from the moth
By watching that its prison thrives.

Albeit, mused Willie, latter-school
Philosophers that creed reverse:—
Let empty pockets prove their rule,
There's Wisdom in the well-stockt purse!
Body & soul, mayhap, are knit   410
As slackly as that sort of wit
In them; but not in me; in me
They joy together; and grieve together,
And are as they should be, one in all weather,
And hail! cry they, to the sight we see.

Whereat he turn'd an eye, as might
Great Hannibal when from the white
Prophetic Alp his hungry gaze
Exulting in its gaunt amaze,

419 gaunt] broad *del.*

Conquer'd Italia!—pastoral gleams   420
Were rippling on her peaceful streams.

And here was honey from the hives,
Of melting amber, such as made
The children near it take their station,
And on it with strange fascination,
Glisten: and here was Ale that drives
Disaster to oblivious shade;
Sending a sun up in the brain,
To blind remembrance, banish pain;
A prime home-brew, but not the primest,   430
Well, farmer, that reserve thou timest!
And here was England's giant joint
Still glowing from the midnight feast:
To which all English ages point
For veneration—not decreased
Tho' Fame upon such splendid fare,
Has waxed too portly to invoke:
Ever proclaim its worth, or wear
Disgraced, an ignominious yoke,
O Englishmen! And here were eggs,   440
Announced at sunrise in a tone
That took the cock nigh off his legs:
For them the hens will warm a stone.
Compassion get they none, I ween:
What egg knows what it would have been;
Or dreams of feathers in that shell
We tap with such deliberate knell.
And here was China's precious plant
Ascending in a fragrant cloud:
Of which the pig-tail'd poets chant,   450
And pig-tailed Emperors pen the Ode;
And little-footed ladies learn
To handle with such easy wrist,
And pour with a bewitching turn
No true celestial can resist.

And here was flesh of swine, for which
As in old chronicles 'tis written,
Full many a princely ancient Briton
In hounds, and beeves, and pastures rich,
And lineage from the Deluge dated,   460
Bled in strife: but rareness made them
Have these Pagan honours paid them,
Contempt came when they propagated.
And here was pie—mysterious—cold;
Let no man name its composition!
The darkness of one small incision
Is all our reverence dare behold.
A faithless Age tells that & this,
By infidel analysis:
For us, we cannot view unblinking,   470
The lustrous morsels darkly winking
Nor wanted aught to fortify
An English heart, for every call
The day might make on it, and all
The tasks commanded from on high:
Whether to work with mind, or muscle,
With elements, or men to tussle,
Bear as loser, bow as winner,
Toil contented—until dinner.

And worthy of such welcome, they!—   480
The low sun-lighted chamber hums
With cheer, while from the cherry spray
Red Robin carols for his crumbs.
And Willie chirrups undeterr'd
By past or future's starving feature;
More like a butterfly, or bird,
Than triple-breathing human creature:
Than one who in a little boat
The mastless hulk of Memory tows
On fathomless deeps; and rows, and rows,   490
And scarce, and scarce can keep afloat.

He sings:—"Mount, mount thy harvest throne
   "Broad Sun! and long delay there.
"The day's our own, the day's our own,
   "And we'll help to make thee stay there.
"Things of Time & his mortal tribes,
    "Are we; and the fore and the after,
"We'll leave to Heaven & all the scribes.
    "For ours is the reign of laughter:
        "Of laughter—of laughter!   500
      "What's gone, claims the pen:
      "What's to come all men
    "Should arm to meet with laughter!"

Then wayward as a thrush, he changed
His notes, and still as blithely ranged:—

—"Up wi' the laverock early, early,
    "High with the laverock early!
"And who would keep the blossom of sleep,
    "Must up with laverock early.
"When field & river wi' freshness shiver,   510
    "And dews are gray & pearly:
"And who would span the measure of man,
    "Must up wi' the laverock early."

Shifting again, with sparkling look,
A different tune his fancy took:—

—"Of Mother Nature's love to us,
"How better can she prove to us,
"Than with her service knowingly,
"To feast us so o'erflowingly?
"Then honour to the table she has spread!   520
    "Nor is the thought irrational
    "To name her favours national.
    "Our fathers at such boards before,
    "She feasted with like hoards before,
"Our children shall not fail them when we're dead!"

523 such] like *or* such

And with an o'erwise nodding head,
That chuckled at the thing he said:—

"—A better faith than this—
    "What man can know, what man can know?
"The like, the like o' this—   530
    "What land can show, what land can show?
"And is there aught amiss,
    "On earth below, on earth below,
"When such a sight as this,
    "Can cheer us so, can cheer us so?"

Dismantled Memory slips the tow,
The little boat leaps high & low;
The wind in every sail is shrill,
Let the wind drive it where it will!

But soon, with deeper feelings swelling,   540
The vision of the hour dissolved:
Far in the past his heart revolved
The morning chase, on Nancy dwelling.
And in a golden haze, and in
A land of glowing plenteousness,
And joyful faces, joyful din,
And mellowing Autumn gorgeousness,
She flew, clad with the sky; and fair
As she the milkwhite doe that flying,
Lured the black Rhenish baron where   550
His innocent Lady languish'd, dying.—

And to his host's uprousing rally
This sweet legend he related:
Telling how, in the wild Rhine Valley
A jealous Lord the Lady mated.
"And with both yearning breasts she loved him;
"And with requiting fervour moved him,
"And made his sullen castle ring
"With joyance in her gentle Spring.

"But ere the bridal dream came true   560
"When bliss & shame mix in one hue,
"And the young mother's pride could flutter
"Round that new name she long'd to utter;
"A trumpet sounding down the flood,
"Stung the dead hero in his blood;
"The wars of his embrace bereft her,
"And to disloyal eyes he left her.
"Left her till the vines were stain'd
"With Autumn thrice, ere he return'd:
"And with a double heart she yearn'd   570
"Towards him thro' the babe she strain'd.
"Up the stirrup as he rein'd
"His war-steed at the gate, she leapt;
"And with a woman's fear unfeign'd,
"Bade the nurse lift his child, and wept,
"She saw not thro' her happy tears,
"The fixt ferocious look he turn'd;
"She heard not in her singing ears,
"Those eager lips of love were spurn'd:
"She knew not there was treason plann'd;   580
"Till at a motion of his hand,
"Two ruffians seized the little child,
"And dragg'd her forth into the wild.
"But God was there: they could not do
"The hest they oft obey'd with ease;
"Nor with the glaze of murder view
"The noble Lady on her knees.
"They went their way, and she was spared;
"Like strangers to themselves they fared;
"And told the tale of blood, and took   590
"The fee, without its red rebuke.
"But little joy of eye had he
"Who graspt the proof, and gave the fee;

572 Up] And del.
576 She saw] Seeing del.
578 She heard] Hearing del.
580 She knew not there was] And witless of the del.

"And never could he lay his head
"Where once her beauty shared his bed.
"All day he chased o'er hill & hollow,
"And felt the wailing echoes follow;
"And in the savage nights he strode
"His steed, and like a spectre rode.
"So, on a noon, when thrice again   600
"The vines were purple, he spurr'd amain,
"And o'er the yellow sandhills drove
"The lither deer in copse and grove.
"And fast he flew, and fast they fled,
"Till each retainer was outrun,
"And nought was near him but the sun
"Behind the sandhills sinking red.
"He curst their tardy hooves in wrath,
"Hallooing to the echoes round,
"When startlingly across his path   610
"A creature like a star did bound;
"And starlike in the stealing dusk
"Wound on, and lured him, faint and lame,
"By caverns of the grunting tusk
"And coverts of the startling game.
"It was a doe, milkwhite, and fleet
"As elves of Elfland thro' the shade,
"All in the coming moonlight sweet,
"It glanced, and doubled, and delay'd.
"When as the hungry huntsman near'd   620
"To deal the death it disappear'd,
"And left him, by the fairy lake
"Where bird wings not, nor thirst can slake.
"A charm'd breeze broke the colouring wave,
"The woods in one mute circle rose;
"He turn'd, and by a brambly cave
"Beheld a glimmer as of twin does

595 once her] her white *or* once her
610 startlingly] suddenly *or* startlingly
612 stealing] gradual *or* stealing
624 A breezy silver dimm'd the wave *or* A charm'd breeze broke the colouring wave

"That on the grass together coucht:
"There by the doe a woman croucht;
"Babe on breast and combless tress,   630
"Shuddering in her nakedness.
"They met as strangers; her perforce
"He knew not from affliction's ravage;
"And he, the quarry of Remorse,
"His hunted eye glared dull & savage.
"And as a stranger, she told him, how,
"Her lover and lord for warrior pride,
"Her husband left her a young bride
"About to be a mother:—how,
"His household favorite had bought   640
"His soul, and her dishonor sought,
"While far her lord was fighting: how,
"She had forgiven him, not to vex
"Her husband, and his mind perplex
"Regarding one he loved:—the rest
"Was known too well in either breast.
"And she in the wild solitude
"Had wander'd with her child to languish,
"When in the loneliness of anguish,
"This fair creature from the wood   650
"Came forth, and at a gentle pace
"Approacht, and lickt her infant's face,
"And offer'd its milk for nourishment,
"This Creature by the Angels sent!
"And eyed her with dumb love, and put
"Strength in her with endearments mute:
"And to the softest moss did guide
"Her tired feet, with many signs
"The very-sadden'd heart divines:
"And never went once from her side.   660
"Making her know that God was by
"Even in a thing so humble, know

629 There] Close *or* There
660 went] stray'd *del.*

"That cheerfulness that's in the sky,
"The faith of innocence in woe.
"And she for sheltering warmth had lain
"Against the doe in ice & rain;
"And in the pleasant season stray'd
"Along the lake, and with it play'd.
"And she upon its milk had fed,
"And fed her child; and on the food   670
"Of wintry birds, and wild fruits shed
"At Autumn, had her life renew'd:
"Wild strawberries, and yewberries,
"And creeping bloomy dewberries,
"And berries of the bramble; fruits,
"And juicy harmless herbs and roots.—"

Here Willie ceased: the children clamour'd
"—Well, father, well? the end! the end!"
And sharp the farmer's fist down-hammer'd,
"—What did the fellow then, my friend!"   680

"—He hang'd the traitor at the gate:
"He brought his Lady home too late:
"She kiss'd their child, and once she sigh'd:
"On their old bridal bed she died."

"—Died!—and the doe?—" all ask'd, much shock'd
To find their happy hopes delusion:
Their eyes on one another lock'd
At this abrupt and sad conclusion.

"—Ah! was it not enough for her
"To prove that Nature is indeed   690
"That Mother we so daily slur
"And never know but in our need!
"To prove that there is still beyond

689 Ah] O del.
693 still] much del.

"The brand of human loves & lies
"A bosom true and deep and fond
"To take the Soul that to it flies,
"Or is thrust forth!—that still doth flourish
"With ever-watchful power endued
"A great, dumb boundless love to nourish
"Innocence and womanhood!—   700
"So let the gentle beastie pass!
"She was this heavenly messenger:—
"Of such a one on yonder grass
"She seems the mission'd harbinger!"

And to the hearts of those who heard,
Made ripe by suffering & pain:
Exalting comfort in his Word,
Came on them as a choiring strain
Of old religious harmony
That sounds far off as one faint voice: 710
For he in Nature's majesty
And mystery made them rejoice.

Silent they were: and in that break
When holiest aspirations wake;
Morn-smitten from Oblivion's blindness;—
Look'd with subtler loving-kindness
Out on the gold-leaved glowing lawn,
Where lay the heroine of the dawn.

694 *Del.:* Affections lost, and traitor's lies,
695 true and deep] ever warm *del.*
697 doth flourish] there is *del.*
699 boundless love to nourish] love to help and kiss *del.*
700 Innocence] Love innocent *del.*
703 *Del.:* And such a one upon the grass
704 *Del.:* Lies yonder! Look on her as here.
705 the] such *or* the
706 suffering & pain] pain and suffering
707 Exalting] There was a *or* Exalting
708 Came on them] Exhalting *or* Came on them

Willie's Dirge on Little Marian

Although there is no indication in the fragments or notes that Willie's daughter Marian was to die, GM interrupted the main text of Canto 2 to draft this song.

Lay the little bud i' the mould;
Lay it low, lay it low,
Lay the little bud i' the mould,
To a flower 'twill never grow,
Never, never tho' for years,
'Twere watered by its mothers tears.

Look at it one last farewell,
Look as clearly as ye may;
Here our little dear will dwell
Quiet when we're far away.   10
Never, never will it cry
To be with us or have us by.

Tears she leaves to those that live;
She so fair & fond of life!
Tears are all we have to give,
Shed them with no bitter strife.
[2 *lines deleted*]

Lay the little bud i' the mould;
Lower it in the green embrace;
Here 'twill keep thro' heat & cold

MS: NB A, [*p. 49*].

6 watered] cherished *or* watered

After 16 del.:

> They when houseless breezes rave
> Will wrap her in a greener grave.

18 Lower] Drop *del.*

That last smile upon its face;   20
Never changed in calm & storm,
Till the angels kiss it warm.

Lay it in its little bed;
Oh! but 'tis so fast asleep!
Drop it not as tho' 'twere dead;
Fear to make its blue eyes peep!
Never, never, nevermore,
Can they open as of yore.

When the moon shines thro' her cloud,
Here she'll see our dear one rest   30
Folded there in its white shroud
With its hands upon its breast.
Never to its parents twain
Will it stretch those hands again.

Summer with the dusky leaves,
Winter with the finest frost,
Autumn with the nodding sheaves,
All will see what we have lost!
Never, never, will the year
Bring us any news of her.   40

In the cool grey twilight hours,
When the ground is glad with Spring
And the air with breathing flowers,

21 Never changed] Changing not *del.*   Never hears it *del.*
21–22 *Del.:*

> Never more with glad surprise
> Will it wake to meet our eyes.

26–27 *Del.:*

> Never will it gaze alive
> Ne'er should we the look survive.

29 *Del.:* Looking where our darling rests
34 hands] arms *or* hands
35 dusky] shining *or* dusky
36 finest] gleaming *del.* shining *del.*
37 nodding] busy *or* nodding
Lines associated with 43:

> Here the linnet, here the lark
> Here the midnight nightingale

Here the happy thrush will sing;
Never will he feel a woe
For the dead child we weep for so.

Notes and Fragments Associated with "Wandering Willie"

Yale NB B, [p. 25]:

1. Barefooted on the desolate highway a girl leads tenderly a little boy. (Willie) the [little *del.*] girl's tale

Yale NB A, [p. 36]:

2. The little girl & her brother & sister whom she reard and how

Yale NB B, [p. 25]:

3. The young man's Tale. (Willie)
Storm autumn woods. Young leveret Virgin's picture

Yale NB A, [p. 36]:

4. The young man in the Autumn wood. Virgin & child Wild Leveret
5. Introduce mention of his Town life
Anecdote

Yale NB A, [p. 37]:

6. London life—the soul that liveth in events becometh a creature of them—great works are completed where (as in Nature all is under certainty & the changes of the season &c &c
7. The honest breezes, the full-faced winds
8. In Nature is no treachery.

Yale NB A, [p. 36]:

9. If rolling bowl & swinging bat
In cottage churls such grace begat,
How much inherent beauty nature
Lends to every filial feature.
10. His heart was green with England

45 we weep for so] so still below *or* we weep for so

Yale NB A, [p. 37]:

11. Achilles in his [*blank*]
    Trod ever in his Elysian doom
12. The hour of Heaven and of Earth
13. And yet behind our loveliest smiles
    Death lurks
14.   —the Soul
    Has thoughts that walk among the Stars.
15. The rooks were baffling with the wind
16. The windings of the river led
    By upland ripe with rustling wheat;
    And all its banks were white & red
    With willow herb & meadow sweet.
17. Death is the shadow of life's tree,
    The coldness & the shade, quoth he:
    But that was shade would not be given
    Without the shining sun of heaven.
18.   (Willie speaks)
    "I've search *or* probed the [hearts *del.*] depths of many
        men
    And I have found, whatever blot
    Defaced their spirit, they were not
    So guilty as myself was then
    In all that I should most condemn
19.   (Some men—)
    "Who understand no gracious act
    Of God's beneficence without,
    Like dogs & beasts, they sniff about
    And ask their senses of the fact.
20. In the lost Eden of her Eyes
21. (Wide in Heaven Love's eye did wake)
22. 'Tis true that Evil holds its Good—
    A kernel in a keyless shell

This poem appears in *The Ordeal of Richard Feverel*, where it is
attributed to Diaper Sandoe, a third-rate poet whom Richard admires. I

have argued in "Richard Feverel, Knight-Errant," (*Bulletin of the New York Public Library* 63 [June 1959]: 339), that it describes Mary Peacock Nicolls, GM's first wife, "a dashing type of horsewoman who attracted much notice from the 'bloods' of the day" (Clodd, p. 142–43). The poem is altogether inapplicable to the girl Carola with whom Richard rides in the park (Mem. Ed., 2:231).

When the poem was salvaged for *Richard Feverel*, the "knights" of line 2 was changed to "squires," and the third stanza was replaced, by a more experienced GM, with:

> And throng to her, sigh to her, you, that can breach
>   The ice-wall that guards her securely;
> You have not such bliss, though she smile on you each,
>   As the heart that can image her purely.

> She rides in the park on a prancing bay,
>   She & her knights together
> Her dark locks gleam from a bonnet of gray
>   & toss with the tossing feather.

> Oh! too proud for a look of pride
>   Is the beautiful face as it passes:
> The cockneys nod to each other aside
>   The coxcombs lift their glasses.

> She goes—she is gone! & turn thou must
>   To the dream she has not riven,   10
> O heart! that would dash her deep dark in the dust,
>   O soul! to soar with her to Heaven.

Song

> Thou tremblest O my love! thy hand in mine
> Is trembling like the moonlight on the deep.
> Thou falterest: O have courage and incline
> Thyself upon my bosom and there weep

SHE RIDES IN THE PARK
MS: NB B, [*p. 47*].
5 too] all *del.* too
SONG: THOU TREMBLEST O MY LOVE!
MS: NB WW, *white scrap pasted therein.*
2 deep] waves *del.*

Tears for the home thou leavest,
Tears for the hearts thou grievest,
Tears for the fate thou weavest;
Tears precious where they fall as wine
To wounded men, or water in the sands—
But come and turn thy smile on other lands—   10
Far from thy fading infancy—
Far from the palace of thy sires.
The old hearth fires,
And all that has been dear & sweet
Before I came to worship at thy feet.
Come and forget them all with me
Or bury them in memory;
Beloved, come! forsake them all,
And tremble not on thy light footfall
Before us shines the untempted sea,   20
Forsake them all & follow me.

Song

Pass we to another land:
Leave the pleasant isle, love!
Help is in my willing hand,
Strength is in thy smile, love.

Fickle was the fleeting kiss;
Life hath nought will last, love:
Here we clasp a faded bliss,
Beggar'd with the Past, love.

Here we heard in sighing bowers,
Wrecks beat on the shore, love: 10
Storms that shook this earth of ours,
Lull'd us but the more, love.

SONG: THOU TREMBLEST O MY LOVE
21 *first written before title*, Song, *with the beginning of a second line:* O love.
SONG: PASS WE TO ANOTHER LAND
MS: Berg, *between pp.* [48 and 49].

Yonder star that was our trust,
 Largening thro' the lime, love,
Laughs to view two things of dust
 Trying to cheat time, love.

Pass we with all things that pass,
 No cold fate up[b]raid, love!
Souls that grow as green as grass,
 See their seasons fade, love.   20

Toil, and pain, and pleasure crost,
 And love, may help us find, love,
What we in our isle have lost,
 In each other's mind, love.

The Ass of Balaam

From Num. 22:21–34. Three times Balaam smote his ass, which recognized the angel of the Lord, as he did not.

A patient brute was Balaam's Ass;
He shook his ears, & ate his grass,
And when he bore his Master's weight,
Complain'd not of the will of Fate.

And Balaam to his Ass was tied
By gratitude and love beside:
Till arrogance beset his soul
And held his spirit in controul.

SONG: PASS WE TO ANOTHER LAND

15 view] see *or* view
16 Trying] Seeking *or* Trying
21 pleasure] pleasures *del.*

THE ASS OF BALAAM

MS: NB A–B, *loose scrap of white paper contained therein.*

❦

She marries the knight she loves—
And she scorns the lord she hates:
And there's dancing in the old castle hall
And dancing under the gates.

❦

These lines probably reveal GM's feelings on moving from London to
"The Limes" in Weybridge, late in 1849.

Beyond the meadow still where sweeps
The greensward to the spreading sun—
And halfway down a sheltering slope
A little village stands—to me
So fair that tho' a stranger until now
My heart leaps to it as an infants home—

How could I rest while suns & moons
Roll by, content that yonder hill
Should take the footfall of the dawn;
Yon vale the days' decline, content   10
With all circling seasons as they pass
For they would not deny me my mild dreams.

SHE MARRIES THE KNIGHT SHE LOVES

MS: NB A–B, *loose scrap of white paper contained therein.*

BEYOND THE MEADOW STILL WHERE SWEEPS

MS: NB A, [*p. 14*].

An abandoned draft of lines 1–3:

       I look athwart a range of earth
       Bright threading streams & [summer *del.*] tedded fields
       And plots of cool embowered shade

2 spreading] setting *del.*
3 Half down the slope & sheltered well, *or* And halfway down a sheltering slope
5 fair] sweet *del.*   until now] to it *or* until now
6 infants] ancient *or* infants
8 Roll] Roll'd *del.*
10 decline] content *del.*
11 pass] pass'd *del.*
12 mild] sweet *del.*

And here in pastoral calm my life
In no rude contrast with its grave,
  Might ebb in song and fill my ears
  With quiet melodies—and here—
Ah! foolish thought both heart & will desire
More than a moment's yearning can divine—

For here as into every nook
Would rumour come of man & all   20
  His triumphs & disasters—all
  His high ambitious hopes—and here
My soul would yearn towards him most & fly
From hill to hill with its branch of peace.

But let me take the joy that smiles
And pluck it like a passing flower
  Whose bloom when withered blooms in thought
  Whose perfume never dies—The scene
When grander Images have past away
Will be a messenger of peace to me.   30

The windmill on the windy height
The watermill that ploughs the stream
  The trembling of the village spire
  Against the western flame—the haze
Of stillness over all will picture forth
A home

5

Or the single path—
    Which the cold moon sheds
From her golden crown
    And her silver lids

BEYOND THE MEADOW STILL WHERE SWEEPS
13 here] while *del.*
24 branch] burden *or* branch
27 blooms] lives *del.*
OR THE SINGLE PATH
MS: NB A–B, *loose leaf therefrom.*

Cold and bright
With silent light
A lonely track o'er the watery night.

6

Or Barley fields in the waves of the wind
When the dusk East with his shadow behind
Spreads out his skirts as he sweeps o'er the wold
Trackt by his shadow so bitter and cold.

7

Or biting flocks of tinkling sheep,
   On the rolling slope of quiet downs,
Scattered half up the grassy sweep,
   And moving at times to choicest mounds—
What time the sun seems half asleep
   And murmurs fail from the distant towns.

8

Or an evening smoke from the chimney pots
Of a peaceful village, where are seen
Neighbour groups round the lowly cots
Watching the calm cool air serene
Deep in the country happy and green—

9

Or meadows at morn from the wintry prime
When the North shines bright upon our slime
   In the crisping breeze
   And the frosted trees
   From the summits hoar
   To the woodland core,
And as the mist clears the Christmas chime
Rings o'er the brooks when the mosses freeze
And the sparkling blades are sharp with rime.

10

Or the foamy fringe which hangs compact
On the plunge of a solid cataract,
That falls forever down one abyss,
From the chin of an aged precipice!

Time

Sure never was heard so berhymed & beriddled!
Why I feel like the man in the forest befiddled
Into the rings of the dancing brides—
Till his featness of foot brought him under the tides.
But hark boys! hark! the merry bells peal,
    And the snowy hills are calling,
The vapours freeze, the mists congeal,
    And the large white flakes are falling—
It is the death of the good old year,
And I must carry him off on his bier.   10
    For the old must make way for the new boys,
    As your fathers made way for you, boys,
    And as you'll make way for those, boys,
    Who will come when you wear the snows, boys.

The Little Foot-Page

This ballad was abandoned after the uncompleted stanza following
line 48, but GM returned to it in 1859 or thereafter because two of the
corrections and stanzas 7 and 8 are written with the bright blue ink that
he started using at that time.

"Hither, come hither, my little foot-page,
    Tell quickly me what ye bear;
O pant at my feet for ye've been fleet
    As the quarry chased down to its lair,

TIME
MS: NB A–B, *loose leaf therefrom, immediately following the preceding fragment.*
2 like] that *Ed.'s emendation*
THE LITTLE FOOT-PAGE
MS: NB B, [*pp. 29–30*]. *Top of* [*p. 1*] Berg: Come hither, come hither, my little foot-
page,
1 Hither, come hither] Hither, and tell me *del.* Come hither, come hither *del.*
2 Tell quickly me] And tell me of *del.*

The message ye gave to his Mother?—
    Ye pluckt the white flower with care?
What said she?—How look'd she?—What did she?
    I see that woman stare!"

"The ferny coverts were wan [?] with Dawn
    As I came to her Castle bower,   10
O ghostly gray in the ruddy ray
    Stood up the turret tower.
I strove to speak, but her presence
    Was like a witch's power;
I could do nought but kneel, Lady!
    And hand her the white wild flower."

"How look'd she, how look'd she, my little foot-page,
    How look'd she at the sight?—"
"—O pale she turn'd, and red she burn'd,
    And like as winter, white,   20
She seized, and shook the blossom;
    As a wind shakes reeds at night;
When thunder tramps the louring hills
    And the sky loses light by light.—"

"What said she, what said she; my little foot-page,
    What said she at the sign?—"
"'O—I have heard of an ill-loved bird
    That sends the foaming brine:

4 chased down] that's chased *del.*
6 Ye pluckt the white flower] The letter ye carried *del.*
8 *Del.:* And shriek'd she not with despair?
11 O ghostly gray] And lovely white *del.*   ray] light *del.*
12 turret] Castle *del.*
13 I strove to speak] I knew not how *del.* To speak I strove *del.*
15 nought] nothing *del.*
17 How look'd she, how look'd she] What did she—What did she *del.*
18 How look'd she] What did she *del.*
20 like as winter] wintry wrathful *del.*
22 at] by *del.*
23 tramps the louring hills] roars in the distance *del.*
27 O—I have heard] I've heard, I've heard *or* O—I have heard
28 foaming] phantom *del.*

The mariner's wraith walks round it,
    And the winds before it whine   30
And the tempest sure will follow, follow—'
    This said she at the sign."

—"What did she, what did she, my little foot-page,
    When she knew—O what did she?—"
"Like a hollow cave to the ebbing wave
    She moan'd, and rock'd her knee.
Her chin began to shiver,
    She opened her eyes on me
Then smoothed aside her thin grey locks
    With fingers wan to see."   40

After 29 del.: Behind it growls the tempest
After 31 del.: And the mariners wraith walks round it:—'
34 When she knew—O] O tell me *del.*
38 *Del.:* And her eyes opened wide on me.
39 *Del.:* Her thin white hands on her thin grey locks   Then] She *del.*
40 *Del.:* She breathed like a wrecking *or* stormy sea.
Between 40 and 41 del.:
    —"No curse. no curse, [my little foot-page *del.*] on a sinful head,
        No curse on a wretched soul?
  Call'd she no curse from Heaven to pierce
      The worker *or* wreaker of her dole?—"
  Del.: "For Malcolm, and for Ronald
      Her voice like a bell did knoll
  Nor [ask'd *del.*] howl'd for angry lightning
      To [strike *del.*] scatter me with the mole."
  Del.: She call'd to God in her distress *or* sore grief
  She howl'd no curse, she called to God
      She curse no wretched soul!

  Thou liest, thou liest, thou *or* Ye lie, ye lie [thou baleful *del.*] ye graceless boy
      Thou liest *or* Ye lie both sad & sore"
  She cursed me twice, she cursed me thrice;
      She cursed me evermore.
  Her snaky curses hiss me:—*or* She hiss'd me with snaky curses *or* Her prayers
        were hissing serpents
      Can I no prayer implore?
  O never the life with love is lost:—*or* never, never now!
      But I did the thing I swore!

"Give ear, give ear, my loved lad,
    I will calm thee with a kiss.
My loved lad, a love I had
    Not like to ye in this.
Nay, never jar so harshly
    The brow I smoothed with bliss:
He knows no longer my warm lip
    From the chilly worm's, I wis.

Tis over, tis over, my little foot-page,
    Tis over & 'tis done.   50
I swore it so, to bring her low,
    And yet our wail is one.
And you must weep, young Maxwell!
    Because our woe is one.
For you a brother, & I a lover,
    And she has lost a son!

My little foot-page, my little foot-page,
    Away & learn to hate:
Go, fly to her knee, & speak of me
    As hell's own fitting mate.   60
I stole you when an infant,
    I stole you from her gate:
O love & life, O life & love,
    You join your hands too late!

42 *Del.:* Rich fee'd with a forehead kiss *Del.:* Thy forehead I will [kiss]
45 never jar so] jar not thus *or* never jar so

Between 48 and 49 del.:

    Give ear, give ear, my orphan'd *or* thou foundling child!
        Mine, mine! for I have none!
    O knight and earl for one young girl
        Held tourney in the sun.
    To catch her crested kerchief:
        They would have died each one:
    O the chargers flew, and the lances flash'd,
        [*line left blank*]

Marian

This lament is not to be confused with the *Marian* printed in the *Modern Love* volume (1862) (see p. 174).

The clouds fly fast across the moon;
 The winds beat on my bosom bare;
My lover will be with me soon,
 And I shall little care.

O little shall I care! for he
 Will take me nestling to his breast
So broad & warm!—and I shall be
 A bird in its own nest.

Will he not start to see me pale
 And shuddering, for the love of him?   10
Now the moon hides, and the cold gale
 Moans o'er the meadows dim.

There is a burden in that sound
 I cannot bear to sit and hear,
So mournfully the hollow ground
 Answers its moaning drear.

And up the meadow path it goes,
 And wrestles with the rooted briar,
As if it storm'd with many throes
 Some stubborn strong desire: 20

MS: Berg, *between pp. 42 and 43.*
4 I shall little] little shall I *or* I shall little
6 take me nestling] let me nestle *or* take me nestling
7 broad & warm] warm and calm *or* broad & warm
11 Now] See *del.*
18 rooted] ragged *del.*

Some hope whose heart is at the root,
    And will not, will not, be uptorn;
O could I know that his dear foot
    Were coming—me forlorn!

Know it, and know that each deep breath
    That blows upon my cheek and hair,
And taunts me in this place of death,
    Had touch'd him darkly there!

My lover! touch! his mouth & throat,
    His neck that I would fret & fawn   30
To clasp, and all I used to dote
    To kiss at early dawn.

To kiss when that gray glimmer woke
    The old reproachful happy room;
And on my wandering slumber broke
    As with an eye of doom.

But I would turn to where he lay;
    His head upon his dreaming arm,
His proud eyes closed, his hair astray,
    His lips as in a charm;—   40

Smiling—and I would wake him—hark!
    —No, no! not he—not he! how fast
The clouds fly on! and the wild dark
    Seems thickening with the blast.

And if he come not, let the rains
    Drown all!—O lover, lover, take
The poor child who has had such pains
    Unsighing for thy sake.

21 whose heart is at the] that has struck hidden *or* whose heart is at the
22 will not, will] shrieks and will *del.*
39 eyes] lids *del.*
42 not he—not he!] it is not he! *or* not he—not he!
46 Drown all!—] Rush down. *del.*

The poor young child!—I seem to hear
    My mother's words:—how poor to me   50
Was pity when her breast was near,
    Now nothing pities me!

Now that I am a mother too:
    No, no! have been! have been! have been!
Waste pity on my head I strew
    Like leaves that once were green.—

My little child lies just below,
    I sit upon its little grave:
My tiny babe that suffer'd so,
    So patient & so brave!   60

'Twas hard to lose it from my sight,
    And hush its merry prattle, too!
With nothing near it day and night,
    But this old silent yew.

And here, they said, he would not heed
    Or in an earthly father joy,
I know, I know my babe must need
    His love—my boy! my boy!

He needs it now! he cannot have
    An infant's peace without it! Come!   70
Oh! it bids to its little grave
    To be a father, come!

Some doubt, who see me nightly here,
    That he will ever come again:
They say, 'Cry not, poor girl! take cheer!
    Go home! sleep! hope is vain!'

56 leaves that once were] dead leaves on the *del.* leaves no longer *or* leaves that once
were
57 just] here *or* just
59 tiny babe] little child *del.*
61 hard] strange *or* hard
66 An earthly Father's love & joy:—*or* Or in an earthly father joy,
71 Come be a Father to this grave! *or* Oh! it bids to its little grave
72 To be a father] My plighted [own dear *del.*] lover *or* To be a father

Ah yes! when hope is vain, go sleep!
    I should be mad as they assert:
Not tho' I never more can weep
    Or feel an earthly hurt.   80

Not tho' I hang upon his name
    And cherish it, who did me ill.
Like a church bride I speak no blame,
    And bend me to his will.

That madness only can forget
    An evil such as mine, they think.
And I feel drowning in a net
    That will not let me sink.

But every touch of it is love;
    And every clutching tangle thrown,   90
Seems all the bliss that swims above,
    Even while it drags me down.

Full of sweet life; of him; of old
    Remembrances of him so sweet:—
Hark now!—my name swells up the wold
    I hear a noise of feet:—

That wind among the wither'd leaves
    Forever will my fancy baulk
With "Marian! Marian!" deceives,
    And mocks his well-known walk.   100

On nights like this it frets me most;
    But when in frost I hold my tryst,
The silence like a glittering ghost
    Stares at me thro' the mist.

78 should be] am not *or* should be
79 Not tho'] Altho' *del.*
81 Not tho'] Altho' *or* Not tho'
88 will not let me] yet will never *or* will not let me
91 all the] full of *or* all the
97 That wind among] Ah no! *del.* No! the wind, *or* That wind among
98 Play traitor to me, mock my talk: *or* Forever will my fancy baulk
100 mocks his well-known] imitates his *or* mocks his well-known
101 nights like this it frets] windy nights they tease *del.*

Chilling my bones, and to my back
    Piercing as tho' with sickening steel:
I sit and hear the hard earth crack,
    And see the dews congeal.

—Like a church bride!—who said it?—bride?
    O sweet, sweet name! God loves it! men   110
Revere it: O with what a pride
    She walks who wears it, then!

And dares to let ungrateful shame
    That is but deeper pride, play o'er
Her lovely marriage face aflame
    While stepping thro' the door;

The door of that old dusky porch
    That looks so happy in the morn:
The blessing of the dreadful church
    Her shield from pain & scorn.   120

And with her finger ring'd, her wrist
    Claspt close, her lover leads her in
To kiss her as I have been kiss'd
    And cannot think it sin.

To kiss her in sweet warmth; while I
    Without my lover sit and moan,
And no one Angel in the sky
    To make me not alone.

110 O sweet, sweet] What a sweet *or* O sweet, sweet
113 ungrateful] a wicked *or* ungrateful
115 marriage face aflame] face like a pale flame *or* marriage face aflame
119 *Del.:* The sacred blessing of the church
120 from pain &] against all *del.* from painful *del.*
122 her lover leads] in his, he takes *del.*
126 and moan] alone *del.*

Hecate

I am Hecate Queen of Hags
    Gather round me maidens bold
Clutch & screw your clouty rags
    And sail against the moonshine cold.

    Breathe ye Love like new dry mould
Hold your frocks below your knees
    Beauty make ye wondrous bold.

Song

Woo me now & you'll win me;
    Woo me now if you choose me;
Woo me now & you'll win me;
    Wait but a day & you'll lose me.
Something is speaking within me,
    Sown by a something without me,
Woo me now & you'll win me,
    I'm never yours if you doubt me.

When shall I hasten to woo her?
    When shall I hope she will wed me?   10
When shall I hasten unto her?
    Tell her the love that has led me.

HECATE
MS: NB A, [*p. 8*].
SONG: WOO ME NOW AND YOU'LL WIN ME
MS: NB B, [*p. 14*].
5 speaking] stirring *del.*
10 she will wed me] to wed her *or* she will wed me

The desert vulture
    jealousy

The sea gull
    love secure

He rests not thro' the flaming day;
    Ev'n in the burning Heaven above
He soars but in the search of prey;
    And that is jealous love.

The sea-gull dips his salt white wings

Desired as Summer rain
    To the offspring of the sun!
Rich, rich as Autumn grain
    Ere the reaping has begun!
The freshness of the spring
As thy dower thou dost bring.
The seedtime & the harvest
    All in one.

Like a blind child is the loving heart
    In its tenderness & trust,
Like a poor blind beggar maid
    That curtseys for a crust.
The simplest thing that has an eye
    May lead it to its wrong
But o! it is the richest [?]
    That doth to earth belong.

THE DESERT VULTURE
MS: NB B, [*p. 16*].
Line associated with stanza 1: The desert vulture's yellow eye
1 rests] sleeps *or* rests
DESIRED AS SUMMER RAIN
MS: NB B, [*p. 16*].
LIKE A BLIND CHILD
MS: NB B, [*p. 16*].
First line appears in Table of Contents, Berg.

〜〰〜

This fragment and the next, jotted closely together, can be dated with the first draft of *Love in a Valley* (see headnote on p. 62), probably 1850. Biographically they are significant, indicating how early in their married life Mary and GM quarreled. Edith Nicolls, Mary's daughter by her first marriage, said later, "They sharpened their wits on each other" (LS, p. 47).

We need some rallying point round which
    To knit the discord & the din
Where [*blank*] shall speak to poor Frich
    And nature know itself akin—

〜〰〜

In all our daily war of words
    Where deadly things are said & [*torn*]
Are there not sure some secret [*torn*]
    When touch'd would make the [*torn*]
    One name when [*torn*]

〜〰〜

He where the great sun looks his last
Seems speaking of the mythic past
Was it in penance for some foul wrong
That baked into blackness he lay so long?

Penance for some obstructing weight
He cast in the way of the human fate
That he who fed on all beams that breathe
Should shadow all things underneath.

WE NEED SOME RALLYING POINT
MS: NB A, [*p. 9*].
IN ALL OUR DAILY WAR OF WORDS
MS: NB A, [*p. 9*].
HE WHERE THE GREAT SUN LOOKS HIS LAST
MS: NB A, [*p. 17*]. *The lines are written over the opening of the fair copy of* "*Mortesto.*"
2 Seems full of the mystery of the past *or* Seems speaking of the mythic past
3 in] for *del.*   for some foul wrong] he lay so long *or* for some [obstructing *del.*] foul
wrong

Penance that to us he pays
Still & in a thousand ways   10
But now if a stave he is still a friend
And will be so until the end
And he will work with all his powers
To warm the hearth & wing the hours.

Fullness of love sleeps in us like a sea
After night's tempest, O thou lovely thing!
The meadow breezes kiss our cheeks, the bee
Hums by us with the honey of the Spring.

These lines and the poems following, through "The Ballad of Lady
Eglantine," all written in pencil, now very faint, can be dated 1850.
Among them are *Sorrows and Joys*, included in *Poems* (1851) (see p. 68),
and "Fireside," retitled *Infancy and Age* for *Household Words* (19 April
1851, see p. 716).

The subject of "Ye noble Lords" indicates that it was written imme-
diately after June 17, 1850. On that date the House of Lords condemned
Foreign Minister Palmerston for mobilizing an attack on Greece in
support of the British subject, Don Pacifico, whose house in Athens was
burned by rioters.

GM plays on the double concept of Protection: protection vs. free trade
and the protection of British subjects.

Ye noble Lords who bravely fight
        The good fight of Protection O!
And back your sturdy arguments
        With many an interjection O!

FULLNESS OF LOVE
MS: NB B, [*p. 36*].
3 meadow] scented *or* meadow
4 Hums by] Is humming *or* Hums by
YE NOBLE LORDS
MS: NB B, [*p. 3*], *canceled.*
1 bravely fight] do uphold *del.*
2 good fight] merits *del.* good cause *del.*
3 back your sturdy] follow up your *del.* back'd *del.*

Why under the Free Traders' wing
    Where shelter is infection O—
Seek ye the very thing ye lose
    With such mad predilection O?

Why—think ye thus in petty spite
    For ends most impolitic O,   10
T' o'erwhelm the noble Palmerston
    And make him in a jiffy go—
Why, peerless paradoxes thus
    With 'larum most horriffic O
Dread ye the bare idea of war,
    Yet scorn all things Pacific O?

Black Richard

Black Richard has a shaggy brow
    His eyes show not a gleam of ruth—
Black Richard is a villain now
    But once he was a bonny youth—

Black Richard in a weedy fen
    Had built himself a lonely house
And there with ghosts of murder'd men
    They hear him loud o' nights carouse—

YE NOBLE LORDS
7 ye lose] they've crushed *del.*
9 in] for *del.*
11 o'erwhelm] assail *del.*
15 Dread] Scout *del.*
16 Yet] And *del.*
Alternative, canceled:

    Ye noble Lords who bravely fight
        The good cause of Protection O—
    And back each sturdy argument
        With many an interjection O
    Why under the Free Traders' wing
        Thus shout & shriek terriffic O
    And while ye shun[?] the warlike thought
        Could use the term Pacific O?—

BLACK RICHARD
MS: NB B, [*p. 3*], *almost illegible pencil.*
2 show] have *del.*

Black Richard hath nor kith nor kin,
  Black Richard never has a friend,   10
He is a midnight man of sin
  Whose weary days would shriek to end—

Black Richard looks upon the sky
  And oftentimes aloud he'll rave:
It were a merry thing to die
  The ghosts speak kindly of the grave—

Black Richard has a field hard by
  In which he sows his crops with care
And if you ask him he'll reply
  "I'm famine" with a ghastly stare—   20

Black Richard is alone, alone,
  No soul dares talk with him save one
A wheezy, feeble, weak old crone
  Who shudders when she sees him gone—

Black Richard had a mother dear
  A father and a sweetheart too;
They died in one dark starving year
  And they will never live anew—

Black Richard has a shaggy brow
  That darkens every glance of ruth—   30
But if he is a villain now
  O once he was a bonny youth.

23 A wheezy, feeble] Who is a wheezy *del.*
After 24 del.: This crone she has a daughter dear
26 sweetheart] brother *del.*

To a Nightingale

In the bowers of the rising moon
    O nightingale with what an extascy
    Pourest thou forth the full rhapsody
Of thy melodious tune—

In the bowers of the rising moon,
From between the twin bosoms of June,
    The throb of thy singing O nightingale
    Doth charm into yearning the twilight pale,
    And the mild gray eye of eve looketh over thee
    Dim with enchantment, the dark leaves that cover thee   10
    Stir not to tell where thou art
For the breezes are hushed & aswoon—
From between the twin bosoms of June.

MS: NB B, [*pp. 4–5*], *three drafts, none canceled. Text is from dr. 3.*
5 rising] roseate *dr. 1*; lustrous *del.* astral *del.* radiant *dr. 2*
After 5, dr. 1: So silvery luminous soon, *dr. 2:* Ascending to nights astral noon
6 *not in dr. 1*
After 6, dr. 2:

        O rapturous nightingale almost to anguish
        The pauses that hear thee not sicken & languish—
        Lifelessly hang the thrilled leaflets and lifelessly
        Sink the [warm *del.*] thick odours adown on the earth
        The warmth of their honeyed wings weighing too heavily
        On the fainting air
        And a sigh that is not of mortal birth
        As it were from the core of the moss'd stems hoar
        Some deep pent spirit agony
        Wild with remorseful memory   10
        And yearning from despair.
7–12 *not in dr. 2*
After 10, dr. 1:

        Stir not to tell where thou art and the stars are all
        Distant and timid as gazers that scarcely dare peer
        At the silence severe
        That enfoldeth the prophetic gloom of some Heaven lipped Oracle
        Such as thou seemest in this sudden deep [sighing *del.*] breathing interval
            Passionate nightingale
        Such as thou seemest this moment, even such, [while *del.*] as I tremble to hear
        While the [air is all *del.*] breezes are hushed and aswoon.   [*Cf. line 12*]

⟅ѺѠѺ⟆

I saw young Spring leap over the hills,
One hand in the Heavens, one foot in the rills,
He was a blushing naked boy,
His eyes were light, his breath was joy—
The clouds drew back as he passed by
And crown'd him with the clear blue sky.
The lark went up to greet the blue
And shower'd down songs on his head like dew—
Crocus and primrose sprung from his feet,
Roses & lilies lovely and sweet.   10
He wept where the snowdrop lay in the snows
And for each warm tear a violet rose—
The ice in the river ran liquid light
At the first gaze of his sunny sight.
And awkward [?] troops of boys & girls
Hung on his shoulders & play'd with his curls—
With his own tender hand he prest
The nightingale's melodious [?] nest
And taught the first clear tune to gush
Quaint from the blackbird & shrill from the thrush—   20
But or ever a merry bird had sung
With fresh green leaves their bowers were hung,
And the March winds made their music be
A rich full foliaged harmony—
Till April came with smiles & showers
And the green Earth was buried in flowers
When in the season on a day
Young happy Spring was married to May.
May with hawthorn on her brows
Blushed roses & lilies & faltered the vows.   30
And in the changes of the moon
She had a daughter whose name was June.
A Beauty was she & fair to view
Rosy & golden & green & blue—

MS: NB B, [p. 7], *almost illegible pencil.*
28 happy] blushing *del.*

And on her white forehead she wore divine
Summer's thriving eglantine—
Then in the deep warmth of the sky
June melted into rich July,
Full glowing noons & twilights long
And the mid [?] season of summer song.   40
Woodbine & jasmine wound around
Her form & with roses her head was crown'd.

"But see what living glory floods the west—"
They turned and all the chesnut trees were drest
In tangled threads of splendour and the sky
Grew rosy from its amber extasy—
"Behold" spake he of song—"In dusk withdrawn
"The rosy sunset prophesies the dawn—
"Fair weather for the morrow—Even thus
"Fair setting systems prophecy to us
"A fairer dawn than if o'erswarthed with storm,
"When even the light that was both loses light & form"—   10
"Well, well! a poets soul may put at ease
"With images and symbols such as these!
"But as for me—and yet I know you John
"This patient spirit is but half put on
"Many's the time I've heard a muttered curse
"Leap like a demon hunted your smooth verse—
"In act to canter thro' Arcadian measures
"And murmur pretty pastorals and country pleasures.
"O then I hear you spur a fiery hoof,
"And laud the blazing rick, the outraged roof,   20
"Pampered oppression put to its own bitter proof!

BUT SEE WHAT LIVING GLORY
MS: NB B, [*p. 9*].
3 tangled] splendour *del.*
19 spur] plant *del.*

"Then madness in the many was a sign
"Of Gods blinding working messenger divine—
"Fair-setting systems then o'erswarthed with storm
"Were promise of the truer light and form!
"What means this change that now so meek & bland
"You have become, I cannot understand."
Spake he of the bright eye and horny hand—
"Then I will tell you" and the poets brow
Flung heavenward beneath the chesnut bough　　　　30
Flushed with the inspiration of his thought.
"In me no common changes time has wrought
"And by no common means—

The Ballad of the Lady Eglantine

O rosy fair and rosy sweet
　　And breathing rosy breath divine
Is she the lady with thorny feet
　　The lovely lady Eglantine.

With thorny feet and beauteous face
　　And lips of budding tenderness,
Among the dewy woodland ways
　　She lavishes her loveliness.

Slowly [?] wakes the summer morn
　　With glow & blue to look on her　　　　10
But wherefore grows the crimson thorn
　　Upon a thing so sweet and fair?

BUT SEE WHAT LIVING GLORY
28 Spake] the *del.*　　eye] clear face *del.*
THE BALLAD OF THE LADY EGLANTINE
MS: NB B, *[p. 13]. The most obliterated of all the faint pencilings in* NB B. *Written in ink
over part of stanza 1 are the lines:*
　　　　　　Alas! the sweetest tunes when played
　　　　　　Together are discord:
　　　　　　Discords alone
Over part of stanza 2:
　　　　　　　Song
　　　　　　Violet & Eglantine

It is a tale of the olden time
    When legends hung round kings & queens,
When fairies charmed the blooming clime
    And danced in rings the circling greens,

When love was deep in fairy lore
    And fairy lore was pledged to love
When keen enchantment thrill'd the shore
    From mystic seas & songs above—   20

When all the [?] possessed a life
    And animated all the earth
And quickened all the budding [?] rife
    To which the blooming clime gave birth.

O Eglantine o'er hill and dale!
    The maiden queen with the golden crown
The fairy looks with the features pale
    O Eglantine o'er vale & down!

And far and wide the rich renown
    Brought silken knights across the sea   30
To win a smile or reap a frown—
    And filled the land with chivalry,

A land that swarmed with spear and plume,
    A land of sunny slopes & hills
And hollows full of moonlight gloom
    And gleams of wizard whispering rills—

A summer land of festive wealth
    And forests hushed with old romance
A land of mysteries and health
    And vines and merry vintage dance,   40

30 silken] glittering *or* silken
34 sunny slopes &] old romantic *or* sunny slopes &
Over stanza 10:
            Tom Tippletoff's Toast

A land of gold & green festoons,
    A land of gray ancestral shapes,
With living glance of suns and moons
    And fountains gushing rich as grapes.

O, Eglantine o'er sea and sky!
    The golden crown with the snowy wreath
The snowy wreath with the blushing dye
    O Eglantine o'er wood & heath!

And far and wide her fame doth breathe
    And sweetens many a distant vale   50
And lightens many a sword from sheath
    And swells out many a midday sail—!

And far and wide from North and South,
    And far and wide from East and West,
Came many a blushing, blooming youth,
    To pluck the Beauty for his breast.

And in the lists and in the field
    With tilt and tourney throng to throng
Lance and steed and brand and shield
    Their prowess served the minstrel's song.   60

The minstrel who with harp and voice
    Would smite the golden quivering chords,
And woo the lovely lady's choice
    With pleading & melodious words.

O Eglantine in glade and bower!
    The fairy locks [?] and the lovely rose,
The lovely rose and the peerless flower—
    O Eglantine o'er sun and snows!

Over stanza 11:

                    Heine
                    British Battle Lyrics
64 pleading] mystic *or* pleading

And far and wide the rumour flows
   Till all young hearts are keen awake   70
And lines [?] of cream white camps enclose
   Her palace by the forest lake.

End of First Part.

Chivalry

We give to chivalry a separate age,
An age of fable, minstrel, & romance,
Of joust and joyance, ladies, knights, & lastly
Love the presiding deity of all:
Within whose temple shine the recorded deeds
Of those that dared & died, but soaring Fame
Has votaries no less numerous than Love's.

〇𝓌〇

Compare GM's definition of Genius in *One of Our Conquerors* (1891):
"It is the lively young great-grandson, in the brain, of the travelling force
which mathematicians put to paper, in a row of astounding ciphers, for
the motion of earth through space; to the generating of heat, whereof
is multiplication, whereof deposited matter, and so your chaos, your half-
lighted labyrinth, your ceaseless pressure to evolvement; and then Light,
and so Creation, order, the work of Genius" (Mem. Ed., 17: 103).
    This fragment fades out with an obvious echo from Milton's *Paradise
Lost*, 1.21.

You ask me what is Genius? 'tis that
Which counts not hours to work its end; nor years.
It is the single living thing unborn
Of Time, or due to Death. The seasons pass—
Time sows & reaps—but from that fallow field
Genius reserves [?], the richer harvest ripens:—

CHIVALRY
MS: NB A, [*p. 3*].
YOU ASK ME WHAT IS GENIUS?
MS: NB A, [*p. 3*].

The harvest that Eternity will garner.
Beware how you condemn sun-drinking sloth—
For it is sacred to an unseen presence;
And over it the Soul of Genius hangs   10
Mute upon breezeless wings;—& as from Chaos
Creation rose—so spring the immortal flowers
And fruit of genius from that brooding silence
Where dove-like

⟨∾ᵂ∾⟩

When stormy day is cold & gray
        And rugged winds do tear the clouds
Little blue breaks look out so gay
        And laugh along their tattered [?] shrouds.

O then the Earth is clothed with mirth
        And sweetly chirp the naked boughs
And the landscape smiles at the fresh Spring birth
        For signs like these are signal vows.

Winter in vain may strive to rain
        And puff & blow with all his might,   10
'Tis only to heat & thaw to his wane
        And he does but more endear the light.

But the triumph so sweet becomes complete
        If wrapt in snows he sleeps secure
When he wakes on a sudden to see at his feet
        The snowdrop smiling strong & pure.

YOU ASK ME WHAT IS GENIUS?
12 so spring the immortal flowers] its deathless offspring *del.*
WHEN STORMY DAY IS COLD AND GRAY
MS: NB A, [*p. 6*].
6 chirp] sing *del.*   naked boughs] watchful birds *del.*
11 He hastens his end & heats his wane *or* Tis only to heat & thaw to his wane

O then with a gleam an ancient dream
    Of glowing Fields will flush his eyes
And as if he would wilt with the very beam
    He rushes headlong to the skies.   20

    'Twas in a glimmering starlight
        When the lamps of Heaven
    Were dimmer than the twilight
        Above a sunset even,
    Three hooded figures
        Stole across the dew
    One was my beloved one
        Strangers were the two.

    How could I tell her

Could we know how kin we are
    With every little drooping flower
With every little distant star
    And every viewless power.

Could we but be content to live
    As flower below, or star above
And in our daily counsels give
    Less logic and more love

The swallow came from over the sea,
Weary with her flight was she,
She fluttered down on a maiden's breast,
That on the sea beach lay at rest;

WHEN STORMY DAY IS COLD AND GREY
17 *Del.:* O then a dream will start & gleam
'TWAS IN A GLIMMERING STARLIGHT
MS: NB A, [*p. 6*].
3 Were] Shone *or* Were
COULD WE KNOW
MS: NB A, [*p. 6*].
THE SWALLOW CAME FROM OVER THE SEA
MS: NB A, [*p. 16*].

O swallow, swallow
Will thy love be hollow?
Lay upon my true heart
Till my true love follow—

The swallow made a Summer nest
In between each little breast,   10
But when the harvest suns had past
She laid her wings on the Southern blast.
    O happy Comer
    Art thou still a roamer?
    Constant unto no love
    But the love of Summer [?]

The swallow flew far, far away
Where feathery lustres flash and play,
But long before the season turned,
Back to the nesting breast she yearned—   20
    Ah pretty maiden
    Breasting, blooming Eden,

Song

The quick bird sings and pierces me
With the shrill sweetness of his bliss:
        O my love!

For me 'twill never, never be
To utter such a joy as his:
        Dear, my love!

Deep, deep in loving shade he sings
Unto his mate who broods aloof:
        My love, my love!

SONG: THE QUICK BIRD
MS: Berg, *between pp.* [74] *and* [75].

But I shall never fold my wings 10
Beneath the blessed bridal roof:
O, my Love!

∽⚹∽

Compare, to Wordsworth's advantage, his lyric, *The Tables Turned*.

From lamplight and an aged leaf,
I turn'd to the night air:
Large Autumn stars bent o'er the sheaf:
A sweet fresh breeze was there.

The gentle freshness fann'd my brow,
And dried some weary dews:
I thought 'in seeking knowledge now;
Great Nature I abuse.

'This Soul speaks from his scornful vault
A language dead & hard: 10
With Nature I am ne'er at fault;
Her gates are never barred:

'And I an infant at her breast
Draw milk of purest life—'
Wise Admonition checkt the rest;
Like bubbles burst the strife.

My spirit like a placid lake
Reflected the great scene:
Scarce thinking, yet with thought awake,
I markt the village green. 20

FROM LAMPLIGHT AND AN AGED LEAF

MS: NB B, [*p. 48*].

4 sweet] soft *del.*

'Beneath the roots of fleeting things
        We pass, & are as they:
But Knowledge gives the spirit wings,
        And Wisdom points the way.

'Or rather pluck with hand that mars
        The daisy of an hour
Or in yon gardens of the stars,
        Gather a deathless flower?

C B M

CBM is, almost certainly, Charles Mansfield, a neighbor of Meredith's
in the early 1850s, a close friend of Charles Kingsley's, and a distinguished
social worker and scientist.

They've covered his face, & he's lost to us
        Shine star in Heaven!
New things & old will blossom & be
But that dear face we shall not see!

Pure was his look—he's lost to us:
        Shine star in Heaven!
His suffering heart he clad in smiles:
The noblest youth of our English Isles.

He strove for the poor & the Suffering
        Shine star in Heaven!   10
Wedded was he to Courage & Truth.
The Poor & the Suffering yearn'd to the Youth.

FROM LAMPLIGHT AND AN AGED LEAF
25 pluck with hand that mars] shall I pluck & prize *or* pluck with hand that mars
27 stars] skies *or* stars
28 *Del.:* Toil up & plant my flower?
C B M
MS: NB B, [*p. 48*].
1 us] our sight *del.*
3 Many a blossom comes new on the tree *or* New things & old will blossom & be
4 not] nevermore *or* not
9 poor] weak *or* poor

Sad was his end: mysterious:
　　Shine star in Heaven!
Forth he strode in the morning aglow:
Ere midday our friend was low.

Our dear friend—he's lost to us:
　　Shine star in Heaven!
Those that loved him like him grew:
Better even than they knew!　　　　　　　　　　　20

In life & in death we honoured him;
　　Shine star in Heaven!
Forty young men stood round his bier,
In every eye there was a tear!

Dirge

　　He has hid his face, and he's gone!
　　　　The grave is green dwelling:
　　Hid his face from all his race!
　　　　It's aye the water's welling.

　　A noble life lived he:
　　　　The grave is green dwelling:
　　A noble life in a whirl of strife:
　　　　It's aye the water's welling.

C B M
16 Ere midday our] Suddenly he was *del.*
20 even than] than even *del.*
23 round] by *or* round

DIRGE

MS: NB B, [*p. 51*].

4, 8, 12, 16 water's] spring keeps *or* water's
7 in a whirl of] that fell in *or* in a whirl of

There's one walks by like a ghost
    The grave is green dwelling: 10
A woman walks by with a shrouded eye
    It's aye the water's welling.

There's one on whose breast was calm.
    The grave is green dwelling:
Wild is that breast, and he's at rest:
    It's aye the water's welling.

ᏇᏇᏇ

I have a hope that's like a star
    In brightness and in peace:
It is that mid my children, far
    From turmoil I may cease.

That I may live my latest days,
    Their laughter in my ear:
Live honour'd, winning honest praise,
    And die just worth a tear.

Jack & Harry

Fair weather for your journey! whither away
At such long seven-league strides; friend Harry?

           Harry

                          Friend?
The name is old and often used. Forgive me!
I am in haste & I must be rude:—

DIRGE
9 walks by like a ghost] like a ghost walks near *del.*
11 *Del.:* One like a ghost, and he is lost!
13 was calm] he slept *del.*
15 wild] lone *del.*
I HAVE A HOPE
MS: NB B, [*p. 49*].
2 brightness] splendour *del.*
JACK & HARRY
MS: NB B, [*p. 27*].

Jack

—What, Hal?

Nay, nay, you shall not go & I will speak.
What! we who thrash'd the usher at our school,
And robb'd the orchard in the owlish moon:
We who bore stripes, gave blows, & were at games
Great rival chiefs. We who in [riper hours *del.*]
Made love to one dear girl just twenty-five   10
When we were ardent fifteen—and I hear
She gave her husband a small crowing thing
Last month of May! sweet Julia Pineney [?]!—we
Old comrades & tried friends part thus? Come, look,
Look the old look! What have I done? O Harry?
How I detest this coldness.

A Carol of Jack Frost

Good night! the gossips cry; Good night!
    And as they turn away, they shiver—
Jack Frost is abroad & he drives down the road
    And leaps over hedge, over field, over river—
Down from the crescent light, comes he.

In at every door I peep—
    Peep and wink
    Thro' every chink—
When the old wife snores & sleeps
Up the shuddering sheets he creeps   10

JACK & HARRY
8 were] shone *del.*
12 small] young *or* small
13 Last month of] A month in *del.*
A CAROL OF JACK FROST
MS: NB A, [*p. 27*], *including later draft of lines 1–4. Text of lines 1–4 is from the later,*
dr. 2.
3 drives] leaps *or* drives *dr. 1*
5 *added in dr. 2*
9 snores & sleeps] lies asleep *del.*
10 he creeps] I'll creep *del.*

Down the flue I blow and turn
All the sparkling embers black
Black the hissing logs all burn,

Fireside

Come sing the name that brings all hearts
 Together and warms them cheerily
However wide the sea that parts
 And the distance lowering drearily—

Come make a circle while we sing,
 Add green logs on the embers,
[*line left blank*]
 Come make a circle while we sing.

Come make a ring and let us sing,
 The good old Christmas story,
The love of praise, whose ancient days   10
 Gain honors as they grow hoary!

Come make a ring and let us sing
 With a pledge & a kindly blessing
To all of those both friends & foes
 Who are far from the hands caressing.

Associated lines:

The bloom flies from the lassie's cheek
And rushes to her nose
From the lassie's cheek the rose
Flies & shelters in her nose.
Huddling round the blazing ingle
 make the embers &
Flare their keenest violet flame

FIRESIDE

MS: NB A, [*p. 18*]. *Associated line*, NB A, [*p. 9*]: Fireside round which all English hearts
6 Add] And *del.* Heap *or* Add

The snow lays thick the ashes click,
    Heap logs upon the embers
[*incomplete*]

'Twas thus our grey forefathers sang
    In the days that went before us—
Thus will our children shout again   20
    When the sweet green grass grows o'er us—

Song

In *The Ordeal of Richard Feverel* Adrian makes fun of the verses young Ricky has been writing: "It shall be admitted that you create the very beauties for a chaste people.

'O might I lie where leans her lute!'

and offend no moral community" (Mem. Ed., 2: 223).

Might I lie where leans her lute,
    When her fingers thrill & thrill
Thrice the wild strings; and, bending mute,
    In her ear they throb, and spill
Music so tremulous; soul-betrothed; panting to death.
    Sweetlier then would I awake
        All the loveliness I know
    Into sweet song; and sweetlier make
        On her bosom overflow
All my great passion in one yearning rapture of breath.   10

FIRESIDE
20 shout] sing *del.*

SONG: MIGHT I LIE WHERE LEANS HER LUTE
MS: Berg, *between pp.* [*16*] *and 17, canceled.*

Song

In contrast to Adrian's mockery of Richard's poetic efforts, Richard's cousin Clare loved his romantic verses and transcribed the verses of this song into her diary (*Richard Feverel*, Mem. Ed., 2: 480–81). The second stanza is quoted in the novel:

> Thou steppest from thy splendour
> To make my life a song:
> My bosom shall be tender
> As thine has risen strong.

> Thy truth to me is truer
> Than horse, or dog, or blade:
> Thy vows to me are fewer
> Than maiden ever made.

Atlas

> Jack with the Sun, is twenty-one
> This day, and all who meet him,
> Make a stand and clap his hand,
> And right gladly greet him.

> "Jack, my boy! we give ye joy!"
> And Jack beams on the givers.
> Bankrupt hosts with cheeks like ghosts,
> Sad lungs and sadder livers.

> Jack elate, feels not the weight
> So huge to all beholders!
> Bend thy back, my honest Jack!
> For the world is on thy shoulders.

10

SONG: THY TRUTH TO ME IS TRUER

MS: Berg, *between pp.* [*38*] *and 39.*
2 dog] lance *del.*

ATLAS

MS: Berg, *between pp. 10 and 11.*
4 gladly] heartily *del.*
7 *Del.:* Bankrupt shoals with bleeding souls,

Song

O they canna' do without it
    Without it, without it:
They canna' do without it:
    Who can with it at a'.
Let Jeanie feign to flout it,
And Jockie think to doubt it.
They canna' do without it
    Who can with it at a'.

Without it, without it,
And that is a' about it,   10
They canna' do without it
    Who can with it at a'.

Song

My darling's love shall close me up
    In bliss from all the world:
Close me like a flowercup
    With starry dew-drops pearl'd.
And nothing but her sweet delight,
    And curtaining of charms,
Shall breathe upon me day and night,
    And keep me safe from harms.

SONG: O THEY CANNA' DO WITHOUT IT

MS: Berg, *between 10 and 11. Most apostrophes added by Ed.*

1, 3, 7 canna'] cannot *del.*
6 Jockie] Jocky *del.*

SONG: MY DARLING'S LOVE

MS: Berg, *between pp. 18 and 19.*

Love they alone the joyful heart
　　The night wind & the leaf?—
That when we are sick with an evil smart
　　They whisper nought but grief.

I thought in my young days to find
　　Relief for breast & brow:
In the mere breathing of the wind,
　　And swaying of the bough.

But now, with no remorseful calm,
　　I look where dead men rest,　　　　　　10
Half jealous of that pallid balm
　　Which sleeps on brow & breast.

Song

Over the ferry, and over the ferry,
　　And over, over, over!
The river runs wide, with an eddying tide,
　　Between the fields of clover.
The fisherman's girl flings back her curl,
　　And rows to fetch the rover,
Over the ferry, and over the ferry,
　　And over, over, over!—

May Song

Come, merry May, on this first day
　　That gives thee to us yearly:
Nothing like thee, so constantly
　　Is loved, and still so dearly.
Come, merry May, with robe & ray

LOVE THEY ALONE
MS: Berg, *between pp.* [26] *and 27.*
SONG: OVER THE FERRY
MS: Berg, *between pp.* [26] *and 27.*
MAY SONG
MS: Berg, *between pp.* [22] *and* [23].
3 Nothing] Nought *del.*

And royal gift & bounty.
Honours due we now renew
    In every English County.

The trees were stirr'd by the wakeful bird
    All night, to give thee greeting.   10
My dreaming heart with a thrill & a start
    Could hear its leafy tweeting.
The trees were stirr'd & the cock was heard
    So blithely bravely crowing:
Leap full-born, from the breast of the morn,
    Thy lavish treasures showing.

Chill breathes the West on the dawning breast
    Where thou, a bud, art blooming.
Over fell, over flood, ope[s] blooming bud,
    Thy wished shape assuming.   20
Warm breathes the West, & from its nest
    The lark spins up to hail thee;
Over dale, over down, come, gather the crown
    Of flowers that never fail thee!

Song

I would be the bounding deer
    That from her breasted shaft doth bleed;
Little hare whose hunted leer
    Dying, sees her weep the deed.

SONG: I WOULD BE THE BOUNDING DEER

MSS: NB B, [*p. 14*]; Berg, *between pp.* [*38*] *and 39, copy-text.*

1 bounding] fleet brown *NB B*; frighted *del.* flying *del. B*
2 from her breasted] flying, from her *NB B*; bounding from her *del. B*

I would be the bow-wing'd hern
  That from her pet hawk dives in fear,
Red fox crouching in the fern
  When the merry pack they cheer.
Anything I'd do or be
So she would but follow me!   10
     Follow me!
Even unto the death I'd flee,
So she would but follow me!
     Follow me!

Song

  Full of thy glory am I,
My adored! and the tales that they tell me,
  Pour thro' my breast like a tide,
    Like a torrent that drinks from the sky!

  Full of thy beauty am I,
My beloved! and swift yearnings impel me
  Thus to sink down at thy side,
    So to gaze on thy face till I die!

To look in thy soul all my love and my pride,
  Hero! to have thee full of me.   10
To wind thee about and be thy bride,
    Thy gathered rose, thy bird of glee!

SONG: I WOULD BE THE BOUNDING DEER

8 *NB B:* When she the merry pack doth cheer. *End of NB B MS.*
9 *B del.:* Any, anything I'd be

SONG: FULL OF THY GLORY AM I

MS: Berg, *between pp.* [50] *and* [51].

Song

When on my faithful charger
    I spur on knightly quest,
And see the star grow larger
    Above the colour'd west,
I halt upon some moorland knoll
    And gaze till all is black;
So like thyself, O stedfast soul!
    It glistens on my track.

The plover whistles by me,
    The hern sails overhead: 10
Night-prowling eyes descry me
    And think me frozen dead.
They circle round my silent steed,
    And slink off to their prey:
I give to all that is no heed,
    But watch that constant ray.

Cold crimson mists rise to it,
    And darkness drinks its light:
But inward fires renew it,
    And still it falls more bright.   20
It falls behind the world's black rim.
    'Tis hidden ere I stir:
Then purely strong in heart and limb,
    I give again the spur.

MS: Berg, *between pp.* [50] *and* [51].

2 on knightly quest] against the west *or* on knightly quest
4 colour'd west] Sun at rest *or* colour'd west
16 watch that] that one *or* watch that
21 behind] upon *del.*

Song

O the wind, the wind, the wind doth blow,
And the world is riper year by year,
And to ebb & flow, & come & go,
Is all that life can fathom clear.
The maids may weep, the mothers wail,
And Beauty wither as she will;
But the ages have one changeless tale,
And the sands slip through, and nought is still.

To conquer earth, and claim the skies
We march at merry morn uncurb'd; 10
Till the sun last eyes that grassy rise
Where friends & foes sleep undisturb'd.
Sweet phantoms round us throb & glow;
Our fathers knew them every one,
And the wind, the wind, the wind doth blow,
They come to all, they stay with none.

Song

My chosen bride shall bless the plough
And be the Queen of harvest hours;
A bindweed wreath shall crown her brow,
All budding round with whitest flowers:
And she by sheaves of leaning corn
Shall sit upon a mound, and say,
'Better one fruit of harvest morn
Than all the blossoms of the May.'

SONG: O THE WIND

MS: Berg, *between pp. 68 and 69.*
4 clear] here *or* clear
13 round us throb & glow;] meet us—friend and foe—*or* round us throb & glow;

SONG: MY CHOSEN BRIDE

MS: Berg, *between pp.* [84] *and 85.*
5 by sheaves of leaning] with wisps of drooping *or* by sheaves of leaning
6 upon a] on sunny *or* upon a

About her as she sits and sings,
    Her lieges we will lounge and lie;   10
Passing the beaker round in rings,
    And pledging her bright ripening eye.
What, tho' a thousand hopes forlorn
    Have fail'd us in our onward way?—
'Better one fruit of harvest morn
    Than all the blossoms of the May.'

[To Lord Palmerston]

GM must have written this sonnet to Lord Palmerston on the occasion of his losing the office of foreign secretary on December 19, 1851. Thought of as the terror of Europe because of his constant involvement in continental politics, he outwitted himself that December when, without approval of the cabinet or the queen, he expressed to the French ambassador in London his pleasure in Louis Napoleon's coup d'état of December 2 by which Napoleon overthrew the government of Louis Philippe. As a proponent of free trade, Palmerston was popular with the people, and his forced resignation made him a public martyr. GM's surmise in the last line of the sonnet that Palmerston might even in time be at the helm came true: he became prime minister in February 1855, as a result of Lord John Russell's failures in the Crimean campaign.

Well may the continental eagles scream,
And flap their carrion wings with joy! for they
No longer see between them & their prey
That all-protecting name, whose fleckless gleam

SONG: MY CHOSEN BRIDE
9 About] Around *or* About
Lines associated with My chosen bride, *NB B*, [*p. 15*].
    Bring a line of bindweed,
        Ring it in a wreath.
    Plait it with its buds & cups
        —Facing the air—
    Her gown shall be like bindweed white,
        Her apron of the cornflower's blue,
    Her kerchief of the poppy's hue
        To hide her blushes bright.
    Her curls shall hang about her [cheek *del.*] neck
        Like grapes upon the vine

[TO LORD PALMERSTON]
MS: NB B, [*p. 11*].

Shone o'er the nations like a desert sun!
Beloved for that in Freedom's bloody field
It served her as a sword & as a shield!
Strong for that with its Country it was one!
Nor victimless, tho' short will be their glee.
Shame to the puny pilots of this realm!   10
Who dared to thwart this honoured place!
But while free-thoughted Englishmen agree,
And noble statesmanship is held in grace,
There shall thou stand again—or at the helm!

A Triad of British Evils

Sentiment, Oeconomy, and Greed;
The vices of old states, as of old men:
These three to certain dissolution lead.

For each to each is more than alien;
And each devoureth each with hungry speed;
Till the doomed habitation is a fen.

Sentiment, the vice of honest heart:
Oeconomy, the avarice of age:
Greed the rapacious monster both do thwart.

Greed for his hungry passions war doth wage;   10
Oeconomy [*blank*]
Sentiment sickens at the bloody page.

[TO LORD PALMERSTON]

7 It served her] 'Twas ever *del.* All felt it *del.*
9 tho'] but *del.*
11 thwart this honoured place] trifle with a name so dear *del.* honoured] proud *del.*
14 or] and *del.*

A TRIAD OF BRITISH EVILS

MS: NB B, [*p. 11*].

1 Sentiment] Mock *del.*
2 states] men *del.*
6 habitation] home they dwelt in *or* habitation
7 Sentiment] Mock *del.*
9 rapacious] hungry *del.*

And each and all have but one niggard sense;
One each and one to all, and all and each
Abuse it to their proper impotence.

[Lines Inscribed to Howes in a Copy of *Poems* (1851)]

GM inscribed these four sets of verses in the copy of *Poems* (1851) that belonged to Henry Howes, who was identified by Forman (*George Meredith and the "Monthly Observer"* [London: privately printed, 1911], p. 6) as editor of Number 11 of "The Monthly Observer" (see Introduction, p. xxix). He was a member of the Adjutant General's Department in the Horse Guards.

Hail, Common Sense! most rare of all!
Long for Thee, I've been panting:
Who buys these 'Poems' from the stall,
In thee is sadly wanting.
That which I meant to line the head,
Will go to line the trunk instead.

"You ask, what Regiment of the Guards,
My Howes has deign'd to choose?
Proclaim it, all ye festive Bards!
'Tis that which *Chased the Blues*."

Read not, my Howes!
With frowning brows,
What verses seem immoral:
Loth were I seen,
For a naked quean,
With a trusty friend to quarrel!

"Sing the famous Ballad
Of the Lion & the Lamb,
And how my Howes 'mong the Farnham hops,
Woo'd & won the old femme de cham'.

A TRIAD OF BRITISH EVILS
15 proper] several *del.*
[LINES INSCRIBED TO HOWES]
MS: inscriptions in copy of Poems (1851), *in the possession of Simon Nowell-Smith. Reproduced in "The Ewelme Collection,"* Book Collector *14 (Summer 1965).*

Tho' he had three young Rivals,
And I was of the Three,
My Howes with the ancient femme de cham',
Walk'd off triumphantly!"

[Lines Inscribed in a Copy of *Poems* (1851)]

I have not discovered the friend to whom this copy of *Poems* (1851), was inscribed; see Introduction, page xxxi.

The rhyme of "shoulders" and "beholders" was running in GM's mind in the early 1850s, as witness the first stanza of *The Head of Bran the Blest* (p. 176) and the hitherto unpublished "Atlas" (p. 1010).

"Poems", says the title:
And for a book 'tis vital
    As is a head on shoulders.
Yet many shoulders going,
And many a book worth knowing,
    Would be to all beholders,
More solemn & more sightly
Decapitated lightly.
Nor would the book be read less,
If I should make it headless.   10

Song

This poem, together with "To the Merry Men of France" (p. 1022), "Despots of Manchester" (p. 1022), "The Three Eagles and the Sleepy Lion," (p. 1036), and "Who says, she is in danger" (p. 1035), reflects the fears expressed in the British press during 1852 of a French invasion. The Poet Laureate, Tennyson, in the *Examiner* of January 31, published an excited poem furthering preparedness entitled *Britons, Guard Your Own*. Apprehensions accelerated as the months passed and were particularly ardent after the death of the Duke of Wellington on September 16, 1852. The same French scare opens GM's novel *Beauchamp's Career* (1876).

"POEMS", SAYS THE TITLE

MS: Berg, *inscription therein.*
9 read/less [*sic*]

Twelve arrows, and a bow, and spear,
    Old British law decreed
That every British householder
    Should keep for Britain's need.
And skill to use, and strength to wield,
    And courage to apply,
Our fathers proved on every field,
    And under every sky.
        All honour to their old renown:
          The law was good & grand [?]!   10

Above the hearth they hung their arms,
    To gather honour'd rust,
Then gave to unreproachful Earth
    Their free & peaceful dust.
To children brave as they, and skill'd
    By them, the land they left;
Secure in soul that, as God will'd,
    It would be safe from theft.
        All praise unto their earnest lives
          And to that Law revered: 20
        The nightmare of a land's dishonour
          Never then was fear'd!

MSS: NB B, [*pp. 15, 18*]*; Berg, between pp.* [*108*] *and* [*109*], *copy-text.*

1 bow] sword *NB B*, [*15*]

After 1 prose note, NB B, [*15*]*:* old Welsh Law that every master of a family be so equipp'd ag^t. foes, foreign &c

4 keep for Britain's] have against his *or* keep for Britain's *NB B*, [p. 18] have against his *del. B*
5 strength] strength *or* force *NB B*, [*18*]

After 8 NB B, [*18*]*:*

Praise reverently their just renoun,	[*Cf. line 19*]
And hold that law revered!	[*Cf. line 20*]
The nightmare of a land's dishonour	[*Cf. line 21*]
Never then was feared!	[*Cf. line 22*]

10 *B del.:* It was a noble law!
11–14 *NB B,* [*18*]*:*

To the Merry Men of France

Cross not, cross not, merry men of France,
　　The sea between us flowing:
For at best you'll have but a miserable chance
　　In the coming & the going.
And the briny waves they have a dance
　　So strange to French tuition,
That long before you reach us, my merry men of France
　　You'll be sick of the Expedition!
　　　　Sick, sick, sick, sick,
　　　　　　Sick of the Expedition!　　　　　　　　　10

Try not, tempt not, South, or East, or West,
　　The wrath of the island nation:
For it's just a whim of hers that she'll not receive a guest
　　But at her invitation.

Despots of Manchester, Oligarchs!
　　That rule as with rods of iron.
Note you what whines & hostile barks
　　The little Isle environ.

In them the [holy *del.*] precious gift of strength
　　Relaxed not, nor took rust,
Their spirits waxed in mightiness, *or* took nobility *del. or* grew in gentleness
[And nobler was *del.*] And mightier waxed their dust.
12 *B:* And when they gathered rust *or* To gather honour'd rust,
13 Then] They *or* Then *B*
After 17 NB B, [*18*]:
　　　　　　'Twas safe from foreign theft.
　　　　　　　Again across their graves ring out
　　　　　　　　The joy in them we feel.
Lines for a third stanza NB B, [*18*]:
　　　　　　The weak breathed hope with England's name,
　　　　　　　The powerful drank *or* respect dread:
　　　　　　She was the light, she was the star,
　　　　　　　As yet she may remain.
TO THE MERRY MEN OF FRANCE
MS: Berg, *between pp.* [*24*] *and* [*25*].
DESPOTS OF MANCHESTER
MS: NB B, [*p. 23*].

The New Era   The Army of the Future
The Egg of an Army

Lord Palmerston, ousted from the foreign secretaryship by the Prime Minister, Lord John Russell, in December 1851 (see headnote to "[To Lord Palmerston]," p. 1017), came back at Russell in what Palmerston called his "tit-for-tat" on the issue of national defense. On February 20, 1852, he succeeded in passing a bill in the Commons to establish a national militia that would be more expensive than the local militia proposed by Russell. A strong national defense was a lifelong concern of GM's.

> How strangely crows the Gallic cock
> Against the star of morning:
> He wakes old England from her sleep.

Richard Lionheart

Richard I was captured and imprisoned by Leopold II (margrave of Austria) in 1192 on his return from a crusade. He traveled back to England briefly in 1194 to raise the required high ransom from his subjects.

> Calm on his charger black and tall,
> He gallops in disguise:
> The sun on the forest slope is all
> Green England to his eyes.
>
> The ferny forest breeze of eve
> Salutes him keenly dear:
> And thro' his curls its fingers weave,
> And a song sings in his ear.

THE NEW ERA

MS: NB B, [*p. 21*].

RICHARD LIONHEART

MS: Berg, *between pp.* [*106*] *and 107.*
6 keenly] strangely *or* keenly

Hail, Richard, hail! and the surging tone
    Of welcome seems to swell.   10
The people's heart within his own
    Is beating like a bell.

O vassal Austria! this one thing
    Too late thou'lt understand:
Whatever his luck, a loyal king
    Will find a loyal land.

O Traitor Austria! this we know
    And thou hast taught it well:
'Tis better to trust in a Paynim foe
    Than such a Christian fell.   20

Song: "Forever"

I am alone in my banishment;
    I cry to thee unhearken'd:
Like Adam from his Eden sent,
    When he look'd where the gold gates darken'd.
Myself I discern in him return
    And plead with a vain endeavour:
In vain he raves where the Angel waves
    The flaming sword "Forever!"

RICHARD LIONHEART
9 the surging] a sea-like *or* the surging
13 vassal] Traitor *del.*

SONG: "FOREVER"
MSS: NB B, [*p. 19*], *stanza 1, canceled;* Berg, *between pp.* [*106*] *and 107, canceled, copy-text.*

2 I cry to thee] Alone I grieve *NB B*; Alone to grieve *or* I cry to thee *B*
4 gold] bright *NB B*
5 Myself I discern] I see *or* discern myself *NB B*
7 In vain he raves] For pity craves *or* In vain he raves *NB B*

And I must sow a homeless lea
    With the sweat of toil & sorrow: 10
Nor in pale hope of joy for thee
    One consolation borrow.
The Paradise in thy sweet eyes
    Still faints with its anguish'd 'never,'
To him who craves where the Angel waves
    The flaming sword "Forever."

It cuts my heart, it blinds my sight,
    It drives me forward friendless;
It turns the fruit of years to blight
    And misery stretches, endless.   20
Yet have we trust beyond our dust
    To meet where others sever:
For sweet over graves the Angel waves
    The flaming sword "Forever!"

A line of eve o'er the moorland
    Lay yellow, & still, & wan:
My steps were turning homeward
    With the hern & the wild-swan.

The hern, & the swan, & the plover,
    Were quiet with their young:
I heard as I walked belated,
    A woman's voice that sung.

SONG: "FOREVER"

11 pale] fair *or* pale
13 The] My *or* The
14 faints] gleams *or* faints
17 cuts] breaks *or* cuts
20 stretches] endless *or* stretches

A LINE OF EVE

MS: NB B, [*p. 22*].

She sung of a wild wild passion
  For one with golden hair: 10
And lo, a gold-hair'd lady
  Stood full before me there.

She took my hand and led me

Song: The Wren

When the shining boughs are bare,
And a blight is in the air,
Nipping all the buds that dare
One faint flush of Spring declare;—
    Little wren, little wren,
       I would be like thee,
    Singing unto weary men
       From a winter tree.

When the Summer Songsters vie,
From the valley coverts nigh,   10
In full chorus, and the sky
Gazes with its kind blue eye;—
    Little wren, little wren,
       Still I'd be like thee,
    Singing unto thoughtful men
       Songs of constancy.

SONG: THE WREN

MS: Berg, *between pp. 100 and [101]*.

2 blight] frost *del.*
3 Nipping] Biting *del.*

She had a secret—bonny Bess!
　　She long'd to make it double.
And who, and who the thing shall guess,
　　He has me for his trouble.

The women mutter'd—shameless minx!
　　And pass'd her bridling stiffer:
But there was something in the Sphinx
　　That made the lads quite differ.

Iconia

Beside the sultry stream he curbs amain his smoking mare.
What shapely girls on yonder grass are sheltering from the glare?

He leans across his saddle bow, athwart his courser's flanks
"And who'll be [?] [blank] thanks

Together like a startled flock of lambs [?] crowd
And some [blank] aloud.

But one, the little fleet Orina [?], [blank]
She hastens to her fathers gate, & brings a cup of wine.

[space left for couplet]

On tiptoe then with outstretched arms she held the ruddy cup;
He lean'd aside, he seized her waist & featherlike swung her up.　　　10

SHE HAD A SECRET

MS: Berg, *between pp. 102 and 103.*

ICONIA

MS: NB B, [*pp. 25–26*].

1 Beside the sultry stream he curbs] He curbs his steed beside the stream [25]
smoking] plunging *del.*
2 Sweet girls are there on the cool green herbs and one is sweetest there. [25] *or* What
shapely girls on yonder grass are sheltering from the glare? [26]

No boats oar slow, no barges pass
    Down the quiet gray canal:
The reed & the rush, & the cotton-grass,
    Stand undisturb'd and tall.
No sound of unrest there alarms
The branch & brown mosses stretch their arms.

A swallow shot falls at my feet:
I muse: If blood must flow in sylvan world
        At least [blank]
        But turn on a stagnant tide [?]

Josepha

I date this poem at 1852, when the California gold rush was much in the news. During the rush most crimes were blamed on Mexicans.

Speak! yellow men who grub for gold
    In rocks & river-slime
What sight is this that I behold
    Of crime avenging crime?

Without a motion to resist,
    Her years yet scarcely ripe,—
A woman by the tender wrist
    Griped in a strangling gripe!

NO BOATS OAR SLOW

MS: NB B, [p. 27].
1 oar] oars del.
Line associated with 2, [p. 26]: Gray to the west lies the long canal
Between 4 and 5 del.:
            Red-stemm'd pines like a wall
            The flowless water darkly [folds del.] fold:
            To the gray sky a glass it [holds del.] hold.

JOSEPHA

MS: Berg, between pp. 6 and 7.
2 In river beds and rocks: del.
4 Among your earthy flocks or Of crime avenging crime

And whither drags she, torn from hope,
    At such a brutal march?   10
"—To yonder bridge, to yonder rope
    "Above the midmost arch:

"For she has drawn her naked knife
    "Against one of our own;
"She took a merry fellow's life,
    "And she in turn shall groan.

"She shall have Law & Justice—she!
    She shall be fairly used!—"
The Judge is Jury-wise, and he
    Is foe to the accused.   20

Far up the town whose mushroom growth
    Gloats in the golden beams,
A slouching throng of vice and sloth
    In motley wrangle streams.

On to the bridge that seaward dips,
    And from its curve descries
Old Europe in her gleaming ships
    Rich with the western skies.

A grimy wretch pourtrays the hurt,
    And flourishes the fact;   30
"—So dropt he in his bleeding shirt,
    —So stood she in the act."

A woman faithless to her sex,
    A boy foregone in years,
Steept both in dross up to the necks,
    Witness what he avers.

19 Judge is Jury-wise] Jury is the Judge *or* Judge is Jury-wise
22 golden] hot noon *del.* lavish *del.*
23 slouching throng] motley crowd *del.*
24 motley] busy *del.*

And some her yellow scarf point out,
    And some her dark blue dress
Dasht with avenging drops—and shout
    To make her doom confess.   40

"—Josepha, girl! what answerest thou?—"
    She gnaws those lips so wan,
And levels round her close black brow
    In scorn—"I kill'd the man!"

Her shining brow she levels mute,
    And bites her thin white mouth,
And stamps her little passionate foot
    In the old crimson wrath.

And crouching not mid the savage rush
    Of rage, uplifts her face   50
All burning with its swarthy blush
    And fierce-defying grace.

"—I kill'd him!"—and they check again
    With much unwilling awe,
The rage that would have rendered vain
    Their masking of the Law.

Then in the Judgment silence, spake
    The voice of a young man;
"Beware what deeper Law you break
    "In this dark Law you plan.   60

"I witness too, and not too late
    "Attest this deed, and swear
"That every woman in such strait,
    "Were well to do like her!

60 dark] harsh *del.*

"Ye who have wives and daughters! Ye
    "To whom a home is all—
"To whom a hearth dishonour'd free,
    "Would wrap earth in a pall;—

"I pray by you Christ's love! forgive
    "This creature so forlorn,   70
"Whose crime is that she would not live
    "Abased by her own scorn:

"Dishonour'd—yea, dishonour'd! prove
    "Her life false, frail, unclean—
"She has the inviolate soul in love,
    "All women cherish keen!

"She has the inviolate right in love,
    "That sanctity to claim
"In which the purest women move,
    "Angel-girt from shame!   80

"Shamed, shamed, and sinful as she is!—"
    —But now with yell & scoff,
"Ho, ho! her paramour is this!"
    They clamour, and hoot him off.

Then in the Ju[d]gment silence, spake
    The voice of an old man:
"—Beware what holier Law you break,
    "In this harsh Law you plan.

"The hand of God is on the girl,
    "And Nature is her screen;   90
"She bears in her breast a living pearl,
    "Quite spotless from her sin!

"She is a mother! men of flesh!
    "Have mercy, and forbear!
"Have mercy, mercy! be not rash!
    "Have mercy on her there!

"Let not the little life she feeds,
   "Thus cease ere yet it wake:
"Let her in spite of her misdeeds,
   "Be sacred for its sake.   100

"Look to her youth, she is so young!
   "O men, with souls to save,
"Dare not to send a soul so young
   "To her redeemless grave!

"Fathers! husbands!—she has none
   "Upon this alien sod,—
"I say this thing shall not be done!
   "'Tis murder, mocking God.

"I say this thing shall not be done!
   "It is a double crime;   110
"The guilty and the innocent one
   "Slaughter'd in solemn mime!

"I say this thing shall not be done!
   "Twill taint the common air;
"'Twill be a brand upon the sun,
   "A spectre of despair!

"A phantom of disgrace! for when
   "The foul revenge is o'er,
"Like men to meet the eyes of men
   "We can turn nevermore!   120

"O listen yet in time! disperse!
   "Take Christ in your decree!
"Nor alienate the universe
   "That marks us from the sea."

105 Fathers! [and *del.*]

And like that sea when thunders sound,
   Or battle smoke rolls thick,
The threatening motion sinks around,
   And hope of life beats quick.

And like that sea when roughened white
   By some lone tossing sail   130
A moment's calm the calm starlight
   Reveals in splendour pale.

Then in the human silence, rose
   A shaggy Judge-elect:
Severely on the victim throws
   His righteous gaze direct:

Uplifts his hands as tho' he drew
   The black-cap from the pit:—
And more of all its horror knew
   Than memory might admit.   140

"She has confest—she is condemn'd:
   "I see no outlet here;
"She has confest—she is condemn'd:
   Our course is very clear."

He lifts his hands, as to his head
   The blackcap he would fit;
And on her fear more terror fed
   Than conscience might admit.

After 128 carets, margin fair hand:
       And love of life with hope of life
         Fair joy of life returns
129–32, margin rough hand, followed by:
       Each savage eye, and threating form,
         And dark daub'd[?] visage feels
140 memory] conscience *or* memory

"—She is condemn'd—she has confest:
    "No paltering, I say   150
"This one example checks the rest;
    "Away with her, away!

"Or shall we for a woman's whim
    "Be stabb'd and stuck at will?"
The subtle home-thrust gains for him
    A most persuasive thrill.

"Or shall this Mexican brood have leave
    "At once to kiss and kill?"
His practised eyes hereat perceive
    A yet more wrathful thrill.   160

"Or shall we shrink to revenge the blood
    "A girl can coolly spill?—"
They seize her in their madden'd mood,
    Scarce held from instant ill.

They doom her to the scaffold near,
    With bitter-coucht rebuke;
The babe leaps in her breast to hear,
    But stedfast is her look.

Once only the old serpent shoots
    Across her mouth and cheek;   170
Twisting to a curse the thoughts
    No mortal tongue could speak:

Then smiling with her smiling lips
    And dead unkindled eye,
All gracefully and firm she steps
    Towards the swinging tie;

172 tongue] speech *del.*

And grasps it tight as she would twit
　　Some object thro' the loop;
And with her fingers fondles it,
　　While she in prayer doth stoop.　　　　　　　　180

While with her chin upon her chest
　　Huddled in prayer she kneels,
Covering with her black locks untrest,
　　Bare neck and naked heels.

Clothing with her long streaming locks
　　Her body bow'd, but bold,
Before those grovellers of the rocks
　　And their brute god of gold.

Song

Who says, she is in danger,
　　While loyal hearts are in her?
　　　　My country!
That dastard fears can change her
　　And beaten foes may win her?
　　　　My country!
Inviolate is she in the sight
Of Heaven, in Freedom's might:
Round her unfetter'd foot is curl'd
The infant hope of all the world:　　　　　　　　10

JOSEPHA

187 grovellers of the rocks] earthy grovelling flocks *del.* black black revengeful grovelling *del.*

SONG: WHO SAYS SHE IS IN DANGER

MSS: NB B, [*p. 23*], *lines 1–8, 2 associated lines;* Berg, *between pp. 46 and 47, lines 1–6; between pp. 60 and 61, fair copy corrected, copy-text.*

2 hearts] hearts *or* sons B *draft 1*
4 fears can] days shall *del.* NB B
5 beaten] hated *NB B, del.* B
7–8 *NB B:*

　　　　　In truth she were a splendid prize,
　　　　　　This Empress of the Western skies.

My country!
How gloriously would each glad son
Join battle for her innocent charms,
Kiss her dear earth & shield it
Clasp the sharp steel & wield it
Win laurell'd life, & yield it
       For England, England, England, my country!

Song

God bless the little Island!
Whatever they may say,
'Tis the finest piece of dry land
That ever saw the day!

The Three Eagles and the Sleepy Lion

The fact that the "fledgling" eagle of line 27 is crowned dates this poem after December 1, 1852, when Louis Napoleon declared himself Emperor of France. The two double-headed eagles are Austria and Russia. In pictures of the period the Austrian eagle occasionally has white polls, but the Russian bird is black, not white. GM's allusion to white feathers in line 17 may have been an attempt to indicate that that power appeared peaceful. The expendable fourth eagle of the Yale notebook draft of line 1 might have been Prussia whom at one time Louis Napoleon had wooed unsuccessfully for what, in *Fraser's* of February 1853, was called a "fifth-rate German princess."

Following the death of the Duke of Wellington on September 16, 1852, *Punch* displayed on October 2 a full-page drawing of the British Lion prone and half asleep below a black-draped portrait of the Duke.

SONG: WHO SAYS SHE IS IN DANGER

12–16 *abandoned but not del. B:*

> [And for her safety *del.*] For her dear sake will every son
> Will rush to *or* join the battle's lull'd alarms,
> Marshall'd upon [the *del.*] her shore as one,
> To stand against that world in arms,

13 innocent] beloved *or* innocent
16 laurell'd] deathless *del.*

Associated line in NB B: Dark days may come upon her,

SONG: GOD BLESS THE LITTLE ISLAND

MS: Berg, *between pp. 62 and 63.*

There were three eagles percht on a rock:
    On each lean head was a crown.
And they cast eye on a browsing flock:
    Derry down, derry down, derry down.
His watch a Lion grim did keep.
But his tail gave sign he was fast asleep.
And he snored as in repletion deep:
    O derry, I derry down.

The first he was double, and with a white poll.
    On each lean head was a crown.   10
When he gorged half he had greed for the whole;
    Derry down, derry down, derry down.
To listen awhile his ear did stoop;
While his wings blacken'd wide for a sudden swoop;
And he fated the Lion's choicest troop.
    O derry, I derry down.

The second was double, his feathers were white.
    On each lean head was a crown.
His claws were bloody; he bark'd for spite.
    Derry down, derry down, derry down.   20
To aid the first, and claim a share;
And to keep his own, was all his care;
His feathers were white, he show'd them there.
    O derry, I derry down.

Single, and silent sat the third.
    On each lean head was a crown.
He was a mighty fledgling bird.

MSS: NB B, [*pp. 23–24*]; Berg, *between pp. 52 and 53, copy-text.*

1 three] four *del.* three *del. NB B*
11 *NB B:* his wings could reach from pole to pole *or* When he had half he wanted the
whole   gorged] swallow'd *or* gorged *B*   had greed for] wanted *or* had greed for *B*
13 ear] head *or* ear *NB B*
14 blacken'd wide] prepared *NB B*
15 fated] singled *NB B*
17 his feathers were] & with a *del. NB B*
21 claim] have *NB B*; have *or* claim *B*

Derry down, derry down, derry down.
What he thought, they could not say,
But they knew right well he wanted prey;   30
While he wetted his brooding beak alway.
     O derry, I derry down.

Said the First to the Second: I've plann'd my game.—
     On each lean head was a crown.
Said the Second full readily: I the same.—
     Derry down, derry down, derry down.
Said the First to the Second: Our brother is wise:
He worried us once; but he sniffs a prize:
And the Lion dreams us his choice allies:
     O derry, I derry down.   40

Said the First to the Second: Such battles have been.—
     On each lean head was a crown.
Twixt Lions fat and Eagles lean.
     Derry down, derry down, derry down.
So we'll wait till the Lion's eyes are peckt:
And our young brother's pinions are broken & checkt:
Then we'll take what they fought for, in peace & respect.
     O derry, I derry down.

30 right] full *NB B, del. B*
33 plann'd] laid *NB B*
35 full readily] to him: and *or* in answer *or* full readily *NB B*
37 brother] friend here *NB B*
41 battles] things *or* battles *B*
45 So we'll] Let us *NB B*   peckt] out *or* peckt *NB B*
46 our young brother's pinions] the Eagle's wings *del. NB B*
After 48 NB B:

         And the Lion he slept, and the Eagles watcht
            On each lean ————
         In dream prophetic, his tail he lasht
            Derry ————

Fusion

The Saint sat down with the sinner:
    All factions fused [?] one of a trade:
It was a magnanimous Dinner,
    And Conscience alone for it paid.

'Twas cheap, they said, and their hunger
    Wax'ed keen as the table they viewed.
Supreme sat the great money-monger
    Surveying his subject brood.

Envision'd by men democratic,
    Long-lineaged Earls were at ease: 10
And garments still rank from the attic
    On costliest cloths rubb'd their grease.

The Song of Drab

Drab look'd long at his neighbour's note,
    Till he conceived a notion:
Drab put on his square-cut coat,
    And cross'd the dancing ocean.

FUSION

MS: NB B, [*p. 25*], *canceled lines and fair copy.*

2 All discords shook hands as they met *del.* Prepared to take all he cd get *del.*
4 Where Conscience alone was *or* fell in debt.

After 4 canceled:

    By the side of the journeyman baker
        The noble Viscount took a seat.
    The Soldier [took *del.*] drank wine with the Quaker;
        They trusted in Heaven to meet.

After 12 fair copy:

    And prove that the land of Fusion
        Would be confronted most
    The Jew is at peace with the porkers:
        The pig turns his snout to the Jews

THE SONG OF DRAB

MS: NB B, [*p. 25*].

Drab gave a knock at the Emperor's gate
As humbly as he was able:
Drab took off his low-crown'd hat
And sat at the Emperor's table.

The birth of GM's son Arthur Gryffydh on June 13, 1853, occasioned
the writing of this poem.

Dear Heaven! for this sweet pledge of life
Thou giv'st me in my boy,
I thank thee, and will meet the strife
With courage & new joy.

That such a breath of innocence
And such a star of light
Should come from me, is warning whence
My Soul came in thy sight.

Ah! little Angel, child of bliss!
Can I believe that little head
That fair-hair'd head that Christ might kiss,
Will come to harm when I am dead?

THE SONG OF DRAB
5 gave a knock at] came up to *del.*

DEAR HEAVEN!

MS: NB B, [*p. 46*].
8 My Soul] Myself *del.*

AH! LITTLE ANGEL

MS: NB B, [*p. 37*].

Reason

In this sonnet GM's concept of Wisdom is closely allied to that of Wordsworth in his sonnet "I grieved for Buonaparté" (1802).

Since Reason, with itself dissatisfied,
Has striven so long to burst the natural chain
Which guards it from the nebulous inane,
There have been many follies deified.
This age has loosen'd an irreverent tide
To wash old landmarks rear'd by Faith with pain:
Love, Law, Religion, these are symbols vain
Since Reason wedded her Arch-Enemy, *Pride*.
Thus while she serves to flatter dunce & fool
She were best banish't for no more is she   10
Wisdom's sweet handmaid at her starr'd footstool,
The champion of secure humility,
The seat of Faith, the source & the guide,
But a blind light that gropes in darkness wide.

Progression

GM's thought follows that of John Stuart Mill in *The Principles of Political Economy* (1848–52). Mill assumed that to his countrymen "progress" meant the accumulation of wealth and an expanding trade, and he deplored this concept.
Compare GM's later sonnet, *Progress*, page 291.

There is a modern term that much would mean,
And gives our orators a mighty peg:
This century laid it like a precious egg,
For watchword against retrospective spleen:

REASON

MS: NB B, [*p. 31*].

7 Law, Religion] honour, country *del.*
13 the guide] Hope *del.*
14 gropes in darkness wide] doth in darkness grope *del.*

PROGRESSION

MS: NB B, [*p. 31*].

But the white oval none will hatch, I ween.
Grammarians with their power on the last leg
Treat it as smugglers the suspicious keg
At midnight when the Coastguard hot are seen.
Startle the sleeping hamlets by the beach:
From globe to globe: let commonplaces breed: 10
When nations retrograde they are undone.
But never until all men march as one,
And it is visible in the Soul of each,
Can I accept Progression as a creed.

Ambition

How little seen, and little understood,
Is high Ambition in our social state.
Envy and Fear have colour'd it for our hate;
A lurid planet with a line of blood:
The phantom of upbraiding widowhood
Follows it, pointing to her slaughtered mate:
Yet do its chariot-wheels the fields of fate
Plough deepest—promise best the fruits of good:
I would have our fresh English youth make choice
For model men of war's most noble names: 10
The highest in all walks let them revere!
But let the calm of eye & purpose, steer
For that ambitious Statesmanship, whose voice
The will of our great commonwealth proclaims.

PROGRESSION
9 Let Science mix her Elements, and reach *or* Startle the sleeping hamlets by the beach:
12 march] move *or* march

AMBITION

MS: NB B, [*p. 31*].
4 They paint *del.*

Song

Buy, buy, buy,
Is the Peace-markt cry:
And the nations are our brothers
If they buy, buy, buy.

Honour's but a windy bag,
And History's a lie;
Nobility's at purchase,
And we'll buy, buy, buy.

The Synagogue's in Parliament;
The Jews are in the sty;   10
Salaam unto the guinea,
And we'll buy, buy, buy.

Young May is in December's bed;
Jack Horner eats his pie;
The Beauty goes to auction,
And we'll buy, buy, buy.

Religion sleeps on its old rags,
The world is all awry,
The Czar shall gulp the Sultan,
And we'll buy, buy, buy.   20

The cheapest thing is flesh and blood,
And hearts that beat high:
So we'll to the market merrily,
And buy, buy, buy.

Buy, buy, buy,
Our new kings cry,
And long live the men of Manchester,
Who buy, buy, buy.

MS: NB B, [*p. 33*].
2 Peace-markt] great Peace *or* Peace-markt
5 windy] empty *or* windy
22 beat] can *del.* beat

Song of the New Zealander among the Ruins of Old London

Writing on Ranke's *History of the Popes* in the *Edinburgh Review*, October 1840, Macaulay said of the Roman Catholic church: "She may still exist in undiminished vogue when some traveller from New Zealand shall, in the midst of a vast solitude, take his stand on a broken arch of London Bridge to sketch the ruins of St. Paul's."

Burra-Boo—Shirra Sha!
Macaulay was a trusty seër,
Barra Poota—Carra Woota!
When he saw me standing here.

The Falling of Sally

Gossips agreed all was wrong with poor Sally!
Things must look baleful when gossips agree:
Late & alone she returned from the valley,
Grasping wild flowers & dead leaves of the tree.
High was her apron, her stocking show'd under,
Weary she walked with the wet in her eye:
Friends look'd her up in a scandalized wonder,
They that once cherished her bade her goodbye.

SONG OF THE NEW ZEALANDER

MS: NB B, [*p. 34*].

THE FALLING OF SALLY

MS: NB B, [*p. 35*].

1 was] is *del.*
2 Things must look baleful when] Gossips are knowing, & *del.*
7 scandalized] sanctified *or* scandalized
8 They that once cherished her bade] Parents took warning & wish'd *del.*

The Capitalist

1

A capitalist was I:
    A mighty King of Cash:
When Stock I would sell, or buy,
    The nation ran close upon smash.
My name on a bundle of rags,
    To the City was Life, or Death.
I had but to tighten my bags
    And London gaspt for breath.
O a fickle race are fools!
    Their worship is profane   10
The capitalist's abased,
    The capitalist's despised
And another Idol rules
    The empire of Chicane.

2

You talk of Peter's will,
    And Russia's vast domain:
Why, the whole world was my mill,
    Mankind the grist & grain.
I ruled without a rod:
    My sovereignty was neat,
For Mammon I set up as God,
    And taught men to compete.
Oh! Mammon, Mammon, Mammon!
    Men worshipped thee profane.   10

MS: NB B, [*pp. 67–68*].

1.2 A mighty King] An Emperor *or* A mighty King
1.13 And] But now *del.*
2.7 set up as] made men's *or* set up as
2.8 men] them *or* men

3

Small Kings in Europe stood,
     And Slaves kneel'd to their thrones:
But mine of Norman blood,
     Best Norman marrowbones.
I spake but three short words
     And 'twas a sight to see
The anatomy of Lords
     A bowing machine to me.

4

Tho' I walk'd in the marriage bond,
     My Lady ogled low,
At cards, the Duchess was fond
     Too fond upon my toe.
A harem of noble Dames
     With languishing eye and a pout [?]
Proclaim'd me the type of Bull:
     They roasted me with flames
And flatter'd me to beef:—
Hung round me breathing flames   10
     And wooing me for scrip.

5

In Parliament I reign'd
     A Prince rever'd & bold:
The doctrine I maintain'd
     That facts are made of gold.
"And facts," said I, "Make laws."
     Thereat I smack'd my breech:
What thunders of applause
     Followed that famous speech!

4.2 ogled low] with ogles would flow *del.* ogled me low *del.*
4.3 was] too *del.* was
4.4 *Del.:* With her amourous foot on my toe.
4.8 flames] their *del.* flames
4.9 And ate me up as beef *or* And flatter'd me to beef:—
5.8 famous] pointed *del.*

'Twas I foresaw the time,
   And understood the Age,   10
Chicanery sublime
   Through me became the rage.

6

'Twas I begot that thing
   Which men a Crisis call:
Likewise I pulled a string
   And Panic o'ershadow'd them all.
Like juggler's balls I toss'd
   This couple in the sun,
The nation paid the cost,
   And thousands were ruin'd for one.

Will Whistle

1

I'm call'd Will Whistle by a throng
   Of those that eat the thistle,
Because whenever a thing goes wrong,
   I pocket my hands and whistle.
It's not because my flesh won't burn,
   Or that I can't feel vexation;
But in all reckonings I discern
   A Law of Compensation.

THE CAPITALIST

6.6 This couple] These monsters *or* This couple

WILL WHISTLE

MS: NB B, [*p. 69*].

After stanza 1, refrain del.:

   So, whistle, lads! & whistle, lads!
   [Learn in good *del.*] And learn in time to whistle:
   When a thing goes wrong, remember the song,
   Pocket your hands and whistle.

3

Now Fortune that keeps Lang so lean,
    Plumps Piper like a goose:
But when Death eyes the couple keen,
    D'ye think he'll stop to choose?
Oh! he's a mighty Epicure
    And loves the fattest ration,
So thus, may Lang the lean make sure
    Of a Law of Compensation.

Philosopher! 'tis said you wail
    Because the earth goes wrong:
Why, that, friend, is an ancient tale
    And matter for a song.

The earth has never yet gone right,
    But while to be it strives
'Tis better in my erring sight,
    To cheer it all our lives.

There's something in the violet,
    There's something in the rose,   10
Which makes me think old earth has yet
    More in her than she shows;

WILL WHISTLE
Between stanzas 1 and 3, stanza 2 del.:
    If Fortune's call'd a fickle Dame,
        The Term of Justice *or* praising savours;
    We should bestow *or* be giving a harder name
        If to one she kept her favours.
    I loved her once: she flouted me:
        One night of proud inflation
    I bared her breast, and learnt to see
        The Law of Compensation.
        So whistle, lads! &c. &c.—

PHILOSOPHER!
MS: NB B, [*p. 53*].
1 'tis said you wail] you've learnt to wail *or* 'tis said you wail
2 earth] world *or* earth
5 earth] world *or* earth   gone] been *or* gone
6 to be it strives] it strives to be *del.*
8 all our lives] with a plea *del.* on with glee *del.*

A cousinship to happy stars
    That burn when all is dark:—
And that 'tis wailful man that mars,
    Philosopher, the mark.

For wailing, though it may be sweet,
    It seldom can be sound:
Crackt instruments one note repeat
    But are as crackt renown'd.   20

Now when my babe this earthly ball
    First visited as man,
The little fellow lookt on all
    Astonisht, & began

To cry, complain, & make a stir:
    He saw that woes prevail'd
Now he was a philosopher
    But twas not long he rail'd.

For learning that despite his cries
    Though loud, change could not come,   30
This little fellow closed his eyes,
    And calmly suckt his thumb.

Meeting

Say nothing: let us sit within arm's reach:
    The silent something passing to the skies

PHILOSOPHER!
13 happy] constant *or* happy
20 But are] One note *del.*
21 babe] boy *del.*
25 complain] & scream *del.*
27 Now he] He, too *or* Now he
28 *Del.:* But of another kind.
29 learning] seeing *del.*   despite] for all *or* despite
30 change could not] no change could *del.*
32 suckt] took *del.*

MEETING
MS: NB B, [*p. 70*].

From heartful earth, more spirit-rich than speech.
And needing not the beam of tender eyes,
Shall breathe between us, dearest soul, & be
A viewless Angel born from you & me.

When my little son leaps in my sight,
And his laughter rings in the air,
Often will pure delight
Surprise my heart with prayer.

I find that my soul has flown
Thro' the future of his days
Has fallen at Heaven's throne
& mingled prayer with praise.

I seize in a central knot,
I grasp in a spark of fire,
The circle of a thought,
The round of a desire.

MEETING

3 more spirit-rich than] we've seen: it is not *del.*
4 beam] light *del.*
5 Shall breathe between] This shall delight *del.*
6 viewless] living *or* viewless
After 6 del.: By this we know we love:

WHEN MY LITTLE SON

MS: NB B, [*p. 70*].

Between 4 and 5 margin:

Will the little blossom of thanks
Bear fruits of a rich content

6 the future of his days] his Future unaware *or* the future of his days

I SEIZE IN A CENTRAL KNOT

MS: NB B, [*p. 70*], *canceled.*

〰️

Believe me, I have studied men,
    Both in myself & others:
I cannot say that in this den
    I'm better than my brothers.

And yet mankind I rank not high
    Nor am I very humble:
Thus always proud philosophy
    Doth at the starting stumble.

〰️

Quake, quake, let us turn Quaker all!
    Bowing to Nicholas, or any other Ass:
Gold is our Idol & money's our maker all,
    Leave us in Peace & we care not what come to pass.

The Red Coats & the Blue

The British expeditionary force sailed for the Crimea in the spring of 1854. This fact, plus the handwriting and ink, has determined the date of a number of these fragments.

Again to measure with the foe,
    The strength that keeps us true,
The gallant sons of Britain go;
    The Red coats & the Blue.

BELIEVE ME
MS: NB B, [*p. 46*].
5 mankind I rank] of men I think *del.*

QUAKE, QUAKE
MS: NB B, [*p. 32*].
1 turn] be *or* turn   Quaker] Quakers *del.*

THE RED COATS
MS: NB B, [*p. 32*].

The Loyal Soldier

1

Just lift me to the window while the British boys march by;
    While they march, God be with them! to the fight:
And Doctor, by your leave, one cheer, if I die;
    One cheer for old England and the right.
Hurrah!—There's not a fellow who steps in yonder ranks,
    Tho' Death is in the front, can go too fast:
For tho' little is his profit and less may be his thanks,
    A British soldier's loyal to the last.

2

They're gone behind the turbans; they're filing in the boat;
    What's this? the old wound burst out anew?
Well, Doctor, if the Russian lead does give me a red coat,
    It proves, when stript, I'm to my colours true.

The Lord of old has dealt in blood
    And not disdain'd to draw the s[word]
And we because our cause is g[ood]
    Will take example by the L[ord.]

THE LOYAL SOLDIER

MS: NB B, [*p. 51*].

1.3 if] tho' *del.*
1.7 For] But *del.*
2.4 It proves, when stript,] It only proves *or* It proves, when stript,

THE LORD OF OLD

MS: NB B, [*p. 35*].

Associated line: We fought in faith: the fight was good:

The world is young, the world is well,
      The world was never better:
And still [?] fool & sage can tell
      That Time remains its debtor.

Observe when yonder shoot of me
      Begins to toddle bravely:
The world's in him, the world is he
      That puts his foot so gravely:
With young delight and laughs the while
      He totters, toddles, tumbles: 10
And looks up with a roguish smile
      While his first word he mumbles.

For he is proud of his first word,
      Nor thinks speech given vainly:
By him his functions are preferr'd
      To fancies all ungainly.

And sure this baby world to see
      So bright-eyed & so rosy
Tis well to think the world is he

A peace conference to try to settle the Crimean War opened in Vienna, March 15, 1855, and adjourned on April 21 without any definite results. Russia was still holding Sevastopol. The principal delegates, GM's "five little men," were: representing Austria, Count von Buol-Schauenstein; France, Baron de Bourqueney; Great Britain, Lord John Russell; Russia, Prince Gorchakov; and Turkey, Aarif Effendi.

THE WORLD IS YOUNG

MS: NB B, [*p. 52*], *canceled.*

8 The world wakes in him gravely: *or* That puts his foot so gravely:
10 He] And *del.*

Between 12 and 13, 4 lines del., first two illegible, ending:

      To imitate the thing he heard
      Is now his constant pleasure.

While Nature mocks her truths with mimic shows,
 And plays the Harlequin when most she weeps,
 What wonder that in Men of State there leaps
Desire to act upon fantastic toes
Their tragic part, and mock a nation's woes
 With grave burlesque? Now Sebastopol rings
 The terrible reality of things,
It is proclaim'd. 'The Conferences close'!

No more, Vienna! shall five little men
 Meet in thy halls,

◦⌇w⌇◦

When Napoleon III visited England in mid-April 1855, he stayed at Windsor Castle. Although one might argue that he was *arrivé*, not "coming," he seems the most likely candidate.

 'Tis I have seen the coming man;
  In pomp he enter'd London:
 The British public cheering ran
  From sunrise unto sundown.

 The Queen & Prince a palace gave;
  To prove him truly welcome
 I heard the arm-chair prophets rave
  Of heaven & of hell come.

WHILE NATURE MOCKS

MS: NB B, [*p. 39*], *canceled.*

'TIS I HAVE SEEN THE COMING MAN

MS: NB B, [*p. 54*].

Abandoned stanza preceding stanza 1:

  The tailor & the cobbler rush'd
   To boot him & to breech him:
  Even Panegyric's self was hush'd,
   And

Glee

What! my friend! you're surely daft
To frown because at you we laught?
Why, ha, ha, ha! good fellow, good fellow,
You're like old wine to us, ruby and mellow.
And is't not a compliment divine
To tap a good fellow like rare old wine?
And laugh at him, laugh at him, ha, ha, ha!
    Till he too laughs like a noble good fellow!
At first half ashamed as the bell-wethers bad
But at last full loud as the mighty bulls bellow!   10
    Ha, ha, ha, ha; had!—

He's a totterer on life's staff
Who can't give & take a laugh:
Why, ha, ha, ha! good fellow! to win us
You've but to pierce to the laughable in us
For they who pretend to be exempt
Instead of laughter meet contempt.

Laughter is that airy whim
Which just makes the vessel swim
Laughter is the good man's wealth   20
And might be the rich man's health.

Gentleman is he, wise elf,
Who leads the laugh against himself
And twill be on a noble morn
When follies are as feathers worn.

MS: NB B, [*p. 44*], *canceled.*
6 tap] rank *or* tap   like] with *or* like
10 But at last] And ends *del.*
12 a totterer on] not worthy of *del.*
13 give & take] give & take *or* furnish us *del.*
14 to win us] such sinners *del.*
18 airy] windy *or* airy

⌒〜⋈〜⌒

I humm'd an air of sweet Mozart,
A tender sigh of love,
With just enough of jealous heart
To make it like the dove.
It haunted me thro' a field of oats
And o'er a thymy down
To where the sea with rocking boats
Wore sunset like a crown

⌒〜⋈〜⌒

GM revised this poem for inclusion in *The Shaving of Shagpat* where it
reads:

Even's star yonder
Comes like a crown on us
Larger and fonder
Grows its orb down on us;
So, love, my love for thee
Blossoms increasingly;
So sinks it in the sea,
Waxing unceasingly.
(Mem. Ed., 1: 53)

See the star yonder
Sink like a crown on us
Fonder & fonder
Grows its beam down on us.
So, love, my love for thee
Blossoms increasingly:
So will it meet the sea
Swelling increasingly.

I HUMM'D AN AIR

MS: NB B, [*p. 49*].

5 It haunted me] I humm'd it *or* It haunted me

SEE THE STAR YONDER

MS: NB B, [*p. 51*].

6 Daily increases: *or* Blossoms increasingly:
8 When my light ceases. *or* Swelling increasingly.

Arabic Poems

Both the subject and handwriting of this draft of poems date the writing of them to be during the composition of *The Shaving of Shagpat* 1854–55.

[1]

Let us sing of our beloved, let us sing of that which is sweetest:
For the sweetest is that desire & desires are the fathers of song.
And Song like the conquering Sun, the great Eagle of light,
Maketh the heavens its own, & soars o'er the dusts of the desert;
Earth in its beam is all gold, and blushes, the wealth of love,
The wonder of men, the last which the hand of Creation
Left upon Beauty's cheek ere leaving Beauty perfect
Blushes awake to it—
                 Is there a drouth over Earth, lo, song
Shall leap like lightening out of the murky heat
And bring from the eyes of men streams of rejoicing tears.   10
Song can bring clouds into the hearts of men & arouse thunder in
    their bosoms.

[2]

When she laughs there is a glitter as of morning before me,
    morning and all its dews; and it is as if beads of
    ivory were flashing from the fresh red of a sliced pomegranate.

[3]

They that love not—are they not as blind camels that behold no
    star in the Desert & must die in it?
    Yea, the coldness of a loveless heart is the coldness of death.

MS: Yale.

1.2 the sweetest is that desire] that which is sweetest the heart desireth *or* the sweetest is that desire

After poem [2]: Names: Novara: Matana:

[4]

When I saw the jewelled girdle tied at her waist I thought of
    the seven-starred silver knot on a side of the heavens.

[5]

As the egg of an ostrich at the bottom [of] a bubbling spring
    seems to swell & tremble, so does thy bosom, my beloved,
    when I dare to gaze on it.

[6]

Her cheeks are as a crystal goblet held to the sun
Her lips red & fresh as the wine of the goblet
Her eyes like the ebbing rivers of light lash'd with darkness
And the torrent of life that speeds thro' her, streams to a broad
    orb of swelling smoothness there when the fluttering bird, her
    heart, sings to itself, rejoices, and palpitates.

[7]

I met at morn a girl of the tribes, bearing a milk-bowl.
Said I: O my soul!
Pluck from your dark-green pomegranate tree
Two of the rounded orbs & fling them straight
Into the bowl
Then wilt thou see in the bowl
Two dancing mounds of milky white
And upon two faintest buds of red
And therein imaged behold the bosom
For which I am sighing.

[8]

Her arms two branches of the almond-tree that sway at morn in the
    time of blossoming

4.2 a side] the waist *del.*
7.4 Two of the rounded orbs & fling them] A rounded fruit ruddy-golden and fling it *or*
Two of the rounded orbs & fling them
7.7 Two dancing mounds] A dancing mound *or* Two dancing mounds

The Fair Bedfellow

I remember, long ago,
　　Ere my teens were twelve & one,
With a fair fair bedfellow
　　I was warm till morning's sun.

Years she had that doubled mine:
　　And I puzzled to divine
When at night I started
Why I always found her crying.
　　She was crying broken-hearted.

By a lamp on the bed,　　　　　　　　　　10
　　Lifting slightly on her knees,
Trembling letter-sheets she read,
　　Clasping beads from foreign seas.

With her forehead on them bow'd
　　Broken words, & half-aloud,
Read she—all her body shaking—
Till my heart nigh burst with aching.

Then her neck I took with a leap
　　In my arms, & sought to know
What it was that made her weep,　　　　　20
　　My own darling bedfellow.

MS: NB B, [*p. 43*].
2 twelve] ten *del.*
3 fair fair] loving *del.*
4 was] slept *del.*
6 puzzled to] could not them *or* puzzled to
7 *Del.:* When I startled from my sleep　　at night] from my sleep *or* at night
10 lamp] candle *or* lamp
13 foreign] distant *or* foreign
14 forehead] head above *or* forehead
15 Broken words] Loud she read *del.*
16 Read she—all] She read slowly *del.*
18 *Del.:* Then I flung my arms about
19 In my arms] Her dear neck *del.*
20 weep] cry *del.*

And she kissed me, made the room
Soft again with tender gloom:
In against her bosom drew me
Till her dear heart panted thro' me.

〜〜〜

Dark on the ridge of the cold salt wave
        The wind-streaks shoot and shiver:
Daylight is gray distant away;
        Thro' the cloud streams a twilight river.

Only the gull on his wet white wing
        Before me wheels in motion:
No sail nears home; but the falls of foam
        Press wearily from the ocean.

Plunging they come to the sandy beach,
        And whiten in circles of thunder: 10
Del.: The fever they hold of a secret untold,
        Del.: Like treasures of beauty untasted.

Love, my beloved! 'tis of love they complain
        I know by what in me is burning:
The heart of the sea like the heart that's in me,
        Is speechless with passionate yearning.

DARK ON THE RIDGE

MS: NB B, [*p. 45*].

1 Dark on the ridge] Darkly over the banks *del.*
3 Daylight] The light *or* Daylight
4 The sky shows *or* clouds bank one pale river *or* Thro' the cloud streams a twilight river.
5 gull on his wet white] white gull wetting *or* gull on his wet white
6 wheels] keeps *del.*
7 falls] tongues *del.*
9 sandy] pebbly *del.*
13 'tis of love they complain] it is love they would speak *or* 'tis of love they complain
16 speechless with] dumb with its *del.*

Yet O for them who have lost—have lost:
Ere their eyes are raised & their arms are crost:
Ere the rainbow rise from the
    tears they weep:
What love see they in the cold
    cruel deep?   20

Nothing but one relentless power
That sprung on their darling in evil hour.
And still, like a beast of the wilds
Plays savage pranks with the hapless dead.

Driving them, driving them,

Yet what is this? the spring returns:
The sun along the furrow burns:
The cowslip gather'd by my boy
Is that which I pluckt once in joy.

Later in his life GM said, "When I was young, had there been given
me a little sunshine of encouragement, what an impetus to better work
would have been mine. I had thoughts, ideas, ravishment; but all fell on a
frosty soil, and a little sunshine would have been so helpful to me"
(LS, p. 46).

DARK ON THE RIDGE
19 rise] has sprung *del.*
20 see they] is for them *del.*
21 relentless] remorseless *or* relentless
22 That look'd alike on weed & flower: *del.*
23 wilds] desert o'erfed *or* wilds
YET WHAT IS THIS?
MS: NB B, [*p. 38*].

Too cold for joy, too cold for woe,
In a girdle of Winter belted,
Fair creature! thou art mountain snow
That eyes the sun unmelted.

An age of petty tit-for-tat,
An age of busy gabble;
An age that like a brewer's vat
Is bursting for the rabble.

An age too fast, an age too slow
An age of vast abuses:
When gentlemen & ladies grow
Too dainty for their uses.

An age that drives an iron horse:
Of earth & skies defiant: 10
Exulting in a Giant force
& trembling at the Giant.

An age of Quaker hue & cut,
That bows to Kings of Cotton:
[line left blank]
By Mammon misbegotten.

TOO COLD FOR JOY

MS: NB B, [p. 46].

AN AGE OF PETTY TIT-FOR-TAT

MS: NB B, [p. 38].

Abandoned stanza 1:

And art thou not a shameless age
& something less than modest?
Declared in the [?] page
The commoner & oddest.

2 busy] silly del. idle del.
4 bursting for] tapp'd for all or bursting for
5 too] of or too   an] &   too] of or too

An age that [*blank*]
[*line left blank*]
Deep-dungeon'd in its own conceit,
    A drunkard's elevation.   20

An age of which to hope the best,
    Will learn it once was crazy:

A kiss, and a clasp, and an eye to eye,
    And a bosom that's heaven to cover,
No maiden need shame herself not to deny
    Unto her parting lover.
With adieu, my dear, & be true, my dear!
    Cry faithful & fickle together:
And let the world break if for once I forsake
    The truth that braves the weather.

I wish'd the world a blindness
    To your beauty & your mind,
I wish'd thee all unkindness
    That you might know me kind.

I dream'd that a King in his bounty,
    A beggar-maid espoused:

A KISS AND A CLASP
MS: NB B, [*p. 41*].
2 heaven to] frankly at *or* heaven to
8 the] every *del.*

I WISH'D THE WORLD A BLINDNESS
MS: NB B, [*p. 50*].
2 your] thy *del.*   beauty] features *or* beauty   your] thy *del.*
4 *Del.:* That I might once be kind.
Line associated with 5–6, [p. 49]: I would that a beggar maid

Squireless Kate

My Knight is over the sea, cried Kate:
The Foe is knocking at the gate:
No living man in my cause can fight:
I must be my own true Knight.
She's buckled her armour, she's met the Foe,
She's swung her blade, & left him low.
They that saw the deed declare,
Never was combat so gallant as there.

Brave Kate! Bonny Kate!
As many a squire as the Queen possesses,   10
All would wait on Squireless Kate
For just one lock of her tresses.

⟨✹⟩

The Lords debate, the Commons brawl,
    The people pay the piper;
There's something wanting unto all,
    And still the Age grows riper.

The Age is doing what she can:
    And barren blooms are falling:
She calls in anguish for her Man,
    And she is hoarse with calling.

SQUIRELESS KATE

MS: NB B, [*p. 63*], *canceled.*
1 over the sea] off to the wars *del.* over the water *del.*
2 is knocking] knocks harshly *or* is knocking
3 can] will *or* can
Lines associated with Squireless Kate, *NB B, [p. 61]:*
                    Kate
        And in the hosts for very life
            She's tilting with the best of us.
                Brave Kate! Bonny Kate

THE LORDS DEBATE

MS: NB B, [*p. 58*].
6 barren blooms] mellow fruits *del.*

A world of Faëry! Saints of Love!
    For one short Season. lend him,   10
For if he come not from above
    The Devil is sure to send him.

◦✦◦

In the time of early love,
    Hill & field with promise blush'd:
Ours flew like a milky Dove,
    And the night was Angel-hush'd.
Heaven open'd east & west,
    Purer feet sped on the green.
Higher creature Earth possess'd:
I have known the bliss of Eden,
    I on Eden's heart have been,
In the hour of Love's awaking,   10
    In the time of early love.

◦✦◦

The poems of disillusion and anguish I date as 1857. By the summer of
that year GM's wife Mary had left him and was visiting Wales with her
lover, the painter Henry Wallis (see LS, p. 58).

In *The Ordeal of Richard Feverel* (1859) GM condensed these two
stanzas into one as an example of the kind of sentimental song that
Mrs. Bella Mount, the seductress, did not like. The version in the novel is
as follows:

Once the sweet romance of story
    Clad thy moving form with grace;
Once the world and all its glory
    Was but framework to thy face.
Ah, too fair!—what I remember,
    Might my soul recall—but no!
To the winds this wretched ember
    Of a fire that falls so low!
        (Mem. Ed., 2: 442)

IN THE TIME OF EARLY LOVE
MS: NB B, [*p. 59*].
6 sped] were *del.*

Once the fair Romance of story
 Clad thy moving feet with grace:
Once the world in all its glory
 Was but framework to thy face.
Over thee Heaven's gorgeous changes
 Roll'd like mantles of a Queen:
In the storm by lightning riven
 Thou glowing Love wert seen.

Sadly is the Idol shattered
 Since we first could learn to part: 10
Every magic gift is scattered
 And thou art the thing thou art.
Fondly might my soul remember
 Something of thy power—but no!
To the winds this tardy ember
 Of a fire that falls so low!

      ❧

A wand of gold from the reaper's moon
 Trembles up the wave of the weir:
And she that is coming, her foot is on my heart,
 And her panting ghost seems near.

ONCE THE FAIR ROMANCE

MS: NB B, [*p. 36*].

6 *Del.:* Like a mantle roll'd in beams:
8 *Del.:* Thou wert seen by Love's lost dreams.
9 is the Idol] now the Idol's *del.*

A WAND OF GOLD

MS: NB B, [*p. 66*].

We stood in the garden alone,
    And not a word we spake:
But all mute things had a tone
    Too terrible to mistake.

Long was the conflict, but now 'tis done:
    Light-hearted fancies are mine no more.
Pain like a sportsman, hides with his gun
    And shoots the fledglings trying to soar.

Terrible sportsman, bagging game!
    Never, it seems, canst thou have enough:
Well could I join in thy curse, and exclaim,
    The old Bird is a world too tough.

Was it wise to count the ranks of teeth
    In the gulf's grim jaws between us there?
And when thou wert above to gaze beneath,
    And shrink from the hope that look'd despair?
    I leapt like a leopard the space of air.

WE STOOD IN THE GARDEN ALONE

MS: NB B, [*p. 56*].

LONG WAS THE CONFLICT

MS: NB B, [*p. 57*].
Line directly above line 1: The game is lost: the race is run
4 fledglings] poor birds *or* fledglings
7 Well could I] I, too, could *del.*

WAS IT WISE TO COUNT THE RANKS OF TEETH

MS: NB B, [*p. 64*].
1 ranks of] ravenous *del.*
5 space of] yawning *or* space of

'Twas the Desert's thirst for a dewy flower,
　　And the Desert's dream of Eden springs:
And the Desert's headlong arrowy power,
　　That gave me the force of cleaving wings:
　　And he who clung to them—now he clings!　　　10

⟨∼∾∾⟩

If thou art sorrowful, hide thy face!
Show it not in the market-place:
And dost thou go where men are gay,
Put on a mask & be as they

Harvest it seems of the loads of woe,
But 'tis a Duty that we owe:
In every day that comes & parts,
So are men made to mock their hearts.

Could we discover the inner breast,
Little should we love a jest:　　　　　　　　　10
And that is what great life demands
To strengthen her oft-failing hands.

Grief is a mirror wherein men view
Too much of themselves that's true.
And when they search for better cheer,
Those who know them do not sneer.

WAS IT WISE TO COUNT THE RANKS OF TEETH
Lines probably associated with Was it wise, *NB B,* [*p. 65*]:

On empty life in my distress
I clasp'd my passionate arms, but to press
Closer the sting of loneliness.

The very hope look'd such despair
That it under the soul of love to dare

IF THOU ART SORROWFUL

MS: NB B, [*p. 61*].

So if thou'rt sorrowful, hide thy face!
Show it not in the market-place:
And dost thou go where men are gay,
Put on a mask & be as they.   20

⊶✠⊷

Blame me not that I refuse
    To sing when racking with despair:
Into my heart I take the Muse
    But not that she may make it bare.

Well she knows me that my love
    Is such as will not clip her wings:
I listen while she soars above
    And from her sovran fancy, sings.

Enough to know that she is mine,
    Unfetter'd by my selfish grief: 10
Made by her happiness divine,
    And better strung to shed relief;

Shed relief, console, exalt;—
    Than if, toucht by our mortal taint,
Taught the dark evils of a fault
    To utter in melodious plaint.

My breast is like that castle old
    Where one forbidden closet stood:
Fair shone the land in sheaves of gold
    Around it many a swelling rood [?]:   20

BLAME ME NOT

MS: NB B, [*p. 62*].
9 *Del.:* It is enough to know her mine
11 That she is all the more divine, *or* Made by her happiness divine.
Stanza associated with Blame me not [*p. 62*]*:*
                    The woe that sad men simulate
                        To cheat their hearts a lengthen'd wail
                    To melt & to upbraid their fate
                        With sweetness of the nightingale.

From every window it was fair
 And fresh with minstrelsy, save one:
On pain of death thou enterest there
 My Muse! into it enter none.

⁓⁕⁓

It is the young fresh rainy leaf
That brushes my cheek as I pass the wood:
And O what a treasure's the tear of Spring
To them that have lost the weeping mood.

The lark sings up in the shower; the brakes
Chirrup the more at the sorrow of May
And O that my heart again were rich
With the wanton grief of my early day

And O that my heart this fragrance gave
And greener grew to the touch of grief;   10
And O that my heart saw Heaven peep thro'
The wreaths of the young fresh rainy leaf!

⁓⁕⁓

Of Robin Redbreast's babes I told,
 Who perish'd in the wood:
My listener was five years' old,
 The first-born of my blood.

IT IS THE YOUNG FRESH RAINY LEAF
MS: NB B, [*p. 67*].
Before stanza 1:

    Warm spring rains have laid the dust:
    The waggon-wheels were yellow with rust:
     Over my head once more
    The rainy fresh young leaf expands.

6 *Del.:* Mock with a chirrup May's sorrowful looks
OF ROBIN REDBREAST'S BABES I TOLD
MS: NB B, [*pp. 39–40*]. *Ed.'s reconstruction of 4 lines on* [*p. 39*] *and 6 lines on* [*p. 40*].
Associated lines, [*p. 40*]:

His dear head has the shape of mine,
    And like his young heart seems:
I seek by Symbols to divine
    His fate, and lapse in dreams.
He is yon river's wavering line,
    In darkness, & in beams.   10

⁓⁓⁓

There fell a sudden rain
    Nigh evenfall.
 The sun is out again,
    And red upon the wall,
Where the tulip-row o'erlooks
The trenches' running brooks
    Through meadows thick with spears
    Of grass, & nodding [*blank*]

The river runs into the sky
The fish is rising to the fly   10

OF ROBIN REDBREAST'S BABES I TOLD
    O may he in his depths be pure
    Yon river winding thro' the vale,
        And flowing from the morn:

THERE FELL A SUDDEN RAIN

MSS: NB B, *MS 1,* [*p. 15*]; *MS 2,* [*p. 41*]; Yale, *loose leaf, copy-text.*
1 fell a sudden] fell a shower of *MS 1*; pass'd a shower of *MS 2*
3 The sun is out] But the sun shone forth *MSS 1, 2*
4 red upon] redden'd on *MSS 1, 2*
After 4, MS 1:
        Ere he died:
    The birds were about & the worm crawl'd *or* came out
    The air was fresh, the view was wide.
        The flowers laugh'd & blush'd,
        A thousand rillets rush'd
            To the tide [?]   *end of MS 1*
After 4, MS 2:
        A thousand rillets *or* Blue rillets leapt & rush'd;
    [The tulips laugh'd & *del.*] The wet-cheek'd tulips blush'd;
    The sky glow'd grey [& fair: *del.*]
    The birds were about, & the worm came out.
        Del.: Freshly flew the air.
        The fly to the fish was prey.   *end of MS 2*

Creation and the Prophet

According to William Hardman, on an unpublished page of his journal-letter, GM intended to include this poem in his *Modern Love* volume (1862) but was dissuaded by friends because "it would have offended a great man, and would have been justly charged with flippancy by those who liked it not" (see Explanatory Notes, p. 1174). The imminent end of the world was seriously feared by many people at that time, the most influential prophet of doom being the evangelist Dr. John Cumming, whose book *The Great Tribulation* was published in 1859.

The appearance of an unnamed comet in 1851 or the reappearance in 1852 of Biela's comet, which in 1846 had split into two, probably occasioned the two early drafts of this poem. Because of the separation of Biela's comet, the smaller of the two may have been the "young comet" of GM's early verses. The appearance of a "great comet" in 1861, however, probably led GM to resurrect his early verses, and, with an eye on the spectacular Dr. Cumming, to change his generic prophet to a specific one.

1

The Prophet at Creation's door
Hath long been humbly dunning:
He swears to us now, that Earth is hoar,
And Time must cease his running.

MSS: NB B, [*p. 19*]; Berg, *between pp. 130 and 131, title:* Song: *C. L. Cline, William Hardman's script: copy-text.*
B title-page: Song: "The good old world is doom'd in space"
1.1–*B:*

> The world is ripe and doom'd in space,
>> She hears her raging prophet; *or* Her prophet greatly rages;
> 'Tis certain Time must yield the race
>> And has warn'd his chosen of it. *or* And has warn'd his chosen sages:
> They show the way, they shriek the day,
>> With dolorous dirges our [path *del.*] life waylay:—

Stanza 1, 2 drafts NB B, dr. 1 canceled:
1.1 *dr. 2* The good old world is doom'd in space,   is doom'd] rolls on *or* rolls round *dr. 1*
1.2 *dr. 2:* She hears the [yearly *del.*] raging prophet
　　dr. 1:

>> Souls spring, and souls pass from it:
>> And souls spring up, & souls pass from it:

1.3 *dr. 2:* 'Tis certain Time [will *del.*] must yield the race,   *dr. 1:* Many's the threat *or* Threats there are many to check its race
1.4 *dr. 2:* And has warn'd his [children *del.*] chosen of it.   *dr. 1:* From prophets hoarse and wild young *or* wanton comet.

He shows us the way: he fights for the day:
He sounds the loud blast of a devil to pay:—
    Still the grass grows,
    Still blooms the rose,
  And the cock crows in the morning.

2

Both Sun & Moon look mild on Earth
  To snare us with reliance;
But they shudder at the monstrous birth
  Of this we christen Science.
The Prophet can raise coming moments at gaze,
When Nature & Heaven change nods in a craze:—
    Still the grass grows,
    Still blooms the rose,
  And the cock crows in the morning.

1.5 *dr. 2:* They point the [day *del.*] way, they dot the hour *or* they scan the day   *dr. 1:*
But still it rolls in its ancient range
1.6 *dr. 2:* When Fire shall fair earth devour:—   *dr. 1:* In the dark whirl of ceaseless
change:
1.7 Still] Yet still *dr. 2*

Stanza 2 not in NB B, B, instead B:

[2]

The fiendish elements we ride
  Are subtle with disaster:
The Slaves of Force *or* These Giant Slaves who work our pride,
  We know not well to master.
With wrath they burn; [and *del.*] they soon will turn
To gather our earth in its funeral urn:—
    Fresh the grass grows,
    Full blooms the rose,
    And the cock crows in the morning.

Lines in NB B associated with B [2] *1–4:*

Fear the great form of
Draw we not darkly from the hearts
  Of elements their forces?
From fiendish elements we draw *del.* what wrath *del.* force,
  We wrest for uses awful!
All things go wandering from their source,
  The rebel lords the lawful.

Before stanza 3, which is [4] *in B:*

3

O vain and stricken hearts who claim
   That ghostly thing, "to-morrow"!
Who nurse young Hope like a child of shame,
   In bosoms charged with sorrow:
Shiver and cark: take refuge dark:
Already the Prophet hath spied the first spark:—
     Still the grass grows,
     Still blooms the rose,
   And the cock crows in the morning.

4

No more the Bard may look beyond,
   For Fame's transfiguration:
The Jew will read his broken bond
   By the vast illumination.
A comet will flail old Earth with his tail,
Till aflame with mad prophets to darkness we sail:—
     Fleet the grass grows,
     Sweet is the rose,
   And the cock crows in the morning.

---

[3]

O vested interests, and vows
   That on a Future reckon!
See ye not young morning's *or* fair nature's brows
   The hand of Chaos *or* A black Oblivion beckon?
Dread the deep ire of the Fates & Fire,
For the [prophets of evil have *del.*] prophet of evil has heard them conspire:—
     Fair the grass grows,
     Rich blooms the rose,
   And the cock crows in the morning.

Stanza 3 not in NB B, [4] in B:
3.1 stricken] foolish *del. B*   who] that *del. B*
3.3 young] sweet *del. B*
3.5 Shiver and cark] Cut loose the Ark *B*
3.7 Still] Aye *B*
3.8 Still] Rare *or* New *B*
Stanza 4 not in B; canceled stanza after stanza 1 NB B:
     By miracle we [last escaped *del.*] chanced to scape   *[Cf. stanza 4]*
       The kick of that young comet
     Who made Creation don [her *del.*] its crape
       For fear we had fallen from it.

5

Old Earth, all saintly men agree, 's
  Foredestined to the Devil:
That's the safe side of prophecy
  Which deals at large with evil.
Ye young and fair who fondle there,
The Prophet forbids, & would have ye beware:—
      Fresh the grass grows,
      Blushes the rose,
  And the cock crows in the morning.

6

His [?] vein'd old Earth had noble blood
  For many a noble story:
We saw the full years in a broadening flood
  To one great ocean-glory.
Then, with a din, of original sin,
Terrible drummings the prophets begin:

How quickly he may come again,
Is furious *or* imminent in the prophet's brain:—
    Yet fresh the grass grows
    Full blooms the rose
    And the cock crows in the morning.
Stanzas 5–7 not in NB B, B; instead in B:
                [5]
    Kick, kick no more this crazy ball,
      Old Time! for swift 'tis rolling
    Down to its sulphurous gulfs, with all
      The spheres like fire-bells tolling:
    [*space left for 6 lines*]
                [6]
  This England! shall she live the storm,
    Her thronging dangers weather?
  Her enemies more thickly swarm,
    Her sons scarce work together:
  Dissension's seed Destruction breed;
  Unanimous prophets declare 'tis decreed:
      Green her grass grows,
      Red blooms her rose,
    And her cock crows in the morning.
  Lines 1–4 of [6] *B a beginning of incomplete stanza* [3] *NB B*
  [6].2 Her thronging] And all her *NB B*

Green the grass grows
Queen is the rose,
And the cock crows in the morning.

7

And was not the story heard before?
And will it not be, after?
Mad prophets have damn'd dear Earth of yore,
And Earth has lent her laughter.
So let us say, like our forefathers grey
When the mad prophets bluster'd: and what said they?
Still the grass grows,
Still blooms the rose,
And the cock crows in the morning.

On Combe Bottom: Surrey

Hardman (see headnote on p. 829), in his account of a walking tour with GM in Surrey, May 1862, wrote of a pause on the morning of May 24 between Shere and Albury. "Presently we began an abrupt descent into a place called Combe Bottom, one of the most lovely spots in creation. Combe Bottom is one of those basins hollowed out of the chalk, with almost precipitous sides, covered with short grass at the base, but crowned with the most luxuriant foliage in every variety of tint" (*MVP*, pp. 132–33). There they lay and smoked pipes while discussing GM's aphorisms.

With tall & silent trees to guard its mounts
And dotted with the juniper & yew
Crown'd with old woods, a slope of sward in view
Runs swelling to the splendours of the South.

CREATION AND THE PROPHET

Lines probably associated with Creation and the Prophet, *NB B*, [*p. 43*]:

When prophets are *or* wax [thick as the *del.*] many as Crows at a feast,
And the long ears that listen are daily increas'd,

ON COMBE BOTTOM

MS: Yale, *pocket NB 3.*

The nightingale sings near the yellow oak:
Lifted as on an [?] cup.
You feel with Heaven alone.
Some poet might the spirit here invoke
    Calling it up,
And so bequeath his own.   10

By the Passeyr

The same Tyrolean scene is vividly described in the first paragraph of
Chapter 27 of *Vittoria* (1867). Although many castles are in view from
the city of Merano, GM probably had in mind the Castle of Sonnenberg
to which Vittoria makes her way.

This was written in the pocket notebook that GM had with him on a
walking tour with his eight-year-old son Arthur and his friend Bonaparte
Wyse in July and August of 1861. See headnote to *By the Rosanna*,
page 192.

Forth from the glaring heat,
Which bakes the mountain walls,
Ah, pleasant to bathe our feet
In the clear green pool in the midst of the falls!
Hither, day after day,
We come, my Arthur & I,
While the sun makes foambows of the spray,
Beneath the castle up in the sky.
& breasting the granite & porphyry rocks,
Streaming, eddying and tossing their locks,   10
Bellowing [?] here & shouldering there
And rounding the stone, & slipping between
And sliding over, & leaping in air,
The bodies of liquid glisten green,
Break to commingle & follow their fellows,
Plumed with foam, to the white abyss
    That through the chasm bellows
    In a passion of watery bliss.

BY THE PASSEYR

MS: Yale, *pocket NB 3.*
1 Forth from] Out of *del.*

I watch the endless flow
   And the mighty will that is here,   20
Till the spirit of waters I know,
   And clasp it without fear.

Move to your destiny springs [?] of life
And sharpen your instincts

⌒∾⌒

As I turn'd into the market-place
What, think ye, I met but a vagabond dog?
He wagg'd his tail & look'd up in my face
And straight at my heels began to jog.

I call'd him a name which he seem'd to know
For he eyed me like a good old friend
'Twas a pitiful sight to see him go;
But his limit was the market's end.

Italy

This poem was written during GM's walking tour of 1861 when Venice
was still in the possession of Austria.

This air & life of Italy
Comes sharp into me & carves clear
My northern nature perfectly.

O what frank animals are here!
With Beauty they have lived & had
Great offspring who make rich our sphere.

AS I TURN'D INTO

MS: Yale, *pocket NB 3.*

Between 3 and 4 del.:

      But I hadn't a penny to give him for pay[?]
      I never knew poverty right till then

ITALY

MS: Yale, *pocket NB 3.*

And Beauty was their mistress glad;
She cannot die; but now she wears
The look that makes a people mad.

ＣＷＭＣＯ

The pasture Alp is webbed with shade,
The white has caught a maiden's blush:
In waves of mist the pinewoods wade,
 The valleys hush.
The waves of mist descending spread
Like fingers of the starved, & show
As held the half-veiled valleys bed
 A wasting snow.

Our upper world is [*blank*]
To breathe, a gift of godhead seems.   10

In the Dry

We have the waking of an eye,
 And soon the shutting follows.
We seem but echoes of a cry
 From hillocks over hollows.
'Tis here & there the battle-dust.
 'Tis then the quiet clearance:
An endless game of cut & thrust,
 To keep a ghost's appearance.

THE PASTURE ALP

MS: Yale.

2 *Del.:* A maiden's blush the white has caught:
7 held] were *del.*

IN THE DRY

MS: Yale.

4 hillocks] mountains *del.*

In the Sap

While intently on ourselves we look,
    Scarce are we stuff for battle;
We read a grand Creation's book
    With less than brain of cattle.
This life of hand & eye & tongue,
    In heritage was given:
And look we forward for the young,
    We plant a star in heaven.

⟨✠⟩

Were men of such importance as they deem,
Earth might look sad on them for being unread
So long: so long perversely written dead;
A stepping-stone, if that, to the Supreme:
More oft a block, or a misleading beam.
She has her wheel to spin, he[r] weft to thread,
And sings the while: her work supplies them bread;
Her gifts comprise the mastery of her theme.
Thus have they life, & labour clear before
Their faces, with the crown of labour shown   10
In glimpses where the tangled woodway thins.
But fables, built of old perceptive sins
Against her laws, have barred an inward door
Between them & their God: each hugs his own.

IN THE SAP

MS: Yale.

1 While] My friend, *del.* While   look] think *or* look
2 Scarce are we] We are not *del.*
3 We read] Across *or* We read   book] brink *del.*
6 In] For *or* In
7 forward for] ever to *or* forward for

WERE MEN OF SUCH IMPORTANCE

MS: Yale.

13 inward] iron *del.*

Ah for that time when open daylight pours
On multitudes that from our clouds emerge,
And men assured of their foundations urge,
Like the discoverers of new seas, to shores
Past thoughts of men who sick with sores
Feel Life as the disease, hail Death for purge.
At seasons we seem nearing to the verge;
Still is it ocean; ply we constant oars.
The faith we have drinks hourly from a source
Plain to the sight as green field & blue vault.   10
Not to that marriage does it cry divorce
Between the mind & senses

Wind & sea are as playmates
    Reviving an ancient affection:
Lovers they are, & the breeze
    Combs out the beard of the wave;
Ripples & smoothes to a mirror
    Its breast, until old recollection
Dreams of the peace of the vale,
    Dance & the pastoral stave.

AH FOR THAT TIME

MS: Yale, *verso of " Were men of such importance."*

2 clouds] wood *del.*
5 Past] Passing all *or* Past   sick with sores] ply their oars *del.*
8 ply we constant] still we ply our *del.*
10 Plain to the] As plain to *or* Plain to the   vault] sky *or* vault
After 10 del.:

                    The senses married to the mind at fault
                    The mind to senses married no divorce

WIND & SEA

MS: Yale.

3 breeze] breezelets *del.*
4 Combs] Comb *del.*
6 breast] face *or* breast
7 vale] valleys *del.*

Prestige

I

In Eastern climes was once a cock, whose fame
Exceeded that of monarchs in their might.
He called the morning, & the morning came;
    He ceased, and it was night.

II

His plunge matched the waters poured aglow
From sunrise, clapping wing or airing leg;
And every time his ladies heard him crow,
    They went & laid an egg.

III

Full sooth he was a jewel bird to own;
The wealth he brought in worship was repaid:
When men beheld him scratching at his throne,
    They kissed the dust he made.

Aimée

On that great night of her success,
When by her mirror she disrobed;
A finger's dubitative press
She laid on her pulse, as one who probed,

PRESTIGE

MS: Yale.

AIMÉE

MS: Yale.
1 that] the *del.*
2 When by] Before *del.*
4 She laid] Laid *del.*

Yet found no shot, nor sounded the deep void;
And sternly at the reflex of her frown
She gazed unthinking, save that unenjoyed
Was now the ripe fruit showering down,
Once coveted, too long witheld;
Sharp with the pain of pleasure dead.   10

Windy Haymaking

'Tis murk upon the hills, but scarce a drop is flung,
Nor down the sombre wood descends the pigeon-breast
Of cloud to moistness turned, with vapour-feathers hung,
As when we look for rain: between the south & west.

Old Richard & his wife have seven children, strong
As little ponies each to help at work & eat.
The host are out afield & tossing with the prong
Their lumps of hay whose wisps fly scattered like to sleet.

John, John of Ottenhaw!
When he was wild he knew no law:
The devil in him drove him round
To plague the lives on English ground.
Away from him ran wife & maid,
And slammed the doors & peeped afraid:
In twos & threes the keepers went:
He thanked them for the compliment.

AIMÉE
9 witheld *sic*

WINDY HAYMAKING
MS: Yale.
1 scarce] not *or* scarce
4 between the south] the wind is high *or* between the south
8 scattered] driven *or* scattered

JOHN, JOHN
MS: Yale.

For any save a lover,
    Your smile might have a meaning;
But naught will he discover
    Who doats to rend the screening.
I see, nor crave it franker,
    Nor claim the glassed emotion,
A smile that rides at anchor
    Upon the smoothest ocean.

Is luring there, & treason?
    And wreck when tempest rages?   10
I make it my glad season,
    And more do not the sages.
Then flowerful glow the garden,
    The orchard-promise fruity!
Though I be not their warden,
    For me is all the beauty.

Sonnet
to J. M.

This sonnet should be related to GM's letter to John Morley of March 23, 1871, in which he answered a letter from Morley that had hurt him deeply. Morley had written that for the past six months GM's manner of speaking had clashed with his own "opinions, ideas, and likings" in such a way that he no longer profited by their conversation. The breach was not healed until Morley began the serialization of *Beauchamp's Career* in the *Fortnightly* in 1874.

Brave is the sight when as a champion tall
You challenge your meek friend's indecent spleen.
Because his countrymen to him have been
In these late days no model wherewithal

FOR ANY SAVE A LOVER

MS: Yale.

SONNET TO J. M.: BRAVE IS THE SIGHT

MS: Yale.

The Muse might sing of them & singing call
The Heavens to witness that their hearts live green
Even as their fields are: Oh! your wit is keen.
Defending them they back you like a wall.

I am o'ermastered: I with modest stealth,
Admire your stand heroic, knowing you try   10
Strenuously with full conscience to resist
Those truths which arm the offended satirist
Who asks for virtue & they show him wealth:
Go: pass your camel through the needle's eye.

Fall'n Is Lucifer

I take this poem to be a tribute to Victor Hugo, who died on May 22,
1885. He and Léon Gambetta, the "Chief" of stanza II, line 1, had been
the republican heroes of the siege of Paris, 1870–71.

GM's manuscript, marked by a printer, is unsigned, and the poem may
have appeared anonymously.

I

Before Sunrise, ere Colour sprang
To fire a people needing spur,
Our Morning Star of Freedom sang:
Before Sunrise, ere Colour sprang.
Name us the voice that now we hear?
——Fall'n, fall'n is Lucifer!

II

His lyre beside his Chief's harangue
Was wine with bread, and he could stir
A lifeless body under fang
(Before Sunrise, ere Colour sprang),
To fling the hideous ravener.
——Fall'n, fall'n is Lucifer!

FALL'N IS LUCIFER

MS: Yale, *fair copy with printer's marks.*
II.5 fling] spurn *del.*

III

No more the lark where vapours hang,
One is he of those hosts which were
Rebels of Light, with metal clang
Before Sunrise, ere Colour sprang
The Singer of the wolf & cur.
——Fall'n, fall'n is Lucifer!

Events in a Rustic Mirror

Because of his financially ruinous extravagances and wild rages, King
Louis II of Bavaria had been declared insane by his doctors. Three days
after his uncle assumed the regency he drowned himself in the
Starnbergersee, June 13, 1886. Although in his own day he was renowned
for his expenditures on public buildings, he is now chiefly remembered
as the patron of Richard Wagner.

I

We heard of that king & his building
Of palaces high overhead,
With fortunes laid out on the gilding:
And just like the ornaments placed on your shelf,
The actors and Plays he had all to himself:
Then agape we all read
He was dead!

FALL'N IS LUCIFER
III.2 of] with *del.*
III.3 metal] cymbals *del.*

EVENTS IN A RUSTIC MIRROR

MS: Yale, *fair copy corrected.*
I.5 and Plays] and *del.* Plays
I.6 agape we all] we gapingly *del.*

II

The gold of Australian diggers
Seemed coppers to what he flung round
On beautiful paintings & figures.
Right over the big snowy mountains at night
His carriage drove flashing electrical light.
Till in horror they found
Their king drowned.

III

His bedroom was awful: to match it
Museums might pour in a tide
And never half floor it or match it.
He walked on a terrace as rich as the Thames;
He looked across earth through a fountain of gems.
And the reason he died?
Suicide!

IV

It came of his reading Romances
And being a king to create
The wonders that jumped in his fancies.
They burst him straight up, like a place undermined.
A wife might have helped, but he hated the kind;
Ran alarmed from a mate.
What a fate!

V

For any such phantasmagory,
The moral is done by a shrug,
To follow the clap of the story.

II.3 beautiful] his *del.* beautiful
II.6 Till] And *or* Till
II.7 Their king] He lay *del.*
III.5 He looked] Looking out *del.*
III.6 And the reason] Now declare how *del.*
IV.6 alarmed] away *del.*

When hearing of millionaires running amuck,
You know they were hoisted to teach us our luck,
    Lift our girl & our mug
    In one hug.

Karl Onyx

GM wrote to George Stevenson on February 16, 1887, "Perhaps, If
I am not driven to the novel, I shall be at a Poem treating of all the
Explosives in the modern mind and manufactories: The Anarchiad. What
do you say?—The hero, Karl Onyx, has as many adventures as Odysseus.
I am at times moved strongly by the theme."

Down lay Karl Onyx for his end of time.
Germania led him at her apron-string,
An infant; Gallia housed him in his prime.
America, beneath her starry wing,
Gave shelter to the fighting man; & last,
The bosom of Britannia let him chafe
For leverage to those upliftings vast,
Whereon he schemed, the giant & the waif.

ᕲᕽᕽᕽᕽᕽᕲ

I looked from the book of the story of men,
To clouds that flew over corn in sheaves.
My look was dropped on the book again,
And clouds went winging across the leaves.

A winnowing breath of our red-veined day
Blew dust from the blood gone dry in deeds.

EVENTS IN A RUSTIC MIRROR
V.7 one] a *del.*

KARL ONYX
MS: Yale.

I LOOKED FROM THE BOOK
MS: Yale.
Between 4 and 5 del.:

        no more on a page
        Then flat on a page no longer[?] gray,
        The story

Fragments of the Iliad in English Hexameter Verse

The following heretofore unpublished fragments of the *Iliad* that are written in ink date from 1890 when GM was busy translating Homer; those in pencil and the penciled corrections are in a more faltering, therefore a later, hand.

On April 3, 1891, just before Clement K. Shorter printed two lots of GM's translation in the *Illustrated London News*, April 11 and 18, GM wrote him that he had more of the fragments and that a review had expressed interest in them. Shorter, however, should have the first option. Although Shorter was enthusiastic about GM's translations, no more of them were printed in the *News* or elsewhere. The fragments that Shorter did print were included in *A Reading of Life* (1901). For the high regard in which GM held them, see headnote on page 695.

The Vengeance of Apollo

i.43

So spake he, supplicating; and him heard Phoibos Apollo.
Down from the peaks of Olympus the God came, ire in his bosom,
Over his shoulders bearing a bow and a close-covered quiver,
Whereof loudly the darts on the back of the God being ireful,
Rattled in onward motion; his coming was like to the nightfall.
Off one stretch from the vessels he sat, forthwith loosed an arrow.
Then was the clang of the argent arc a resounder terrific;
Mules, as it happed, & the fleet-foot dogs were the first of his
     victims

FRAGMENTS OF THE ILIAD
MSS: Yale.

ILIAD i.43: THE VENGEANCE OF APOLLO
Two MS drafts, both fair copies corrected; MS 2, copy-text.
1 supplicating] supplicatory *MS 1*   and him] him [then *del.*] *MS 1*
3 Over his shoulders bearing a] Bearing *or* Armed, flung o'er his shoulders, [a *del.*] with *MS 1*
4 back of the God] shoulders of him *MS 1*
6 forthwith] & forthwith *or* away *MS 1*
7 resounder] resounding *del.* resound *MS 1*
8 fleet-foot] darting *MS 1*

But, full soon, now, the God, letting fly a keen barb at the armed
    men,
Smote; aye then on the pyres smoked burnings of numberless
    corpses.   10

[Assembly of the Achaians]

ii.87

Even as when you behold hot swarms of the tribes of the wild bees
Burst from their nest in a hollow rock incessantly outward;
These fly forth o'er the meads & in clusters fall on the Spring-
    flowers;
Lo, & the hosts of them fly this way; & they fly away yonder;
So those numerous tribes of the people from ships & from shelters,
Fronting the deep strand, marched in their companies orderly forth
    right
Up to the place of assembly; glittering Fame, too, among them,
Messenger of the God, urged them on; so together they gathered.
Tumult reigned in the place when the hosts took seats, & the earth
    groaned
Under them, loud was the uproar; then did the cry of heralds   10
Strive with shrill shouting to tone them to silence, if that their
    clamour
Could be held in, & the people hearken their kings who were God-
    reared.

ILIAD ii.87: [ASSEMBLY OF THE ACHAIANS]

Working draft, in pencil.

1 hot] thick *or* hot
2 a] the *del.*
3 o'er the] in their *del.*
6 strand] shore *or* strand   forth right] onward *or* forth right
8 the God] Zeus *or* the God
10 the cry of] nine *or* the cry of
12 reared] led *or* reared

Helen on the Skaian Gates

iii.141

Forthwith readily swathing her head in a sheeny fine linen,
Quick out stepped from her chamber, & dropped a big tear so
    doing:
Not unattended, for handmaids twain did her footing close follow.
Aithre, daughter of Pitthêus, she, Klymené, too, the ox-eyed.
Soon thereupon in their haste they approached the Dardanian
    gateways.
So now gathered round Priam & Panthoos, therewith Thymoites,
Lampos, Klytios tall, Hiketaon, a scion of Arés,
Oukalegon, therewith too Antenor, both very clear-headed,
Sat o'er the gates named Skaian assembled the chiefs of the people
    in council;
Resting from war, in the years' full measure, but speakers
    persuasive   10
Were they, like to cicadae, which up some tree of the woodland
Sit on a branch, where they chirp forth notes lily-sweet, lily-slender.
Such ranked there on the tower were the Council-heads of the
    Trojans.

Working draft, corrected in pencil.

1 readily] quickly *del.*   fine] white *del.*
2 Quick out stepped] Hastened *or* Quick out stepped   from her] out of the *del.*
3 Not] Nor *del.*   did her footing close follow] her footing close followed *del.*
5 in their haste they approached the Dardanian gateways] *or* the place where the high
Skaian gates were *or* came they to the place of the high Skaian gates *or* did they come to
where were the Skaian gateways *or* they came to where were the Skaian gateways *or* in
their haste they approached the Dardanian gateways
6 So now gathered round] Now encompassing *or* So now gathered round
7 Klytios tall] & Klytios *del.*
8 therewith too] therewith *del.*
9 gates named Skaian] Skaian gates *del.*   the chiefs of the people in council] assembled
the people's elders *or* the chiefs of the people in council
10 years' full measure] course of the years *or* years' full measure
11 like to cicadae, which up] & like to cicadae that up in *del.*
12 where they] & *del.*
13 ranked there] seated then *or* ranked there

So now when these had looked on Helen beneath them
    approaching,
Low the winged words breathed they & in hearing the one of the
    other.

"Blame can we not the Trojans nay, nor the bright-greaved
    Achaians,
"That for the sake of yon woman, long they have suffered such
    evils.
"Fearfully like in her aspect she to the Goddesses deathless!
"Still even so, she such as we see, let her back in the vessels,
"Rather than bring us ruin, to us & our dear children
    thereafter."   20

    So then they spake. And Priam meanwhile by her name called
        to Helen:
"Here in the front take seat, dear my child, since that thou hast
    come hither,
"Here look on thy first husband, thy kinsfolk, & all thy beloved
    ones
("Guilty to me thou'rt not, 'tis the Gods in good truth who have
    wronged me.
"They who have brought upon me this much-bewept war with
    Achaians),
"So can'st thou name me now the towering warrior yonder;
"Who may he be, this Achaian hero so grand & excelling:
"True, there are others about exceed him in tallness of stature,

15 breathed they &] they breathed *del.*
16 nay, nor] nor either *or* nay, nor
17 long] so *del.* long
18 aspect] appearance is *del.*
19 she] & *del.* she
20 ruin, to] to ruin *del.*   dear children thereafter] children after *or* dear children
thereafter
21 her name] name *del.*
22 take seat] be seated *or* take seat   that thou] thou *del.*
23 look on] to behold *del.*   & all thy] & thy *del.*
24 thou'rt not, 'tis] thou art not *del.*   who] 'tis *del.*
25 this] the *del.*

"But until now these eyes have not looked upon any so
     handsome,
"Nor so impressive: a royal man is he truly to look on."   30

     Helen, then, peerless of women, to him in these words made
          her answer:
"Thou, dear sire of my lord, thou art reverend to me & awful:
"More should have pleased me bitter death, when that I followed
     hither
"Him thy son, forsaking my nuptial bed, & my brothers,
"Darling my daughter, & them, those dear fellows in age, full of
     graces!
"But it was not so; and that it was not, I sicken with weeping.
"Let me now tell thee the things thou askest of me for instruction.
"Yon is Atreidés, he the broad of rule lord Agamemnon,
"Good full sure as a ruler & strong as a warrior he, both:
"Brother by marriage of mine, me shameless, if such one was
     ever."   40

     So ran her words: & the old man marvelled to gaze on him,
          crying:
"Happy art thou, Son of Atreus, blest at thy birth, heaven guided.
"Many in truth are the numbers of those young Achaians, thy
     subjects.
"I too in the old time unto Phrygia, land of the vine, came,
"Where did I see the Phrygians plentiful, men of fleet coursers,

29 upon any] upon one *del.* on one *del.*
31 her answer] answer *del.*
32 thou art reverend to me & awful] by me art revered & dreaded *or* thou art reverend to
me & awful
34 bed, & my] bed, my *del.*
35 those dear] my *or* those dear
36 I] do *del.* I
38 he the] the *del.*   broad of rule] wide-ruling *del.*
39 full sure] indeed *del.*   ruler] king *or* ruler
40 shameless] wanton *or* shameless
42 guided] favoured *del.*
43 those young] young *del.*
44 unto] to *del.*

"People of Otrêus and the men too of eminent Mygdon,
"Who down lengths of the banks of Sangarios had their
            encampment:
"For, I being then an ally, they counted me one of their number,
"On that day when the man-like Amazons came to attack them:
"Yet not they were so many as many the glad-eyed Achaians."   50

        Secondly, there on, sceing Odysseus, the old man did
            question:
"Come now, dear child, & of this one tell me, & who may be
            this one;
"Shorter he by a head than Atreidés, Agamemnon,
"But to behold in the measure of shoulders & chest fully bigger.
"He on the pregnant earth has laid down the weight of his armour,
"While, and like unto a ram, those warriors' rank-lengths he
            ranges;
"Striking my sight as a very ram of a thick growth of fleeces,
"Busy to form here, there, a great flock of sheep whitely shining."

        Then unto him did Helen, the daughter of Zeus, make her
            answer:
"That one next is the wary Odysseus, the son of Laertes,   60
"Reared on the hard-rock soil of Ithaca, though 'tis so barren,
"He at command holds every wile & the counsels of wisdom."

46 People] Teeming people *or* People   and the men too of eminent] & eminent *or* &
them too of eminent *or* and the men too of eminent
47 down lengths of] alength down *or* down lengths of   their encampment] encamp-
ment *del.*
48 I being] being *del.*   one of] of *del.*
50 so many] many *del.*
51 on] upon *del.*   did question] questioned *del.*
52 & who] who *del.*
53 Atreidés] the son of Atreus *del.*
54 fully] far *or* mighty *or* fully
55 pregnant earth has laid down] bountiful earth has laid *or* pregnant earth has laid
down
56 unto] to *del.*   those warriors' rank-lengths] the warriors' ranks *or* those warriors'
rank-lengths
58 here, there] here & there *del.*   whitely] white *del.*
59 the daughter] daughter *del.*   her answer] answer *del.*
61 hard-rock soil] rocky ground *del.*   'tis so] so *del.*

Then responding to her did utter clear-headed Antenor:
"Lady, the word thou speakest, it is most truthfully spoken:
"Hither in past days once did journey the godlike Odysseus,
"Missioned to treat in thy case, & with Arés-beloved Menelaos:
"Them in my halls I welcomed as guests & I did entertain kindly,
"Whereby learned I the nature of each in his counsels of wisdom.
"Now when the two stood mixed in all the crowd of the Trojans,
"Standing upright, Menelaos was marked for the breadth of his
    shoulders,
"But, when the two took seats, then the far more majestic
    Odysseus.
"Natheless when in our presence they wove at the web of their
    speeches,
"True, Menelaos then had consecutive flow in haranguing,
"Brief, truly, but to the point, for he was a man most laconic,
"Not of the emptily voluble, though in his years he the younger.
"Yet when rose in his turn to address us the wary Odysseus,
"Still he stood, & down did he look, with his eyes fixed
    earthward,
"Swayed not the sceptre backward & forward, but had it stiff out
    so;
"You would have said he was dumb in a fury, perchance idiotic;

                                                  70

62 holds] has *del.*
63 did utter clear-headed] said thoughtfully *del.* thoughtful-minded *or* did say *del.* utter clear-headed
65 in past days once did journey the godlike] already of old [has come the divine *del.*] *or* once in old days did journey the godlike *or* in past days once did journey the godlike
66 in thy case] for thee *or* in thy case   -beloved]-loved *del.*
67 I did entertain] entertained *del.*
69 in all the crowd of the] among the assembled *or* in all the crowd of the
70 the] his *del.*   his shoulders] shoulders *del.*
71 took seats] were seated *or* took seats   then] the *del.*   the far more] more *or* the far more
72 Natheless when in our presence] When however before us *or* Natheless when in our presence
73 then had] had then a *del.*
74 most laconic] laconic *del.*
76 Yet when rose in his] But when had risen in *del.*
77 Still] Blunt *or* Still
79 perchance idiotic] & likewise witless *or* likewise idiotic *or* mayhap idiotic *or* perchance idiotic

"But when indeed came forth his mighty voice [from] his bosom,   80
"On it the words which seemèd to fall as the snows fall in winter
"Then with yonder Odysseus none could dispute among mortals:
"Then that form of Odysseus no way more excited amazement."

     Thirdly, further, observing Aias, the old man did question:
"Who may then be this Achaian hero so splendid & mighty,
"Who by a head & broad shoulders outdoes all the crowd of the
       Argives?"

     Him then that long-robed Helen replied to, the peerless of
       women:
"This is the towering Aias, bulwark he of all Achaians:
"Idomeneus on the farther side, mid his Cretans, & god-like,
"Stands: & around him throng the principal chiefs of the Cretans.   90
"Often has Menelaos, Ares-beloved, entertained him
"In our house, whensoever from Crete to our land he made voyage.
"Now one & other are clear to me, all of the glad-eyed Achaians,
"Whom I could read right well, & tell off their names in
       succession.
"But I have failed to set eyes on that pair of chiefs in the army,
"Kastor, tamer of horses, & Polydeukés, the brave boxer,
"Brothers of mine, whom to me did the one sole mother give
       birth to.

80 came forth his mighty voice] he had sent [his grand *del.*] voice [forth of *del.*] his & *or*
came forth his mighty voice
81 snows fall in winter] wintry snowflakes *del.*
82 yonder] that *del.*   none could] could no other *del.* could none *del.*
83 that] the *or* that   way more] longer *del.*
84 did question] questioned *del.*
86 crowd] rest *del.*
88 he of all] of the *or* he of all
89 & god-like] god-like *del.*
90 throng] are gathered *del.* crowd *del.*
92 In] There in *or* Home in *or* In   land] shores *del.*   made voyage] voyaged *or*
made voyage
95 that pair of] those two *or* that pair of
97 the one] one *del.*

Night Watch of the Trojans before Troy

viii.542

Tennyson had translated this passage into blank verse (*Cornhill*, December 1863) with a prose note declaring his allegiance to blank verse rather than hexameters for the translation of Homer into English. It was included in the *Enoch Arden* volume (1864).

Hector spake to them thus, & the Trojans cheered with applauses.
Straightway then from the yoke did they loosen their ranked
    sweating horses;
Then tethered they with the thongs each one to the lock of its
    war-car.
Oxen, good grand sheep of a size, did they drive from the town-
    gates
Speedily; heart-enlivening wine too they fetched from their
    homesteads;
Bread therewith, & moreover they gathered them bundles of
    firewood.
Forth on the winds from the plains to the heavens went up the
    sweet savour.
These now big in their minds lay stretched on the field of the
    conflict
All through night, & mid-army the flames rose of many a
    watchfire;
Even as when in the heavens seen high do the stars round the
    lustrous   10
Moon shine glorious out, when the air it has fallen to windless;
When all the hill-tops clear shadow forth, & the horns of the
    headlands,
Into the glens, too, & deep ope the heavens to infinite aether,

Fair copy.
4 good] & good *del.*   the] their *del.*
10 in the heavens seen high do] seen high in the heavens *or* in the heavens seen high do

Hosts of the stars shine forth, and the shepherd's heart it is
    gladdened;
So in like numbers between beached ships & the Xanthian
    streamlets,
Shone against Ilion's face those fires lit ablaze by the Trojans.
Fires, bright thousands burned on the plains, & the men in their
    fifties
Sate there nigh by the flames, in the light of the strong burning
    firebrands.
Meanwhile the close-tethered coursers, standing ranked by their
    war-cars,
Champed the white barley & spelt, there waiting the fair-thronèd
    morning.   20

Odysseus Encircled

xi.411

Now as he rolled these matters within him in heart & in spirit
During the space came under their round shields the Trojans.
Him they shut up in their midmost, pulling a scourge in among
    them.
So, as when round some boar the dogs & the lithe blooming
    youngsters
Quicken their steps, & when he forth out of his lair in deep
    forest,
Whets him the sharp white tusk twixt the crook of his jaws, &
    around him

———

14 Hosts of the stars shine forth] Showing hosts of the stars *or* Hosts of the stars shine
forth

ILIAD xi.411: ODYSSEUS ENCIRCLED

Working draft, in pencil.

2 *Del.:* Meanwhile behind their shields came on the ranks of the Trojans.   under]
covered *del.* under
3 midmost] centre *or* midmost   scourge in among] bane amid *or* scourge in among
4 some] a *del.*
5 steps] pace *or* steps   when he forth] he from *del.*
6 him] the *del.*   twixt] between *del.*

Rushing they press, & the hard-ground of tusks as they gnash
    sounds from under,
They meanwhile hold their ground, for the look of him
    seemeth most fearful;
Thus then the cherished of Zeus, him Odysseus, the Trojans
    encircled.

xi.462

Thrice gave he cry, full loud as the head of a mortal can hurl
    forth;
Thrice was it heard by the great Menelaos, the cherished of Ares;
Thereat forthwith he spake unto Aias, close at his elbow:
"Aias, issue of Zeus, son of Telamon, captain of numbers,
"Up round my ears there has come like the cry of stout-hearted
    Odysseus
"Like unto that, as though ringed-round he stood mid the
    Trojans, & single,
"Harried, cut off in the last fierce press of the fight, from his
    fellows,
"Into the thick let us go, for our part it is now to stand by him.
"Brave as he is, I fear me that mid of the Trojans a mishap
"May have befallen him, then were a heavy grief on the
    D[anaan."]   10
    Saying it, forth stepped he, & the godlike man at his heels
    went.

---

7 hard-ground] grinding of *del.*
8 their] to *del.* their   seemeth] being *del.*
9 *Del.:* Thus then the Trojans beset the cherished of Zeus, Odysseus.

ILIAD xi.462: ODYSSEUS ENCIRCLED

Working draft, in pencil.
1 full] as *del.* & *del.*   forth] its *del.*
3 unto] to *del.*   close] even *del.*
5 come] come *or* broke[?]   stout-hearted Odysseus] Odysseus seems *or* stout-hearted
Odysseus
6 & single] single *del.*
9 mid of the] among those *del.*   a mishap] an evil *del.*
10 were a heavy grief] would a great grief be *or* were [a] heavy [grief]
11 stepped he] he stepped *del.*   at his heels went] followed with *or* at his heels went

Soon came they on Odysseus, the cherished of Zeus, by the
    Trojans
Dogged all about, as the bloodied jackals that round on an
    antlered
Stag on the mountains, the which now a man with a shaft from
    his bow-string
Sorely hath struck, & in sooth with the speed of his feet then he
    flees it
Long as the blood it is warm, & long as his knees they will bear
    him:
So & so on till he drops at the last, by the fleet dart is mastered.
On a dark wood on the heights then him do the flesh-gnawing
    jackals
Rend: & so thither is fate-led then fate a great ravageing lion;
Sooth, and the jackals are scattered right left, but the meal is
    the lion's;   20
So thus rounding the wary Odysseus, the crafty in counsel,
Many numbered & stout were the Trojans; but ever that hero
Warded the pitiless day with the quick-rushing thrusts of his ˙
    spear-head.

Achilles over the Trench

xviii.202

Under the same title Tennyson had translated this passage into blank
verse (*Nineteenth Century*, August 1877). It was included in *Ballads and
Other Poems* (1880).

ILIAD xi.462: ODYSSEUS ENCIRCLED
12 came they] they came *del.*
13 bloodied jackals that] bloody jackals *del.*
14 *After* mountains,] wounded *del.* thick *del.*   now] doth *del.* now
17 So] On *or* So   he drops at the last] at last he drops *del.*
19 fate-led] led by *or* fate-led
20 and] then *del.*   but] & *del.*
21 rounding] round *del.*
22 numbered] number *del.*

Thus having said, forthwith on her way went quick-footed Iris.
Then did Achilles, dear unto Zeus, uprise; and around him Athene
Over his powerful shoulders planted her bright-fringèd aegis;
She, the most holy of Goddesses, rounding his head then a
    golden
Cloud spread, kindling the flame of it into a wide-raying
    brilliance.
Now, as when up from a town comes a smoke forth, mounting to
    aether,
Out of an isle far distant, set round about it with foemen,
All through day do the townsfolk carry on hideous warfare,
Makeing their sallies; but they full soon at the sun's going
    downward
Light up their close-rowed beacon-fires, so that the blaze of them
    high lifts,   10
Thence to be seen of the neighbour coastmen, hopeful if, mayhap,
Those in their vessels be drawn to protect that town from
    destruction;
So from Achilles' head went the radiance shooting up skyward.
Now having come to the trench outside of the wall, there he stood
    fast,

Nor with Achaians mixed, for wise knew he his mother's
    injunction.

Sole there standing he shouted; his voice then did Pallas Athene
Double afar; & the Trojans roused he to terrified tumult.
Even as when sharp clear, when a clarion's note has resounded
Out of the midst of the foemen rounding a city, destroyers,
Not less clear o'er the host did the shrill voice of Aiakides ring.   20
So when the brazen shout of Aiakides then had these heard,

Fair copy.

4 most holy] the divinest *or* most holy
12 that] their *or* that
16 Sole there standing] Standing sole there *del. This correction was made years later in
GM's shakiest hand with the purple crayon that he used for correcting proof.*

All in their souls were aghast; & the fair-maned horses for presage
Bodeful took it at heart, & they swung round their chariots
    backward.
Frighted the charioteers were to see the inveterate fire rise,
Terribly off that head of the great-hearted issue of Peleus
Burning, kindled to blaze by the Goddess, blue-eyed Athene.
Thrice then over the trench big shouts raised god-like Achilles;
Thrice fell the Trojan host & their brilliant allies in confusion.
There too perished then by the jam of the spears & the car-wheels
Twelve of their choicest heroes. But now the exulting Achaians   30
Drew Patroklos out of the flight of the darts; on a litter
Laid they him; & about him, bewailing him, stood his dear
    comrades;
Mid them swift-footed Achilles followed, hot tears from his eyes
    poured
Streaming at sight of his faithful comrade prone on the bier there,
Pierced by the sharp bronze through; whom he sent with his horses
    & war-car
Forth to the fight, no more his returning to greet with the welcome.

The Shield of Achilles

xviii.478

First then made he a big strong shield, with his cunningest
    craft-skill
Wrought all over, and thereabout round it all put he a
    threefold
Bright shineing rim most brilliant, & there hung a fair silver
    baldrick.
So, now, the shield itself was of five layers made, & so made he
Cunning devices thereon full many from out his own shrewd wit.

ILIAD xviii.202: ACHILLES OVER THE TRENCH

31 darts] shafts *or* darts

ILIAD xviii.478: THE SHIELD OF ACHILLES

Fair copy.

On it wrought he the earth, & the heavens, also the sea-waters;
Wrought he the inexhaustible sun, the moon waxing to fulness;
Wrought he the various constellations there crowning the sky-vault,
Pleiades, also Hyades, & with them too the might of Orion.
There too the Bear, that is likewise known for the Wain, for a
    surname,   10
Turning, she, in her place, & Orion ever observing;
She of them all there the sole one barred from the baths of the
    Ocean.
      On it moreover he wrought two beautiful cities of menfolk.
So, now, further, in one were espousals, festival banquets;
Forth under flameing torches the brides were led out of their
    chambers
Down through the streets, & a many-voiced bridal-song rose
    around them;
Youths whirled there in the dance, & from out of their midst
    lutes and lyres rang
High, & the women each one at their doors hung looking with
    wonder.
There in the market-place was a crowd of the folk, & a quarrel
Surged: two men had a quarrel between them because of a ransom 20
Due for a slain man; one of them vowed he had given the whole
    price,
Showing it so to the folk; that other denied aught for handfast.
Both then shouted for having an end of it, fronting an umpire.
So, now, the crowd took sides there, & pleaded for each one with
    outcries;
Then did the heralds tone down the people, & so then the elders
Sat upon smooth stone seats in the circle inviolate, seated
Holding up in their hands those staves of the shrilly-voiced
    heralds;
Therewith, followed it, rose they in order, delivering judgement.
Now there were placed two talents of gold in their midmost, the
    guerdon
Placed to be given to him whose cause the best answered to justice. 30
    Round, now, the second city two armies of men had
      encampment,

Splendid in arms. And between them they urged two different
     projects,
Either to doom it to sack or to share fair measure in portions
Whatso for plunder the pleasant city contained within walls there;
Nay, but of yielding thought not the men therein, stealthy for
     ambush
Armed they, sooth, while their own dear wives & their little
     ones, infants,
Mingled with men that were aged, stood up on the walls to defend
     them.
On came the others; their heads were Ares & Pallas Athene,
Both gold figures, & having to clothe them both golden vesture,
Goodly & grand to behold with their arms, right fully to Gods
     like,   40
Seen most eminent round o'er the field, & the troops were
     diminished.
So, then, when these reached the point where an ambuscade
     seemed inviteing,
Hard by a stream's ford, down where the cattle had water in
     common,
There did they make their seat, clad all in a metal that glittered.
So, now, they placed two scouts of their body away at a distance,
Look-outs, watchful for seeing the crook-horned oxen & sheep
     come.
Soon, then, did these come on, & in company followed two
     shepherds,
Cheered by their play on the reed-pipes, little foreseeing a trap
     laid.
Right so ran, having spied these things, all the rest, & delayed not
Straightway to cut off the oxen-herds & the flocks of the fair white   50
Sheep; furthermore did they slay those shepherds. When the
     besieged ones
Heard, being then in the place of debate, great noise of a tumult
Raised by the pasture-beasts, on the instant sallied they outward,
Mounted on high-stepping chargers fleet, & were speedily present.
There, taking place by the stream's banks, ready they stood for the
     combat.

Each then smote at the other with thrusts of the bronze-pointed
    spear-heads.
'Mid them was Strife, 'mid them Discord there, & the cruel Death-
    Goddess,
Grasping one with a quick wound, one unharmed, & she dragged
    one
On by his feet through the dust-raised length of the battle, a dead
    man;
She round her shoulders a garment wore all bloody with man's
    blood.   60
So, then, they hurtled even as do live mortals, & battled,
So dragged on & along there of each one's slaughtered the corpses.
    Moreover, thereon set he a field, fat fallows for tillage,
Broad, thrice ploughed, & of husbandmen in the field there were
    numbers
Turning the yoke's course, pushing it up & down onward before
    them.
These, when came they close on the verge of the field for the
    wheel round,
Straightway met them a man, & he into their hands gave a goblet
Charged with a honey-sweet wine; but the foremost turned to
    the furrows,
Longing to get to the term of their hard day's work in the plough-
    field.
Now, all this, sheer gold though it was, dark stood at its
    background,   70
Seeming a ploughed field verily; that above all was the marvel.
    Moreover, thereon set he a close of tall grain, & the reapers
Plied at their reapers' work, with the sharp-edged sickles in hand
    there,
Armfuls thick on the lines of the furrows their lengths to the
    ground fell;
Some lay strewn, that the sheaf-binders gathered & bound-up in
    straw-bands.
Three of the sheaf-binders on one side, & ever behind them

63 fat fallows] soft earth, fat *or* fat fallows
72 close] square *or* close

Boys fast gathered the cornstalks, ceaselessly bring their armfuls
Up to be bound; & the lord of it stood mid-field where the
      swathes lay,
Holding his staff in attentive silence, in heart very joyful.
Now, hard by did the heralds dress the feast under an oak-tree,   80
They having killed a big sacrificial ox; and the women
Mixed much meal of the barley white for the labourers' supper.
    Moreover, thereon set he, with vines of large clusters, a
        vineyard,
Golden, lovely to see, & the grapes up the rows they were black
      ones;
Nay, but of solid silver for them to cling to were the vine-props.
Round it a steel-blue ditch he drew, over about was a fence-work
Fashioned of tin; & there led to the vineyard one single pathway,
That which the bearers took at the vintageing time in the
      vineyard.
Maidens & adolescents, cheerfully-minded, were there, too,
Bearing the sweet fruit piled high up in the fair-plaited baskets.   90
Them did a boy in their midst enchant with a silvery hand-lute,
Makeing a pleasant music; he sang them a sweet song of Linos,
Pitched in a delicate voice; & then those all strikeing in
      common,
Followed with song & with hum, & with jumps of their feet to the
      measure.
    Also a herd of the kine having high-raised horns, on it made
      he;
Wrought all of gold & of tin were the kine, which bellowing
      dashed forth
Out of the stables & on to the pastures, nigh where a stream
      rushed
Noising on beside beds of the slender bordering reed-blades.
So, now, after the kine four shepherds came, & there followed
Close at their masters' heels nine dogs nimble-footed behind them.   100
Lo, then, a couple of frightful lions amid the kine foremost,

81 and] furthermore did *del.*
82 Mixed] Mix *del.*
99 after the] forth with *del.*

Fast held a roaring bull of the herd; & it mightily bellowed,
Tugged by the lions, & after him ran all the dogs & the
    youngsters.
Sooth, having rended the big bull's hide, did the lions devour
    him,
Swallowing entrails & black blood, vainly assailed by the
    shepherds
Crying the swift dogs on, for these shrank from the lions, not
    dareing
Bite, & they barked in a ring set close round about them, but
    held off.
    Thereon further was done by the art of the glorious Lame-
      God,
Down in a beautiful valley, a pasture spacious for white sheep,
Stables were there, too, & well-roofed huts, & were also
    enclosures.   110
    Craftily, on it the glorious Lame-God fashioned a dance-place,
Like the device, which in old time Daidalos worked with his
    cunning,
Over in spacious Knossos, for beautiful-tressed Ariadne.
Sooth, then, were there young men seen, & maidens costly for
    wooing,
All holding hands by the wrist, all stepping it out to the measure.
So, for the damsels, they wore fine veils, & the youths they
    wore tunics
Spun of rare tissue, faintly with sprinkle of oil rendered shineing;
Beautiful garlands, troth, did the girls have on, & the lads wore
Golden daggers, that hung at their sides from the silver-worked
    belt-strap.
These would now quicken their steps to a run, good sooth,
    deftly-footed.   120
Even as when at his work some leg-stretched potter his wheel holds,
Trying it, twixt both hands, so to see in the run if it goes well;
Now, at another while, ran they ranked, one another engageing.

103 ran] hied *or* ran
107 ring set] circle *or* ring set
121 leg-stretched] seated *or* leg-stretched

These, then, a numerous band that dance enchanting encircled,
Joying to view; & among them sang a most heavenly minstrel,
Strikeing the lyre; & behold, mid-circle a couple of tumblers
Played at their antics just when the note of the song was
          beginning.
          Thereon set he besides, near the thick shield's outermost
          margin,
Made so solidly strong, the full might of the river of Ocean.

[Nourishment before Battle]

xix.146

          Then unto him responding answered fleet-foot Achilles:
"Atreides, most famed of the chiefs, king of men, Agamemnon,
"Thine is the power to bestow these gifts, if thou will, as in justice,
"Or to retain them. Now, though, bethink we & quick, on the
          instant,
"How to give battle; behoves not to use fine words, here
          assembled,
"Nor to delay; yet, yet is the work to be done unaccomplished;
"So that once more be Achilles sighted ahead, mid the foremost,
"Wreaking with his bronze spear-head ruin on the ranks of the
          Trojans
"Whereof may each one of you have thought when he grapples
          his foeman."
          Then unto him responding answered the crafty Odysseus.   10

ILIAD xviii.478: THE SHIELD OF ACHILLES
128–29 *Iliad 18.607–8, also written verso of 19.146, next fragment*

ILIAD xix.146: [NOURISHMENT BEFORE BATTLE]

Working draft, in pencil.

1 fleet-foot] swift-footed *or* fleet-foot
6 to delay] be delaying *del.*   yet, yet] for yet *del.*   work to be done] great work to
do *or* work to be done
7 be Achilles sighted] shall be seen Achilles there *del.*
8 Wreaking with his bronze spear-head ruin] Dealing wrath with his brazen spear *or*
Wreaking with his bronze spear-head ruin

"Drive not thus, though of valour unequalled, godlike Achilles,
"Forth against Ilion's ramparts fasting the brave sons of
          Achaians,
"Bent to encounter the Trojans; not a short bout will the fight be
"When once meet in the shock of the strife those masses of armed
          men
"Filled by God with the fury of battle each other to slaughter.
"Rather, bid thou the Achaians now on the decks of their swift
          ships,
"Take food, drink wine; that is the fountain of strength and
          endurance;
"Empty of nourishment no man face to face fighting can hold on
"Right through the long day's length till the hour of the sun's going
          downward.
"He, though indeed he may have good heart for the strife, in his
          members   20
"Heavily weighted will feel, unwitting, & he will be sharpest,
"Stricken by hunger & thirst, & his knees in his going will give
          way.
"No, but the man well sated with wine & sufficient of victuals,
"He through the length of a day engages the foemen unwearied.
"He having, truth, in his bosom a lion's heart, & his members
"Will not fail him first, not before all have gone from the combat."

12 Forth against Ilion's ramparts fasting] Fasting, forth against Ilion's walls *or* Forth
against Ilion's ramparts fasting
16 bid thou] command *or* bid thou
18 Empty of food [there is none *del.*] no man through the long day's length can sustain
him. *or* Empty of nourishment no man face to face fighting can hold on
19 Face to face fighting throughout, till the sun's down going to darkness. *or* Right
through the long day's length till the suns going down to darkness. *or* Right through the
long day's length till the hour of the sun's going downward.
21 sharpest] stricken *or* sharpest
26 have gone] withdraw *or* have gone

What makes it hard to understand
The wailings of this modern fry?
We two have dwelt in Skylarkland,
And that must be the simple why.

We fell when time was ripe, but fell
So soft we neither knew of pain
As leave of sun the pimpernel
Takes humbly ere his cloak is rain.

Hear now the mission of good wine,
And waves to the wind our hearts respond.
If I walk earth I look for a sign
Of the journey's rest & a gleam beyond.

Dalila

Between my husband & my people, Samson,
The choice was on me like a knife's sharp edge;
And I a woman. Think of it. Either way
For me the black abyss. O, think of it! see
What narrow ridge I footed: thou, my husband;
They my own people fearing thee for life.

WHAT MAKES IT HARD
MS: Yale.
3 dwelt] been *or* dwelt
6 we] that *del.*

HEAR NOW THE MISSION OF GOOD WINE
MS: Yale.
1 Hear now] Name [me *del.*] us *or* Hear now

DALILA
MS: Yale.
1 people] country *del.*
2 knife's sharp edge] sharp-edged knife *del.*

As from the fall of candlelight
On eyelids of a dreamer, sight
Arises out of deeps to see
God, the one Reality.
Him the long Visioned; half the human aim;
Of whom in creeds we spell'd the name;
By whom were driven to do our cleansing task;
We read through Nature's callous mask,
And dreaded more than dog the whip:
More seeking to be loved of him   10
Than love to give, except by lip
Propitiating wrath & whim.

In the clear dark lake a lady dived;
And a milky meteor clove the deep,
The messenger bubbles she sent survived
For her laugh ere foam on the ripples' leap.

Gone to the Naiads, she might seem,
Counting by breath; & a sweeter one.
Something of mystery born of a dream,
She wore when she rose, though her face was fun.

AS FROM THE FALL OF CANDLELIGHT

MS: Yale.

1 As from] Lo, as *del.*
3 out of] from the *del.*
5 Him the long] The *del.*

IN THE CLEAR DARK LAKE

MS: Yale, *identical hand and ink to that of MS of the late " Youth in Age."*
2 And a] A *del.*

We see the farther in the far
At every step we take with her.

A restless rebel Lucifer
Again shall be her Morning Star

And what bright founts to sky will spout
When, like the Winter's vernal bear,
Our strange old monster Self comes out
To take his breath of common air.

The Miracle

The kernel escaped from the nut uncracked.
    'Twas a wonderful thing; & they tell
    That it might have been caught in the act,
    Had the squirrel kept eye on its shell.
The squirrel was cocking his tail on a bough.
    With an eye for a coming foot-fall
So believe it, nor rattle of how
That there never was kernel at all.

Unindexed Fragments

The selection of this unindexed material has been subjective. The fragments have been arranged and numbered in the same roughly chronological order as the unpublished poems and fragments in the main text, and because, with the exception of four labeled "Berg," they are all at Yale, Yale has not been named after each one.

WE SEE THE FARTHER

MS: Yale.
8 his] the *or* his

THE MIRACLE

MS: Yale.
2 wonderful thing] miracle, truth *del.*
5 But *del.*
6 *Del.:* Having heard a dull foot at the fall
7 nor rattle of] 'tis better than *del.*

[1]   She laugh'd a merry laugh to mock   NB B, [47]
                My daring her to do it:
            She sat herself upon the rock;
                A [stream *del.*] brook went bubbling thro' it.

            The stockings from her dainty feet
                She drew & laid them dankly:
            Her look was more than I could meet,
                And I felt aught but frankly.

[2]   Your ringlets that so wildly flew,   NB B, [47]
                All in a [knot *del.*] bun you braided:
            The stockings from our feet we drew
                And in the waters waded.

            Our fingers knotted into one

[3]*   She plunges in the rolling sea:—   NB B, [47]
                Push off! the winds are high:
            Another land shall bloom for me,
                For me another sky.

            And I will let the tempest rock
                A stormier soul to rest:

[4]   I would have life within thine eyes,   NB WW, scrap
                A life as blue as Heaven—

[5]   The vine bends to her where she sleeps   NB WW, scrap

[6]   They stand upon the battlefield   NB B, [15]
                Two armies of red-handed men;
            The morning sun on [spear *or*] sword & shield
                Shines with a bright [prophetic *or*] & wistful ken.
            Silent they breathe the breath of life

            The trumpets sound, the war steeds prance,

* Fragments 1–3 can be dated about 1849. See "She rides in the park," p. 972 and note.

[7]   Blossoms have fallen   NB B, [15]
                 Fruits have failed;
            Friends have departed,
                 Foes prevailed.

[8]   Pledge me twice and pledge me thrice   NB B, [15]
                 Pledge me till the moon grows double.

[9]   There was a young lady who sat on the sea, NB B, [7]
            Her face was handsome as handsome   canceled
                 could be;
            So full of good humour & laughter & smiles
            I guess you would call her the Queen of the Isles.

[10]   Eternity before   NB A, [18]
            Eternity behind

            Grandeurs[?] of all space
                 Boundless [blank] orb'd
            Spans of clear[?] grace
                 In one light absorb'd

            Stars in bright profusion—
                 Leading[?] the dark skies
            But the one is wanting
                 To the mortal eyes   10

[11]   By the dim [light del.] beams of a lonely   NB B, [5]
                 light
            Over the dusky German page,
            An old man softly snowed with age
                 Sat reading thro' the night.—
            It was a new philosophy
            Fresh minted from the teeming brain
            That films the eye of Allemain

[12]   **Throstle to the Swallow**   NB B, [7]

[Floating *del.*] Sailing high in the warm
                blue sky,
        Or winging the cloudy wind—
Shooting himself like an arrow
        'Twas his own wayward bow

[13]   Like a maiden near a mirror   NB A, [5]
                Is the merry April sky

[14]   Come maiden from the morning hills   NB A, [6]
        Come little maid and dancing down—
        No rocky rivulet so blithe,
        No merry breeze so full of joy

[15]   A golden orb in a crimson mist   NB A, [9]
        Sinks slowly down the

[16]   Mowers in the meadows,   NB A, [12]
                [And *del.*] Reapers in the fields,
        Dust [upon *or*] on the roadways
                Rain upon the hills—

[17]   Will not the dead leaf sing in its fall   NB A, [18]
        While thus it takes flight like a bird?

[18]   So sad on such a merry [day *del.*] morn   NB A, [18]
        Said a grandam to a [lady gay *or*] maid forlorn
                As curtseying she stood.
        The maid was clad in silks & furs,

[19]   **Dirge**   Berg, *Poems*, 114–115

            Deaf to wailing words,
                Is the ear.

[20]   Song   Berg, *Poems*, [118–119]

As I came thro' the breezy wheat,
A pretty girl I chanc'd to meet,
A rounded shape, from face to feet.
Fair as a field-rose, and as sweet.

[21]   Song   Berg, *Poems*, 120–121

What we would be; what we are:
What we shall be, if we dare

[22]   Song   Berg, *Poems*, [122]–123

In the days when we are gone,
        And our boys that play about us,
Proudly walk in Freedom's dawn,
        Won by us, but worn without us:

[23]   Plant pines around the graves of mighty
                men!   NB B, [11]
        Or bury them in pine-woods, where the noise
        Of the one murmuring, vast, melodious voice—

[24]   The eagle builds his eyrie on the rock   NB B, [11]
        Baffling the winds and the white leaping main.
        The eagle doth not build upon the plain,
        And power is his to give and take the shock.

[25]   O, and down the great river see go—   NB B, [21]
        The banker he bows to the [noble *del.*] ancient Lord.

        The banker bows low to the noble Lord
        As the noble Lord to Time bows low.

[26]   Ione   NB B, [21]

Across the bay the moonlight came,
    And kissed our feet with ripples:
My Nereid

The moonlight [rode *del.*] swam on the ripples
    As they [broke along *or*] sparkled & broke the bay:
The soft eve-song of the pebbles
    Was sweet to us where we lay:

[27]   The Ghost's Confession   NB B, [25]

Belied are not who think that cunning Death
Cuts from Immortal life the race of fools.

[28]   Pale down the stream came the [trembling *del.* NB B, [19]
            quivering *del.*] pointing beam,   canceled
        Pale were our cheeks at the parting:
    Sadly we gazed with our [faces *del.*] heads upraised
        And wiped not the tears of our smarting.
    Del.: The sorrowful queen of the night advanced
        Del.: And we knew her the queen of sorrow
    [Brightly the moon glanced as her shape advanced *or*]
    The moon glanced wide as she rose o'er the tide
        The night crown'd her the Queen of sorrow:

[29]   Freshly on the world she looks   NB B, [23]
            As Eve on Eden skies:
        The boundless light of April brooks
            Is like her laughing eyes

[30]   Light of my household! how I love   NB B, [42]
        Light of my household! My music of life   NB B, [43]
            Star of my future Seal of my past

[31]   If that we are but common clay,   NB B, [35]
                  The maxims of the world are wise
            That man shall live his little day
                  & be the day that dies.
            But maxims are a narrow sort
                  Of Tyrant that the truth constrain

[32]   The Emigrants' House   NB B, [68]
                                                          canceled

                              1

            Dayly and more desolate
                  The old House looks on the village green;
            Wide on its hinges swings the garden gate
                  But none go out, & none go in.
            Hawker & Pedlar gravely pass
                  Without a halt; an eye askance
            On gravel-paths sown thick with grass,
                  Tells the sad story at a glance.

                  Gone are the dwellers! loth to roam!
                  Exiled is the happy Home   10
                  Del.: Often we gaze & drop a tear
                  There is no gazing without a tear
                  Del.: For the House where we held lusty cheer!
                  We held in that House such lusty cheer!

                              2
                  Laurentians & lilacs bloom

[33]   Those must who play the Game of Chance NB B, [35]
                  Believe in hidden Laws.

[34]   And he must never fail in test   NB B, [5]
                  Who firmly would achieve.

[35]   Old Vernon was once a brisk boy in his class,   NB B, [32]
            And a bachelor as brave as could be:
        But now he's a weary old man, with, alas!
            [A poor wife that's *del*] A wife more weary than he.

        His Fortune coursed after the fox, & no more
            Will old Vernon [unearth them again *or*] either unearth,
        The friends at his table were daily a score,
            And now not a dinner he's worth.

[36]*   Twas on that second glorious morn   NB B, [59]
            When England charged with France

[37]   Now on a single plot of earth   NB B, [43]
                The Drama of the world is play'd:

[38]   Islanders, who on the tide,   NB B, [39]
                Freedom dare proclaim your bride,   canceled
            Now be worthy of her choice,
                Daunt the Despot with one voice:

[39]   A man with one Idea, who with that key   NB B, [52]
                Had open'd of the Halls of Knowledge one
            Wherein he sat enthroned himself to see
                In mirrors vast outsun the outer sun:

[40]   On golden ladders up & down   NB B, [55]
                    The sun's bright purpled[?] motes

[41]   London at morn   NB B, [55]
            When thro' its streets the fresh sweet country air
            Breathes as in pity, sighing for its sins

[42]   Forever & forever & forever   NB B, [51]
            Those starry lights will shine
            When we in earth recline,
            But we, too, are divine.

* September 20, 1854: to gain a victory over the Russians at the Alma River.

[43]   My darlings! you have learn'd to grow   NB B, [49]
                      Familiar with my pallid face:

[44]*   From the back falling night of dark hair   NB B, [12]
                  Her forehead shines like morning.

[45]   She threw away the book she read;   loose leaf
                  Why this is I, 'tis I, she cried:
                  & pressed her hands against her head,
                  & in a frenzy stretched them wide.

[46]   *Del.:* Give ear, all ye of low degree,   NB B, [43]
                      To a singer of your sort:
                      For Song's of humble birth, d'ye see,
                          Tho' it bobs sometimes at Court.

                  But while we crawl on Mother Earth
                      We'll sing & cease to moan
                  For Song's a thing of humble birth
                      And so ['tis *del.*] the people's own.

[47]   So let me lift my mind   NB B, [42]
                      Not ruled by an awful rod:
                  And learn to face mankind
                      As Nature faces God.

[48]   I dream'd that on a noble ship   NB B, [45]
                      Del.: We two were on the deep:
                  We twain into the Orient steer'd:
                  No word of love had pass'd my lip:
                      We talk'd of things that neither fear'd

[49]   When Nature & man shall work together   NB B, [50]
                      And he become her perfect flower,

* Used in *The Shaving of Shagpat* (1855), Mem. Ed., 1:57.

[50]   Well, then, I love her, tho' I'm but dust   NB B, [50]
                    Underneath her haughty foot:
                Love her I will, love her I must.

[51]   'Tis over, 'tis past!   NB B, [49]
                        No more will it be:
                    The first & the last
                        Twixt thee & me!

                    'Tis seal'd in the years,

[52]   The Old Dramatist   NB B, [54]

        Full many songs I've made my puppets sing;
            Merry and sad! now let me sing my own:
        [Pardon a crazy *del.*] Age has a fault of dwelling on
                    one string,
            [And what Age *del.*] Pardon it, and some squeaking
                    in the tone.

[53]   From Europe for her sins of late   NB B, [66]
                    Has Britain much to be forgiven:

[54]   In smooth grey rings the westward stream, NB B, [60]
                Beneath our ash's fountain'd bower,
            Sweeps on to glow in one deep gleam
                Of Heaven's forefinger on the hour.

[55]   To eyes that ignorantly see,   NB B, [61]
                    We are a drear anatomy:

[56]*   The Bells of Ouseley   Pocket NB 3

                Says Ted it is the evening time
                    & we've been rowing briskly:
                Methinks I hear a distant chime
                    And it must be the Bells of Ouseley.

        * Ouseley Lodge, Old Windsor, Berks.

[57]   Solomon Riddle   Pocket NB 3

Sol, says my father, you're naught but a fool
I lifted my cap & I bow'd quite cool:
If I'm a fool, father, I'm sure you'll agree
I'm one of a very large family:
    For hey, diddle, diddle
    Who isn't a Riddle?

So to see my relations I took a long walk

[58]   A senseless generation marr'd in age   Pocket
                    From wantonness in youth: NB 3
               They cry to all from pulpit and the stage
                    For comfort, not for truth.

[59]   Delicious glades   Pocket NB 3
               Where crouch'd on one bent arm
                    Great Pan has spied
               Diana's whiteness with a sunny wink

[60]   A poet   Pocket NB 3
         [*line left blank*]
         Manured with praise, with censure raked & hoed.

[61]*   as when the moon   Pocket NB 3
             Throws her full [light *del.*] ray upon an Alp
             The dweller in the heavens
             Takes all its whiteness on to look at her.

[62]   The language of tongues I think I've learnt   Pocket
                                                               NB 3

    * These lines and the next five fragments date from a walking tour in the summer of
1861. See headnote to *By the Rosanna*, page 192.

[63]* Sunset on the Piazza Saint Mark's   Pocket NB 3

> Fire tipp'd the Campanile's swinging bells.
> Like swinging torches

[64]†   Venice   Pocket NB 3

> The star of cities shines along the sea

[65]   O silver lands of morning   Pocket NB 3
>   That lie in the white cloud!
>   Therein have I most stainlessly walk'd
>   When I was young & proud.

[66]   as sure   Pocket NB 3
>   As primroses will look on April's face

[67]   As when at eve the last faint breeze of day   Pocket
>   Lisps swiftly to the water's shuddering gray.   NB 3

[68]‡   Hendecasyllables   Pocket NB 3

> The [sweet *or*] fresh smell of the woodland haunts me ever.

---

* Associated simile: "Sunset dying out 'Like to the last lines of some old Romance.'"

† See WMM, p. 34.

‡ Tennyson published 21 lines in this metre of Catullus, *Cornhill*, December 1863.

[69]* Up the water, moving to Aurora from the shade,   Pocket
     Grew a branching light that with a golden foliage   NB 3
       play'd.
     Down the water streaming rings of Naiads, floating, sang,
     Fear the wrath of Dian
       'Dian, Dian,' shrilly[?] rang.

[70]   I saw her figure in the beams, all sulphurous   Pocket
       phantom white   NB 3
     As stands a gorsebush mid the buds, grey in a web
      of blight.

[71]   The early moving of the dawn   Pocket NB 3
     Like a great thing done in secret.

[72]†   Sow in thy heart the seed of future flowers   Pocket
     But let not thy desires outstrip the hours   NB 4

[73]   John Axle's Holiday   Pocket NB 4

     I've been a thinker more than half my life
     So long, I can't remember the beginning,
     But that it was before I took a wife,
     Seems doubtful.

     I met a gentleman upon the road,

[74]‡   From thymy Motterone   Pocket NB 4
               peaks
     Peaks & high crags, green pastures & brown slopes

* Followed by: "Cambridge 4th Oct 1862." The next two fragments are from the same part of the notebook.

† This fragment and the one following are in the notebook used on a brief walking tour with Lionel Robinson in northern Italy and Switzerland, August–September 1863.

‡ After a prose note dated Aug. 31, 1863.

[75]   A Summer swallow, as I write,   loose leaf
                With open window, has come in.
                Against the pane he sees the light,
                And sets his flurried wings at spin
                By fits

[76]   "The Parting of the Hour"   Yale, top half,
                He who made age [more *or*] as beautiful   verso
                    to see,   of p. 387; a
                More tolerable to bear,   fragment of
                [Than *or*] As in the flash of morning   *The Amazing*
                    youth's green tree,   *Marriage*
                Than youth's light load of care.

[77]   Yon flask, that stands like sable Dis   loose leaf
                   Enwreathed by Proserpine pale:
                As the fir-tree under the clematis:
                A ghostly thing on misted eves,
                When the chill woodland drips dead leaves

[78]   Tell me, would you seek to win   loose leaf
                   Columbine from Harlequin?

[79]   Who had that power of soul to shatter the   loose leaf
                   yoke of Creeds,
                The shadow of quaking Fear on the mount of
                 Ignorance.

[80]   We read not earth by looking down;   loose leaf
                Best is she read with heaven in eye.

[81]   The cat gave a curl to her tail   Pocket NB 6
                The dog took his nose in his paws.
                There was peace in the house of the male,
                Till

[82]   For nought is in the highest earthly single,   loose leaf
            And creatures bent on rapture know that truth
            When pleasure touches pain & the two mingle

Appendix I

A Poem Possibly Attributable to Meredith

"Let them go with the cheers of their country to speed them" appeared in *Fraser's* 49 (June 1854), signed with the initials "G. M." The attribution is supported by the fact that GM did write patriotic verses on the departure of troops for the Crimean War (see pp. 1051–52) and that in the summer of 1855 he offered to his first publisher, John Parker, the manuscript of a volume to be called "British Songs." (The manuscript was rejected and presumably destroyed.) Moreover, two of GM's poems had previously been printed in *Fraser's*; see pages 741 and 742.

I.

Let them go with the cheers of their country to speed them,
    The gallant, devoted, and flower of the land;
We well may be proud that Old England could breed them,
    And match her past heroes at Freedom's command.
By the Angels of Heaven! our Cause is so holy,
    That dread of the Sequel is God to distrust:
At home, in His Presence, we are not less lowly,
    Because we here chorus Success to the Just!

II.

Preach no more this new doctrine that Valour confiding
    In Duty and sovereign Justice, offends;
That we should be dumb while our bosoms are priding
    In countrymen manfully fighting for friends.
At the pompous array of their Power, they who stumble
    Are such as serve Ruin, and arm not to save;
But hearts that beat highest may yet be most humble,
    As ours while we're singing Success to the Brave!

III.

In the face of the motherly fears that alarm her,
    The Might she must grapple, the numbers defy,
Old England serenely has girded her armour,
    The Foe of Tradition her faithful Ally.
They have joined honest hands for the Future of Nations,
    The grandeur of Law, and Humanity's due:
Belief that God's blessing through all their relations
    Is with them, inspires our—Success to the True!

IV.

On the fields of renown when the iron rain rattles,
 And red through the smoke flash the long lines of flame,
They will not forget that the great God of Battles
 Requires a pure soul and a chivalrous aim.
And they bear it—the men of our blood and alliance—
 To thunder its tidings on land and on sea;
O, far is our confident joy from defiance
 Of fate, when we echo Success to the Free!

V.

Let them go, while behind them their country is cheering,
 Prepared for Disaster, secure from Defeat:
If stanch we continue as they are unfearing,
 There's Victory somewhere for Army and Fleet.
By the Angels that see us! this Cause is so holy,
 We'll send our last ship and last man to the fight:
Still singing, while Faith in our bosoms prays lowly,
 Farewell, gallant brothers, Success to the Right!

G. M.

Appendix II

Titles or First Lines of Projected Poems

Jotting down tables of contents was one of GM's favorite pastimes. Several such tables appear in the early notebooks, as well as a long one in Berg. In addition, lest he forget an idea, he would occasionally jot down a title at the top of a page used for drafts. A few of these titles were fulfilled as poems that appeared in the *Modern Love* volume (1862), but most of them were apparently bubbles in the air. Inspection of the files of many periodicals that flourished in the 1850s has failed to reveal them. All titles noted by GM, including some half dozen mentioned in letters, are listed here not only because they show GM's wide range of interest in poetic subjects but because someone else may happen on an accomplishment that I have not discovered.

Arad
Argus
Armada, The: Song
Astrel
Ballad of the Locust-wing
Battle of Llongborth, The
Belshazzar, The Writing on the Wall
Between us, Ireland! they shall put: Song
Blessed Burden, The
Bridget
British Battle Lyrics [Destroyed by GM; Cline, Letter 1282]
Cadair Idris
Carol of Vagrant Will, A
Christmas day is coming on
Clara Desboro'
Coalition, A
Constance: Song
Dancing girl, The
Diana [See Fragments 59, 69.]
Dream of Mrs. Bloomer, A: Song
Echo
Eglantine: Song
8th September
Ellen Dewberry
Emigrants, The (plan for a ballad)
Emilia
Emir A Omarim
Enthusiast, The

Ethel & Arthur
Evening in Spring
Ex-Champion's Lament, The
Fairy Mab
Fame
Figleaf, The
Fisherman, The
For us they won the flower of Peace
France and England: Song
From one and for all; From all and for one
Fugitives, The
Geraint ap Erbin
The good ship Britannia
Harper, The: Ballad
Has she ever like a doe: Song
Heine
Hie blithely over hill and brook
Hungary
Hungry air that feeds on us, The
In the dropping round of the Sun
Into the pits of hell we hurl'd: Song
Jenny Averel
Jessy's night watch: Song
Josephine
Juana[?]
Lady Marjory: ballad
Lady Olivia: ballad
Laurian: ballad
Lime tree, lime tree, under thee
Lost Leg, The (Capt. Love): Song
Margaret
Marriage Verses for Miss Eveleen Mary Smith
Martha
Melanghel
Memory
Moll Flanders' hornpipe
My Nereid [See Fragment 26.]
My true love's ring
Nonn[?]: Song
Nourmahal
Odds, The: Song
Ode on the death [or funeral] of Arthur, Duke of Wellington
Ode to Beethoven
Ode to Death
Ode to Europe
Ode to Garibaldi
Ode to the Napiers
Ode written in Venice, Summer 1861
Olber[?] Redlight
Old Man of War laid up in dock, The: Song
Olympia
On Poland: Sonnet

One [?] of the Sussex downs
Painters, The
Peace: Sonnet
Prayers for children [1866]
Present Crisis, The: Song
Prophecy of Merlin, The
Raleigh
Recruit, The (plan for a ballad)
Resignation
Revenge and Remorse
Rhiannan
Richer with to-morrow is today
Roman, Saxon, Celt: Song
Rosanara
Sappho
Secret Love
Sieur Beliot: Song
Sir Gawain's Burial
Sir Humphrey Gilbert
Sir Richard Grenville
Strange in her bliss the young bride moves
Tears of Enid, bride of Geraint, The
Thames, The
To Cornelia*
To Jack at Greenwich
Tom Tippletoff's Toast
Tombelène
Turkey: Song
'Twere well for me could I lie down
Under the Cliff
Valley of Avalon, The
Violet and Eglantine: Song
Virgin Picture
The war[?] of creeds
Water-rat, The: Song
We fought in faith: the fight was good:
We stood on the cliff in the time of dew
When I would vision thy features
When the first cold tear on our changing sight

---

* S. M. Ellis (p. 70 n.) reported:

The late Rev. H. G. Woods, Master of the Temple, possessed a copy of the second edition of Tennyson's *The Princess*, 1848, which contained on the flyleaf an original manuscript poem of ten lines by George Meredith, and his autograph inscription: "To Cornelia—as the Lady most ambitious and best endowed to take fair Ida for prototype." The book was sold in 1915 for £39.

The sale was by Hodgson on November 10, and the catalogue presumed, wisely, that GM presented the volume to his future wife, Mrs. Mary Peacock Nicolls. The volume was presented by

> One who trusts some day to sing her praises
> Albeit in humbler measures . . . .

In spite of my efforts, I have failed to find this volume.

Explanatory Notes

THE WILD ROSE AND THE SNOWDROP

GM's letter to his printer, James Vizetelly [? February 1851], implies that the poet Richard H. Horne (see p. xxx) had made some corrections in this poem before it went to press.

JOHN LACKLAND

On December 1, 1849, GM offered *Chambers's Edinburgh Journal* some sonnets on "Two Kings of England," saying that "they would do very well if taken as a series and I have a great many already finished." *John Lackland* is the only one of them that survives, and GM struck it out in his corrected copy of *Poems* (1851) in Berg (see p. xxxi). He retained it, however, in the Edition de Luxe.

14 *symbols of the Lord*: churches and monasteries that King John (1199–1216) confiscated during his long dispute with Pope Innocent III.

THE SLEEPING CITY

See Explanatory Note to *London by Lamplight*, below.

1–56 This long analogy is suggested by "the eastern tale" told in the *Arabian Nights* (New York: Harper, 1948) by the "First of the Three Ladies of Baghdad" (1:100).

REQUIEM

7 See headnote. The Hobhouses may have broken their sad journey from Southampton to Erle Stoke at Lower Halliford, Peacock's home.

THE RAPE OF AURORA

In his letter sending the bulk of *Poems* to the publisher, John W. Parker, December 12, 1850, GM wrote of this poem: "I have followed the idea of Ariosto and invented a little mythology—The union of the Sun and the Dawn—."

DAPHNE

GM's letter to the printer, James Vizetelly [? February 1851], implies that the poet Richard H. Horne (see p. xxx) had made some corrections in this poem.

When GM sent the bulk of *Poems* to the publisher, John W. Parker, on December 12, 1850, he noted that in *Daphne* he had "avoided mention of Dan Cupid." Under the title of the poem in Berg Copy 1 of *Poems* GM wrote "not Ovidian." Cf. *Metamorphoses* 1.450–571.

383 This ungrammatical use of "sure" was habitual in the early poems of Keats.

SONG: SHOULD THY LOVE DIE

This poem was dropped from the "Poems Written in Early Youth" in volume 3 of the Edition de Luxe (1898), but was brought back in an adjunct to volume 4 of this edition, "Poems Written in Youth" (1910 posth.).

LONDON BY LAMPLIGHT

11 For "the human form divine," see Blake, *The Divine Image*, in *Songs of Innocence*; also Milton, *Paradise Lost*, 3.44, "the human face divine."

74 The "Scriptured rock" must allude to the rock in Horeb which, when Moses smote it, sprang water so that the Israelites might drink (Exod. 17:1–6).

PASTORALS I

In sending the first batch of MSS to his publisher, December 12, 1850, GM wrote John W. Parker: "The two 'Blank verse metres' beginning 'How sweet on sunny afternoons' are selections from half a dozen of the sort, and will be, *I* think, the most original feature in the volume." By "blank verse" he obviously meant "unrhymed."

PASTORALS IV

12 *in his mother's eye*: that is, at day-break when the first rays of the sun striking the celebrated statue of Memnon in Egypt elicited from it a melodious sound.

PASTORALS V

After one of his first meetings with GM, William Hardman recorded, in September 1861, that the poet had shown him "the place where he composed and wrote" this poem; "it was on an eminence surrounded by pines on the St. George's Hill estate [Surrey]" (*MVP*, p. 50).

SORROWS AND JOYS

According to the account book of *Household Words*, the guinea paid for this poem was split between GM and R. H. Horne (see p. xxx and MBF, p. 147).

SWATHED ROUND IN MIST

22–30 GM evidently had in mind Shelley's *Mont Blanc*.

NO, NO, THE FALLING BLOSSOM

The third stanza echoes Tennyson's *Love and Death*, lines 9–15.

THE TWO BLACKBIRDS

GM wrote a postscript to his poem in *The Ordeal of Richard Feverel*. The wise youth, Adrian, Richard, and Richard's uncle Hippias are listening to a blackbird. Richard speaks:

> 'You know that bird I told you of—the blackbird that had its mate shot, and used to come to sing to old Dame Bakewell's bird from the tree opposite. A rascal knocked it over the day before yesterday, and the dame says her bird hasn't sung a note since.'
> 'Extraordinary!' Hippias muttered abstractedly. 'I remember the verses.'
> 'But where's your moral?' interposed the wrathful Adrian. 'Where's constancy rewarded?
>
> > "The ouzel-cock so black of hue,
> > With orange-tawny bill;
> > The rascal with his aim so true;
> > The Poet's little quill!"

Where's the moral of that? except that all's game to the poet! Certainly we have a noble example of the devotedness of the female, who for three entire days refuses to make herself heard, on account of a defunct male. I suppose that's what Ricky dwells on' [Mem. Ed., 2:224].

According to the account book of *Household Words*, the guinea paid for this poem was split between GM and R. H. Horne (see p. xxx and MBF, p. 147).

THE SHIPWRECK OF IDOMENEUS

21–25 *the Shape*: Idomeneus. Here GM indulged in amateur etymology. He evidently figured that the "Ido" of Idomeneus's name was derived from εἶδοσ 'shape,' and that "men" was from μέν ... δέ construction 'as well ... as': both in councils and in battles. Liddell and Scott's Greek Dictionary defines "Idomeneus" as "the strength of Ida" (in Crete).

PICTURES OF THE RHINE

I.1–10 Cf. Shelley's lyric, "Music, when soft voices die."

IV The "little Isle" of Nonnenwerth lies in the Rhine between Bonn and Linz. The legend is that when Roland, one of Charlemagne's paladins, was summoned to battle, he left his betrothed Hildegard there. Assuming death to be the only reason for his long absence, she became a nun in the convent of Nonnenwerth. When Roland finally returned, he built a tower on the hill overlooking Nonnenwerth, which he never left thereafter.

MODERN LOVE (1862)

In the Edition de Luxe GM placed the following poems from *Modern Love* (1862) among the "Poems Written in Youth":

Grandfather Bridgeman
The Meeting
The Beggar's Soliloquy
Cassandra
The Young Usurper
Margaret's Bridal-Eve
The Head of Bran the Blest
By Morning Twilight
Autumn Even-Song
Unknown Fair Faces
Phantasy
Shemselnihar
A Roar through the Tall Twin Elm-Trees
When I would image
I chafe at darkness
By the Rosanna
Ode to the Spirit of Earth in Autumn
The Doe: A Fragment

XIV–XXIII The battle of Inkerman was fought on November 5, 1854. "It was a 'soldier's battle' pure and simple," won by the allies after heavy losses. (*Enc. Brit.*, 11th ed., s.v. "Crimean War.")

In a letter to Maxse, January [?17], 1862, GM asked his friend: "By the way, tell me, do army men—ensigns, fight in undress uniform? Did any at Inkermann? Or is the full dress *de rigueur*?" In his next letter to Maxse, GM thanked him "for the Guardsman's dictum. What other people but Britons would fight in full dress?"

MODERN LOVE

I.1 Cf. the syntax of this opening line with the deleted words after the unpublished verses, "Meeting," p. 1050.

IV.1 The apparatus criticus notes the misprint "joy" for "joys" in the reprint of *Modern Love* (1892). On February 3 of that year GM wrote to Frederick Macmillan: "*Modern Love* has gratuitous ghastly printers' errors. I spoke of wishing to see the book before it appeared. We might as well insert the Errata in the unbound copies, for though the errors are inexcusably obvious, I have had queries addressed to me." MBF notes no errata leaf for this volume, nor have I seen one.

XIII.16 The condemnatory review of *Modern Love* in the *Spectator*, 24 May 1862, had taken particular exception to the line, "Sounds thro' the listless hurricane of hair!"; hence, perhaps, GM's rewriting of it.

XIV.5–8 From this point on a reading of *Modern Love* is facilitated by noting that the "gold-haired lady" is alluded to as "Lady," see especially sonnet XXVII, and the wife as "Madam," as in XIV.12.

XVII.12 *ephemerioe*: flies that live but a day. The customary spelling is *ephemerae* or the genetic *ephemeridae*.

XVII.14 Cf. Keats's *Ode to a Nightingale*, line 5: "'Tis not through envy of thy happy lot."

XVII.16 For the "corpse-light," see headnote to *Will o' the Wisp*, p. 29. It is similar to the *ignis fatuus*.

XVIII.11 GM had in mind Tennyson's *Amphion*, in which the poet conjures up the "days of old Amphion" (line 10) who, by his music, made trees dance. Among them: "The gouty oak began to move, / And flounder into hornpipes" (lines 23–24).

XXIII.16 Cf. *Shemselnihar*, line 22; *A Preaching from a Spanish Ballad*, IX. 1; *Diana of the Crossways*, Mem. Ed., 16:410.

XXVIIff. William T. Going, in "A Note on 'My Lady' of *Modern Love*," *MLQ* 7 (September 1946), properly took issue with Sencourt's blunt statement that "none other than" Janet Duff Gordon (see n., p. 822) "can be the 'lady' of *Modern Love*" (p. 109). Janet was a girl very dear to GM, 1858–60, after his wife had left him. He modeled his young heroine Rose Jocelyn in *Evan Harrington* after her. In 1860, the year that the novel was published, Janet married at the age of eighteen. She would never have been willing to serve as GM's mistress.

XXXI.9–10 Carl H. Ketcham notes in the *Explicator 17*, no. 1 (1958), n. 7: "Lines 9–11 seem to contain a reference to the celebrated 'Count' Borowlaski (Borulwaski, Boruslawski), a Polish dwarf who, after successfully exhibiting himself for many years, died in Durham in 1837, aged ninety-eight. Walter Scott, in a letter to B. S. Morritt, July 24, 1814 . . . remarks that if Waverley had married Flora, 'she would have set him up upon the chimney-piece, as Count Borowlaski's wife used to do with him.' The comparison, appropriate enough in itself, becomes markedly ironic if we assume that Meredith may have known the tiny Count's reputation for being witty, handsome, and successfully amorous—everything that the husband would wish to be in the eyes of 'My Lady,' reduced, in his abrupt mood of self-contempt, to ridiculous miniature."

XXXIII.5–6 It would seem that GM meant the Romans of Pompey's army rather than "Pharsalians." In the battle of Pharsalia in Thessaly (June 48 B.C.) Julius Caesar won a conclusive victory over his rival and former son-in-law, Pompey the Great. The inexperienced young aristocrats in Pompey's army were given to luxury, self-indulgence, and fear of disfigurement. They were slow to join battle and quick to retreat.[1]

XLII.13 Not the goddess of wisdom but the goddess of youth.

XLIX and L Blunt reported in *My Diaries*, November 7, 1905 (2:120–21), that Wilfrid Meynell read *Modern Love* to him and Sydney Cockerell and "expounded it" to them "as Meredith had expounded it to Mrs. Meynell. According to this the last two stanzas mean that the wife, 'Madam,' commits suicide so as to leave the poet free to marry 'My Lady.' Cockerell thinks that to have been an afterthought, and that the poem really ended before the last two stanzas, and that the wife eloped with her lover. Meredith, Meynell says, seems to have persuaded himself that his wife, in real life, left him for some such altruistic motive."

L.9–10 GM's distrust of questioning is repeated in *Beauchamp's Career* (1875) where Beauchamp is said to have "drunk of the *questioning* cup [GM's italics], that which denieth peace to us, and which projects us upon the missionary search of the How, the Wherefore, and the Why not, ever afterward" (Mem. Ed., 11:155).

JUGGLING JERRY

XII.5 S. M. Ellis identified The Mound, usually capitalized, as Round Hill, right by Copsham Cottage near Esher where GM lived from 1859 to 1864. Phiz pictured it in his illustration for *Juggling Jerry* in *Once a Week*, and there is a charming photograph of it in Ellis, facing p. 130.

THE OLD CHARTIST

IV.1 The park was probably Claremont Park where King Louis Philippe had lived in exile. It is about a mile from Esher, GM's village, 1858–59, and a brook runs along the road between Claremont and Esher.

XV.6 "Cleanliness is, indeed, next to godliness." John Wesley, *Sermons*, 93.

PATRIOT ENGINEER

49–60 The motivation for the engineer's return to England from Hungary is the Austrian suppression of the Magyar revolt in 1849. GMT explains:

"The 'traitor' refers to Görgei, the general who effected the surrender of the Magyar army at Vilagós on August 13, 1849. The 'two despots' were Russia and Austria. Their combined forces rendered the submission at Vilagós necessary in the eyes of Görgei, who was therefore long regarded as a traitor by his countrymen—unjustly, as Meredith himself thought in later years when he had read the history." (Trevelyan was a young friend of the elderly GM.)

"Following on the surrender of Vilagós, the Austrians shot four and hanged nine of the surrendered Magyar generals."

1. Caesar, *Civil Wars* 3.92–97; Plutarch, " Pompey," " Caesar," *Lives*.

74 The Austrian two-headed eagle.

130 *aspect more sublime*: from Wordsworth's *Lines Composed a Few Miles above Tintern Abbey*, line 37.

133–34 The mother of Coleridge's *To a Young Ass, Its Mother Being Tethered near It* has now presumably been liberated.

CASSANDRA

I.4 *Futurity*: Lempriere's word for the gift that Cassandra had asked of Apollo, who was enamored of her. Once having received the gift of prophecy, she refused him her favors, and he "effected that no credit or reliance should ever be put upon her predictions, however true or faithful they might be."[1]

XII.4 *the grand majestic ghost*: Agamemnon who, in Cassandra's prophetic mind, is as good as dead already at the hands of Clytemnestra.

MARIAN

In the Edition de Luxe, this poem was moved from the *Modern Love* poems and placed under the heading *Verses*, in Volume 3 (1898).

PHANTASY

I See headnote, p. 182. The "village lily" in the ballet was Giselle.

II.1 *cynical Adrian*: this seems to be GM's friend, Maurice FitzGerald, nephew of Edward FitzGerald, of *Omar Khayyám* fame. He was the model for the "wise youth," Adrian, in *The Ordeal of Richard Feverel*.

II.2 Bruges, see XXX.4. GMT identified the "carol" with the "famous chimes in the belfry of the Halles."

IV.1 *Hawking ruin*: cf. *Rhine-Land*, line 78, p. 764, an earlier poem that tells of GM's wedding trip with his first wife, Mary.

VI.1 Wordsworth had been struck by these garments, and in one of his sonnets on Bruges, *Memorials of a Tour on the Continent, 1820*, wrote of the "nun-like females" who "with soft motion, glide!" In his prose note to the sonnet he conjectured, "the long black mantle universally worn by the females is probably a remnant of the old Spanish connection, which, if I do not much deceive myself, is traceable in the grave deportment of its inhabitants."

XVIII, XIX.3, XX.1–3 See headnote, p. 182. Ketcham informs us that the details of water-lilies, "languid twining girls," "long locks disarraying," the circling motion, the sedge, and the convolvulus are all to be found in the lithograph by Fanoli.

XXXI.4 The "la, la, la!—Largo al factotum della città" aria of Figaro in the first act of Rossini's popular comic opera *The Barber of Seville* (1816).

BY THE ROSANNA

99 *Buon' mano* in this context means a "handout".

159 Captain Maxse, R.N., had fought in the Crimean War by the Black (Euxine) Sea.

175–78 Cf. lines 9–12.

1. *Classical Dictionary*, 2d ed. (London: Cadell, 1792), s.v. "Cassandra."

ODE TO THE SPIRIT OF EARTH IN AUTUMN

112 For the Anakim, see Deut. 2:9–11.

122 and 177 For the "winged seed," compare Shelley's "wingèd seeds," *Ode to the West Wind*, line 7.

158 *Bacchante Mother*: Bacchus, unlike his fervent followers, was benevolent as well as gay. GM had used the same concept earlier, in "Wandering Willie," Canto 2, lines 342–58.

190–208 This is GM's only tribute to the Noble Savage; cf. Pope, *An Essay on Man*, 1.99–112. The text is from "Wandering Willie," Canto 2, lines 366–80, p. 924.

THE DOE

2 The farmer's name is Gale. See "Wandering Willie," fragment 3, line 367.

11 Joan is Willie's wife.

41–88 The idea of a doe comforting a human being stems not only from folklore but from Wordsworth's *White Doe of Rylstone* (1815). I have stated elsewhere (see hn., p. 893) that the loose plan of "Wandering Willie" imitates Wordsworth's *Excursion* (1814).

91–93 and 140–96 The trouble with Bessy, the farmer's daughter, can be easily deduced from the unpublished fragments 2 and 3, pp. 943–67. She has loved out of wedlock and been deserted; hence she cannot bear the thought that her pure, dead sister Nancy looked forward to a reunion with her in heaven.

135–36 This hope of meeting the doe in heaven was attributed to the farmer himself in a fragment of "Wandering Willie," lines 146–48, p. 949.

189 The "sinless child" refers to Joan's baby, whom she was carrying with her on the morning of the chase.

THE WOODS OF WESTERMAIN

IV.60 By adding this line to the original version of *The Woods of Westermain*, GM emphasized the attachment that he had formed early in life to the doctrines of Thomas Carlyle, who had declared in *Sartor Resartus* (1838) that the "Annihilation of Self" was "the first preliminary moral act." GM's important modification of Carlyle's attack on Self was his evolutionary belief that Self could be changed rather than annihilated. To aid this process he constantly revealed the inflated ego in his novels, and it is of course the central subject of *The Egoist* (1879).

IV.243–44 *Some . . . damps*: For the light of marsh-damps, see headnote to *Will o' the Wisp*, p. 29, and note to *Modern Love* XVII.16, p. 1138.

THE DAY OF THE DAUGHTER OF HADES

II Cf. *The Appeasement of Demeter*, pp. 415–19.

V.35 *rud*: archaic for 'ruddiness', or a 'blush'.

VI.14–15 *Briareus*: the giant who defended Jupiter when other gods threatened to dethrone him and who was later bound under Mount Etna in Sicily.

VI.62–65 *The Beneficent*: Demeter; *that Other*, Pluto.

VII.47 *her of the wells*: probably Arethusa.

VII.95–100 The reference is to the Homeric heroes Achilles, Agamemnon, Odysseus.

IX.65 According to GMT, "the Three" are Demeter, Persephone, and Pluto.

THE LARK ASCENDING

Contrast the early poem *To a Skylark*, p. 68.

11 "Changeingly" is the first appearance in GM's verse of the internal *e* that became a studied practice with him.

93–94 Of these two lines, often quoted, Ernest de Selincourt drew a comparison with stanza 7 of Keats's *Ode to a Nightingale*: "apart from its song [the nightingale's], it has no life for him."[1]

PHOEBUS WITH ADMETUS

Clodd (see hn., p. 874) noted on February 23, 1893, that GM "assesses *Phoebus with Admetus* higher than *Earth and Man*, which I always praise highly" (*TLS-I*).

I.7–8 Phoebus's sister sphere was the Moon.

MELAMPUS

V and VI The sudden awakening of Melampus to an understanding of the language of birds after the young snakes had licked his ears is charmingly described by Lempriere in the *Classical Dictionary* that was probably the chief source of GM's poem.

LOVE IN THE VALLEY

118 This line is derived from Ruskin's chapter, "The Truth of Chiaroscuro," in *Modern Painters*, 2.2.3, "especially such a remark as 'For no outline of objects whatsoever is so sharp as the edge of a close shadow' (John Ruskin, *Works*, 3.304)."[2]

197 *the wild white cherry*: see note to *A Faith on Trial*, lines 218–94, p. 1148.

200 GM was abundantly fond of the verb "swim" as a metaphor for the actions or emotions of his heroines. On one page of *The Egoist* (1879), for example, Clara Middleton swims "on the wave in her bosom," and thereupon "swam for a brilliant instant on tears, and yielded to the overflow" (Mem. Ed., 13:188).

THREE SINGERS TO YOUNG BLOOD

III The Rose is that of the alchemists in Rosicrucian doctrine. "It was said that whenever this wonderful drink [the Elixir of Life] was made in a laboratory, there would appear in the liquid the ghostly image of a luminous Rose."[3]

III.12 For the accent on "Immortal," see note to *The South-Wester*, p. 1147.

A BALLAD OF FAIR LADIES IN REVOLT

I.2 This metaphor appears in the early NB B, [p. 12] as: "An ever falling fountain of green leaves (birch)."

III.5 "Ritornell" is the German spelling for the Italian *ritornello*, 'anything "returned to" in music' (*Oxford Companion to Music*, 9th ed., s.v. "ritornel").

1. *The Poems of John Keats* (London: Methuen, 1905), n. 1., p. 475.
2. Geoffrey Tillotson, *Criticism and the Nineteenth Century* (University of London, 1951), p. 33 n.
3. Lafcadio Hearn, "The Poetry of George Meredith," *Pre-Raphaelite and Other Poets*, ed. John Erskine (New York: Dodd, 1922), p. 370.

XXX.3 *the white wife of Lot*: Gen. 19:26.

XXXVIII.5–6 For the resemblance of men and women cf. "An Essay on Comedy," delivered 1877 (*Miscellaneous Prose*, Mem. Ed., 23:15).

THE STAR SIRIUS

13 GMT claims that the lord of the Earth is the Sun.

THE DISCIPLINE OF WISDOM

3–4 In a time when hammocks swung between trees have gone out of fashion, it may be useful to point out that this is the image.

THE WORLD'S ADVANCE

9 According to GMT the "memorable Lady" was "presumably Mrs. Browning (or Aurora Leigh)":

> What is art,
> But life upon the larger scale, the higher,
> When, graduating up in a spiral line
> Of still expanding and ascending gyres,
> It pushes toward the intense significance
> Of all things, hungry for the Infinite?
> Art's life,—and where we live, we suffer and toil.
>
> (*Aurora Leigh* [1857], 4.1151–57)

THE GARDEN OF EPICURUS

The famous garden of the philosopher Epicurus (341–270 B.C.), was in Athens.

THE POINT OF TASTE

13–14 Tony Lumpkin sings a tavern song in Act 1, Scene 1 of Goldsmith's *She Stoops to Conquer* (1773).

CAMELUS SALTAT

Camelus saltat: 'the camel dances'.

11–12 The allusion is to the nursery exercise in articulation: "Peter Piper picked a peck of pickled pepper."

THE TWO MASKS

I.7 Mount Athos rises at the southern tip of the easternmost peninsula of Chalcidice, in the north-eastern part of Greece.

I.8 Cape Leucadia (now an island, Leucas) is off the coast of Acarnania, a region of ancient Greece between the Achelous River and the Ionian Sea.

ARCHDUCHESS ANNE

I.VI.2 In folklore Kraken was a huge sea monster.

A PREACHING FROM A SPANISH BALLAD

II.1 The Prado in Madrid is the most famous of all Spanish promenades, but the term is used for the fashionable walking place in any Spanish town.

IX.1 Although the lady in Lockhart's popular ballad (see hn., p. 325) briefly lists the personal services that she will offer her young lover, they do not include the warming of his footsoles. Cf. *Shemselnihar*, line 22, *Modern Love*, XXIII.15–16, and *Diana of the Crossways*, Mem. Ed., 16:410.

XX–XXI In the popular ballad the lady asks her lord to spare the youth and to bury her in the orange garden with the following legend on her tombstone: "Ladies shrink from love unholy, warned by her whose tomb you see."

KING HARALD'S TRANCE

GM's Harald must stem from the same folk source as Johann Ludwig Uhland's poem *Harald*.[1] In Uhland's poem Harald is left sitting on a stone in a permanent sleep; occasionally he brandishes his sword.

VIII–X The chiefs chose a "kingling," the young wife's lover, instead of waiting for the birth of his legitimate son.

XIII–XVIII Lafcadio Hearn explained that burial for the "lord of war" would have been cremation on a beach and that Harald's body had been carried there, armored, with his sword by his side on the bier. Hence he was strengthened by the smell of brine to kill his pregnant wife, but he died before he could demolish the kingling.[2]

MANFRED

I Throughout most of GM's novels the Alps were a symbol of spiritual restoration, so that Manfred's climb in order to jump to destruction was repellently theatrical: the "bile and buskin Attitude." Vernon Whitford, the ideal antagonist of *The Egoist* (1879), modeled after Leslie Stephen who was a mountaineer as well as a scholar, was GM's supreme exemplar of the Alpine ideal.

THE NUPTIALS OF ATTILA

XVI A warrior cries "Vale" (lines 1–2) to remind Attila of his intention of returning to Italy to capture Rome. In 452, after capturing and burning the cities of northern Italy, Attila encamped "at the place where the slow-winding Mincius is lost in the foaming waves of the Lake Benacus" (Gibbon, chap. 35)—XVI, lines 9, 22, and 25–28 in the poem. There Pope Leo I (line 10) eloquently persuaded him not to enter Rome, and was aided in his effort by a vision of Peter and Paul—the "Two" of line 12—who threatened Attila with instant death if he did not heed Leo's words.

GM wrote of line 9 in a letter to Richard H. P. Curle, January 3, 1905. The subject of the letter was Curle's forthcoming article, "George Meredith," in *The Poets and the Poetry of the Nineteenth Century: Charles Kingsley to James Thomson*, ed. Alfred H. Miles (1905). "I may say that I noticed praise of a line, 'Where gleams [*sic*] the sapphire lake', which has little quality. It must have struck you from its coming abruptly in a barbaric poem."

XXII According to Gibbon, Attila died of a burst artery and as he "lay in a supine position, he was suffocated by a torrent of blood, which, instead of finding a passage through the nostrils, regurgitated into the lungs and stomach." But the report soon reached Constantinople that Ildico had killed him.

A recent historian, using the same sources as Gibbon, adds the fact that Attila was prone to nose bleeds, but was too drunk on this wedding night to raise himself. "His body bore no trace of a wound."[3]

1. *Gedichte* (Stuttgart: J. C. Cotta, 1853), pp. 304–6.
2. "The Poetry of George Meredith," *Pre-Raphaelites and Other Poets*, ed. John Erskine (N.Y.: Dodd, 1922), p. 321.
3. E. A. Thompson, *A History of Attila and the Huns* (Oxford: Clarendon, 1948), p. 149.

XXVII and XXVIII Gibbon tells that the captives who had dug his grave were massacred, so that no one knows where Attila is buried.

ANEURIN'S HARP

GM probably read *Y Gododin: A Poem on the Battle of Cattraeth* when it was published in Welsh with an English translation by the Reverend John Williams Ab Ithel in 1852. The battle lasted a week and Aneurin was present as an official Welsh bard. Gododin is a place where the heroes come and go. A later editor, Thomas Powel (1888), argued that the battle took place in North Britain and confidently dated the week-long battle 603. After the battle, which the Welsh lost, Aneurin retired to Wales to write his elegy.

II.8 *hirlas*: 'a drinking horn'.

X.5–6 Cf. *The Sweet o' the Year*, lines 1–2, p. 614.

XI.8 *I*: GM, who was proud of his Welsh blood.

XII.8 "The 'Norman nose' is the type of England's aristocracy—once a reality in the days of the Conqueror, now a title to gild wealth." [1]

FRANCE, DECEMBER 1870

II.2 The French Revolution; see GM's ode, p. 553.

II.15 The theme of "Angel and Wanton" is taken up in the later *Odes*.

III.7 The fall was from the revolutionary ideals of 1789 to Napoleon I.

IV.31–32 Cf. Gal. 6:7.

VII.62, 74 The "Dishonour" and "trickster" was Napoleon III. The change made from "Dishonourer" to "Dishonour" for *Odes* (1898), was probably to improve the meter.

X.1–5 The "flame" was the revolutionary hope for Liberty, Equality, and Fraternity in 1789. "The Man" is Prometheus; see part XIV from the *Fortnightly* version in Supplementary Textual Notes.

XI.25–54 Cf. Shelley's *Lines Written on Hearing the News of the Death of Napoleon* (published with *Hellas*, 1822), in which Mother Earth says that her "heart grew warm" by the spirit of the dead: "I feed on whom I fed" (line 32).

THE LAST CONTENTION

GM wrote to Mrs. Louise Chandler Moulton on December 9, 1887, "You are the first to notice anything of value in 'The Last Contention'; and your remarks on it would of themselves prove to me that you have thought closely and fruitfully upon life."

PERIANDER

IX.4–6 Lycophron would not speak to his father because he had been told by his mother's father Procles that Periander had killed his mother (Herodotus 3.50).

X.1 *The Island*: Corcyra (Herodotus 3.52).

XVII The Corcyreans had killed Lycophron to keep Periander from coming to their island (Herodotus 3.53). But, according to GM's poem, they were "dismayed" by the size of the fleet.

1. George Macaulay Trevelyan, *The Poetry and Philosophy of George Meredith* (London: Constable, 1906), pp. 204–05.

BELLEROPHON

IV.1 frag. A: Alëius Campus in Lykia was the place where Pegasus threw Bellerophon.

PHAÉTHÒN

In 1887, the following note was appended to this poem.

The Galliambic Measure

Hermann (*Elementa Doctrinae Metricae*) [i.e., Godofredi Hermanni (Lipsiae, 1816), p. 505], after citing lines from the Tragic poet Phrynichus and from the Comic, observes:

Dixi supra, Phrynichorum versus videri puros Ionicos esse. Id si verum est, Galliambi non alia re ab his differunt, quam quod anaclasin, contractionesque et solutiones recipiunt. Itaque versus Galliambicus ex duobus versibus Anacreonteis constat, quorum secundus catalecticus est, hac forma:

$$\overline{\overline{u u}} \ \underline{\prime} \ \underline{\prime} \ u u \ \underline{\prime} \ \underline{\prime} \quad \Big| \quad u u \ \underline{\prime} \ \underline{\prime} \ u u \ \underset{\smile}{\prime}$$
$$\overline{\overline{u u}} \ \underline{\prime} \ \underset{\smile}{\overline{}} \ \overline{\overline{u u}} \ \overset{\smile}{} \ \underline{\prime} \ \underline{\prime} \quad \Big| \quad u u \ \underline{\prime} \ \underset{\smile}{\overline{}} \ \underset{\smile}{\overline{\overline{u u}}} \ \overset{\smile}{} \ \underset{\smile}{\prime}$$

The wonderful *ATYS* of Catullus is the one classic example. A few lines have been gathered elsewhere. The Laureate [Tennyson]'s *Boadicea* rides over many difficulties and is a noble poem. Catullus makes general use of the variant second of the above metrical forms:

Mihi januae frequentes, mihi limina tepida:

With stress on the emotion:

Jam, jam dolet quod egi, jam jamque poenitet.

A perfect conquest of the measure is not possible in our tongue. For the sake of an occasional success in the velocity, sweep, volume of the line, it seems worth an effort; and, if to some degree serviceable for narrative verse, it is one of the exercises of a writer which readers may be invited to share.

53 The Phaethontiades (to be read in the plural) are more correctly known as the Heliades.

THE SOUTH-WESTER

1–3 This naval metaphor appears as early as Canto 2 of "Wandering Willie," see line 438, p. 927. In the back of his mind may have lurked Tennyson's "airy navies grappling in the central blue" (*Locksley Hall* [1842], line 124).

16 GM had in mind the Black Briony, a vine commonly called "Lady's Seal." In a notebook that he used in part for jottings on his novel *Emilia in England* (1864), he remarked that his heroine wears a black briony wreath and asked himself the question: "Is it nightshade?" The answer is no. Cf. *The Sage Enamoured and the Honest Lady*, IV.154.

87 At the highest point of rhetoric in his "Essay on Comedy" (1877) GM associated silver with laughter. The Comic Spirit looks down on all pretentious men and casts "an oblique light on them, followed by volleys of silvery laughter" (*Miscellaneous Prose*, Mem. Ed., 28:47).

106–16 Iris, the rainbow, was the Dream-messenger of the gods.

116 In *A Reading of Earth* (1888), the noun "immortal" was incorrectly printed without the accent. In a letter to G. W. Foote, February 25, 1889, GM wrote: "as to 'immortal', there should have been an accent on the initial syllable,—the stress opposing it to 'mortal'. Properly *im* is long, the sense should make it so; in this instance, the sense demands it. The word is an anti-Bacchic foot—immŏrtăl. On this I take my stand." (The *bacchius* is a foot of three syllables, one short and two long.)

Cf. *The Three Singers to Young Blood*, III.12 (p. 258) and later poems, passim.

127-28 Cheer contrasted with violence: the "forest gong" is reminiscent of Pan; the serpent Python had attacked Apollo's mother while she was pregnant, and the young god's first great deed was to kill the monster.

130-33 Combining an understanding of pantheism and a belief in the value of re-collection, this is probably the most Wordsworthian sentence in GM's nature poetry.

THE THRUSH IN FEBRUARY

24-25 GMT identifies these images as "the cirrus clouds at sunset."

157-60 These lines recall a two-line fragment in NB B, [p. 48]:

> As at morn after a frost the crocus
> Is found leaning her yellow cheeks to the earth.

THE APPEASEMENT OF DEMETER

V.3 Iambe was Metanira's merry maidservant, who was hospitable to Demeter during her search for her daughter. She cheered Demeter, and from "the jokes and stories which she made use of, free and satyrical verses have been called Iambics" (Lempriere, s.v. "Iambe").

IX.7 *the realms of gold*: Keats, *On First Looking into Chapman's Homer*, line 1.

WOODLAND PEACE

2 and 25 GM had used the compound epithet "Eden-sweet" in an early poem, *South-West Wind in the Woodland*, line 112 (see p. 28).

THE QUESTION WHITHER

III.7 GM probably took the thought and phrasing of this line from Goethe. Cf. *Truth and Poetry*: "all we can do in the light car of our destiny is 'in cool self-possession to hold the reins with a firm hand, and to guide the wheels, now to the left, now to the right, avoiding a stone here, a precipice there.' We don't know whither or whence."[1] See also Eckermann's *Conversations with Goethe*: "Man is a darkened being; he knows not whence he comes, nor whither he goes; he knows little of the world, and less of himself. I know not myself, and may God protect me from it!"[2]

When on April 5, 1906, GM obliged a correspondent by enumerating his "readings of the formative kind," he gave place of honor to "the noble Goethe, the most enduring."

DIRGE IN WOODS

14-15 The emphatic "Even so" runs throughout *The Shaving of Shagpat* (1855), and there is even one "Even I!" (Mem. Ed., 1:62, 137, 192, 215, 264, and 293).

---

1. James Stone, "Meredith and Goethe," *University of Toronto Quarterly* 21 (January 1952): 157–66.

2. Trans. S. M. Fuller (Boston: Hilliard, Gray, 1839), p. 309.

A FAITH ON TRIAL

56–62 "At Nonancourt, in Normandy, on the Avre, Mrs. Meredith's three brothers lived and owned wool-spinning mills" (WMM, p. 214 n.).

65 During the Hundred Years War, 1337–1453.

215 *awag*: a neologism.

218–94 In the second version of *Love in the Valley* (1878), line 197 (see p. 256), GM's lover says that the girl he loves is fairer "than the wild white cherry." He could scarcely have been more hyperbolic. GM's particular feeling for the wild white cherry tree was firmly expressed through the consciousness of Clara Middleton in *The Egoist* (1879). At the end of chap. 11, "The Double-Blossom Wild Cherry-Tree," she sees Vernon Whitford sleeping under the flowering tree with its "load of virginal blossom" (cf. line 256). Clara looks up "from deep to deeper heavens of white" (cf. lines 283–84) and reflects, "'He must be good who loves to lie and sleep beneath the branches of this tree!'" (cf. lines 261–62 and 593–97) (Mem. Ed., 13:134–35).

227–35 GMT: the medieval way of the Canterbury pilgrims "runs along the southern slope of Boxhill."

306 For "the Whither whose echo is Whence," repeated in line 602, see *The Question Whither*, III.7 and note, p. 1147.

340 *acerb*: properly an adjective.

467 *glisterlings*: a neologism.

HYMN TO COLOUR

III.1 On May 14, 1907, GM wrote to J. C. Smith about this image: "If you observe the Planet Venus at the hour when the dawn does no more than give an intimation, she is full of silver, and darkness surrounds her. So she seems to me to fly on dark wings. . . . 'Black Star' is common in classic poets. It is true I push the epithet farther."

THE EMPEROR FREDERICK OF OUR TIME

1 Alfred the Great, king of Wessex (871–99?) was a renowned scholar-king. France's Louis IX (1226–70) was a patron of Gothic cathedrals and helped to found the Sorbonne. He was canonized in 1297.

THE YEAR'S SHEDDINGS

Cf. *A Faith on Trial*, lines 10–12, p. 428.

In *The Egoist* (1879), Laetitia Dale compares herself with dead leaves: "Last year's sheddings from the tree do not form an attractive garland. Their merit is, that they have not the ambition" (Mem. Ed., 13:188).

THE EMPTY PURSE

133 ff. The "Gourd-like" image for the "Lord of the Purse" recalls GM's earlier description of a gourd in chap. 25 of *Beauchamp's Career* (1875) as a symbol for the elderly marquis, husband of the young French heroine Renée.

182 Pythagoras, a native of Samos, sixth century B.C., believed in the transmigration of souls between men and animals for purification or punishment.

330 See headnote, p. 483.

366 See lines 614–21 and note.

449–68 In MS 1, line 12, the "Elgin front" is probably the flattened face of one of the warriors sculptured on a frieze of the Parthenon, brought to England by Lord Elgin and bought for the British Museum in 1816. "Caestus fists" are hard-hitting fists because the fists of Greek and Roman boxers were bound with leather thongs, the *caestus*, in order to harden their blows.

499 *Batrachian croak*: a frog-like croak. GM undoubtedly capitalized "Batrachian" because he had in mind the *Batrachomyomachia* 'battle of the frogs and the mice,' a mock-heroic poem that used to be attributed to Homer.

545–54 GM contrasts the maddening noises of Phrygian celebrations in honor of the country's chief goddess Cybele with the proper music of Measure.

584–621, *frag. S, line 2 nous*: Greek for 'mind'; a colloquialism in the nineteenth century for intelligence or common sense.

585–87 See note to lines 545–54. Cybele's beast was the lion, recalled by GM in fragments Y, W, and X.

586 *thermonous*: GM's neologism for 'heated.'

591–92 These lines, voicing the main text of GM's sermon to the prodigal, keep reappearing in the MSS.

614–21 According to Servius in his note to Virgil's *Aeneid* 3.57, "whenever the people of Massilia [Marseilles] were burdened with pestilence, one of the poor would volunteer to be fed for an entire year out of public funds on food of special purity. After this period he would be decked with sacred herbs and sacred robes, and would be led through the whole state while people cursed him, in order that the sufferings of the whole state might fall upon him, and so he would be cast out. This account has been given in Petronius."[1] GMT remarks that "The young man of the *Empty Purse* had no choice in the matter, as the law forced him to start life handicapped with riches."

624 GM follows Carlyle in using the color pink for sentimentality. In the first chapter of *Diana of the Crossways* (1885) GM wrote that when the novelist's art "attained its majority. . . . Rose-pink and dirty drab will alike have passed away. Philosophy is the foe of both" (Mem. Ed., 16:15).

638–40 Luke 15:15, 23.

672–76 Although not a practicing Christian, GM believed in the good of prayer. As Dr. Shrapnel wrote to Nevil Beauchamp: "'it makes us repose on the unknown with confidence, makes us flexible to change, makes us ready for revolution—for life, then! He who has the fountain of prayer in him will not complain of hazards. Prayer is the recognition of laws; the soul's exercise and source of strength; its thread of conjunction with them.'"[2]

JUMP-TO-GLORY JANE

XV.2 *pen*: a small enclosure, as for sheep.

XVIII.6 *Satan's pounds and quarts*: that is, of meat and of beer. See IV.6 and XXIII.4, MS 1.

XXXI.5 For the meaning of "charger" as 'salver' (MS 1 and frag. B), the word GM first used, cf. Matt. 14:8.

1. *Petronius*, trans. Michael Heseltine, Loeb Classical Library, p. 325, fragment 1.
2. *Beauchamp's Career* (1875), Mem. Ed., 12:5–6. See also WMM, pp. 237–38, 350.

XXXIV.2 There is no Fredsham in Bartholomew's *Survey Gazetteer of the British Isles*. Fredley, however, is two miles north of Dorking, GM's home.

TO THE COMIC SPIRIT

20 The phrase "trodden weeds" echoes Keats's *Ode on a Grecian Urn*, 5.3.

58 The "throb" is a metonymy for the heart that should not be "lord" of our behavior.

73 Cf. description of the Comic Spirit in "An Essay on Comedy": "It has the sage's brows, and the sunny malice of a faun lurks at the corners of the half-closed lips drawn in an idle wariness of half tension" (*Miscellaneous Prose*, Mem. Ed., 23:46).

97–214 Douglas Bush writes of this long passage: "The mythology seems to be largely Meredith's. For Momus' criticism of the gods" he cites Lucian.[1]

This passage apparently was conceived before the rest of the ode. A sketch of titles on a loose leaf at Yale includes "The Banishment of Momus." Momus, the god of pleasantry who continually satirized the gods, was lamed (line 109) by his fall from Olympus.

116–214 According to GM's myth, when the Olympians fell to earth after the expulsion of Momus they became a band of musicians at a summer seaside resort. Momus is leader of the band and dazes the listeners when he drops the great names of the members of the band. GMT worked out the members of the band as follows: "His Trombone [131] is Father Zeus; strong Heracles beats the drum [134]; Ares, god of war, is his bugler [135]; the Harp [139] is played by Apollo, god of the lyre and of the sun at dawn, now 'rayless' [140]; the Triangle is played by his twin-sister Artemis, the moon-goddess of chastity, 'the gibbous prude' [141]. (Gibbous = humpbacked, of a person; particularly of the moon, if it exceeds a semi-circle but is not as large as a circle.) His Tambourine [142] is Hebe, the graceful cup-bearer of Olympus, now blowzy and run to fat. The long passage beginning with 'O but now . . .' [149] refers to Aphrodite, goddess of love and beauty, 'the Dame of Dames' [151]. Like all the other gods and goddesses, she has come 'to this' [160] from rejecting the correction of Momus' Comic Spirit when on Olympus. The 'fatal kick' [166] Zeus gave to Momus has ruined Aphrodite also."

167–71 From love to lust: Aphrodite is now on the level of the enchantress Circe and of the Phoenician goddess Astarte.

174 For GM's use of the gourd image, see note to *The Empty Purse*, lines 133 ff., p. 1148.

202 Cf. line 58 and note.

340–52 According to Georg Roppen, this passage is "the twilight of the gods which Swinburne celebrated in *Hertha* [1871]. The passage looks back upon a great deal of what had happened to doctrinal structures since the beginning of the century, through the influence of Feuerbach and Strauss, through Comte and Stuart Mill, through Spencer, Darwin and Huxley."[2]

YOUTH IN MEMORY

11 *shepherd boy*: Ganymede.

57–59 Cf. these lines to a sentence from a famous letter by Keats to Benjamin Bailey, written at what is now the Burford Bridge Hotel at the foot of Box Hill, on November 22,

1. *Mythology and the Romantic Tradition in English Poetry* (Cambridge: Harvard, 1937), p. 391 n.
2. *Evolution and Poetic Belief: A Study in Some Victorian and Modern Writers* (Oslo: Oslo University Press, 1956), p. 265.

1817: "The setting sun will always set me to rights—or if a Sparrow come before my Window I take part in its existince [*sic*] and pick about the Gravel."[1]

79 The dragon is GM's symbol for Self; see *The Woods of Westermain*, IV.37 (p. 213), and throughout the novels.

PENETRATION AND TRUST

I.1–2 These lines had their genesis in the same pocket notebook at Yale, numbered 3, that contains four lines for *By the Rosanna*, written in the summer of 1861 (see hn., p. 192).

> Quick as a lizard under a stone
> The thought of her eyes shot out & in.

NIGHT OF FROST IN MAY

This poem is alive with memories that evidently meant much to GM. In his first novel, *The Ordeal of Richard Feverel* (1859), young Richard passionately desires to bend "above a hand glittering white and fragrant as the frosted blossom of a May night," and the day after he imagines this vision he meets Lucy Desborough who holds out her hand in saying "Good-bye." "The hand was pure white—white and fragrant as the frosted blossom of a Maynight." Hs kisses it (Mem. Ed., 2:111, 125). Chapter 58 of *Emilia in England* (1864), later *Sandra Belloni*, is titled "Frost on the May Night." In this chapter there are "white jewels" and "in the bright silence the nightingales sang loud." "The frost on the edges of the brown-leaved bracken gave a faint colour. Here and there, intense silver dazzled" the characters' eyes. Emilia and Tracy Runningbrook, the pleasant impersonation of Swinburne, advanced on the scene "amid the icy hush" (*Sandra Belloni*, Mem. Ed., 4:295). That this chapter was especially dear to GM is indicated by a letter to Captain Maxse, written just before the novel's publication [? March 11 or 18, 1864], saying that he would visit him and Mrs. Maxse in the spring. "And we will go and hear the nightingales, as you and I did, my dear fellow, when they chuckled a love-snatch and your heart had not found a home. Note 'Frost on the May-night' close to the end of 'Emilia.'" The nightingales' chuckles reappear in the poem, line 18.

Between the time of *Richard Feverel* and *Emilia*, he jotted in a pocket notebook (Yale 3), used in 1861–62:

> Frost on a May Night
> the larchwood & nightingales

15–36 This is the most accurate description of the nightingale's song that I know of in English poetry. GM had analyzed it in *Farina* (1857). There, twice, are the "four long notes," as well as the "chuckle," the "sob" and the "throb" (Mem. Ed., 2:93–94).

Part ii of "The Poets' Night," *MS 3*: 17 ff. The idea of " The Poets' Night" may have sprung from Elizabeth Barrett Browning's *Vision of Poets*, a poem in which a night scene leads to an array of poets from Homer to Coleridge. GM discarded the artifact while retaining, in *Night of Frost in May*, the lines inspired by memory. His catalogue of poets is not esoteric: Chaucer of *The Canterbury Tales* [22], Shakespeare in *The Merchant of Venice* [23], Milton in the sonnet "O Nightingale" [24], Coleridge in *Kubla Khan* [26], Keats in *Ode to a Nightingale* [27], Wordsworth in "Three years she grew" [29–30], Shelley of *The Cloud* [30–31], and Tennyson of *The Lotos Eaters* and *The Brook* [31–34].

---

1. *Letters*, ed. Hyder E. Rollins (Cambridge: Harvard University Press, 1958), Letter 43.

Part ii of "The Poets' Night," *MS 3*: 22–39 These lines were reproduced from Sotheby's Catalogue, 1 December 1910, by MBF, p. 106.

Part ii of "The Poets' Night," *MS 3*: 38–39 The inclusion of the author of *Atalanta in Calydon* among the poets is pleasant evidence that GM wanted to heal the long breach between himself and Swinburne.

THE TEACHING OF THE NUDE

II.7 GM felt strongly about the accent on "immortal." In writing to Frederick Macmillan, September 24, 1892, about the printing of *The Empty Purse*, he said that he had twice directed the printers to place an acute accent over this syllable, but it "has only at best a blunt dab of ink. They did the same in a previous volume; and if they have not the type for doing differently, I must change the word." See note to *The South-Wester*, line 116, p. 1147.

II.8 *Meliboeus*: a shepherd in Virgil's *Eclogues* 1.7.

EMPEDOCLES

I.8 Matthew Arnold, "his poet," celebrated Empedocles and his suicide in the boiling crater of Mount Etna in *Empedocles on Etna: A Dramatic Poem*, 1852, 1867. GM's poem is a curt rejoinder to Arnold's sympathetic treatment of Empedocles' despair.

TO COLONEL CHARLES

II.1 *Grisnez*: cape point in France, nearest to England; *Dungeness*: headland on the southeast extremity of Rye.

VII.3 Léon Gambetta (1838–82), lawyer, statesman, and orator, drew up the constitution of France's Third Republic (1873). He opposed the monarchistic President MacMahon (1808–93) and in 1877 was instrumental in forcing his resignation.

IX.1–2 GMT identified the quotation in Homer's *Odyssey* 19.13.

X.4–XI.5 A fragment at Yale apparently foreshadows these lines:

> And they on her, my cannonier:
> She has that instinct of the fowl.

> And they on her, my cannonier:
> She hears her military dog,
> And shares his instinct

Cf. the "military dog" with fragment between stanzas I and II.

XII The battle of Königgrätz on July 3, 1866, was the decisive engagement in the Seven Weeks War. General Benedek, heading the Austrian forces, observed that two Prussian armies had made a junction, a wedge. Foreseeing his defeat, he telegraphed the Emperor urging him to make peace, but Francis Joseph ordered him either to join battle or retreat. GMT explains that Chlum "was the village in the centre of the Austrian position. . . ."

ENGLAND BEFORE THE STORM

III.1 *Lord of Hosts*: Isa. 13:4.

ODES IN CONTRIBUTION TO THE SONG OF FRENCH HISTORY

GM probably derived his uncouth title for this volume from a concept of Thomas Carlyle, who wrote to Emerson on August 12, 1834, that he was "constantly studying . . .

for a Book on the French Revolution. It is part of my creed that the only Poetry is History, could we tell it right."[1]

THE REVOLUTION

I.1 and thereafter. The metaphor of the French Revolution as a volcano seems to have been a commonplace, used by Thomas Carlyle in *The French Revolution* (1837).

I.2 Cf. the "giant-limbs" of France in Coleridge's *France: An Ode.*

II.3 Cf. GM's "Essay on Comedy" (1877) in which he described the French courtiers in Molière's *Le Misanthrope* as "gilded flies" (*Miscellaneous Prose*, Mem. Ed., 23:22).

III.1, 21 The "unanticipated day" was the storming of the Bastille on July 14, 1789.

III.15–30 and IV The "young Angelical" of IV.1 is the bridegroom Liberty of III.16–17. See later in the poem, VII and XIII.9 ff.; also *Napoléon*, III.3, VI.50, XIII.124; *Alsace-Lorraine*, III.11, X.2.

IV.19–23 A foreshadowing of the Terror.

V.15–22 This vivid picture of the people of France before the Revolution may have come from Arthur Young's *Travels in France* (1787–89), republished in 1889 when it was reviewed by GM's friend Frederic Harrison.[2] Cf. Wordsworth's *Prelude* 9.502–532.

V.48 Probably the "Lucifer of the Mint," III.24.

VI–VIII Instead of drinking earth's dew (cf. V.1), France drank blood during the Reign of Terror, 1793–94.

VII.5–6 The laughter was not the laughter of the Comic Spirit, which had been one of France's great gifts, but demonic laughter. For the "heavenly lover," see III.15–30, IV, and note.

VIII.8 The lion suggests England; the snake, Royalist intrigue within France.

IX France's untrained peasant army repulsed the invading Austrian and Prussian forces at Valmy, September 20, 1792.

IX.11 The hiss is from the snake of VIII.8; see note.

IX.13 The *Marseillaise.*

IX.22 The "novel scythe" is the gun. In this section GM seems to have been influenced by Carlyle's descriptions of this Revolutionary army.

X.10 *tonant*: see note to *Napoléon* XIII.62.

X.16 The "shift of the hunt" occurred when, under the Directory, France turned her war of self-defense into wars of conquest, 1795. It is not clear what myth GM is alluding to in Titan climbing Olympus. According to Lempriere, Titan as a specific instead of a generic name comes to us from Lactantius, a Christian writer. He was the oldest son of Coelus and Terra who gave his younger brother Saturn the earth to reign. Perhaps in this sense he "clomb" Olympus.

XI.1–2 The eighth edition of Baedeker's *Paris* (p. 262) states that these banners, once in the Hôtel des Invalides, were accidentally burned in 1851.

XII.15 By 1797, after his successful Italian and Austrian campaigns, "the iron lord," Gen. Napoleon Bonaparte, had won the hearts of his countrymen.

XIII.7 *the Just*: cf. II.9.

    1. *The Correspondence of Thomas Carlyle and Ralph Waldo Emerson*, 1834–1872, 3rd ed., 2 vols. (Boston: James R. Osgood, 1883), 1:25.
    2. "France in 1789 and 1889," *The Meaning of History and Other Historical Pieces*, new ed. (London: Macmillan, 1908), pp. 208–10.

XIII.9 See III.

XIII.69 '*I only; I who can*': Carlyle's definition of Kingship.[1]

NAPOLÉON

I.1–2 and thereafter. During two uprisings in Paris, 1792 and 1795, Napoleon had recommended the use of cannons against the mobs and had personally employed them in 1795. He knew well how to use them and how to capture them during his campaigns. (They do not feature in contemporary cartoons of Napoleon.) The cannon, moreover, links Napoleon I with Napoleon III, who features in the next ode, *Alsace-Lorraine*. Napoleon III was an expert on munitions, and in 1849, while President of the Republic, had established the use of light cannon by the French armies. It was known as the "Napoleon gun" or "cannon" and was adopted by the United States.

I.14 For the metaphor of the volcano see *The Revolution*, I.1–2, III.1–3.

II.17 Charlemagne not only created an empire but established a dynasty. Napoleon emulated him in both of these respects. He restored "Order" (line 26) after the French Revolution and the Terror as Charlemagne had restored order in Europe after the dissolution of the Holy Roman Empire.

II.42 The eagle was Napoleon's ensign, just as it had been a symbol of Jove.

III.3 For France's "heavenly lover," see *The Revolution*, IV.1–2 and note.

III.25 *vivisectionist and knave*: enemies foreign and domestic.

III.33–37 The eagles carried on poles. Cf. VI.28.

IV.38–40 Cf. *The Revolution*, III.5–14.

V.16 *Earth's fluttering little lyre*: as GMT explained, this is the lark, GM's symbol of "the voice of liberty and humanity."

VI.13 *cloak connivent rains*: the rains cloak his movements.

VI.18 *opal puffs*: cannon smoke.

VI.39–54 Byron, in *Childe Harold's Pilgrimage*, Canto 4, stanzas 95–98, made the same comparison between the American Revolution and the French Revolution and between George Washington and Napoleon. Napoleon himself had said that had he been across the Atlantic he might have been another Washington.[2]

VII.1–21 The battle of Eylau was fought on February 8, 1807, against the Russians in a snowstorm "of spectral gloom" (line 5). "The slaughter was frightful—'sheer butchery,' said Napoleon later. 'What carnage,' said Ney, 'and no results,' thus accurately describing this encounter."[3] GM imagines Napoleon recalling after this drawn battle his visit to the tomb of Frederick the Great at Potsdam the previous October, before his triumphal entry into Berlin. The visit to the tomb was a gesture of admiration. "He had the execrable taste, however, to take the dead Frederick's sword and sash and send them to Paris as trophies. 'The entire kingdom of Prussia is in my hands,' he announced."[4]

    1. "The Hero as King," *Heroes and Hero-Worship*, Edinburgh ed. (New York: Scribner's, 1903), 5:196.
    2. "Le Comte de Las Cases," *Le Mémorial de Sainte-Hélène*, ed. Gerard Walter, 2 vols. (Paris: Gallimard, 1956), 1:233.
    3. Charles Downer Hazen, *The French Revolution and Napoleon* (New York: Holt, 1917), p. 313.
    4. Ibid., p. 312.

Napoleon had cause to meditate at Frederick's tomb. Frederick II, absolute monarch of Prussia, 1740–86, described himself as "the first servant of the state" and acted the part. Known for his enlightened spirit and his fine sense of justice, he was the most illustrious European sovereign of his day, and by strengthening Prussia he laid the foundation for the German Empire.

See GM's epitaph, *The Emperor Frederick of our Time* and headnote, p. 462.

VII.21 *battle's dice-box*: the Treaty of Tilsit, made in the summer of 1807 by Czar Alexander I and Napoleon. Cf. III.29–30.

VII.24 *the Seaman*: England.

VII.35 *Macedonian*: Alexander the Great, who conquered northern India in 326 B.C.

VII.37 If "immarcessible" is derived from *mark* or *march* 'a border', as GMT believed, it is a neologism, but there is an adjective, now rare, *immarcescible*, meaning 'unfading' or 'imperishable'. This meaning would be apt for the more glorious Charlemagne that Napoleon imagines he will be.

VII.52–57 Napoleon will be led into the fatal Russian campaign of 1812.

VIII.14 France's critical faculty had been a concomitant of her Common Sense.

VIII.17 *Solon-Mars*: that is, the lawmaker as well as the war-maker. The Code Napoléon (1804), a modification of the Roman or Civil Law, is, with amendments, still the law of France.

VIII.18 Cf. a metaphor in *One of Our Conquerors* (1891) that describes Victor Radnor as having "the cataract's force which won its way by catching or by mastering, uprooting, ruining!" (Mem. Ed., 17:470.)

IX.18 *devolvent*: a neologism.

IX.32–39 Cf. Napoleon on policy: "*Events ought not to govern policy, but policy events*" (1797).[1]

After IX.37 MS and between IX.45 and IX.46 TS. Lycurgus, king of Sparta, hypothetically in the seventh century B.C., was famous as a lawmaker. The *SOED* defines "Frate" as a 'friar', but here GM must be using it in its basic meaning as 'brother'.

IX.89 *his Euclid mind*: Napoleon excelled in mathematics.

IX.135 Napoleon's "Tyrant" was ambition.

X.17–19 Napoleon was not as well schooled as the Greek hero Achilles, leader of the industrious Myrmidons.

X.44 For Napoleon's daemon, see note to IX.135.

X.51 Cf. III.39–43.

XI.13–23 England, suffering economic hardship from Napoleon's continental blockade (November 21, 1806), was trying to persuade Russia (the Scythian, line 19) to open the Baltic ports to her shipping. Napoleon's distrust of Czar Alexander's relations with England was a precipitating factor in his invasion of Russia.

XI.19 The Russians had not abided by the Treaty of Tilsit. See note to VII.21.

XI.20 Still England, the meteorite with water in the brain.

XI.45–57 Napoleon's army crossed the River Niemen, lines 54–55, the night of June 24, 1812 through June 27.

XI.47 Among the barbarian invasions, GM probably had chiefly in mind Attila's of 451. He had made a study of the Hun for his poem, *The Nuptials of Attila*, p. 345.

1. William Hazlitt, *Works*, Centenary ed., 13:322.

XI.49 Caesar's Gallic Wars, 58–49 B.C.

XIII.14–68 After Napoleon's defeat in Russia he campaigned in Prussia and Austria in 1813, and in November of that year refused to accept a peace from the coalition of Russia, Prussia, Austria, and England that would have left France with her natural boundaries. In February and March of 1814 he fought a brilliant defensive campaign when the allies invaded France.

XIII.62 *tonant*: 'thundering, loud-sounding'. This line and line 5 of *Clash in Arms of the Achaians and Trojans* contain the only examples of the word in the *OED*; see also *The Revolution* X.10.

XIII.64 See X.47.

XIII.69–92 On March 31, 1814, Czar Alexander and Frederick William III, king of Prussia, entered Paris and forced the abdication of Napoleon and his exile to the island of Elba. His reappearance at Cannes on March 1, 1815, and triumphal march to Paris with his former soldiers flocking around him he later thought to be the happiest time of his life.

XIII.92 The battle of Waterloo was fought on June 18, 1815, a hot Sunday.

XIII.99 *flaminical*: pertaining to a *flamen* 'a priest devoted to the service of a deity'.

XIII.109 The "bow" metaphor is Napoleon's own, uttered on what proved to be his deathbed (Hazlitt, *Works*, 15:346).

XIII.118 *Earth's fluttering little Lyre*: see V.16 and note.

XIII.119 *the raven's . . . croak*: GMT, "the voice of the Cossack and of the Holy Alliance."

XIII.124 *young Angelical*: see *The Revolution*, III.15–30 and note.

Following *Napoléon* in *Odes in Contribution to the Song of French History*, GM reprinted his much earlier ode, *France, December 1870*, which had appeared in the *Fortnightly*, 1 January 1871. In the present edition this ode is to be found with the contents of the volume in which it was first collected, *Ballads and Poems of Tragic Life* (1887), p. 369.

ALSACE-LORRAINE

The notes in GMT should be consulted for *Alsace-Lorraine* because Trevelyan "had the advantage of the poet's instruction as to the meaning of some of the more difficult passages. . . ." The poem records the recovery of France after the Franco-Prussian War; see *France, December 1870*, p. 369.

I.1 The personification of the Hours (*Horae*) is classical, made memorable in English poetry by Spenser's *Epithalamion* and Shelley's *Prometheus Unbound*. Here the Hours are linked as on the face of a clock.

I.5–10 Cf. *France, December 1870*, IV.31–32 (p. 372) and note.

I.15 The "Book of the River of Life" is only one of GM's many tutelary books. See the epigraph to the first printing of *Modern Love*, in headnote (p. 116). In *Richard Feverel* there is "The Pilgrim Scrip," in *The Egoist*, "The Book of Egoism," and in *The Amazing Marriage*, "Maxims for Men."

II.63 *respersive*: 'tending to scatter', the only example in the *OED*.

II.67–69 Cf. the quatrain from *Vittoria* (1867), lines 31–34 (pp. 852–53) and note.

III.2 *darkness on that Eastward side*: lost Alsace-Lorraine.

III.5–8 Prussia waits to see if France will rearm.

III.11 For the "Angelical" see *The Revolution*, IV.1–2 and note.

III.16 See *The Revolution* XII.4. The "Auroral ray" of the Revolution has been darkened.

III.34–47 The indemnity agreed upon in the Treaty of Frankfurt, January 21, 1871, that France would repay Prussia within the stipulated three years.

IV.4 The "one" is MacMahon, monarchist president of France, 1873–77. Cf. *To Colonel Charles*, lines VII.3–5, p. 547.

IV.16 In the previous odes France was described as a "wanton" because she deserted her true lover, Liberty, for the Terror and the two Napoleons, I and III.

IV.18 *Phrygian caps*: conical with the peak turned over in front, now identified with the cap of liberty.

IV.20 Austria, Germany, and England. (The Guelphs were the ancestors of the House of Hanover.)

IV.21–22 *belly-god*: Phil. 3:19.

IV.36 *treasure-galleon*: revival of Bonapartism; see *Napoléon*, XIII.131–32.

IV.37 *cannon-name*: see *Napoléon* I.1 and passim.

V.2 GM would have been gratified to know that Joan of Arc, who was beatified in 1909, was at last canonized in 1920.

V.31 *mastodonized*: a neologism; see *Napoléon*, III.43 and X.51.

V.33 *treasure-galleon*: the Napoleonic legend. See *Napoléon*, XIII.131–32.

V.44 '*I who can*': see *The Revolution*, XIII.69 and note.

V.48 Vercingetorix, a leader of the Gauls, led a great revolt against the Romans in 52 B.C. but was ultimately defeated by Caesar, who led him in triumph to Rome and had him put to death in 46 B.C.

VI.1 Cf. Renée in *Beauchamp's Career*, chap. 40: "'There is no step backward in life'" (Mem. Ed., 12:133).

VI.17 *that one word*: Sedan. The battle of Sedan, fought on September 2, 1870, was the decisive disaster of the Franco-Prussian War. The disorganized French army was totally dispersed, and Napoleon III, who had been in the thick of the fire, was taken prisoner after capitulating to William I.

VII.1 *credible ghost*: Napoleon I overlooking the battle of Sedan.

VII.7 *Expugnant*: a neologism from *expugn*, 'to take by storm'.

VII.13–14 The Dardans are the Trojans in Homer's epic, but it is not clear what poet GM had in mind, distinct from Homer, as the Rhapsode of the Greeks (Achaeans).

VII.31–34 The description is of Adolphe Thiers (1797–1877), a statesman and historian, who published his *History of the Consulate and the Empire* in 20 volumes, 1840–55. It appeared in an English translation, 1845–62. The work is regarded now, as GM regarded it, as an inaccurate eulogy that helped to create the Napoleonic legend. Thiers knew, however, that Napoleon III was over-optimistic about the strength of his army, and he was one of the few deputies who voted against France declaring war on Prussia in 1870.

GM's disgust for Thiers is also vividly expressed in two letters. On October 25, 1870, he wrote to his son Arthur: "There is talk of an armistice, but Paris must fall before the French will seriously treat for peace. Count Bismarck gives audience to-day to that deleterious little Frenchman Thiers, who has been poisoning his countrymen for half a century, and now runs from Court to Court, from minister to minister, to get help to undo his own direct work." Seven years later, on November 16, 1877, he wrote to John Morley: "Senior's Thiers is a lasting picture to me of the Devil's own Infernal Imp. Statesman, yea, begotten by Machiavelli of the Vivandière of the Regiment! Had I time, I would compose a La Bruyère abstract of it.—Born with Satan's blessing too! His kettle-drum taps marched France to Sedan. His more than Louis Napoleon's. The Thiers-fed French really thought at the sound of the bugle that another chapter of the Windy History was to be written."

VII.47 *Lopped of an arm*: Alsace-Lorraine. This refers back to III.9.

VII.56 This line echoes Shelley's "The desire of the moth for the star," in the lyric "One word is too often profaned."

IX.10 The "revolving Twelves" refers to the Hours of I.1 ff.

IX.21 *one tall spire*: of Strasbourg Cathedral.

IX.36–38 Mount Helicon was sacred to the Muses. For GM's early translations of German lyrics, see pp. 808–12

IX.45 *belted Overshadower*: Germany.

IX.46 GM's concept of "Force" was set forth in one of his earliest poems, "Force and His Master"; see p. 718.

IX.51–52 Before being defeated first by Saul and then by David, the Amalekites ranged through a wide territory. During the reign of Hezekiah, king of Judah, five hundred Simeonites captured the last Amalekite stronghold, Mount Seir. The analogy is between the French as possessors of Alsace-Lorraine (Amalekite) and the Germans (Simeonite).

X.1 *Jeanne*: see section V and note.

X.2 *young Angelical*: see *The Revolution*, IV.1–2 and note.

X.6 '*she who can*': Cf. V.44 and *The Revolution*, III. XIII.69 and note.

X.7 *Heliaea*: judgment-court.

X.20–21 GM's faith in France was expressed in *France, December 1870* (p. 369), written during the Siege of Paris.

X.33 *double name*: Alsace-Lorraine.

X.35 For France's Angel bridegroom, see *The Revolution*, III.13–30 and note.

X.43 "History's Ætna" was GM's metaphor for the French Revolution. See *The Revolution*, I.1 and note.

X.87 France must not go to war to recover Alsace-Lorraine as the Greeks did to recover Helen of Troy.

X.91–99 France is blind to the danger of the Napoleonic legend.

X.98 The myth of Cadmus.

X.123 The Seaman, as in *Napoléon*, is England.

X.125 *Neva*: the Russian river in the delta of which lay St. Petersburg, now Leningrad.

X.130–34 Cf. *France, December 1870*, XI.54–54.

LINES TO A FRIEND VISITING AMERICA

V and VI The "blunderers" were the British upper classes who had supported the South in the recent American Civil War.

XXVIII.3 Cf. the "noble Norman lip" with the "Norman nose" in *Aneurin's Harp*,

XII.8 (p. 367) and note.

XXXI.4 *belly-god*: see Phil. 3:19.

XXXV and XXXVI GMT identifies the "poet" as Thomas Carlyle, "who a few months before this poem was written had published his *Shooting Niagara, and After*, in which he expressed his sympathy with the slave-owners in America, and the 'titular aristocracy' in England."

TO CARDINAL MANNING

1 *the skylark voice in men*: see *The Lark Ascending*, lines 92–122, pp. 241–42.

TO CHILDREN: FOR TYRANTS

I–IV GM wrote to his daughter Marie on July 24, 1886, about Koby's jealousy over a new dachshund puppy.

V–X The story of the Shannon spaniel closely parallels one related in V. Sackville-West's book *Faces* (London: Harvill Press, 1961). She writes that "no mention" of the Irish water spaniel "occurs until 1845, when he plunges into a rough sea to save the life of a boy, and subsequently endeavours to rescue a drunkard who dragged poor *Bagsman* under water with him when they were both drowned" (p. 24).

XIV–XV Which history books GM had in mind is not clear, but the story of Lord Llewelyn ap Iorweth ap Owain Gynedd, Prince of North Wales, who died in 1240, was familiar. Llewelyn mistook the blood of the wolf that the dog had attacked for the blood of his child.

A STAVE OF ROVING TIM

II.8 Sailors call petrels, "Mother Carey's chickens," having derived the term from the Latin *Mater Cara*, because they believe that these birds are protected by the Virgin.

THE RIDDLE FOR MEN

I.1 and II.1 GM intended this play on the verbs "rede" and "read," but GMT emended the verb in II.1 to "rede." GM may have been recalling Carlyle's "rede" in the sense of 'interpret': "The secret of Man's being is still . . . a riddle that he cannot rede" *Sartor Resartus* (1838) 1.8 (*NED*).

THE VITAL CHOICE

A Reading of Life was published in May 1901, and on June 4 GM wrote to his son William Maxse, who acted as his agent in the firm of Archibald Constable & Co.:

> 1st page of Poems, 1st verse, last line but one, is printed
> "Each can torture if divided" which has no meaning.
> It should be
> "Each can torture if derided."
>   I am sure this error was not in the *New Review* [*Monthly Review*].
>   —This page must be cancelled in all the unbound copies, and the erratum added to the bound copies.

GM was right in his recollection that the *Monthly Review* had correctly printed "derided." The word was restored in Constable's second impression of *A Reading of Life* (1901). Simon Nowell-Smith in *TLS*, 25 July 1942, described his own copy of

A Reading of Life that has an erratum sheet: "Page 1, line 5, *for* 'divided' *read* 'derided.'"

WITH THE PERSUADER

125–59 Aphrodite (passionate love) looks scornfully at the followers of the huntress Artemis. They have roses in their cheeks because they exercise (GMT), but these are not the roses of love.

236 *Laurel God*: Apollo.

273 GM was probably thinking of Euphrosyne, one of the Graces who represents Mirth, as in Milton's *L'Allegro*, line 12.

THE TEST OF MANHOOD

17–18 The "Huntress" is Artemis, the "Persuader" Aphrodite. See *The Vital Choice*, lines 1 and 2, p. 640.

91–121 In the course of man's advance, God, who had early appeared as "shrouded" (line 94), finally was "discerned" (111).

THE CAGEING OF ARES

71–79 See headnote, p. 663. After Ares had been encased in the "vessel of bronze" for thirteen months he was freed by Hermes, "the Dexterous."

THE NIGHT-WALK

27 The mantle of Night echoes Shelley's *To Night*: "Wrap thy form in a mantle gray" (2.1).

SONG IN THE SONGLESS

The printer wrote on the MS, "To follow Caging [*sic*] of Ares," but GM instructed him, "Let 'The Hueless Love' precede this."

1 For a very early suggestion of music from the "sedges dry," see two lines associated with "Wandering Willie," Canto 2, line 276, p. 919.

THE MAIN REGRET: WRITTEN FOR THE CHARING CROSS ALBUM

For the bibliographical explanation of the canceled leaves alluded to in the apparatus criticus, see MBF, p. 137.

On March 26 [1901], GM wrote William Maxse that *The Main Regret* was not to be published in *A Reading of Life* if it had not already appeared in the *Charing Cross May-Day Album* [*sic*], due to appear at the end of April. "In any case, print under the title, in small caps, 'Written for the Charing Cross Album'." Soon thereafter, sometime in April, he wrote again:

> It may no longer be possible to delete "The Main Regret." But I will pay the cost for alterations that must be made for the lines to be classical Elegiacs.
> Second line of 1st verse, for "strike men ruthlessly" etc., put "strike us all ruthlessly" etc.
> 4th line—for "past all hope" etc., put "past the one hope" etc.
> 2nd verse, 4th line, for "back to acceptance of life" etc., put "back to a half-sloughed life" etc.
> If the back is not in binding this may be done. It is a question of correcter metre.

Obviously the reading of the cancel has priority. There is no reason for the correction of I.2 in the errata of the Edition de Luxe.

FOREST HISTORY

II.1–2 and XXVII.1 Here the Dragon is the primitive Dragon of fear, not the symbolic Dragon of Self as in *The Woods of Westermain*, IV.60 (p. 214) and note.

II.4 *devorant*: a neologism. After man had made roadways through the forest, he changed places with the Dragon.

X.4 The Garden of Eden "half restored" for the nuns.

XIX.1 *hallali*: GM's onomatopoetic neologism.

XXVI.1 *the one*: Shakespeare.

XXVIII GM alludes to Shakespeare's Forest of Arden in *As You Like It* where Duke Senior

> Finds tongues in trees, books in the running brooks,
> Sermons in stones, and good in every thing. (2.1.16–17)

A GARDEN IDYL

7 GM's study, above the garden beside his home at Box Hill, was built in the shape of a chalet.

FORESIGHT AND PATIENCE

136 For GM's concept of Lucifer, see *Lucifer in Starlight*, p. 285.

166 For the metaphor of the full trough—i.e. the "grunters" (line 173) and the "'troughsters'" (184)—describing the upper classes as distinct from the "toilers" (184), compare the ebullient, opulent, and poetic Captain Con in GM's unfinished novel *Celt and Saxon* (*ca*. 1888): "We're wash in a hog-trough for Father Saturn to devour; big chief and suckling babe, we all go into it, calling it life! And what hope have we of reading the mystery? All we can see is the straining of the old fellow's hams to push his old snout deeper into the gobble, and the ridiculous curl of a tail totally devoid of expression!" (Mem. Ed., 20:78).

Between 208 and 209, National Review *line 3* For GM's extended use of Momus, see *To the Comic Spirit*, lines 97–214 (pp. 521–25) and note.

Between 212 and 213, National Review *line 17* The demi-god Silenus, attendant of Bacchus, is always represented as fat, jolly, and intoxicated.

255–57 This metaphor for the fate of some philosophers stems from GM's poem *Empedocles*; see p. 544 and note.

ILIAD i.225: INVECTIVE OF ACHILLES

GM had quoted this passage from the translations of Chapman and of Merivale in his article of 1869; see headnote, p. 696.

ILIAD xiv. 394: CLASH IN ARMS OF THE ACHAIANS AND TROJANS

The draft in the Cochran Library is the one sent to Pollock; see headnote, p. 695.

5 *tonant*: not derived from the Greek text; see note to *Napoléon*, XIII.62.

THE MARES OF THE CAMARGUE

20 *Vacarés*: a salt bog in the Camargue.

TIME

According to the account book of *Household Words*, the ten shillings and sixpence paid for this poem was split between GM and the subeditor, W. H. Wills (see MBF, p. 147, and LS, p. 32).

QUEEN ZULEIMA

10 *old City*: Scodra (modern Scutari), the capital of Illyria.

47–48 These lines echo the refrain of Wordsworth's poem *The Thorn*: "Oh misery! oh misery! / Oh woe is me! oh misery!"

A WASSAIL FOR THE NEW YEAR

51–56 Following Louis Napoleon's coup d'état of December 2, 1851, when he declared himself Napoleon III, Emperor of France, the fate of the country was uncertain.

57–62 GM favors the Sultan of Turkey because he allowed the famous Hungarian Lajos Kossuth to visit England.[1] Kossuth had fled to Turkey after the failure of the Hungarian revolution and had been confined there for two years.

63–68 He approves of Hungary because it joined in the revolutionary uprisings of 1848, and he is down on Austria because of its occupation of northern Italy.

71 *Gorgon's countenance*: King Frederick William IV of Prussia who failed to carry out constitutional reforms promised in 1848 and reestablished the reactionary Germanic Confederation of 1815.

73–74 Poland, in spite of her revolutionary endeavors, was in the possession of Austria and Russia.

75–80 Italy yearned to break her Austrian chains.

81–86 A toast to the freedom of Britain and the United States of America.

WAR

According to the account book of *Household Words*, the guinea paid for this poem was split between GM and R. H. Horne (see p. xxx and MBF, p. 147).

II.12 Isa. 2:4.

MOTLEY

65–88 Fair Rosamond, the mistress of Henry II (1154–89), is best known through Deloney's ballad in *Percy's Reliques*. She was "embowered" by Henry in a labyrinthine stronghold at Woodstock, near Oxford, where she died ca. 1176. The farcical details of the Scotch colonel being tripped by his ladder into the "billow" and of the flower-pot falling on the King's head are indeed wondrous transformations wrought by the Clown's art.

RHINE-LAND

GM probably refreshed his memory of the Rhineland from this poem for his tale *Farina* (1857). In *Farina* we find the sandhills to the south of Andernach (Mem. Ed.,

---

1. In 1849 GM offered, unsuccessfully, to *Chambers's Edinburgh Journal* an abridged translation of a biography of Kossuth (LS, pp. 28, 31).

2: 87, 107), in *Rhine-Land*, line 20; the silver arrow that "our German girls slide in their back-hair," (p. 36), *Rhine-Land*, lines 51–52; and the "careless" song of a Water-Lady (p. 96), *Rhine-Land*, line 71 ff. "Farina caught no words, nor whether the song was of days in dust or in flower, but his mind bloomed with legends and sad splendours of story, while she sang on the slate-block under sprinkled shadows by the water." See also *Pictures of the Rhine*, pp. 97–100.

25 Mary Peacock Nicolls's sister and foster-sister may have served as bridal maids at her marriage to GM in St. George's Church, Hanover Square, on August 9, 1849.

MONMOUTH

21–22 During the Great Rebellion, the northern army, supporting Charles I, was destroyed by the parliamentary and Scottish armies at Marston Moor on July 2, 1644. On September 3, 1651, Oliver Cromwell's forces won the great victory at Worcester, thus ending the Civil War that had succeeded the Great Rebellion.

25 The admiral was Robert Blake (1599–1657), who had occupied Taunton during the Civil War, becoming its governor. Later he was made an admiral of the fleet.

27 *October*: the name of the ale brewed in that month.

31–32 According to George Roberts's *Life, Progresses and Rebellion of James, Duke of Monmouth* (London: Longman, 1844), 1:303, on this gala day of June 19, twenty-seven young virgins had presented as many colors to Monmouth, "worked with their own hands, though the expense of the material was defrayed by the inhabitants of the town."

96 James II, a Catholic by conversion, alarmed the British by his open championship of Roman Catholics.

118 *Tone*: the river that flows past Taunton.

121 Monmouth was "king" on June 20–21.

Berg MS 124 Charles II was known as the "Merry Monarch." He had many illegitimate children of whom he declared Monmouth to be one.

Berg MS 127 Lord Feversham led the royalist army that routed Monmouth.

THE STORY OF SIR ARNULPH

"The Story of Sir Arnulph" was not included in the Edition de Luxe, although GM did not cancel the poem in the proof sheets. It was to appear between *A Crown of Love* and *Lines to a Friend Visiting America*.

IN THE WOODS

In their catalogue for a sale of *First Editions of George Meredith* [1912], Dodd & Livingston of New York described a copy of *In the Woods*, extracted from the *Fortnightly*, "with important corrections and alterations in the author's autograph. . . . The purpose . . . in making the alterations on the present sheets cannot now be traced" (p. 11). I have not found these sheets.

THE LABOURER

GM sent *The Labourer* to Edward Tyas Cook, editor of the *Westminster Gazette*, on February 3, 1893, stipulating for good space and type and forbidding a facsimile of his manuscript. He had a chance to correct proof and after publication wrote Cook on February 10 about one misprint and two emendations, in case the poem should be written "in an album." In the present edition the poem is corrected according to GM's instructions.

2–12 GM addresses the men and women of the Primrose League, a conservative political organization, so named because of Benjamin Disraeli's affection for the primrose.

8 *Dog*: Cerberus.

TRAFALGAR DAY

This poem was probably prompted by GM's visit with Mr. and Mrs. Seymour Trower at Weybridge in August, 1896, inasmuch as Mr. Trower was "associated with the Navy League and with the observance of Trafalgar Day."[1] GM sent the poem to Mrs. Alice Meynell on September 25, 1896, saying that he would send it to the *Daily Chronicle* if she approved: "Poetry so so, but remember, it is a battle trump, and not a threnody." On October 20 he let her know that he had "amended" the poem before sending it to the *Chronicle*.

IV.4 At the Battle of Austerlitz, December 2, 1805, Napoleon I defeated the armies of Russia and Austria. This most brilliant of his victories was won on a sunny, cloudless day.

AT THE FUNERAL

1 *tenement*: used here to describe the Queen's body, the same word that GM used in an epitaph for a pet dachshund, *Islet the Dachs* (see p. 461).

THE CRISIS

15 *red Sunday*: On Sunday, January 22, 1905, in St. Petersburg, a band of laborers, led by a priest, marched to present a petition to the czar and was fired upon by troops.

20 After his conversion to the principles of Christian love, about 1876, Tolstoy preached the doctrine of nonviolence.

OCTOBER 21, 1905

This was the second poem GM wrote on Nelson and Trafalgar; see *Trafalgar Day* (p. 781) and note. Two days after its publication he wrote Miss Louisa Lawrence, "If you see *The Outlook*, correct on 4th Stanza, 1st line 'fears' for 'tears'—a horrible disfigurement, causing me pain almost as sharp as the bandage on my erring leg." (He had broken his ankle.)

When the Sunday *Observer* reprinted the poem five days after GM's death, it did so with the observation that the poem was "as appropriate to Empire Day." A letter to me from the *Observer*, May 18, 1962, says that the paper has no record of what happened to the manuscript from which it made a facsimile of stanzas 2 and 3.

THE CENTENARY OF GARIBALDI

The centenary of Giuseppe Garibaldi's birth was July 4, 1907. Then, as now, he was the most popular hero of the Risorgimento. On May 14, 1907, GM sent this poem to his son to be typed "speedily." Within two days he had corrected the typescript and wanted a fresh copy to send to Rome.

Many years earlier [May ?4, 1864], GM had written William Hardman that he was at work on an ode to Garibaldi. The poem has never come to light.

1. *The Letters of George Meredith to Alice Meynell* (London: Nonesuch, 1923), p. 36.

6–7 Camillo Benso Cavour (1810–61) was the political "Brain" behind the unification of Italy under the House of Savoy. Giuseppe Mazzini (1805–72) was the unfaltering republican "Soul" of the Risorgimento, whose attitude toward the common aim of national unification was deeply moral and spiritual. Under sentence of death, he conducted his propaganda chiefly from London, although he made frequent secret visits to Italy and in 1849 led the short-lived republican government in Rome. GM portrayed him at the beginning of the second chapter of his novel *Vittoria* (1867). Giuseppe Garibaldi (1807–82) was the military genius whose "Sword" was always ready to help the cause. Perhaps his most brilliant and heroic exploits were the defense of Rome in 1849, in which he was defeated only by French intervention, and the conquest of Sicily and Naples in the summer of 1860 with the support of only a thousand volunteers.

IL Y A CENT ANS

GM complained to his son William Maxse in letters of March 29 and April 19, 1908, that he wrote this poem under duress. Although he had been too ill to receive Maj. H. F. Trippel, editor of the *Flag*, he had been reluctantly persuaded by his nurse to write something for the Union Jack Club. See also Butcher, p. 145.

Copy of the poem for *LP* was evidently set up from uncorrected proof sheets.

III.1 *bulk of Power*: Napoleon I; cf. GM's ode, *Napoléon*, p. 564.

Stanzas XII and XIII summarize GM's life-time warning to Britain. The metaphor of XIII. 3–4 must have been a truism with GM. Lady Butcher reported: "He used to say that when war did burst upon us—and we were unprepared—England would be like a hermit crab, without a shell, fighting with terrible odds against a fierce enemy crustacean protected by an armoured and scaly shell, and he dreaded the result" (p. 131).

THE CALL

6 *Exercitus*: 'a disciplined body of men, an army' (Europe).

7 *Salsipotent*: 'one that rules the waves' (Britain).

YOUTH IN AGE

Cf. the early eight lines *To a Skylark*, p. 68.
GM sent the MS of this poem to William Maxse Meredith on May 29, 1908.

ON COMO

5–7 Gen. 6:1–4.

MILTON

27–30 Since Ida is a mountain near Troy, this is the voice of Homer telling of the Trojan War.

34–35 GM means that this Age repeats the cry of Wordsworth in his sonnet, *London, 1802*,

> Milton! thou shouldst be living at this hour
> England hath need of thee;

36 *Belial*: see *Paradise Lost* 2.108–228.

37–38 *Mammon*: PL 2.228–83.

38–41 *Moloch*: PL 2.43–105.

TO R. H. H. WITH DAPHNE

33 *giant bright*: Horne's epic *Orion*, named after the constellation. See Introduction, p. xxx.

I LOOK'D FOR MY POET

7 For the Friar, William Hardman, see headnote, p. 829.

13–14 Wyse was a grandnephew of Napoleon through a French-Irish marriage.

DEAR, MY FRIEND

23 Ellis noted (p. 176) that this line was "An allusion to a kitchen courtship in Jessopp's household."

THE JOLLY YOUNG CARPENTER

7 John William Colenso (1814–83), Bishop of Natal, created a public sensation when his book, *The Pentateuch and the Book of Joshua Critically Examined*, was published in 1862. He had come to the conclusion that the first six books of the Old Testament could not be taken literally as the Word of God.

TUCK, MY TREASURE!

2 *Lucas*: Samuel Lucas of *Once a Week*.

2–3 *Cheshire Cheese*: a restaurant renowned for its most famous patron, Samuel Johnson.

7 *Quodque cupit sperat* (Ovid, *Metamorphoses* 1.491): 'And what he desires, he hopes' (Cline, Letter 188, n.3).

10–11 Mrs. Hamilton, nee Vulliamy, was of French origin, "First . . . of Bonny" (Bonaparte) (Cline, Letter 192, n.1).

ADIEU, ADIEU

6 Hardman had so large a paunch that he posed for a portrait of Henry VIII. See *The Hardman Papers* (*1865–1868*), facing p. 318.

THE IRENE

7 *St. Bernard*: the nickname for Morison derived from the biography of the saint that he had just completed.

9 *James Parthenon*: was James Virtue who owned the journal, the *Parthenon*.

12 Hardman, the "Tuck" of the party (line 3), identified Charles Austin as "A writer on *The Saturday Review* and *The Standard*," adding that "He was too ill to accompany the yachting trip" (*MVP*, p. 243, n.3).

13 *Argue-nots*: according to Cline, a dig at Morison, who was fond of arguing.

24 *Cubitt*: the builder of Gordon Street on which the Hardmans lived in Bloomsbury (see line 37).

38 Francatelli was a famous chef and author of a cookbook. GM broke off his verses at this point with the addendum: "Here the Friar ventures upon familiar and non-admissable rhymes. He threatens this Island with strange foul winds, if he is not quickly landed. He is dismissed to seek companionship with the 'Flying Dutchman'" (Cline, Letter 202).

FRIAR UXORIOUS!

1.4 "Detroïa" is a shortening of GM's usual nickname for Mrs. Hardman; "Demi-troïa," invented because Hardman had courted her for five years, half the time of the siege of Troy.

O HAVE YOU SEEN MY TUCK?

10–16 Cline, Letter 217, note 1, explains that these lines allude to the *Ode of Welcome* that Martin Farquhar Tupper (1810–89) had written for the marriage of Princess Alexandra and the Prince of Wales, an ode that Hardman had parodied.

12 *Northern Lass*: Alexandra was the daughter of the king of Denmark.

[VERSES BY GM AND LIONEL ROBINSON]

"Tuck is he named," line 7: Cline reports that a marginal note by Robinson identifies the "*poor young man*" as "Robin," GM (Letter 239, n. 12).

21 After Poco's (Robinson's) "Grenoble" Cline records a marginal comment by GM:

> His verses run and that's a fact
> ('Twere better would they tarry)
> But where they ran was never track'd
> Nor what the sense they carry.

20–21 The marginal note in Latin following the bracket means "Take whichever of these you prefer" (Cline, Letter 239, nn. 4, 5).

CLEOPATRA

90–107 Lady Butcher wrote of a discussion in the early 1870s about "which features of a woman's face were most expressive of her character. . . . Mr. Meredith averred that the feature above all others that most betrayed a man's or a woman's disposition was the nostrils. He disliked and distrusted any one with tall narrow nostrils; on the other hand, a sensitive wide nostril like a race-horse he professed to admire. We all began to examine each other's noses, and decided that his own was the only one present that stood the test" (pp. 34–35).

91 *Actium*: The sea battle off the promontory of Actium, from which Cleopatra so ignominiously fled with her unwanted ships, was won by Octavian in 31 B.C.

TUCK, THOU GRACELESS SINNER!

4 I quote Cline's note (Letter 337): "John Bengo, Jr., of Combe Lane, Norbiton, was charged in Borough Court with using a shed on his premises as a slaughter-house without licence, and shortly later his father was charged with maintaining on his premises a heap of manure containing a quantity of offal which gave off an unbearable stench."

15–16 Cline has identified the Latin quotation: Horace, *Odes* 1.24.19–20, to Quintillius: "that which cannot be changed will be made lighter by submission."

[VITTORIA CONCLUDING "CAMILLA"]

With the exception of four lines, I repeat my reluctance to reproduce verses apart from the novel in which they are incorporated: *Vittoria* (1867). The quatrain, lines 31–34 of the duet, said by Lady Butcher (p. 53) to be GM's "best loved lines," is chiseled on the open book that is his tombstone in Dorking Cemetery. The place and time of the songs GMT included are La Scala, Milan, 1847, on the occasion when

Vittoria ends an opera with a call to Italy to rebel against her Austrian possessors (Mem. Ed., 7:251–55).

31–34 See preceding note and *The Question Whither*, III.1–4 (p. 424) and note. This quatrain also suggests Goethe: "To me, the eternal existence of my soul is proved, from my need of activity; if I work incessantly till my death, nature is pledged to give me another form of being when the present can no longer sustain my spirit."[1]

SWEET JUSTICE OF NORBITON

1 *Jones*: a London solicitor, had taken over the lease of GM's house, Kingston Lodge, Norbiton, when the Merediths moved to Box Hill, Dorking.

4 *Princess of Teck*: the former Princess Mary of Cambridge, whose first child, born in 1867, was to become Queen Mary, wife of George V.

PALGRAVE

Professor Cline has suggested to me that the most likely subject of this quatrain was [John] Palgrave Simpson (1807–87), a dramatist and novelist, whom GM knew well at the Garrick Club. The verses are written on mourning paper in black ink, so I assume them to have been written in 1885 or 1884, when GM used this paper and ink following the death of his second wife.

On February 21, 1908, GM wrote Gilbert Farquhar that his friend's recollection of this quatrain "flatters me with the belief that I did some good portraiture in my time."

REMEMBER WHAT A NIGHT OF STORM

6 *Ossian*: the legendary Gaelic bard, made famous in the eighteenth century by the forgeries of James Macpherson.

I WOULD I WERE WITH JEAN

6 *Riette*: GM's daughter Marie, who had married Henry Parkman Sturgis in July, 1894.

7 *Walter*: Jean's husband, Walter Palmer.

SHALL I AGAIN

12 *Lobby*: Alice Meynell's daughter Olivia, aged six.

15 *Monica*: another daughter.

18 Alice Meynell, poet and essayist (1847–1922), had written a paper on "Daughters' Portions" in the *Daily Chronicle*. GM wrote her on May 31, 1896: "'Daughters' Portions' wars excellently, in the best of causes. Where I have stood grumbling at injustice and shooting jibes, you have done the work required."[2]

THOU PIRATE NESTED OVER ALDE!

8 Clodd's home was at the sea resort of Aldeburgh, described by George Crabbe (1754–1832) in his poem *The Borough* (1810).

9–12 Aldeburgh had been a favorite resort of Edward FitzGerald (1809–83), translator of *The Rubáiyát of Omar Khayyám*.

1. Johann Peter Eckermann, *Conversations with Goethe*, trans. Gisela O'Brien (New York: Ungar, 1974), p. 270.
2. *Letters of George Meredith to Alice Meynell* (London: Nonesuch, 1923), pp. 24–25.

IRELAND

Although this poem did not appear in a periodical until after GM's death, he had wanted it published. On November 19, 1908, he wrote tersely to his son: "The enclosed poem 'Ireland' for type. You will not easily get it accepted, owing to the subject."

John Morley, who had been Secretary for Ireland in Gladstone's administrations of 1886 and 1892–94 and who was a staunch Home Ruler, wrote of GM: "When our prospects in the Irish battle were darkest, Meredith stood firm to our drooping green flag" (Morley, 1:41). Captain Con in the unfinished novel *Celt and Saxon* is vivid evidence of how well GM understood the rebellious Irish and their grievances. The Irish battle was darkest in 1886 when Gladstone, in office as Prime Minister for the third time, produced the Home Rule Bill that split the Liberals and returned the Conservatives to office for six years. GM had written two articles on the subject: "A Pause in the Strife" for the *Pall Mall Gazette*, 9 July 1886, and "Concession to the Celt" for the *Fortnightly*, October 1886. He approved of Gladstone's view of the future but deplored his lack of strategy.

OPEN HORIZONS ROUND

Edward Clodd in his *Memories* (p. 147) gave a version of "Open horizons round" that GM wrote into Clodd's copy of *A Reading of Life*.

3 Clodd gives "waltz" for "walk," an understandable misreading of GM's late hand.

THE SOUL

At the beginning of NB A, [p. 3] GM wrote in clear, copybook hand a table of contents which reads:

> —Requiem
> —St. Therese
> —The Soul   Part 1
>   Part 2
>   Part 3
> —Love
> —Mortesto

Shortly thereafter GM must have considered all of these poems, except *Requiem*, expendable. *Requiem* was evidently torn out for use in *Poems* (1851) (p. 20). What remains of the rest of the poems is scribbled over. Various short fragments are written in the top margin of the only remaining page of "St. Thérèse" (p. 805). The first draft of *Love in the Valley* (p. 62) is crossed over the first four stanzas of "The Soul" (see the frontispiece of vol. 2). Stanzas 1–4 of Part 3 of "The Soul" are torn out vertically down the middle, and other stanzas of the poem are torn out completely. The end of "The Labouring Giant" is written over Part 3, stanza 9 of "The Soul." Stanzas for *The Olive Branch*, *Poems* (1851) (pp. 3–7) are written in the margin of "Love," overlapping stanzas 5–8. Similarly, the lines beginning with "He where the great sun looks his last" (p. 989) overlap the first seven lines of "Mortesto." All of these neatly copied remains were probably taken over from "The Monthly Observer" (see Introduction, p. xxix).

LOVE

See preceding note to "The Soul."

MORTESTO

See above note to "The Soul." These verses read like the ending of a longer poem. As Latin, *mortesto* is impossible. GM probably intended *mors esto*, 'let there be death.'

WANDERING WILLIE

As designated in the Textual Notes, the present text of "Wandering Willie" is pieced together from drafts in NB A and NB WW (see also pp. 200 and 968). The aim has been to achieve the most plausible narrative sequence.

The end of NB WW that faces the bookplate belonging to the Altschul Collection at Yale was to have been devoted to this poem, and trial runs of a title page indicate that there were to have been five cantos:

> The Muse and Willie
> Willie in London
> The Harvest Home
> The Inspiration of the Great West Wind
> The Doe

Of "The Muse and Willie" four fragments upside down on NB WW, leaf [11] remain:

> Wandering Willie
> Canto 1.
> Shall the star have name
> Come to us here, O single
> O for that London thick with laurels!
> Show[?] forth O [shiny *del.*] northern minstrel star:
> Thy shining head

These jottings and a prose note on NB A, [p. 37] (see p. 970) show that Willie went to London to make his name as a poet, but if any part of "Willie in London" was written, it is not extant. "The Harvest Home" and "The Doe" were evidently not conceived as separate cantos when first composed and copied. In NB WW they are run together. GM published a rewritten passage: *The Doe: A Fragment* "(From 'Wandering Willie.')" as the last poem in his *Modern Love* volume (1862) (see p. 200). "The Inspiration of the Great West Wind" appears in a rougher, and I think later, draft in NB A, [pp. 39–58] than the passages in NB WW.

The scheme of these five cantos does not include "The Last Wandering of Poor Willie" that appears as Canto 1 in NB A, [pp. 29–37]. GM evidently altered his tentative plan in order to start near the end of the action.

Canto 1, *lines associated with 169–70, [p. 37]:* For GM's interest in the tale of Sir Gawain's marriage, see his published poem, *The Song of Courtesy*, p. 616.

Canto 2. For later treatments of Willie's theme in this Canto, see headnote to *South-West Wind in the Woodland*, p. 25.

Canto 2.19–56 The "roofless House" was suggested by bk. 1 of Wordsworth's *The Excursion* in which the "Author," having heard the tale of the "roofless" (line 30) Hut's or Cottage's last inhabitant, was comforted by the "secret spirit of humanity" (line 927), as was Willie in the family's one-night abode. For Willie's association with *The Excursion* see p. 893 note. To Willie's son, on the other hand, a roofless house "was naught" (Canto 1.58).

80 ff. For the relationship between the rest of this Canto and *Ode to the Spirit of Earth in Autumn*, see headnote p. 193.

82 For the altered diction in this line, "breath," "yellow," "fevered," cf. Shelley's *Ode to the West Wind*, lines 1–5; for the altered word "scattered" in line 90, cf. Shelley,

line 66; and for the "commotion" in line 94, cf. Shelley, line 15.

109–10 For the promised victory and the "trumpet," cf. Shelley's *Ode to the West Wind*, line 69.

160 The "fevered" or "frenzied" is again suggested by Shelley's *Ode to the West Wind*, line 5: "Pestilence-stricken multitudes"; and GM starts his array of colors with "Yellow," line 164, as Shelley did in line 4; while the "winged seed" of line 174 is from Shelley's "wingèd seeds," line 7.

314 An echo of the Queen's description of Ophelia floating down the stream: "Which time she chanted snatches of old tunes" (*Hamlet*, 4. 7.178).

364–78 Having revised them slightly, GM used these lines for the conclusion of *Ode to the Spirit of Earth in Autumn*, lines 190–208 (see pp. 199–200).

Between 406 and 407 del., lines 16–17 The chief of these bards was Coleridge in his lesson of "The Ancient Mariner."

436 Cf. *The South-Wester*, line 1, p. 405.

479–82 Cf. Shelley's *Ode to the West Wind*, lines 57–61.

Before 503 del. Lines 3–6 recall Wordsworth's *Ode. Intimations of Immortality*, especially lines 203–04.

560–63 Matt. 19:14, Mark 10:14, Luke 18:16.

585 Canto 2 of "Wandering Willie" breaks off here, but there is a plan in NB A, [p. 46] for its extension: "The height above the village—Willie meditates how to turn his handicrafts to account—they descend and meet a man who after conversation offers them to come to his harvest home & for Willie to play the fiddle. Willie's reflection— They go—Third Canto begins with the Harvest Home." The man in this note is the farmer of the long fragments for "The Harvest Home" and "The Doe" that follow.

WANDERING WILLIE: FRAGMENTS FOR THE HARVEST HOME AND THE DOE

A prose note, NB A, [p. 36], indicates that at one point GM intended "Harvest Home" to be the second canto: "Canto 2nd Little Willie & Janet harvest home" On the next page is a sketch for an episode: "In 2nd Canto the pledge of the Forget-me not for the snowdrop of next spring. In the last Joan gives this to Willie preserved."

Fragment 1. GM's dalliance with the motif of Chaunticlere was inspired by Chaucer; see GM's *The Poetry of Chaucer*, p. 15, and Chaucer's *Nun's Priest's Tale*.

206 The narrative is resumed at this point. Willie and his family are at the home of the hospitable farmer.

Fragment 2. 1 *Bessy*: the daughter of the farmer who harbored Willie and his family in the unfinished Canto "The Harvest Home."

Fragment 3. 67 *Nancy*: the farmer's other daughter, now dead.

97 GM echoes Owen Glendower's boast: "I can call spirits from the vasty deep" (*I Henry IV*, 3.1.52).

167 The doe had been christened "Nancy" after the farmer's dead daughter; see *The Doe: A Fragment* at the end of the *Modern Love* volume (1862), line 88.

204 According to *The Doe: A Fragment* (1862), the doe is protected by a circle of horned cows, lines 97–106. Cf. later in this unpublished fragment, lines 282–83.

367 The bee was the regal device for Napoleon III, as it had been for Napoleon I.

378 Penny postage came into existence in 1839, followed by the issue of the first stamp in 1840.

406–07 The most impassioned contemporary philosopher to decry personal wealth was Thomas Carlyle, in "Stump-Orator," *Latter-Day Pamphlets* (1850).

408–09 GM himself, when his purse was sufficiently "well-stockt," reversed this verdict in his didactic poem *The Empty Purse* (see p. 483).

416–20 The great Carthaginian general, Hannibal, conquered the greater part of Italy, but not Rome, in the Second Punic War, 218–201 B.C.

506 "Up with the laverock early, early" is listed as a separate title in NB B, [p. 32].

552–684 Willie's Rhenish tale is related to the same medieval legend that was the basis for Robert Schumann's only opera complete, *Genoveva* (1850). As folklore, however, it is atypical: there are not multiple offspring; the abandoned wife dies after being recovered by her husband.

NOTES AND FRAGMENTS ASSOCIATED WITH "WANDERING WILLIE"

3, 4 It is curious to find in these notes the genesis of Chapter 42 of *The Ordeal of Richard Feverel*, "Nature Speaks." In that chapter Richard encounters, in a Rhineland forest, a fierce summer (not autumn) thunderstorm, picks up a frightened leveret, holds it to his breast where the small creature licks his hand, passes a little chapel within which he sees an image of the Virgin and her Child, and is so purified by the experience that he can return to his wife Lucy.

OR THE SINGLE PATH

The Or . . . Or . . . Or . . . pattern of this detruncated fragment irregularly follows the pattern of lines 91–124 in Tennyson's *Palace of Art* (1832, 1842).

TIME

1–4 See *Phantasy* (p. 182) and headnote.

SONG: WOO ME NOW

These verses may have been prompted by the refrain of a love song attributed to "the late Mr Graham of Gartmore" by Walter Scott in his *Minstrelsy of the Scottish Border*.[1]

> Then tell me how to woo thee, love;
> O tell me how to woo thee!
> For thy dear sake, nae care I'll take,
> Tho' ne'er another trow me.

THE BALLAD OF THE LADY EGLANTINE

3, 5 *thorny feet*: so called because of its prickles.

[LINES INSCRIBED TO HOWES]

The verses beginning, "Read not, my Howes!" probably allude to the review of *Poems* in the *Guardian* (9 July 1851), a Church of England weekly, which decreed that GM must "mend his morals and his taste." "Ovid is bad enough, but 'Daphne' and 'The Rape of Aurora' in this volume are worse, from their studied and amplified voluptuousness, than anything in the Metamorphoses."

1. Second edition, 3 vols. (Edinburgh: Ballantyne, 1803), 2:330.

SONG: WHO SAYS, SHE IS IN DANGER

5 *beaten foes*: the French. The English fear of a French invasion derived from the supposition that Louis Napoleon would want to avenge the French defeat at the Battle of Waterloo (1815).

SONG: BUY, BUY, BUY

13 GM was probably thinking of the adulterous *Merchant's Tale* in Chaucer's *Canterbury Tales*, in which the old man is January rather than December. The implication is that young England is sleeping in the arms of old England, not alert to what is going on.

14 *Jack Horner*: here the nursery rhyme figure represents England lulled by its own abundance.

19 This line dates the poem late 1853 or early 1854, when the English press alerted the nation to Russia's designs on Turkey, the first warnings of the Crimean War.

THE CAPITALIST

2.1 *Peter's will*: the power of the Roman Catholic church.

QUAKE, QUAKE

2 *Nicholas*: Nicholas I, czar of Russia, whose attempts to dominate Turkey provoked the Crimean War.

ARABIC POEMS

4.2 *the seven-starred silver knot*: the Pleiades.

AN AGE OF PETTY TIT-FOR-TAT

A completed version of this poem appears in *The Ordeal of Richard Feverel* (1859). Written by the despised poet Diaper Sandoe, it was a song about the "Age of Work."

> An Age of petty tit for tat,
>   An Age of busy gabble:
> An Age that's like a brewer's vat
>   Fermenting for the rabble!
>
> An Age that's chaste in Love, but lax
>   To virtuous abuses:
> Whose gentlemen and ladies wax
>   Too dainty for their uses.
>
> An age that drives an Iron Horse,
>   Of Time and Space defiant;
> Exulting in a Giant's Force,
>   And trembling at the Giant.
>
> An Age of Quaker hue and cut,
>   By Mammon misbegotten;
> See the mad Hamlet mouth and strut!
>   And mark the Kings of Cotton!

> From this unrest, lo, early wreck'd,
>   A Future staggers crazy,
> Ophelia of the Ages, deck'd
>   With woeful weed and daisy!

(Mem. Ed., 2: 48–49)

I WISH'D THE WORLD A BLINDNESS

This fragment is corrected in the bright blue ink that GM adopted in 1859.

BLAME ME NOT

17–24 The allusion is to the story of *Faithful John* in the Brothers Grimm.

CREATION AND THE PROPHET

Because the MS of this poem in the Yale notebook is a very rough draft and the fair copy in Berg is incomplete, I have used as copy-text the version in seven stanzas that GM's friend William Hardman copied from a MS that GM gave him. The text comes from some scattered pages of the journal that Hardman wrote monthly to a friend in Australia. They were given to Cline by a London bookdealer, and Cline adduces that they were not included in *MVP* because they are partly illegible. The xerox copy, however, has brought out the poem so that it can be read. Inasmuch as the poem is a copy in which the punctuation is inconsistent, I have regularized it.

SONNET TO J. M.: BRAVE IS THE SIGHT

14 Matt. 19:24.

Supplementary Textual Notes

LOVE IN THE VALLEY

MS: NB A, [*pp. 7–8*].

Abandoned fragments [*p. 7*]:

[1] Can we count on kisses as of [firm *del.*] bridal pledges?
      Then is she mine for the kisses that I drew,
   Mine for those kisses that I stole while she was sleeping
      For my lips clung fast till to hers they almost grew.
[2] Sunning her soft palms
[3] How often will the birds couple & the years
   Complete themselves and she still be untamed
   Hundreds of maidens long for young lovers
             and feel no shame
[4] As her [empty *del.*] bed when she leaves it in the morning
   Emptied of its treasure am I out of her
   Sight

Abandoned fragments [*p. 8*]:

[1] Near the ruddy hearth-floor hung about with holly
[2] All things are dearer for the love I bear her
   Each shows a likeness to the thing I love
[3] *after 80:*

   Once when she pluck'd a rosebud from the rose tree—
      From a mothers bosom took *or* drew the dimpled child,
   Deep on her cheek did I fix my earnest glances
      Till [above *del.*] beside her fondling she hid her head & smiled.

   Soon the pretty babe grew fretful for its mother,
      Stretch'd its tiny fingers to leave its alien nest—
   Did not the thought then work her heart & chide her
      That the little thing felt the snow upon her breast.

BY THE ROSANNA

The poem originally was much longer.

21–178 *OaW, 1862: not in de L or Mem. Ed., but in GMT.*

        I find it where I sought it least;
        I sought the mountain and the beast,

        The young thin air that knits the nerves,
        The chamois ledge, the snowy curves;
        Earth in her whiteness looking bold
        To Heaven for ever as of old.

        And lo, if I translate the sound
        Now thundering in my ears around,
        'Tis London rushing down a hill,
        Life, or London; which you will!   30

And men with brain who follow the bubble,
  And hosts without, who hurry and eddy,
And still press on: joy, passion, and trouble!
  Necessity's instinct; true, though unsteady.

Yea, letting alone the roar and the strife,
This On-on-on is so like life!
Here's devil take the hindmost, too;
And an amorous wave has a beauty in view;
And lips of others are kissing the rocks:
Here's chasing of bubbles, and wooing of blocks.   40
And through the resonant monotone
  I catch wild laughter mix'd with shrieks;
And a wretched creature's stifled moan,
  Whom Time, the terrible usurer, tweaks.

Between 44 and 45 OaW:

And yonder a little boy bellows the Topic;
  The picture of yesterday clean for a penny:
Done with a pen so microscopic
  That we all see ourselves in the face of the many.

Business, Business, seems the word,
  In this unvarying On-on-on!
  The volume coming, the volume gone,
Ghosts, glancing at Beauty, undeterr'd:
As in the torrent of cabs we both
Have glanced borne forward, willing or loth.

Is it enough to profane your mood,
  Arcadian dreamer, who think it sad
If a breath of the world on your haunts intrude,
  Though in London you're hunting the bubble like mad?

For you are one who raise the Nymph
  Wherever Nature sits alone;   50
Who pitch your delight in a region of lymph,
  Rejoiced that its arms evade your own.

I see you lying here, and wistfully
  Watching the dim shape, tender and fresh;
Your Season-Beauty faithless, or kiss'd fully,
  You're just a little tired of flesh.

She dances, and gleams, now under the wave,
  Now on a fern-branch, or fox-glove bell;
Thro' a wreath of the bramble she eyes me grave;
  She has a secret she will not tell.   60

But if I follow her more and more,
  If I hold her sacred to each lone spot,
She'll tell me—what I knew before;
  For the secret is, that she can't be caught!

She lives, I swear! We join hands there.
But what's her use? Can you declare?
If she serves no purpose, she must take wing:
Art stamps her for an ugly thing.

Will she fly with the old gods, or join with the new?
    Is she made of the stuff for a thorough alliance?   70
Or, standing alone, does she dare to go thro'
    The ordeal of a scrutiny of Science?

What say you, if, in this retreat,
    While she poises tiptoe on yon granite slab, man,
I introduce her, shy and sweet,
    To a short-neck'd, many-caped, London cabman?

You gasp! she totters! And is it too much?
Mayn't he take off his hat to her? hope for a touch?
Get one kind curtsey of aërial grace
For his most liberal grimace?   80

It would do him a world of good, poor devil!
And Science makes equal on this level:
Remember that!—and his friend, the popular
Mr. Professor, the learned and jocular,
Were he to inspect her, and call her a foam-bow,
I very much fear it would prove a home-blow.
We couldn't save her!—she'd vanish, fly;
    Tho' she's more than that, as we know right well;
But who shall expound to a hard cold eye
    The infinite impalpable?   90

A Queen on sufferance must not act
    My Lady Scornful:—thus presuming,
If Sentiment won't wed with Fact,
    Poor Sentiment soon needs perfuming.
Let her curtsey with becoming tact
    To cabman caped and poet blooming!—

No, I wouldn't mix Porter with Montepulciano!
    I ask you merely, without demanding,
To give a poor beggar his *buon' mano*:—
    Make my meaning large with your understanding!   100

The cicada sits spinning his wheel on the tree;
    The little green lizard slips over the stone
    Like water: the waters flash, and the cone
Drops at my feet. Say, how shall it be?
    Your Nymph is on trial. Will she own
Her parentage Humanity?
Of her essence these things but form a part;
Her heart comes out of the human heart.

99 *See Explanatory Notes.*

Tremendous thought, which I scarce dare blab, man!
    The soul she lacks—the illumination   110
    Immortal!—it strikes me like inspiration,
She must get her that soul by wedding the cabman!

Don't ask me why:—when Instinct speaks,
    Old Mother Reason is not at home.
But how gladly would dance the days and weeks!
    And the sky, what a mirth-embracing dome!
If round sweet Poesy's waist were curl'd
The arm of him who drives the World!

Could she claim a higher conquest, she?
And a different presence his would be!   120
I see him lifting his double chin
    On his three-fold comforter, sniffing and smirking,
And showing us all that the man within
    Has had his ideas of her secretly lurking.

Confess that the sight were as fine—ay, as fair!
As if from a fire-ball in mid-air
She glow'd before you woman, spreading
With hands the hair her foot was treading!

'Twere an effort for Nature both ways, and which
    The mightier I can't aver: 130
If we screw ourselves up to a certain pitch,
    She meets us—that I know of her.

She is ready to meet the grim cabman half-way!
    Now! and where better than here, where, with thunder
Of waters, she might bathe his clay,
    And enter him by the gate of wonder?

It takes him doubtless long to peel,
    Who wears at least a dozen capes:
Yet if but once she makes him feel,
    The man comes of his multiform shapes.   140

To make him feel, friend, is not easy.
    I once did nourish that ambition:
But there he goes, purple, and greasy, and wheezy,
    And waits a greater and truer magician!

Hark to the wild Rosanna cheering!
    Never droops she, while changing clime
At every leap, the levels nearing:
    Faith in ourselves is faith in Time!

And faith in Nature keeps the force
    We have in us for daily wear.   150
Come from thy keen Alp down, and, hoarse
    Tell to the valleys the tale I hear,

152 hear] bear *OaW*

O River!
   Now, my friend, adieu!
In contrast, and in likeness, you
Have risen before me from the tide,
Whose channel is narrow, whose noise is wide;
Whose rage is that of your native seas;
Buzzing of battle like myriad bees,
Which you have heard on the Euxine shore
  Sounding in earnest. Here have I placed   160
The delicate spirit which you adore
  Dame Nature in lone haunts embraced.
Have I affrighted it, frail thing, aghast?
I have shown it the way to live and last!

How often will these long links of foam
Cry to me in my English home,
To nerve me, whenever I hear them bellow,
Like the smack of the hand of a gallant fellow!

I give them my meaning here, and they
Will give me theirs when far away.   170
And the snowy points, and the ash-pale peaks,
Will bring a trembling to my cheeks,
The leap of the white-fleck'd, clear light, green—
Sudden the length of its course be seen,
As, swift it launches an emerald shoulder,
  And, thundering ever of the mountain,
Slaps in sport some giant boulder,
  And tops it in a silver fountain.

ODE TO THE SPIRIT OF EARTH IN AUTUMN

Between 174 and 175, 1862:

   Hark to her laughter! And would you wonder
   To hear amazing laughter thunder
   From one who contemplateth man?—
    Knowing the plan!

  The great procession of the Comedy,
  Passes before her. Let the curtain down!
  For she must laugh to shake her starry crown,
  To mark the strange perversions that are we;
  Who hoist our shoulders confident of wings,

BY THE ROSANNA

159 *See Explanatory Notes.*
163 affrighted] frighted *OaW*
175–78 *See Explanatory Notes.*

When we have named her Ashes, dug her ditch;   10
Who do regard her as a damnëd witch,
Fair to the eye, but full of foulest things,
We, pious humpback mountebanks meanwhile,
Break off our antics to stand forth, white-eyed,
And fondly hope for our Creator's smile,
By telling him that his prime work vile,
Whom, through our noses, we've renounced, denied.

Good friends of mine, who love her,
And would not see her bleeding:
The light that is above her,   20
From eyesight is receding,
As ever we grow older,
And blood is waxing colder.
But grasp in spirit tightly,
That she is no pretender,
While still the eye sees brightly,—
Then darkness knows her splendour,
And coldness feels her glory.
As in yon cloud-scud hoary,
From gloom to gloom still winging,   30
The sunset beams have found me:
I hear the sunset singing
In this blank roar around me!

Friends, we are yet in the warmth of our blood,
And swift as the tides upon which we are borne.
There's a long blue rift in the speeding scud,
That shows like a boat on a sea forlorn,
With stars to man it! That boat is ours,
And we are the mariners on the great flood
Of the shifting slopes and the drifting flowers,   40
That oar unresting towards the morn!
And we are the children of Heaven and earth,
We'll be true to the mother with whom we are,
So to be worthy of Him who afar,
Beckons us on to a brighter birth.

Before deleting this passage for de L, GM had made the following changes:

8 To mark] Marking
17 Whom] Which

THE ORCHARD AND THE HEATH

In Macmillan's *the poem formed Part I of a poem in two parts. Part II, omitted in* Poems and Lyrics of the Joy of Earth *(1883), was as follows:*

My pace is quick on foot, till as a lyre
The wind sings in my ears, and homeward bent,
    I heard an ever-lifting quire
    Of children by that smoky tent,
Who praised the union of the pot with fire.

More loved of Heaven, I thought them, though less fair,
Less blest of earth, than those who played at morn
    Like sun-spots in the scented square;
    To pleasant narrow spaces born,
Unknowing other fruits bloom otherwhere.   10

But is there love in Heaven which turns aside
From Heaven's good laws to flatter want or grief?
    Blind pity, and self-pity, and Pride,
    Clamour for it to bribe belief.
Let earth know better lest her woes abide.

Few men dare think what many have dared say—
That Heaven can entertain elective love,
    And narrow to our yea and nay
    The august great concords roll'd above.
I felt them, and went reverent on my way.   20

Yet fancy (the quick flutter of young thought
Above the flower, sensation) would not rest:
    From hues and lights of evening brought
    Rich symbols to make manifest
What recompense is for the houseless wrought.

Sweet recompense! thereat the ascetics aim.
Self-exiled from the orchard-bounds, they purge
    Poor flesh of lusts which bring them shame,
    And with the rigour of the scourge
Transfuse them to their souls in keener flame.   30

Surely I know the houseless little ones;
My spirit is among them all its days:
    Like them, 'tis of the changing suns;
    Subsists, like them, on waifs and strays,
Well chasten'd by the wild wherein it runs.

So that we find sufficient we can sleep,
Considering recompense scarce fit for dreams[.]
    No hushing songs of lambs and sheep,
    No highway trot of harness'd teams,
Lull us: we rock upon a tuneless deep.   40

We cannot cherish, like the folded throng,
Belief in sustenance, as frail as breath:
    Our faith is in our hunger; strong,
    Therefore, and constant is our faith:
A roaming force 'twixt morn and even-song.

But we divide; no likeness is complete:
For when it comes to seeing, they are blind.
    This is the mystery I meet
    At every corner of the mind;—
Twice cursed are they whom earth doth ill-entreat!   50

Ere yon sky orchards drop their golden key,
'Tis recognition Heaven demands, I know.
    Shall earth, then, bid its chosen see,
    And seeing grasp the fruits that grow
In Heaven as well as earth? How may this be?

My light of Heaven answers: 'Eye for fruits
'Have many: they are pluck'd by favour'd hands[.]
    'Is such a craving of the brutes
    'The recognition Heaven demands?
'Am I the Tree which has in earth its roots?   60

'Those fruits are gifts of heritage, not mine.
'The virtues garden in some lines of men,
    'And eminent and large they shine
    'As captains of the host, till when
'Much flatter'd flesh has drugg'd the soul divine.

'For of the fruits enjoy'd new seed should spring;
'And of their vantage station men shall make
    'A place of sacrifice, and cling
    'To sacrifice for man's dear sake,
'Or perish: 'tis the choice of sage and king.   70

'You waves of life go rolling o'er and o'er;
'And some will toss the uppermost foam, and fall;
    'And here and there the sky will pour
    'Illuminating rays, but all
'Are one great ocean rolling without shore.

'Never till men rejoice in being one
'Shall any of them hold a perfect heart.
    'Nearer to me shall gather none
    'That from their fellows climb apart.
'An evil is a common evil done.   80

'Make strength your weapon, purity your mark;
'Keep shrewd with hunger, as an edge of steel.
    'An army marching in the dark
    'Are men; but forward, while they reel,
'Still they bear forward some faint rescuing spark[.]

'By service they must live who would have sight:
'The children of the Orchard and the Heath
    'In equal destinies unite,
    'Serving or fattening beneath;
'But thank them best that trim in thee my light.'   90

A crown of darkness on the yellow west,
Where day and night took hands in union brief,
    And sat in sober splendour, press'd:
    I clasp'd as one full harvest sheaf
The thought of the poor children I thank'd best.

Far back I saw the flames of scanty wood
Upon the closing shadows cower low.
    The meal was done, and it was good;
    And now to huddling sleep they go.
May food supply them! They have given me food.   100

FRANCE, DECEMBER 1870

The following parts in the Fortnightly (*1871*) *were omitted from* Ballads and Poems of
Tragic Life (*1887*).

VIII

Behold the Gods are with her now, and known:
And to know them, not suffering for their sake,
Is madness to the souls that may not take
The easy way of death, being divine.
Her frenzy is not Reason's light extinct
In fumes of foul revenge and desperate sense,
But Reason rising on the storm intense,
Three-faced, with present, past, and future linked;
Informed three-fold with duty to her line.
By sacrifice of blood must she atone,   10
(Since thus the foe decrees it) to her own:
That she who cannot supplicate, nor cease,
Who will not utter the false word for Peace,
May burn to ashes, with a heart of stone,
Whatso has made her of all lands the flower,
To spring in flame for one redeeming hour,
For one propitious hour arise from prone,
Athwart Ambition's path, and have and wrench
His towering stature from the bitter trench,
Retributive, by her taskmasters shown,—   20
The spectral trench where bloody seed was sown.

Between 1887 parts X and XI in F:

XII

Once more, O earthly fortune, speak!
Has she a gleam of victory? one
Outshining of her old historic sun?
    For awhile! for an hour!
And sunlight on her banner seems
A miracle conceived in dreams,
The faint reflux of orient beams
    Thro' a lifting shower.

XIII

Now is she in the vulture-grasp of Power,
And all her sins are manifest to men.
Now may they reckon with punctilious pen
Her list of misdemeanors, and her dower
Of precious gifts that gilded the rank fen
Where lay a wanton greedy to devour.

XIV

Now is she in the vulture-grasp of Power.
The harlot sister of the man sublime,
Prometheus, she, though vanquished will not cower.
Offending Heaven, she grovelled in the slime;
Offending Man, she aimed beyond her time;
Offending Earth, her Pride was like a tower.

XV

O like the banner on the tower,
Her spirit was, and toyed and curled
Among its folds to lure the world—
It called to follow. But when strong men thrust
The banner on the winds, 'twas flame,
And pilgrim-generations tread its dust,
And kiss its track. Disastrously unripe,
Imperfect, changeful, full of blame,
Still the Gods love her, for that of high aim   [*Cf. X.8*]
Is this good France, the bleeding thing they stripe.   10 [*Cf. X.9*]

PERIANDER

MS: Huntington HM6766, *working copy. Variants are from this MS.*

I.1 dares shape] has shaped
I.5 bread] bread *del.* crust

II.1 There is] Men know *or* There is   the] yon *or* the
II.2 the] he *or* the
II.3 In magnanimity] Magnanimous *or* In magnanimity   in rule] infallible *or* in mind
del. laws *del.* rule
II.4 on] in   he] there *or* he

III.1 *Del.:* He of his princely judgement in youth's glow; He of the judgement [never
del.] rarely tyrant lacks,
III.2 [Distinguished *del.*] Discerning how the governed straighter [grow *del.*] wax
III.3 Than moss ungoverned, wrought [& to make *del.*] so that the seeds
III.4 *Del.:* Of his good rule a garden clipped & trim.
III.5 [Ruthless he put *del.*] Sagaciously *or* Electively he drove the hoe at [wanton *del.*]
weeds
III.6 And [raised *del.*] reared fair flower-beds [lifting *del.* turning *del.* showing *del.*]
raising face to him.

IV.1 This Corinth, stately growing, duly bent
IV.4 moved] signed *del.*
IV.5 At whiles] Now as *del.* Was now *or* At whiles

IV.6 At whiles] Now *del.* And now

V.4 Contested] Dared question *or* Contested
V.6 gave] had *or* gave

VI.3 Reviewing, saw him hold] Advanced, & found him in
VI.4 Age asked, Who follows? & no answer had.
VI.5 Age, grayer, pointed at the pallid *or* its reflex hour.
VI.6 To come] He saw   dried] dry *del.*

Between stanzas VI and VII stanza VIII deleted

VII.1 of his male issue] among his children
VII.2 stride] hold *or* stride
VII.3 This] As   he sole] none else *or* he sole
VII.4 Fired] Gave   strong tide] long stream *del.*
VII.5 right] proof
VII.6 support] endure *del.*   yea] a

Stanza VIII was originally vii, deleted, rewritten as viii.

VIII.1 Glad waters giving life, himself the *or* from fount to fount *dr. 1*   Himself the
prince beheld] The prince beheld himself *or* Himself the prince beheld *dr. 2*
VIII.2 back unto] backward to *dr. 1*
VIII.3 *dr.: 1* But of the thirsty onward was no sign. *Del.:* But of the thirsty onward was
no sign, But the fleet onward waved no thirsty sign
VIII.4 stood] rose *drs. 1, 2*

IX.2 A figure shunned along the] Alone, & shunned, along a
IX.3 Perforce] By stress *or* Perforce
IX.4 him] that *del.* the
IX.5 look that proved] one that showed *or* proved

X.2 from the hushed] & from the *del.*
X.3 had] bore   on] on *del.* blown
X.4 a] an iron *del.*   sapphire] purple
X.5 *Del.:* The seasons like a troop of billows rolled; *Del.:* The seasons rolled like troops
of billows on; Like troops of billows rolled the seasons on; The seasons &c [*blank*]
billows blown; Against &c——& on
X.6 To spraymist] To shatter *del.*

XI.1 Deaf] Then *or* Deaf
XI.2 from] in   not done] undone *del.*
XI.3 *Del.:* Undone his whole life's work! A [mournful *del.*] thin sad name. *Del.:*
Historic echoes [choked[?] *del.*] a [sad, thin *del.*] thin sad name, *Del.:* Historic echoes
uttered for his own; He heard historic echoes [breathe *del.*] cry *or* moan his name,
XI.4 *Del.:* The husky trumpets of the one he bore; *or* that source of laws: [The last of
his great race *del.*] As of the princes in whom this race had pause;

XII.1 exile now appeared] sullen exile seemed *or* exile now appeared
XII.2 from the shadow cleared] though of glory sheared
XII.3 With those unburied brows of his. The youth
XII.4 [And ceremonies unappeased *del.*] Shone of him under *or* Princely behind cloud
[to be breathed clear *del.*] he owned it loth,
XII.5 He owned him conquered, & in sign of ruth *or* Yet was he conquered, & to move
the truth
XII.6 Sent him *or* Despatched the messenger [to both most dear *del.*] most dear to both

XIII.1 *Del.:* Soon from his daughter followed tidings glad:
XIII.2 halycons o'er] doves across
XIII.3 *Del.:* In recognition of the tie of blood
XIII.4 and rejoiced] & it would sail *del.*
XIII.5 a prince] in state *or* a prince   [close the flood *del.*]
XIII.6 & forth [his *del.*] in many vessels met the gale *or* Commanded man the oars, the anchors *or* white sails hoist

XIV.1 *Del.:* Grandly they swept along, till Corinth sands. *Del.:* He waved the fleet upon its way & dreamed, Musing he waved the fleet upon its way,
XIV.2 *Del.:* The islands & that son *or* harbour wharves before him beamed. The [purple *del.*] sea-lined hills [above *del.*] the stone wharves beamed *or* o'er the white harbour beamed
XIV.3 Soil of those] His mark *or* Soil of those
XIV.4 Whom now his heart] Whom his heart thanked *del.*   honour to] cherishing
XIV.5 They should learn] And they shall *or* They should see *del.*
XIV.6 happiness enjoins him] he is humbled down to *or* happiness enjoins him

Between stanzas XIV and XV del.:

> He landed, & as waters the crowd fled;
> Advanced; they crested: Lycrophon take dead

XV.1 worn with haste] long he paced *del.*
XV.2 revived, and, close] returning, &
XV.3 Pardon] Receive   who had subdued him] the pardoned *del.*   gained] won[?] *del.*

XVI.1 unperceived] masked[?] *del.*
XVI.2 his] this
XVI.5 States and people fretting] States around, & frettings *or* vassal States, vain frettings *or* States or People fretting
XVI.6 fleet brown-flocked on] vessels darkened

XVII.1 They [came *del.*] pulled, they entered harbour; without roar
XVII.2 For greeting shadowed round the thing they bore.
XVII.3 whose approach in such rare pomp and] at whose nearing *or* whose approaching in their pomp & *or* such bright
XVII.4 dismayed] had fear *or* dismayed
XVII.5 At] That *del.* At *del.* Lest   come] come *del.* drew
XVII.6 breathless] lifeless *or* breathless

XVIII.6 her served; they lay] in life, in death,

Stanza XIX was originally written after XVII and was unnumbered. Rewritten as xix.

XIX.1 Demand] Tears, tears, *del. dr. 1*
XIX.2 *dr. 1 del.:* What were they for such quenching of his years,   Sharper] Fiercer, *drs. 1, 2*
XIX.4 *dr. 1:* And did such *or* his work of smoke & blood *or* blood & shame; to show; *dr. 2:* And did his work of blood & shame, for proof
XIX.5 prompt the Tyrant for] quickly *or* promptly Tyrants take *dr. 1*; promptly Tyrants take *dr. 2*
XIX.6 *dr. 1:* Standing black shapes in [that *del.*] their historic row.   *dr. 2:* Standing black shapes, from humankind aloof.

THE SOUTH-WESTER

MSS: Yale. *MS 1, working draft; MS 2, fair copy; frag. A, title;* South-West, *lines 1–4
+16 lines; frag. B, fair copy of lines 51–93; frag. C, fair copy of lines 123–29½ + 1½;
frag. D, fair copy of lines 123–30 + 8½; frag. E, 11½ lines not used, with an earlier version
of the same.*

After 4 frag. A:

        Now do the heavens & earth unite
        Their sweetest unto sound & sight;
    Del.: And [who shall *del.*] shall we say they are not one,
           Who hear the woods & eye the sun?
        [And hear *del.* Hear but *del.*] Hear we the woods & eye the sun,
             As harp & harper are they one.   [*Cf. lines 60–61*]
        This nerve or that] The nerve she strikes *del.* & 'tis alike
        To such quick joy that she may strike

        We know not if 'tis *or* whether heard or seen,
        We know but music on a tide;
            For Nature quivering golden-green,   [*Cf. line 36*]
        Has opened all our Soulways *or* Window & doorway opens wide.

        [And *del.*] She sets the inner life aflame,
        And draws it forth to join her rout,
        Interminable, of wild & tame

        And them that sing & them that shout,
        Push they in earth *or* with grunt a truffle snout,
        Or swan-winged & swan-voiced acclaim

8 To] For *MS 1*
9 As] Like *del. MS 1*   or] as *del. MS 1*
10 tossed to fly] [lost to eye *del.*] drawn to fly *or* hurled to fly *MS 1*
11 caverned peal] cavern-peal *MS 1*
16 to watch thee lie] till thou wert rosed *or* to watch thee lie *MS 1*
18 till in the braid *not in MS 1*
19 *not in MS 1*   purpled] purpling *del. MS 2*
20 Till that new] The slumbering *or* Till that new *MS 1*
22 beat] flush *del. MS 1*
25 they flew the breast] the breasts they flew *or* they flew the breast *MS 1*
26 But] But *del.* Ah *MS 1*
27 none guessed] none knew *del.* who guessed *MS 1*
29 straining] drawn *or* strained *MS 1*   eager] to glittering *MS 1*
30 Lightened, and high] High *or* Flew & high on *MS 1*
32 Name] He, *MS 1*
34 Beauteous] Grandly *MS 1*
36 quivered] quivering *MS 1*
42 in the fluttering sheen] next a pallor, strange *or* in the thrilling *or* fluttering sheen
MS 1
43 the slate air that] it was the sky that *del.* that slate sky which *MS 1*
44 reindeer's] reindeer *MS 1*
45 *MS 1:* The falling *or* frowning & the fallen snow.

46–47 *MS 1:* Next minute: hooded, [nunlike stoled *del.*] stol'd in strange Device:
                Del.: In garment of the blot[?], snows,
                      And lo,
                      In garments of the Season's dirge:

48–50 *not in MS 1*
51 Anew: and through quick] Lifeless *or* Bechilled; & [with *del.*] through her *MS 1*
54 *MS 1:*

                But noon saw heaven & earth unite,
                Their sweetest in the ear & sight,

55–57 *not in MS 1*
55 our] earth's *frag. B*
57 inner sweetest] sweetest treasures *frag. B*
60 *MS 1:* And heard we woodland, eyed we sun,
62–71 *not in MS 1*
62 *frag. B:* We saw the cloud the cloud assail,
63 *frag. B:* The milky fair the murk elude,
64–71 *not in frag. B, instead:*

                And in our hearing had the tale;
                A flitted scene, a varied mood.

72 did each movement rouse] at a motion woke *MS 1, frag. B*
73 minstrel's] glorious *or* minstrel's *MS 1*
74 *MS 1:* To rouse the spirit, & evoke
75 bathe them] have us on *MS 1, frag. B*
77 vapoury] cloud in *MS 1*
78 western pile] mounded bank *or* bank to bank *or* pile to pile   to eastern rack]
to lengthened rack *or* from rack to rack *MS 1*   *frag. B:* From pile to pile, from rack
to rack
79 on] 'twere *MS 1*
80 It peeped &c *MS 1*   youngness] youth has *del. MS 1*
81 When songful] And when the *MS 1, frag. B*
83 *MS 1:* And when the clouds were rolling waves;   When the ranked] And when
the *frag. B*
84 *MS 1:* Of eagle's breast & albatross; Breast of swan] Of swan-breast *frag. B*
85 ordered lines] order close *or* ordered lines *MS 1*
87 *MS 1:* It peeped, it promised, played & laughed; silver] very *frag. B*
88 *MS 1:* Lyric it thrilled the leaves, & shot; Lyric it thrilled *frag. B*
89 *MS 1:* And slew the gloom with golden shafts; Slew the huge] And slew the *frag. B*
90 *MS 1:* Uncoil'd the knotted *or* volumed Python Club
91–98 *not in MS 1*
91 *frag. B:* The flying palace built, & clove
92 the flying nests] saw we not *frag. B*
93 *frag. B:* Whose hands the glory-garland wove?
99 Only at gathered] But only at grand *MS 1*
100 The marvels of the day] What wonders had been done *MS 1*
101 Mount upon] Mountain on *MS 1*
102 spacious] startled *MS 1*
103 sublime] divine *MS 1*
104 towering] mightest [*sic*] *or* towering *MS 1*

After 106 MS 1 del.:

> And lest our mortal sight should bound
> The credible

107 *MS 1:* [Wafted they Iris *del.*] They wafted this Dream-messenger,
109 That] The *MS 1*

After 109 MS 1 del.:

> In sunlight, who, not wingëd, shaped
> By chrysalis wrappings, under dome
> Undid

110 sun-rays] sunlight *MS 1*
114 *MS 1:* Poised & dispieced, dissolved to *or* in threads,
115 Melting she] And melting *MS 1*
115 immortal *no accent MS 1*
117 was known] knew I *MS 1*
120 old bards] the Greeks *MS 1*
122 undyingness] undying soul *MS 1*
124 His grand] [The *del.*] His great *MS 1*
126 *end of MS 1*
130 We could believe] & ever young *frag. C*

frag. D:

> The lyre, the dance: a day untired
> In transformations wild as sea
> At catch of wind: a day inspired
> To vivify in brook & tree
> And cloud old fables: day of the fleets
> Full sail, & over them at peace,
> Long feathers laid on azure streets;
> Breather of keenest-scented sweets,
> And brush to conjure fair as fleece
> The city shining.

frag E., rejected conclusion:

> Hail! farewell,
> O day of life! Farewell, & hail.
> If alone
> For quickening city childrens' limbs
> Like meadow lambs', thou should'st be known
> O Day of [life *del.*] grace! [or holiday *del.*] & sung in hymns,
> *Del.:* As Earth inviting holiday;
> As Earth that on her river swims
> *Del.:* The freër, cheerer, come to bless;
> Inviting life to holiday.
> *Del.:* The painter of the various ray;
> The freër, cheerer, winging wide,
> And *or* Yet striking through *or* down each dark recess,
> Our ancient Mother, young as May,

> If alone
> For lifting city-childrens' limbs
> Like meadow-lambs', thou should'st be known,
> O Day of Grace! & sung in hyms [sic],
> As Earth that down her river swims,
> Inviting life to holiday:
> Our ancient Mother, young as May:
> *Del.:* The singer on the shifting tide,
> The painter of the various ray *or* rosy prime:
> And, freër, cheerer, wings she wide,
> Or strikes to scour each dark recess,
>
> Our freër, cheerer, teacher

THE EMPTY PURSE

MSS: Huntington. *MS 1,* HM7467, *working draft: MS 2,* HM7468, *fair copy corrected; 39 fragments (the numbers in square brackets are GM's pagination):*

Fragments associated with MS 1: frag. A [1], lines 1–9; frag. B [4], lines 60–110; frag. C[4] lines 63–99; frag. D [4, 4a, 5], lines 63–124; frags. E, F, G, H, I, J, six unnumbered frags., verso of two early leaves, lines 83–88, 97–99; frag. K [5], lines 111–124; frag. L [5a], lines 111–124; frag. M [5b, 6, 7, 8, 9], lines 152–367; frag. N [16], lines 319–333, 355, 363; frag. 0 [16a], lines 345–346, 355, 363; frag. P [17, 18], lines 366–491; frag. Q [17], lines 366–399 + 2; frag. R [18], lines 435–477; frag. S [11, 12, 13], lines 438–621; frag. T [18a], lines 438–453; frag. U [19], lines 478–492; frag. V [20], lines 491–592; frag. W [20, 21], lines 491–587; frag. X [20, 21, 22], lines 491–592; frag. Y [21], lines 567–592; frag. Z, unnumbered, lines 614–621; frag. AA [25], lines 622–624 + 20; frag. BB, unnumbered, 12 lines; frag. CC, unnumbered, 14 lines; frag. DD [26], lines 640 + 22; frag. EE [26], lines 686–692.

Fragments associated with MS 2: frag. FF [19, 20], lines 354–421; frag. GG [20], lines 376–417; frag. HH [20], lines 376–411; frag. II [20], lines 376–392 + 7; frag. JJ, unnumbered, verso of frag. MM [29], lines 385–392 + 9; frag. KK [22, 23], lines 435– 479 + 3; frag. LL, unnumbered, lines 593–609; frag. MM [29, 30], lines 593–640.

The large number of fragments from *The Empty Purse* and their relation to the two extant completed drafts require explanation. There are thirty-nine fragments on forty-six leaves. Thirty-six of the leaves are thin, cheap, white paper, measuring $7\frac{1}{4} \times 8$ inches. These are parts of drafts written before *MS 1,* which is on the same paper. Ten of the leaves are thicker, slightly larger, and creamier-white paper, measuring $7\frac{1}{2} \times 9\frac{3}{8}$ inches. These are parts of drafts written between *MS 1* and *MS 2, MS 2* having been written on the same larger paper. The ink on the thin paper is a brighter blue than that on the thicker.

In spite of the many discarded passages recorded in the apparatus criticus, the poem grew by accretion. Conspicuously, the 141 lines 480–621 grew from a draft of only forty-two lines. *MS 1* is thirty-two pages; *MS 2* is thirty-four on larger leaves.

All but eleven of the fragments are left over from paginated drafts, numbered by GM. Number <u>20</u> (GM usually underlined his page numbers) is the most complicated example of his discards. Seven of the forty-six leaves are numbered <u>20.</u>

It is impossible to determine how many times GM rewrote this poem. The seven <u>20</u>s plus the two completed drafts add to nine versions that one can count for sure, and there must have been a final one for the printer. One draft was completed before *A Reading of Earth* (1888); in estimating the number of pages for that volume GM included twenty-two for *The Empty Purse* and then deleted the entry (MS, Yale). At the end of *A Reading of Earth*, Macmillan advertised a "*Forthcoming Volume*. THE EMPTY PURSE: A Sermon to our Later Prodigal Son."

Subtitle, frag. A: A Sermon to Prodigal Son

1 *frag. A:* O bird without feather! fish without fin!   [*Cf. line 330*]

MS 1: [O bird without *del.*] A bird stripped of feather! [a fish without *del.*] a fish clipped of fin!

2 *frag. A, MS 1:* O vessel, of crew & sails bereft!
3 Quenched] Sad *frag. A, MS 1*
4 limp] a limp *frag. A, MS 1*
5. gale upon spikes] winds on a spike *frag. A;* [winds *del.*] gale on a spike *MS 1*
6 *not in frag. A, MS 1*
7 *frag. A:* For flag [*or* sign *MS 1*] of the life gone out [*or* forth *MS 1*], is thine:
14 *MS 1:* Through the devious ways it has come to this,
15 consecutive] unbroken *MS 1*
17 waves] waved *MS 1*
18 at the] in *MS 1*
19 shadow] devil *MS 1*
20 Of] Not *MS 1*
21 souls] the soul *MS 1*
22–30 *not in MS 1*
31 over] in *MS 1*
32 of blossom] it blossomed *MS 1*
33 This] Our *MS 1*
35 *not in MS 1*

Between 36 and 37 MS 1: Ere the dream had flown to thee there,

37 room of the toys] field of thy games *MS 1*

After 37 MS 1: When it came on a day of the fluting merls,   [*Cf. line 28*]

38–45 *not in MS 1*
41 A] Their *del. MS 2*
46 *MS 1:* The field was a realm, & the dream   magician] poetic[?] *del. MS 2*
47 Was] True *MS 1*
48 himself] thyself *MS 1*   his] thy *MS 1*
49 *MS 1:* (A lily at seek with pearl) *del. MS 2*
51 kisses a locket] lockets an infant *MS 1*
52 cherub] boyish *MS 1*
60 With] In *MS 1*
61 And high] Away *frag. B, MS 1*
66 light] star *frags. C, D, MS 1, MS 2*
67–77 *not in frags. C, D, MS 1, instead:*

> Woman, the one, perchance!
> The marvellous effluence shed
> To be mover of all romance.

72 Led on by] Allured from *del. MS 2*
78–99 *not in frag. B*

78–84 *not in frag. C*
78 Did] And did *frag. D*
79 Nested warm] Richly for thee *frag. D*
80 *not in frag. D. MS 1:* It waited the morrow to fly: and for thee
81 tuned, refined;] made them kind. *frag. D, MS 1*

Between 81 and 82 frag. D:

> Hers was the magic that quickened old creeds,
> Pagan, & saintly, & knightly: a swarm

82 Drowned sharp edges] Alien, homely *frag. D*
82 *not in MS 1, instead:*

> *Del.:* Formless she drew to the lure of a form. Various, drew she to lures
> As were it the wings that alight or flee
> Unseizable, thy fierier needs,
> Under awe at a beauty divined
> When the sun's [last *del.*] red ebb recedes,
> When the pearly flow is blind.

Frags. associated with 83–88, 97–99; all six begin with: She beckoned, she whispered in reeds *continuing:*

E

> On the bow of the foam-fall leaped
> With the waters at limpedest ran.

F

> She was the light over light
> In the wave where it fell, where it ran

G

> She drew to the warmth *or* lures of a form
> Formless, aloof from our needs,
> Unseizable, all of thee warm
> Under awe at a beauty divined;
> Only seen where the day recedes,
> Where yet the young dawn is blind.
> Shy she was; light over light
> On the wave where it fell, where it ran
> [Lucidly *del.*] Lucid: & when the wild hue
> Gathered shape

H

> *Del.:* She ran in the foam
> In the lightest breeze astir
> She was audible

I

> She ran on the foam of weirs,
> She widened her wings or sheathed
> Where

J

> *Del.:* On the foam of the rivers she ran. On the foam-falls
>   she was the bow,
> *Del.:* She was shy
> And shy she was, oftener night
> Than day, [-beams *del.*] save the day that[?]
> Leaving one ember to wane *or* glow.

84 on] from *frag. D, MS 1*   winging] leaping *frag. D, MS 1*
85 *frag. C:* She wave[d] the keen witchery, whispered in reeds, *frag. D:* She quivered in legends *or* on ruins, she whispered in reeds, *or* With her witch-whisper on ruins, in reeds o'er] on *MS 1*
86 *not in frag. C*   low the] the low *frag. D, MS 1*
88 *frag. C:* Astream to the forest where innerly bleeds   woodland] forest *frag. D, MS 1*
89 on] in the *frag. C;* from *frag. D*
90–93 *not in frag. C*
90 valorous deeds] valour: she led *frag. D; MS 1:* Hers was the magic to quicken old creeds,
91–92 *not in frag. D*
91 *MS 1:* Pagan, & saintly, & knightly: a swarm,

Between 91 and 92 MS 1: Aliens, homely beneath her cloak.   [*Cf. line 82*]

92 *MS 1:* Remember her summons to valour: she led
93 more than] besides *frag. D*
94 *frag. C:* She waved her impalpable yoke; *frag. D:* Waved her impalpable yoke
95 *not in frag. C*   Whither] Wide: where *frag. D*
95–96 *not in frag. C, instead:*

> Elusive, up woodlands most,
> Eye of the waters & throb of the tree.
> Ghost, but with blood to illuminate ghost,
>   She drew to the lures of a form
>   Formless, aloof from our needs,
>   Unseizable, all of thee warm
>   Under awe at a beauty divined;
>   Only seen where the day recedes,
>   Where yet the young dawn is blind.

96–99 *not in frag. D, instead:*

> The lover, that turbulent ran
> From the blood at the flood delayed,
> Through the heart of thee surgeing to man.

96 Ere] Ere yet *del. MS 1*
97–99 *frag. C:*

> And shy of her bosom she was as a maid
> Bathing: her treasury plunged into night
> At a thought that sprang up of itself afraid.

97 secrets] bosom *del.* secret *MS 1*   under deeps] as a maid *MS 1*
98–99 *MS 1:*

[Bathing her treasury *del.*] [Startled *del.*] Alarmed at the bath; she plunged into night
[At a thought that sprang up *del.*] At a throb in thy heart itself afraid;

After 99, frag. C:

> And still [still *or* she *MS 1*] when the flitting wild hue
> Gathered shape, [was she *del. MS 1*] she was light over light

After 99, frag. C, MS 1: In thy loftiest fancy, & shone to subdue
MS 1:

> Thy lower, whose turbulence drove
> Through blood at the flood-gate stayed,
> [In *del.*] Where the heart of thee surging for love

100 into [to our *MS 1*] uttermost heavens it flew *frags. B, D*
102 the] a *frag. B*
104–5 *not in frags. B, D*
104 puffed and] was puffed *MS 1*
105 *MS 1:* Thy dream of the beauty fled;
106 brayed] blew *frag. B*
107 seized] took *frags. B, D, MS 1;* caught[?] *del. MS 2*
108 *not in frags. B, D, MS 1*
111 keen] wild *frags. K, L*
113 greenblade] green young *frag. K;* green sweet *frag. L, MS 1*
114 flowerful] flowering *frag. K*
115 Orient] rosy *frag. K*
116 a] the *frag. K*
117 was it] it was *del. frag. L*   breast] bosom *frags. K, L*
118 windowless world without] world without window or *frags. K, L, MS 1*
119 Only darkening jets] Save the jets from below *frag. K;* Save the darkening jets
frag. L, MS 1
120 over] amid *frags. K, L, MS 1*
122 along] down *frags. K, L, MS 1*
123 and] with *frag. K, MS 1*
127 Stalked] Did *MS 1*
128 *MS 1:* Reign monarch of pantomine?   For] Reign *del.* Stalk *del. MS 2*
131 the] our *MS 1*
135 And for] For *MS 1*
136 Despised] Disdained *MS 1*
155 flesh] things *frag. M, MS 1*
156–78 *not in frag. M*
157 goblet] winecup *MS 1*
159 grisly] shameless *del.* flaunting *MS 1*
163 stuck in] lured to *MS 1*
166 glory of banquet] moment of beauty we *MS 1;* moment *del.* glory of banquet [we
del.] *MS 2*
167 creature] thing *MS 1*
168 Our pursy] The young *MS 1*
169 still] yet *MS 1*
171 blindfold] simple *MS 1*
175 the] our *MS 1*
179–80 *frag. M:*

Del.: We have him: 'tis he, our quarry, the hooved, 'Tis he, our quarry, the hoofed,
Del.: The horned: who else? [& *del.*] though he twists awry. The horned, we have him.
      He twists
        But feeling our grip [on him *del.*] *or* Not to be thrown[?] till he stands unmoved.
        Shackled at feet & wrists
        And Eye [*sic*] him: the features behold

180 scan] eye *MS 1*   inspect] behold *del. MS 1*
182 I] thou *del. frag. M*

Between 182 and 183, line 186 del. frag. M

184 hieroglyph] antic *del. frag. M*
185 *not in frag. M*
186 Thou! will] And *del.* Thou! does *frag. M*
187 Thus] Such *frag. M, MS 1*
189 Anew] Again *del. frag. M*   all of thy like] any *frag. M, MS 1*
191 man, clean] man again *frag. M, MS 1*
192 grip] wand *MS 1*   Sorcerer] Sorceress *frag. M*
194 his] its *frag. M, MS 1*
199 *frag. M, MS 1:* That issue of both enfold;—
200 A morn] Which is light *frag. M*; A light *MS 1*   all] our *frag. M, MS 1*

After 200 frag. M, MS 1:

        Of the images coined [of *MS 1*] emotions untaught
          Or instructed dispensers of speech.

        MS 1:
        Unknown [to thy mind *del.*] in thy head hitherto
          'Tis the dawn of a mind, that yet
        Has openings widened for few.

201–02 *not in frag. M, MS 1*
203 it, 'tis] it is *frag. M*; it is *del.* with 'tis *MS 1*
204 *frag. M:* To those having little 'tis mist;   who are misty]having little *MS 1*

After 204, frag. M: [Yet it *del.*] It lives in the life of thought.

205–24 *not in frag. M*
205 billow] wave *MS 1*
208 Ay] Yea *del. MSS 1, 2*
209 pricking the blind] trimming our sight *MS 1*; pricking the sight *MS 2*
210 This is thy gain now the] Such is the gain when thy *MS 1*
211 *MS 1:* To read with the soul from its topmost height
212 Is man's chief lesson] In the mirror of mind *MS 1*
217–22 *not in MS 1*
221 The] Yet the *del. MS 2*
223 *MS 1:* True, & philosophy, careless to soothe;   thoughtless] careless *del. MS 2*
225 good sooth] 'tis true *or* good sooth *frag. M*
226 *frag, M:* Craggy, we know it; [& *del.*] hard for the tooth.   flint] hard *MS 1*
227 *not in frag. M*
228 *frag. M del.:* Manful has met it, & manful will meet.   But] Yet *MS 1*
229 *frag. M:* Think of thee, *or* Radiant out of the hog!   & in youth *not in MS 1,*
instead:

> And think of the dower thou hast,
> In the natural glory of youth:
> No other than bright new birth.

frag. M del.: [Pure *del.*] A real new birth is the dower thou hast.

230–46 *not in frag. M, instead:*

> If naked, why, that [must be *del.*] even is at a birth,
> And thou, new born with a visible past,
> Art richer than children, than senior chiefs,
>   For these we see dragging a log,
>   Those to be wrecked on the reefs.

230 To have sight] With a glimpse *MS 1*
231 fouling thee] inhabited *del. MS 1*   jumping] doomed, lost over *MS 1*
232 *not in MS 1*
234–46 *not in MS 1*
236 more an] longer *del. MS 2*
241 prince or] monarch[?] or *del.* and the *del. MS 2*
247 strike Earth] touch Earth; [feel truth. *del.*] *frag. M*
248–53 *not in frag. M, MS 1, instead MS 1:* For whom touches Earth in his shallow-vast
For] And *del.* For *frag. M*
254 And thou com'st on] He is sure of *frag. M, MS 1*
255 *frag. M:* For a root-planted worth   thy] his *MS 1*
255–56 *reverse order MS 1*

After 255 frag. M:

> Be it clean, be it mud
> Dispenses the personal fog. *or* To scatter his egoist fog

256–70 *not in frag. M*
256 flint, mud, or the] be it mud, be it *MS 1*
257 *MS 1:* He is bound to the hard-exact: grasp] hold *del. MS 2*
258 sinners deluded] sinners *MS 1*
259 Dry] Good *MS 1*   bruises] scratches *MS 1*
260 *MS 1:* Fast is he linked to the common heart,
261 nips] grips *MS 1*
262 *MS 1:* At his nakedness, learns he; & thus to smart,
263 And we] To *MS 1*

After 263 MS 1:

> Enlarges the ring of his mean little I
> Tyrannical, source of our circles of hells:
>   Teaches him wisdom in act,
>   The service to brotherhood; swells,
>   From the soul of him fixed as a mast,
>   Sails for all weathers & waves
>   Between the black nether & sky.
>   Yea; stripped by some resolute blast,
>   With the ire of the elements packed

264–68 *not in MS 1*
269 *MS 1:* To engulf him, the creature is firm: Thus] So *del. MS 2*

270 *not in MS 1*
271 [No more will he follow his *del.*] He follows no longer his *frag. M*   We follow]
He follows *MS 1*   a] his *MS 1*
272 *frag. M:* To trot where the brute is tracked   hog] brute *MS 1*
273 *not in frag. M*   wriggle] wriggles *MS 1*
274 Thou wilt spare us the] Avoid the poor *frag. M*

Between 275 and 276 frag. M: Above all, be thou careful *or* watchful to cast

276 *frag. M:* No villain anathemas about—   *MS 1:* [Let *del.*] No rascal anathemas
[be *del.*] cast
277 women] men, & *del. frag. M*
279–83 *not in frag. M*
279–80 *not in MS 1*
282 sad] poor *del. MS 1*

After 288 frag. M: We are written in [what *del.*] that we have sown. *MS 1:* We are
printed [by *del.*] in that we have sown.

289–92 *not in frag. M*
289 nursing] having *MS 1*
291 finished] ended *MS 1*
292 vessel] bottom *MS 1*
293 *frag. M:* [Be thou *del.*] Rather go [of *del.*] where the demagogue [troop *del.* band
del.] roars
294–306 *not in frag. M, instead:*

> [That *del.*] Who by clamour the ears of the angels [refresh *del.*] invites
> To listen for pleasing diversion of snores,
>> With his thump on the wrongs & the rights.
>> Assist him their ears to refresh,
>> They are sick of that lullaby hymn
> Of the fat songsters[?] in praise
>> To our Arch-seducer of flesh,   *[Cf. line 311]*
>> If he will *or* That he may sustain men to swim,
>> Consentingly lengthen their days,

295 Hurrah to] Join in *MS 1*
296 that smokes] discerned *MS 1*
297 sin's death-dyes] sins in [matching size *del.*] death's dyes *MS 1*
301 snore] snores *del. MS 1*
307 Then] And *frag. M*   the] their *del. frag. M*
308 Thy] The *frag. M*
309 heart] breast *frag. M, MS 1*
310 things] deeds *MS 1*
311 *not in frag. M*   the] our *MS 1*
312 the] all *frag. M*   at women and] at men & at *frag. M;* at men or at *MS 1*
313 Confess] Admit *del.* Avow *MS 1*
314 of our wanton, our weak] for *del.* of the *or* our wanton, the *or* our weak *frag. M*
315 Of] For *del. frag. M*

Between 315 and 316 frag. M, del.:

> A contrary course to the mood[?] of mankind
> Speak, for the weal of the soul in thee speak:

Between 315 and 316 insert, MS 1, del.:

> That the devil's own piper thou wert
> To lead the way down to his mesh,
> And the joy of our nature pervert.

318 on grandmotherly] of old barbarous *or* Grandmotherly *frag. M*
320 their] our *del. MS 1*
322 And] To *MS 1*   banquet's] Siren *frag. M*; banquet *frag. N*
325 Thereat] And here *frag. M*; Whereat *frag. N, MS 1*
326 sick] void *frags. M, N, MS 1*
327 as] e'er *or* a *frag. M*
328–30 *not in frag. M, instead:* And sins channelled slides for sin!)
329–30 *not in MS 1*
330 *Cf. line 1 of frag. A, MS 1*
331 And commend] But thank *frag. M*   torrents of wrath] tides *del.* torrents *del.*
torrent *frag. M*
332 *frag. M del.:* That will dash at thee, boulder & froth That will hurl, foe of the dearest
men   Which] That will *frag. N*; Which will *MS 1*
333 Rough-rolling] Thundering *del. frag. N*
334 *not in frag. N, but* Gigantical enginery *in margin*
335–65 *not in frags. M, N, instead:*

> Lo, such [Such *frag. N*] do they bear who civilize!   *[Cf. line 355]*
> For them are the stripes or [the *del. frag. M*] chains.   *[Cf. line 364]*

Between 336 and 337 MS 1: Be at least of the passively wise!

337 Men's] Their *del. MS 1*
338 creatures they] fields they have *MS 1*
340 fast] secure *MS 1*
341 by prudent devices appeased] by *del.* in death, through the law, unappeased *MS 1*
prudent] happy *del. MS 2*
342–45 *not in MS 1*
343 perceive] can see *del. MS 2*
345–46 *frag. 0:*

> Till [you *del.*] thou shalt have pointed their hungers to skies
> Beyond [& *del.*] far now [fruitfull *del.*] fruitfuller, [& *del.*]
>   less overcast!
> So take thou the sting of the scourge for thy pains.   *[Cf. line 354]*
> Such do they bear who civilize!   *[Cf. line 355]*
>   For them are the stripes & chains!   *[Cf. line 364]*

345–65 *MS 1:*   *Cf. lines:*

> Till thou shalt have pointed their hungers to skies   *[346]*
> Beyond, far fruitfuller, less overcast;
> Where savages marvelling learn of a debt   *[347]*
> They have owed since they drummed on their hollows for war;   *[348]*
> Where the more that they give, ever more do they get;   *[349]*
> And their old tyrant-monster—now father of flies!   *[352]*
> Once the sun of their systems!—themselves most abhor.   *[353]*
> For this, take the sting of the scourge unashamed: *[354]*
> Such do they bear who civilize;   *[355]*

> Who teach the thing novel & true: [356]
> That the brutal antique of our growth must be tamed; [357]
> That the God of old days may be Satan of new, [359]
> If we keep him not still at development aimed; [360]
> That the feeding fat Self to be dominant, heaps [363]
> Dust on the soul. Take stripes and chains. [364]
> Clutch fast to thy standard reviled [365]

350 For] And for *del. MS 2*

352 Their adored] That the proud[?] *del. MS*   a] is *del. MS 2*

353 their] this *del. MS 2*

354 good] brave *frag. FF*

357 springs] growth *del. frag. FF*

359 time will act] days be the *del.* time act *frag. FF*

361–62 *not in frag. FF*

362 where] and *del. MS 2*

363 *frag. FF:* And that feeding fat Self into dominance, heaps

365 Grip at] Hold to *frag. FF*

366 what] how *frags. M, P, Q, MS 1*   from the steeps] to the deeps *frags. M, P, Q, MS 1, frag. FF*

367 Our] The *del. frag. M*

369 ah] *not in frag. Q*

370 down the Ages! to] & to love it & *frags. P, Q*

372 thread of] work for *frag. P;* work in *frag. Q*

373 *frag. P:* May it show braver to face [hot *del.*] hard shot;   May] And may *MS 1, frag. FF*   be] show *frag. Q, MS 1*

375 *not in frag. P. Frag. Q, MS 1:* The uprising of novel Powers! *frag. FF:* The rising of Stranger Powers.

376 *not in frag. P*   how] when *frag. Q*

377 *not in frags. P, Q, MS 1, frag. FF*

378 *frag. P:* The slumber on precedents shun,

379 *frag. P:* On an earth leaving heaps in the path of the hoof;   print] stamp *frag. Q, MS 1*

380 *not in frag. P*

381 *frag. P:* Where Change is the promise of sun. *frag. Q:* Bids welcome to Change as the promise of sun;   And should prompt us] Bid welcome *del.* And should bid us *MS 1;*   as to] as the *del.* as a *MS 1*

382–97 *not in frag. P*

383–97 *not in frag. Q, MS 1, frags. FF, GG, HH*

383–84, 387 *not in frag. II*

385–86 *and* 388–95 *reverse order frag. II*

385–92 *frag. JJ:*

> That forefather print of the hoof, mark well.
> It had right meaning in time gone by,
> When the wolf was abroad or lurked up sleeve.
> But now on an animate morning it stamps
> The lines of a sombre eve.
>
> That forefather print of the hoof, mark well.
> It had fair meaning in days gone by.
>
> Shall an animate morning be stamped
> By the lines of a sombre eve?

> Of old the good forefather ramped
> For authority, much did achieve.
>
> *Del.:* Of old the good forefather much did
>
> When lion effulgently ramped,
> And the wolf was a visible [lurker up sleeve *del.*] fang under hood
> The snake a lithe lurker up sleeve
> Our forefather hoof did its work in the wood.
> *Del.:* By conquest authority claimed
> But still it was hoof where the conqueror tramped,
> And wrote the decrees for the brutish subdued.

386 *frag. II:* [May *del.*] Shall an animate morn be stamped . . . ?
388 the hypocrite] a visible *frag. II*   the] a *del. MS 2*
391 Then our] Our *frag. II*

After 392, frag. II:

> He wrote his decrees for a brutish subdued,
>   Not for the breathers of mind:
> Would we sever connection? rather compute
> By morning's beams what the old day [wrote *del.*] penned
> The despot in usage detect *or* reject as brute,
> The only[?] breath of our nostrils the friend
> Unshackled the uses

398 *frag. P:* Precedents, printed so coldly [icy *frag. Q, MS 1*] aloof,   on high] aloof
frags. FF, GG, HH
399 *frags. P, Q, MS 1, frag. FF:* Challenge the tentatives hot.   hot to rebel] ever too
hot *frag. GG*
400–34 *not in frags. P, Q, MS 1, instead:*

> Whereof may [shall *frag. Q, MS 1*] a trifle of wisdom be spun,
> *frag. P:* Though better if battle were not.
> *frag. Q del.:* Though Better [*sic*] if battle were not
> *margin:* Whichever the winner

MS 1:

> [When *del.*] If the battle [is *del.*] grow earnest with shot
> For Youth needs a bleeding, & Age
> Dispossession [of *del.*] from one fixed seat.
>   No senile kings of a time past page,
>   Over men who the new day meet!

400–09 *not in frags. FF, GG, instead:*

frag. FF:

> Whereof may a trifle of wisdom be spun;
>   A trifle, & none can tell what.
> 'Tis the whirligig way to a road hard won.
>   Still, if Youth needs a bridle, & Age
>   Dispossession from one fixed seat,

frag. GG:

> A step in progression, a slip in relapse,
> Has come when their battle waxed earnest with shot;
> > And under a clouding perhaps,
> > We counted an inch hard won!
> Free of the tug of a blood run dry,
> A blood running fire, may our offspring run.

400–03 *not in frag. HH*
400 who] that *del. MS 2*
403 O loose] More free *del.* Loose *frag. HH*
404 flame] fire *frag. HH*
405 *not in frag. HH*
410 *frag. FF:* May the senile kings of a time past page;   Let] May *frag. GG*
411 *frag. FF:* And the merry young turbulents drunk of the morn;   generous] merry
young *frags. GG, HH*
412–13 *not in frags. FF, GG*
414 *frag. FF:* Together cast eye on a Roman street   *frag. GG:* Cast eye on the map
[of *del.*] where a Roman street
415–16 *not in frags. FF, GG*
416 a] the *del. MS 2*
417 To see across] Running rapid through *frag. FF;* Shoots rapid through *frag. GG*
418 *not in frag. FF*
419 *frag. FF:* The ruler's direct, from the head to the mark.
420 route] course *frag. FF*
421 the stride of his] his footing of *frag. FF*

After 421 frag. FF:

> Not [the *del.*] lumberer's logs nor [the *del.*] cataract's force,
> It is head wins [the crown *del.*] men in the wars we wage.

434 affairs to be] that things should be *del. MS 2*
435 *frag. P:* Since, however, thou'rt young take thy place in the fray   *frag. R, MS 1:*
Then thou being young take thy place in the fray   natural] rightful *frag. KK*
437 Our lullaby word] That lullaby name *frag. P;* Our lullaby name *frag. R*
438–73 *not in frags. P, R, instead:*

frag. R:

> For sloth to have infinite lease.
> Against it the young have a right to declaim;
> And the purseless are fitted to speak like the wind
> > Which informs them & whips them to flame.
> Should they make thee, as haply those forces behind
> Pressing urgent will do, the loud mouth of a sect,
> > Divert the decree in thy mind
> > For the opposite order's decease.   [*Cf. line 439*]
> > Believe it not recklessly wrong,
> > If foolishly stationed & decked.   10
> Perceive that we marched this way;

Variants in frag. P:

1 In a world where the questions increase!
2–4 *not in frag. P*
6 Pressing urgent will do] Will do
7 decree in] intent of
8 For] From
9 recklessly] utterly
10 If] Though
11 marched] grew *also frag. S*

438–41 *not in MS 1, instead lines 1–4 from 438–73 frag. R, continuing:*

Shall an evil digestion of poisonous facts,
O paunch of the world! be as Peace defined?
And O when the senile king attracts
To the backward march of the loyal kind,
Brain of the world! thou knowest what leads.
Stout thews they may have, brave watchwords, & tread   10
The barren way of our grain's decrease,
  Where Palsy nods over [the death *del.*] its bed.

But thou that art heir of the flowering seeds
Of the senile king in his fruitful prime,—
Having animal vigour to carry them on,
Despite him, & prove thee a truer to time,—
Test thy soul to perceive you share merits apiece;
In the strength of thee feel his bequest to his heirs;   [*Cf. line 453*]
  See that Time is both father & son.   [*Cf. line 457*]
  —This had I to say on the stairs;   20

17–20 frag. T:

17 Test thy soul to perceive] Acknowledge a leash *del.*
   Admit that *del.*
18 And he may have done the best work [of *del.*] in his day!
19 See that] Only *del.*

Between 19 and 20 del.: And to measure his instruments—vain?
To quadrate his instruments surely is vain?

20 This had I in passing to say, *del.:* This had I to say
as a hint of police. As it were a mild hint of police.   [*Cf. line 442*]

438–41 *not in frag. KK, instead:*

  The sluggard's long century lease.
It is good: then observe thine antagonist, con   [*Cf. line 449*]
His reasons for rocking the lullaby word.   [*line 450*]
You stand on a different stage of the stairs.   [*line 451*]
He fought certain battles; yon senile lord.   [*line 452*]
In the strength of thee, feel his bequest to his heirs.   [*line 453*]
Does it knock at thy head very hard if I say,   [*line 456*]
  That Time is both father & son?

439 *frag. S:*

> *Del.:* And should'st thou be a mouth of a sect,
> *Del.:* Believe not the order opposing *or* opposite order all wrong;
> Yet should they have made thee
> Contrive not the opposite order's decease:
> Believe it not utterly wrong.

442 And accept] As it were *MS 1*   word] hint *MS 1, frag. KK*
444 puffings] temptations *del. frag. T*
445 even as the merchant] eke with our merchanty *frag. T*
even as the] as with our *MS 1*
446–47 *frag. T:* A temperate gale for a haven seeks.
447 haven] a haven *MS 1*
449–68 *not in MS 1, instead:*

> And bear with me further: those forces behind,
> Should they, as they urge, make thee mouth of a sect,
> Divert the immediate decree in thy mind
>> For the opposite party's decease.   [*Cf. line 439*]
>> Suppose it not recklessly wrong,
>> If sillily stationed & decked.
> Advise thee [of *del.*] on methods for winning sweet peace
> In a blade's flash, which others more swiftly may try;
> And what of thee then, & thy cause? Reflect
> How chapters of History drape them in mists;   10
> How the bust of the Muse of men we spy,
> With an Elgin front as from caestus fists!
> That aspect she has; & not walking erect,
> With the showered [crimson *del.*] red spots on her peplum awry,
> When she takes up the march of her armies. Reflect,
> What a dreary see-saw we have made her sit,
> [Through chapter & chapter *del.*] With those weighty
>> blood-buckets! as though she pumped
> The daggered grey ghosts from [the *del.*] our pit;—
> The bags of vendetta eternally humped;
> And scarce better business had hers! But thou   20
>> Wilt help to her straighter advance,
>> Wilt put a new morn on her brow,
>> Wilt rescue from impious Chance
>> Her steps, nor consenting allow
> Dismemberment to them of old or hence.
>> As thou know'st the paternal of Now   [*Cf. line 459*]
>> Must father thy present tense,   [*Cf. line 460*]
> Be filial; not with satiric respect   [*Cf. line 463*]
>> Bow to thine elder, whose bow   [*Cf. line 466*]
> Is to backward likewise, for a thunderous back   30 [*Cf. line 467*]
>> Upon thee! but forgive him & thank.
> And thank the bright God of the pictures in shade,
> For this he presents of a low tide's blank—

449–68, line 12. *See Explanatory Notes.*

An intellect dead in a frame undecayed:
'Twixt the breadth of those shoulders a mud-desert's lack
Of the [animate life *del.*] wave or the wheat hailing Day. Be
    thou warned:
Give & take with the deeps: let it never be said
By thy sons, who are not of the hooved & horned:
'His mind it is moveless—a clot in the veins.
"'Tis moveless, or else were it maniac.'   40
    No, hold not thine scorned!

1–8 frag. T:

1 And bear with me further] And should they, which haply
2 Should they, as they urge] Pressing urgent will do
6 sillily] foolishly
7 Advise thee on methods for] And thy method of
8 which others more swiftly] another

    After 8:

    [Perceive *del.*] Reflect that we marched this way;
    Where bearing his banner full high,

458–64 frag. KK:

    There are giants to slay, & they call for their Jack.
    But cast off the cloud of thy senses & sense;   [*Cf. line 458*]
    [Know the paternal *del.*] Hard lesson!—discern of Now   [*Cf. line 459*]
    As the sire of thy present tense;   [*Cf. line 460*]

458 Tough] Hard *del. MS 2*
460 Then] sire *del. MS 2*
461–64 *not in frag. KK*
463 So] And *del. MS 2*
465–67 frag. KK:

    And be filial; nor with satiric respect,
      Bow to thine elder, whose bow
    Is backward too, for a thunderous back

467 as well] too[?] *del. MS 2*
468 his] that *del. MS 2*
469 strove] reached *MS 1*
470–73 *not in MS 1, frag. KK; MS 1 instead:* Was rebuilded of battle, of hopes & pains.
474 Yet thy] that *MS 1, frag. KK   frag. R:* [On *del.*] Where a road where thine
enemy once did work; *frag. P:* On a road where thine enemy once did [good *del.*] work;
frag. S: On a road both troubled & long,
476 and] with *MS 1   * reject] to reject *MS 1; frag. R:* Having gold to retain with the
dross to reject; *frags. S, P:* Having much to retain, with the much to reject,

After 476 frag. R: To cherish [more often than *del.*] as well as to slay.   *frags. P, S:*
To cherish [nourish *frag. S*] more often than slay.   *frag. S continues:*

    Ideas, my friend, that are not in song,
    Must be suited the wearers to fit
    [The wearers *del.*] like uniform clothes, or they kick.
    Mathematical tailors are wanting in wit
    When they rig present men to the cut of a stick,

On the *or* a model of future: & they are the bruised;
For men to their fashions allied will deem
    Unholy the new unused,
    Wherewith heads of demagogues teem.
And men of the fashion are multitudes: Power   10
    They are: 'tis a thing to conceive
    Before taking action an hour
    You advance but *or* only by their leave.
[Right *del.*] Hard Reason in [soft *del.*] gentle Persuasion arrayed
    Is woman & man to the mind
    Of manly & womanly made:
    And these appealing may find,
When working *or* moving as one they may find a door
    Thrown open for audience kind,
    Was barred to the demagogue's roar.

477 humour, not aiming to quash] cherish him rather than slay *MS 1*; humour him rather than [slay *del.*] quash *frag. KK*

478 Detest] Abhor *frags. P, U*

479 And] But *frags. P, U, MS 1*

After 479 frag. KK:

    Our game is the rock & the wave's wild wash,
    If we play impolitely. He hath a stout lair.
    He is tricksy with many a pit for the rash.

After 479 frag. U, MS 1: Even youth is half fashioned in clay. *MS 2:* Much bedded in clay.

480–88 *not in frag. P*

480–88 *and* 489–92 *reverse order frag. U*

480 brains] mind *frag. S*   full] stout *frag. S*

481 *frags. S, U:* Ere thou thunderest: also beware; *MS 1:* Ere thou thunderest cool to beware

483 *frag. S:* Where extremities fierily snare.   horrid] yonder *frag. U*

484 juice for] wine of *frag. S, U*   for] of *MS 1*

485 *frag. S:* [Which knows *del.*] Who know not a generous grape; *frag. U:* Which knows not a generous grape   a] more *MS 1*

486 Oft] How oft *frag. S*

487 *frags. S, U:* When the torrent it roused was a rape;   *MS 1:* When the cataract roused was a rape

488 a] the *frags. S, U, MS 1*

After 488 frag. S:

    Remember thy case & the devil thou wert:
    From another dark form of him hold thee deterred.
        And should the fount press for a spirit,
        Choose the discriminate word,
        Instead of the voluble spout:
        Whereby may come health from thy dose.
    The trick in reserve of the traitor within,
        Transfers our deeds done in the gross,
        To a spotted [old *del.*] fat world without,
        That we rage to make thinner than this,   10
        For appeasement of conscience, no doubt.

489 'Tis known how] For, mark you, *frag. P*; For mark how *frag. U, MS 1*

Between 490 and 491 frags. P, U:

> At a summons of armies [And shifty their issue: *frag. U*] foundations
> are wrecked;

frag. U: The land becomes ocean & gong,

491 *frags. P, U, V, W, X:* Obscured by the fumes of the pit. *MS 1:* And shifty their issue: foundations are split.   Shifty] And shifty *del. MS 2*

Between 491 and 492, MS 1:

> The land becomes ocean & gong,
> Obscured by the fumes of the crimson pit,

491–92 and 516 *Long after the preparation of these notes, an uncatalogued fragment appeared at Yale:*

> Obscured by the fumes of the pit,
> At a call to a game that our brutes best play
> Silence the old ding-dong
> Before the shrill jangle is loud,

492 *frag. U:* At [a *del.*] the call to a game that [our *del.*] brutes best play;   To the game] At a call to the game which *MS 1*; At a call to the game that *frags. V, W, X*
493–504 *not in MS 1, frags. V, W, X*
497 light] strike *del. MS 2*
499 croak] strike *del. MS 2*
502 write] pay *del. MS 2*

Before 505 frags. V, W: Question thee spouting [seething *W*] in throng   [*Cf. line 511*]
After 505 frags. V, W, X: And ask of thyself: This word I say,
> *frag. V:* The cause at my heart I would have prevail; *frags. W, X:* The cause I would have prevail; *frags. V, W:* Can it be shaped to song?; *frag. X:* Is it accepted of Song?   [*line 521*]

> *frag. V:*

> Then if, ay, the good answer, my friend,   [*Cf. line 555*]
> Not as Cybele's beast will thy head lash tail,   [*line 585*]
> With a zeal so lionly thermonous   [*Cf. line 586*]
> The musical God & the savage will seem
> Divided yet farther than hands that erect,
>   From the furious paws that rend.
> Then thou, who art hardly the stubbornest-necked,
>   To the musical God will bend,
> When he sings: Keep the young generation in hail,   [*Cf. line 591*]
>   Nor hand it a tumbled house,   [*Cf. line 592*]

506 hot mobs] the mob *frag. V*
508 will rank] accept *MS 1*
510 *MS 1:* Just humanly speckled, half enginery steam):
511 amid the] in *MS 1*
514 and roundelay] that *del.* which blesses a day *MS 1*
515 *MS 1:* [Without any *del.*] And that with no terminal wail?—
516 *MS 1:* No funeral's mournful ding-dong!—

517 This furious Yea] This word I say, *MS 1*
518 *not in MS 1*
519 In the] The *MS 1*
521 Can it be shaped to Song? *del. frag. X*

After 521 frag. W:

> 'Tis a test, & conclusive, I deem.
> It kisses or else it bites.

522–44 *not in frag. W*
522 *frag. X:* Does it sound into mind & ear
523 *frag. X:* Sane: has it orderly feet?; *MS 1:* Pure sane? has it orderly feet?

After 523 frag. X:

> 'Tis a test, & conclusive, I deem: [*Cf. line 534*]
> It kisses or mortally bites.—

524–25 *not in MS 1*
524–38 *not in frag. X*
526 *MS 1:* Rings it to melody sheer?   clear] sheer *del. MS 2*
527–33 *not in MS 1*
534 The test is] 'Tis a test, & *MS 1*
536–38 *not in MS 1*
539 And no] No *frag. X*
540 The] The [great *del.*] *MS 1*
541 a] a *del.* the *MS 1*
542 A law that] The law which *frag. X*
543 *frag. X:* That the passions no longer contend.—   Forbidding] In forbidding *MS 1*
544 *not in frag. X, MS 1*
545 *frag. W:* Then if, nay, the dark answer, my friend;   And if] If *frag. X, MS 1*
546 sharp] quick *frag. W*; alert *frag. X, MS 1*   ramping] rabble *frag. W*; rampant *frag. X*
547 hoar-old] ancient *frag. W, X*
549 those] the *frags. W, X, MS 1*   that] that *del.* who *frag. X*; who *MS 1*
550 For frenzy the] The *frag. W*
553–54 *not in frag. W*
553 to] on *MS 1*
554 Shorn] Cut *frag. X, MS 1*
555 *frag. W:* But thou, if thy answer be, ay,
558 tune] & tune *frag. W*
562 *frag. W:* For the Master of Measure is he from whose throne

After 562 frag. W: Hangs [the *del.*] balance of false & true.

563–71 *not in frag. W*
563 arms] bounds *frag. X, MS 1*
565 voice is a] echo is *frag. X, MS 1*
566 numbered long] long *frag. X, MS 1*

Lines associated with 567–92, frag. Y:

> The musical God & the savage will seem
> Divided more widely than hands that build,
> From the furious paws that rend.

569–84 *not in frag. Y*
569 *not in frag. X, MS 1*
572 pertain] belong *frag. X*
575–77 *not in frag. W*
580–82 *not in frag. W*
580 Over-run] Over-roll *frag. X, MS 1*
583 Yes, the] The *frag. W*; Yea, the *frag. X, MS 1*   off] from *del. frag. W*
584 furies] frenzies *frag. W*
584–621 *frag. S:*

> Let not *or* never the state of thy purse be clue
> *Del.:* To that of a head bearing word[?] for *nous.*
> To that of a head having fury to rend
> *Del.:* Join not the ranks of the therminous:
> *Del.:* With the tigerly zeal of the therminous
> With a zeal too tigerly therminous   [*Cf. line 586*]
> Keep the Young Generation in view: [*Cf. line 591*]
> Nor hand it a tumbled house.   [*Cf. line 592*]
> So, good: & away on thy mission start,
> And accept no pennies for preachments, friend.
> A warning, they call thee: contend
> That victim was rather thy part.
> The task of thy leisure, the word of thy heart,   10
>   It must be to serve *or* hit a right end.
> Proclaim to the world [that *del.*] which loves not vice,
> While virtue is likewise unbeloved,
> That thou art the Pagan sacrifice
> We offered to Custom's Gods: proclaim
>   How now on our Young is proved
>   The rite once having for name
> Massilia's; where, when raged *or* settled a pest   [*Cf. lines 614–21*]
> A poor volunteer of [their *del.*] the town
> Perchance from the bagnios loosed   20
> Was taken [& plumped *del.*] stuffed with its best,
> To propitiate Deity's frown.

Between 584 and 585, frag. X: In the musical God's fair beam,

586 *frags. Y, W:* In a zeal so lionly *thermonous; frag. X:* Thermonous, lionly ther-
monous,
587 far fled] far *del.* flown *frag. Y*   Attis] Atys *MS 1*
588–99 *not in frag. Y, instead:*

> Then thou less frenziedly willed   [*Cf. line 584*]
> To the musical God [will? *del.*] mayest bend,
> When he of the lustrous brows
> Outlasting all lights; on his throne
>   Overlooking all seas; supreme
> Above mortal excesses, the bliss & the bale,
> Shall sing the one couplet for men at their strife:

590 cry] voice *frag. X, MS 1*

584–621, line 2. *See Explanatory Notes.*

591 generations] generation *frags. S, Y, X, MS 1*   hail] view *frag. S*
592 And bequeath them no] Nor hand it a *frags. S, V*; And hand it no *frags. Y, X, MS 1*

After 592 frag. Y:

> Lo, there is the word of the active life.
> Perchance, O my purseless! my personal theme
> Rightly should hold thee

593 sacred] sacredest *MS 1*
594 *not in frags. LL, MM, MS 1*
596 In vision] In the vision *MS 1*
598–613 *not in MS 1*
598–605 *not in frags. LL, MM*
599 With] Follow her with *del. MS 2*
607 desires] demands *frags. LL, MM*
608–13 *not in frag. MM*
609 *frag. LL:* The plural about us, we have her spur.   warm round] about *del. MS 2*
612 letters] features[?] *del. MS 2*

614 *frag. Z:*

> A whole year through was he Strasburg-Goosed.
> And when (for the wretch was a volunteer:
> He bargained & counted the odds)
> When in plumpness he had no peer,
> Processionate rounds, with my lord in the van,
> (Sat trolling from pricks & prods)
> To the high cliff [over *del.* topping *del.*] heading the harbour mole
> Arrived, & delivered him up to the priests,
> Who took the poor wheezy & lob-livered man,
> For the Grandfinale of all his feasts,   10
> Anointed him out of the incense bowl;
> He bobbing inebriate nods;
> Then toppled him over, for food of the [waves *del.*] wave,
> A mouthful to terrible gods.
> So was it with thee: let thy purse be a grave,
> [And arise *del.*] Arise from it, dowered to speak in soul,
> And a young generation save.

614 *MS 1:* And as for thy case, O [friend, I needs *del.*] my friend, one must think
As for] For *del.* As to *frag. MM*

Between 615 and 616, frag. MM del.: For the carnival

616–19 *MS 1:*

> For a carnival season, knew worse, though he
> [Had alternatives *del.*] Alternatives had, making choice;
> And for thee, by our ruling, none were:
> It was write ere thou camest to a voice.

617 *frag. MM:*

> Knew worse in the end; though he
> Was offered alternative choice:

618 For] And for *frag. MM*

620–21 *not in MS 1, instead:*

> Since we danced thee not over the brink,
> So to finish thy goose-liver year,
> Parade thee [our *del.*] that sacrifice, be thou [our *del.*] that Plague,

622 *MS 1:* With the tongue or the weapon of ink.

Between 621 and 622 frag. MM: A sacrifice, not a decoy.

622–24 *frag. AA:*

> Insist upon the great expiation in ink,
> Our journalists harry to fish in the vague,
> And offer their catches, the not too pink,

622 thy lean as] the tongue or *frag. MM*

Before 623 frag. MM:

> Attack as murderous, stoutly devote   [*Cf. line 625*]
> Thy fragments that curse of the Gods to destroy.

623–29 *not in frag. MM, instead:*

> Though they deal thee the whip or contemptuous whiff,
>   Persist in thy wakeful note:
>   Taken thee[?] they cannot refuse
> *margin:* Persistence will rival Samsonian thews

623 Though they] Let them *MS 1*

After 624, frag. AA:

> Unto Parliaments angrily; only for peace,
> (Be thou plague enough, plague enough!)
> We shall see a law pitch'd to its mangle below,
> As the wretch in the colony, issue of Greece.
>   [Then *del.*] Now adieu. Thou hast heard me assert
>   That our blood is a tuneable stuff;
> Over-active, a danger; more deathly insert.
> Its hue of right health is the rose without crape.
> [Away with *del.*] Then, away with the pallid repression of Woe!
> And live, but not lusting to live, nor agape   10
> For condolences, cherishings, tea-tear & sniff.
> Life gives not the whole, not the tenderer half,
> Of the kind legend's dues to its marrowbones boy
> Repentant on knee-caps: it points to the cliff:
> To the cliff or this harness; & yet it means Joy,
> Although Wisdom, the reading of Life, must be rough,
> And a Sermon thy share of the Scriptural calf,   [*Cf. line 640*]
> Thy father confessor much wanting in heart,
>   O son of the silver spoon!
>   In the golden cradle nursed!   20

625–26 *not in MS 1, instead:*

> Let them angrily threaten the cliff;
> But hold thou to thy task, nor admit a rebuff;

627–28 *reverse order MS 1*
628 our] The *MS 1*   in] & *del. MS 1*

629–38 *not in MS 1, instead:*

> And (be thou but plague enough, plague enough!)
>   Only for peace, blessed peace,
>   At last will their toughest of tough
> Disintegrate down to the final mite!
> They will pitch their plump law for its mangle below,
> As the wretch in the colony, issue of Greece,
> Whom the priests beheld smashed, with approving phlegm.
>
>   For there, spite of usage, they know
>   That law is the savage in them:
> A glutton, a [drunkard *del.*] toper; a driver insane,   10
> Overwheeling [the *del.*] humaner; composed to destroy;
>   A sign of their wilderness plain,
> If we look beneath surface, where wild weeds grow.
>   This world, my poor marrowbones boy,
> Repentant on knee-caps!—& not meeting half

629–37 *not in frag. MM, instead:*

> It is thy expiation, my Prodigal boy!
> Thy straight second step in the fleshly spurned.
> And thy first has been exercise in the polite,   [*Cf. line 629*]

629 Yet] But *frag. MM*   with] & *frag. MM*
635 poor] my poor *del. MS 2*
637 forgiveness is] & forgiveness *del. MS 2*
638 *frag. MM:* At a strain trying patience: denied thee thy half
639 blessing] feast *MS 1, frag. MM;* [the *del.*] young swineherd *MS 1*

Lines associated with 640, frag. BB,

> Hopefully so! Meanwhile,
> Dost thou solicit advice,
> I counsel thee cling to thy theme:
> The Purse of the aureate pile,
> Bequeathed to their Young; & the price
> They pay for the *or* an impish bequest:
> With the whole soul oft for [the *del.*] their sacrifice,
>   Instead of a saveable half:
>   Here in this Mammonite Isle,
>   Where, to give the lean dinner a zest,   10
> Jeers are the service to brighten *or* that brightens the board,
> Sermons our joints of the Scriptural calf,   [*Cf. line 640*]
>   *Del.:* And the special injunction, to hoard,
>   *Del.:* Wags loose for legitimate vice,
>   *Del.:* Gluttony, pride, & the rest.

Variants in frag. CC, beginning with the same lines:

4 aureate] golden
5 their] our
6 the *or* an] that
7 their] that
9 Here] There *del.*   this] our[?] *del.*
10 Where to give the repentant *or* Where to give the lean dinner a zest   *Del.:*
And make more impressive the board,
11 Jeers are [the *del.*] our welcoming banquet prepared,
12 our] the *del.*
    While the low levelled[?] wretch by his legasy [*sic*] snored[?],
    Is raised for a Warning to them at the board[.]

640 slice] share *frag. DD, MS 1, frag. MM*

After 640 frag. DD:

[And nothing *del.*] Nothing other to fill thee before well earned;—
This world of its congregate Many in loom,
Has now got it a conscience: there hast thou thy joy,
Thy feasting to-come: & forgive [a gloom *del.*] it some   *[Cf. line 676]*
At proposals to pull down instead of support.
It best loves its pillars: no wonder that curst
The shorn little Samson—create to construct—
We deem, & can think that thy motive was first
A bitter inside of the acorny sort.
New temples we need; let the pillars be plucked.   10
There is but one God, be it understood.

And O thou son of the silvery spoon!
    In the golden cradle nursed!
Our God in the conscience of Many to feel,   *[Cf. line 665]*
    Is to feel deep to Earth at her heart.   *[Cf. line 666]*
    Perceive, & thou feelest: then brood: *
Then give into harness thy best & thy worst;   *[Cf. line 669]*
Forth on the trot of thy servitude start;   *[Cf. line 670]*
Delicious desire for a sustenance meal,
Thy mind & thy body will know full soon;   20
The wheaten of Wisdom accept in the rough
To be nourished as none

641–68 not in MS 1, instead:

Nothing other to fill thee, before well earned;—
This world of its congregate Many in loom
From the threading together [of *del.*] for colours to match,
From the rubbing together of needs, from the signs
Of a likeness unseen at [the *del.*] their bowier[?] bloom,
An egg of a conscience has got, & will hatch,
With encouragement; fear not; there's feasting to come.   *[Cf. line 641]*
One hears a faint crow of the cock of [the *del.*] a brood,
    As down the new shafting of mines   *[line 649]*
    A shout from the metally gnome.   10 *[Cf. line 650]*

And meanwhile it will pelt thee, & kick thee, & cuff:
'Tis the family greeting [for *del.*] to novel designs;
A temporal show of antagonist mood.
Only be thou but plague enough, plague enough,
If the world cannot crush us, we're fruitfully cursed.
Persistence will equal Samsonian thews;
And the shorn, & the dwarf, [may *del.*] pull pillars to dust,
Ay, the temples of marble as well as of wood,
When the God has gone out of them. [These *del.*] Them we disuse,
In these days, if we see their gold vessels take rust.   20
The temples are even as the billows that burst
There is but one God, be it understood.

That God in the conscience of Many to feel   [*Cf. line 665*]
    Is to feel deep to Earth at her heart.   [*Cf. line 666*]
    Perceive, & thou feelest: then brood.

644 gives] gave *del. MS 2*
646 wonders] marvels *MS 2*
652 With the] For a *del. MS 2*
654 gates] doors[?] *del. MS 2*
655 For the] See them[?] for *del.* We shall see *del. MS 2*
669 Yield] Then give *MS 1*
670 Away] And forth *MS 1*
671 *MS 1:* Delicious desire for a sustenance meal.
672–75 *not in MS 1*
677 To a mind and a] The mind & the *MS 1*
678 *MS 1:* [Both *del.*] Well mated, embracing, will know full soon:
679 Earth's] Our[?] *del. MS 1*   dispensed] accept *MS 1*

680–82 *not in MS 1, instead:*

    To be nourished as none of the silver spoon,
    Unto whom the world's pertliest Plenitudes kneel.

683 And] Now *MS 1*
685–86 *not in MS 1*

Before 686 frag. EE: I remember that I have stood,

686 No] And no *frag. EE*
687 I looked on] Observing *frag. EE*
688 By] At *del. frag. EE*   wayside] roadside *del. MS 1*
690 *end of MS 1, torn*

691–92 *not in frag. EE, instead:* Take him into thy thought,
    uncatalogued frag. Yale:

    Food for me, food: such as first
    Drew my soul to things lowly for food.

NIGHT OF FROST IN MAY

MSS: Huntington HM6761, *title:* The Poets' Night. *MS 1, fair copy corrected; MS 2, fair copy corrected; MS 3, fair copy corrected; frag. A, lines 1–6 + 6; frag. B, on MS 1,*

3 verso, draft for A lines 7–8; frag. C, lines 1–6 + 4; frag. D, lines 1–6 + 8; frag. E, lines 46–48 + 1.

Part ii of The Poets' Night, *70 lines, not printed. See after* Night of Frost in May: *frag. F, lines 23–32; frag. G, 24–50; frag. H, lines 43–46; frag. I, lines 43–48; frag. J, lines 51–66; frag. K, lines 65–68; frag. L, lines 67–69.*

2 A] The *MS 1, MS 2; frags. A, D*
4 close] vast *or* close *MS 1*

Between 6 and 7, frag. A:

    1 A serious breath of young surprise
    2 Went over grass blades watching skies
    3 The desert brilliance had around,
    4 Thin semblance of a web of rose,
    5 Arrested chill; and [nearer *del.*] near to ground,
    6 A harder colour through it froze.

    1–2 frag. B:

        Along grey meadow-grasses crept
        A seriousness, that faced to sky   [*Cf. lines 77–78*]
        Expectant

        Del.: Young meadow-grasses look the coat
            Of serious

        A serious breath went over meads,
        Grey meadow-grasses, stiffened weeds.

    1–2 *not in other drafts*
    3 *MS 1 del.:* Around the desert brilliance heaped[?]
    3–6 *after 14 MS 1*
    3 around] overhead *frags. C, D, MS 3*
    4 Thin semblance of] Afar & dim *or* Thin semblance of *MS 1*

    4 frag. C:

        A glimmer of a furnace-[hue *del.*] red,
        For sharpness, midway under [shed *del.*] threw,
        Round earth was mist on metal-blue.

    MS 2:

        A glimmer of a furnace-hue,
        For sharpness, [round below it *del.*] midway under
        Del.: Round earth was haze in metal blue.

8 jewelled] brilliant *MS 1*
16 severing] coming *MSS 1, 2*; neighbour- *MS 3*
17 sound] sound *del.* stir *MSS 1, 2, 3*
18 a warble] low chuckles *MSS 1, 2, 3*
20 Near by the] Beside its *MS 1*; Beside the *MSS 2, 3*
23 not] nor *MS 1*
26 with] through *MSS 1, 2*
28 In throb] With beat *MSS 1, 2*; In beat *MS 3*
29 at] on *MS 1, 2*
32 ruffle] stir it *del. MS 1*

35–36 *not in MSS, instead MS 3:*

  1 And higher now does one ascend,
  2 As in the blissful garden home;
  3 And thick below the warbles blend,
  4 As were they piling honeycomb:
  5 A measured tumult of quick leaps
  6 Emulous, urged from under deeps.
  7 Where swift the bubble-water wound,
  8 To pillars luminous in sound;
  9 [As out of *del.*] Out of the breast of earth to sky;   *[Cf. line 45]*
10 The voice of earth & sky; astrain
11 For pain of joy, for joy in pain: *frag. E*
12 And they were secret, they were nigh. *frag. E*   *[Cf. line 46]*
13 A hand the magic could disperse; *frag. E*   *[Cf. line 47]*
14 The magic held my universe. *frag. E*   *[Cf. line 48]*
    1–4 *not in MSS 1, 2*
  6 from under] by deeper *del. MS 1*
  7 swift] thick *MSS 1, 2*   bubble-water] water-gurgle *del. MS 1*
  9 Out of the] As out of *MSS 1, 2*
11–14 *frag. E*
11 in] of *MS 1*

After 14 margin MS 1:

    They poured by fits for me to heed;
    The many [to excel *del.*] swarm with young him strove
    In one to make their passion bleed.
    Excelling, yet one song they wove.

38 Our] The *MS 1*
41 Or now a legion] It seemed the countless *MS 1*; It seemed a thousand *MSS 2, 3*
43 In] For *MSS 1, 2, 3*   high] there *MSS 1, 2, 3*
45–48 *See passage following 34.*
49–76 *not in MSS, except:*
                 70 *cf. Part ii. 53*   And] When *MSS 1, 2, 3*
77–78 *See between 6 and 7, frag. B.*
79–82 *See Part ii, 59–62*
80 On leaf and meadow-herb] On wood & meadow, & *MS 3; Part ii, 60*
82 spinning] growing *MS 3; Part ii, 62*

Part ii of The Poets' Night, *MS 3:*

    Now when that night, the very queen
    Of earthly nights, remembered shone,
    The tower of beauty it had been
    Discarded hues too much my own:
    Nor suffered human heart to stress
    The song with throbs: aside it flung

1 Now] But *MS 1*   that] the *MS 2*
4 Discarded] Forbade all *del.* Disclaimed all *MS 1*
5 human heart] me the song *MS 1*
6 The song with] With human *MS 1*

Our anguish & our happiness,
For simple glory seen & sung.
I had it pure of our strong wine,
Which flushes to dissolve the pearl.   10
Imagination thus was mine,
Beyond emotion's drowning whirl.
I have it as it shone unstained;
Because devoutly straight, where curved
The lureful fancies, I observed,
And my beguiling sprite contained.

So that fair night the years prolong.
I people it with my most dear,
Our nightingales of English song;
The truthful, forceful, fervent, clear;   20
Whose notes in ear are day to sight:
With him on Canterbury's way:
With him who harped 'On such a night';
With him who tuned 'the bloomy spray':
And welcome he who gave to ear
'A damsel with a dulcimer';
And he of 'Faëry lands forlorn',
The voice beneath the hovering shroud;
Hear him who piped the 'beauty born
Of murmuring sound'; & hear the Cloud   30
Songfully fly: hear him who roused
To chant those Lotos-Eaters drowsed;

10 Which] Which *or* That *MS 1*
After 12 MSS 1, 2:
   So knew I what the soul of things,
   Conceived in soul, [of fadeless *del. MS 1*] recurrent brings:
   MS 1:
   How fleetingness, where'er[?] is cast
   [Full heart *del.*] Warm thought remains a throbbing Past
13 *not in MS 1; inserted after 17 MS 2*
14–16 *not in MS 1*
14 Because] For that *del. MS 2*
17 *See Explanatory Notes.*
18 I] To *del.* And *MS 1*
19 Our] My *MSS 1, 2*
20 The] Our *MS 2*
21 day] day *or* dawn *MS 1*   dawn *MS 2*
22 on] on *or* down *MS 1*
22–39 *See Explanatory Notes.*
23 harped] sang *MS 1*
25–26 *not in MS 1*
26 A] The *frag. F*
27 And he] With him *MS 1*
28 The voice beneath the] Whose voice was under his [early *del.*] *MS 1*
29 Hear him] With him *MS 1;* And he *frag. F*
30 hear] who *MS 1*
31 Songfully fly] Sent singing on *MS 1;* [Swim songful on *del.*] Songful swim on *frag. F*
hear] with *MS 1;* he *del. frag. F*

>Who passed into the Brook, & rhymes
>Our tongue with limpid water-chimes.
>
>My palace of the night they fill;
>Not jealously the gates to new
>Forbidding: emulous, not chill.
>He with the feet of Hermes, who
>Sang Atalanta, enters there.
>No gate rebuffs: if true the song,   40
>Can never be too close a throng
>To rival light, to quicken air.
>And more, for making many one,
>>Shall follow as a river's run.
>>Or in our isle, or where their seed
>>Beyond Atlantic nature read,
>>The Maybirds of our English tongue
>>Will leave no coming Age unsung.

After 32 MS 1:

>Since youth was mine for haloeing May,
>Since that frost hush of silver day

   MS 2:

>[but that night is theirs *margin*]
>Since youth was mine to halo May;
>Since that frost-hush of silver day,   [*Cf. line 51*]
>When serious breath [the *del.*] our woodland held,   [*Cf. line 52*]
>And hoar with crust the field-flower *or* cowslip swelled,   [*Cf. line 53*]
>
>I have had many *or* foreign loves, in truth;
>[But *del.*] Yet faithful I to the loves of youth.
>How the white mother-muteness pressed   [*Cf. line 59*]
>On tree & grass-blade, [until *del.*] and how shook,   [*Cf. line 60*]
>Nigh speech of mouth, [sparkling *del.*] the sparkle-crest   [*Cf. line 61*]
>Seen growing on the bracken-crook.   [*Cf. line 62*]
>Until our border woodland rang,
>Again I feel, &, like it, hang
>Attentive while my chosen pour   [*Cf. line 65*]
>Their song through memory young in hoar.   [*Cf. line 66*]

33–34 *not in MSS 1, 2; frag. G*
35 the] pure *MS 2*
37 emulous, not chill] & they *or* these enter still *MS 1*; these enter still *MS 2*
39 Sang Atalanta] The *Atalanta* sang *MSS 1, 2*   enters] is *MS 1, 2*
39 *See Explanatory Notes.*
40 No gate rebuffs] Wide are the doors *del.* My doors are wide *MS 1*
42 to quicken] enliven *del. MS 1*
43–66 *not in MS 1*
43 *MS 2:* For they, the many being one,
44 Shall follow] Are taken *MS 2*; Will follow *frags. G, H*; Are following *frag. I*
After 44 MS 2:

>And make the musically dumb
>Of their long issue sweet to come,
>Expected, half evoked are sent,
>By shining eyes intelligent.

43–50 *not in MS 2*
45–46 *not in frags. G, H, I*
47 The] These *frags. G, H, I*
48 *frag. G:* Will leave no English Age unsung. *frag. H:* No English Age will leave unsung.
coming] future *del. frag. I*

Happy the youthful dowered to hear,
Note they but well the far & near.   50

Since that frost-hush of [silver *del.*] night made day,
When serious breath our woodland held,
And hoar with crust the cowslip swelled,
To me they are a household May:
My boyhood glistens in the scene
Of soaring thoughts on breathing keen;
[And *del.*] In the sheer beauty that may claim
Be natal home for these[?] I name.
How the white mother-muteness pressed
On wood & meadow, & how shook,   60
Nigh speech of mouth, the sparkle-crest
Seen growing on the bracken-crook.
But would I now revive it, nought
Of fancy gives it me in thought
I feel while my dear chosen pour
Their song through memory young in hoar.
There, too, a rillet's halting drip,
An owl's halloo, a leaf on tree,
That curls or lets the crystal slip,
Are homely aids to melody.   70

FORESIGHT AND PATIENCE

Copy-text: A Reading of Life (*Constable, May 1901*). *Previously printed in the* National Review 23 (*April 1894*). *MSS:* Huntington. *MS 1, HM7464, fair copy of an early draft lacking the last leaf or leaves; MS 2, HM7463, fair copy, corrected, of the* National Review *version;* Yale, *clipping from the* National Review *corrected for* A Reading of Life. *As will be evident, MS 1 was cut drastically before the poem was printed in the* National Review. *Variants in MS 2 from the printed text start with line 17 of the text.*

NIGHT OF FROST IN MAY

After 48 frag. I:

Or in our isle or, it may be,
Beyond Atlantic

49 youthful dowered] young who stand *frag. G*
51–66 *See after 32, MS 2*
51 night made] silver *frag. J*
55 *frag. J:* I have them there, & all the scene
56 on] in *frag. J*
57–58 *not in frag. J*
63–64 *not in MSS 1, 2; frag. J*
65–66 *not in MSS 1, 2 but in frags. J, K*
67 *MS 1:* And even a rillet's thinnest fall,   halting drip] limping fall *frag. K*; thinnest fall *frag. L;* thinnest drip *MS 2*
68 on] from *del. MS 1*
69 *MS 1:* That crisps in curl, is welcome; all
70 *MS 1:* Are welcome, make they melody. *MS 2:* Have welcome, join they melody
After this line in MS 3, GM indicated by signing his name that the poem was finished.

Before line 1:

     MS 1:

In The Woods.

———

Foresight and Patience.

———

Foresight & her blind sister Patience walk
These woods at night, & I have heard them talk.

—How different was it ere we stepped as one,
The prouder unrestrained, the meek outrun!

—But now earth sings her quiet rounding air
Of lights that change & seasons that repair.

—O you, [what *del.*] who in the timeful soil take root,
Your name is wisdom, rich you bear the fruit!

—But you, beloved leading me, have eyes
For fruits more golden than in present skies.   10

—Not that fair faith which [quenches *del.*] bridles overhaste,
Have I, who straightway seeing burn to taste.

—What strength we have to cleave our way you give,
And yours the only life the soul can live.

—Too much I trust, from reading in the dark,
That we may fly as arrows to our mark.

—We scarce should move nor one of us beat wing
Save for the harvest-tidings that you bring.

—The wrecks are of my sowing, & I store
Tears, with no other harvest on the floor.   20

—The promise of the vision which endures
For me through darkness day by day is yours.

They passed, I followed. Then, on a deep sigh,
The brighter figure heard I make reply.

—Some sure To-Be is planted on my brow,   [*Cf. line 29*]
But you, blind sister, spell for us the How.   [*Cf. line 30*]
I scribble wildly where a far blank page
Invites me, reckless of my anchorage,
And in strange havens find unhomely rest,
While here my little daisy, with her breast   30 [*Cf. line 31*]
To the bright sun laid open, reads him through,
Is nearer him than eagles up the blue.   [*Cf. line 32*]
Eye him they can, they are not in his heart,
As she who sleeps with him & wakes, apart,
Yet closely knit: the milk of the sweet hour
Unto her withering cherishes my flower.
She has the secret never fieriest reach   [*Cf. line 33*]
Of brain shall master till they hear her teach.   [*Cf. line 34*]

—Ah, liker to the clod flaked by the plough,   [*Cf. line 35*]
My lesson when I have you not as now.   40 [*Cf. line 36*]
The quiet creatures who escape mishap,   [*Cf. line 37*]
Seem pictures of the things that speed green sap; [*Cf. line 38*]
Which have their struggles too; 'tis not all sloth;
But human means another kind of growth,
Wrestlings & bitter stranglings done within
Silently, rarely ceasing, till we win
The face we show to men, not quite our own,
Yet of self-conquest some true frontal shown
For their inscription of our titles. Who
Most human is, I know not, of us two: 50
I know the one diviner, & my life
Revives with your heroic shout to strife,
Since, as the running blood, the constant breath,
The rolling day, instruct us, truce is death.
Of earth we come, & sweet of earth may be;   [*Cf. line 51*]
Foul carrion if very earth are we.   [*Cf. line 52*]
And I would rather feel the world in arms   [*Cf. line 59*]
Than stagnant while the sensual piper charms [*Cf. line 60*]
Each drowsy malady & coiling vice   [*Cf. line 61*]
With dreams of ease whereof the soul pays price. 60 [*Cf. line 62*]
Our banner flying speaks of youthful wealth,
And battle in a world like ours is health,
Truth's brawny brother, oft persuading truth,
For service wrought, to lend her eyes to youth.
I have no heart for peace while evil breeds,   [*Cf. line 63*]
While error governs, none: and must the seeds [*Cf. line 64*]
You sow, you that for long have reaped disdain, [*Cf. line 65*]
Lie barren on the threshold of the brain   [*Cf. line 66*]
Till they are springs of blood & tongues of flame,
Look farther, dearest, not forget my name,   70

—In solitariness I pace this land.

—Not while you have the linking of my hand,
To feed my soul with our inheritance.

—I look [upon *del.*] down on a world where men advance [*Cf. line 72*]
No step, but vilely circle when much stirred   [*Cf. line 73*]
Like dead things on dead water: for a word   [*Cf. line 74*]
Prompting their appetites they bravely march,   [*Cf. line 75*]
As to band-music under victory's arch.   [*Cf. line 76*]
More comfort might one have in gazing back.

—And even while you spoke your grasp grew slack. 80
But good is the gaze rearward for a term;   [*Cf. line 79*]
Far back to the first twisting of the worm.   [*Cf. line 80*]
Thence look this way: from space to space revealed,
See how [where[?] *del.*] that bigger worm, the slaughter-field,
Shows dyed in Moloch the poor human beast,
Gored for his tyrant & white auguring priest,
Those prickers of the herd on either side,
Both claiming God as [warrior[?] *del.*] weapon of their pride.

The bloody way of saying yes & no,   [*Cf. line 82*]
Prevails when dark the realm where we two grow: 90
Yet [when[?] *del.*] if they hail the viewless for mere weight
To mend their scales, they prove a clearer state,
And you were wakened then: perchance you blinked
Painfully, still you saw; while I, unlinked,
Knew not the name's red dawn on humankind,
As densely to the spirit was I blind:
No home had I save in the narrow round
['Midst *del.*] 'Mid famished sweaters delving niggard ground.

1 Sprung] Born *del. MS 2*
17 headlong world's imperious] world's imperious headlong *del. MS 2*
21 ff. [*Foresight*] *and* [*Patience*] *were added by GMT in his edition of the* Poetical Works *and are retained for clarity.*
30 must I] I must *del. MS 2*
38 pure] the *del. MS 2*
49 'tis little] it is not *del. MS 2*

Between 62 and 63 MS 2, NR:

> Their banner flying sings of generous wealth;
> 'Tis their fresh Youth, that offers life for health:—
> Truth's brawny brother! he persuading Truth,
> For service done, to lend her eyes to Youth.

73 A doubtful foot] Their doubtful feet *del. MS 2*
75 hungers, and] appetites *del. MS 2*
79 down rearward] regard[?] them *del. MS 2*
80 twistings] twisting *MS 2*
90 learning is] trick is now *MS 1*
92 casts the burden of] ends the strife, accepts *MS 1*
93 *MS 1:* This Age has challenged earth.

>   —And heaven.
>   —[Not *del.*] Nor less

94–99 *MS 1:*

> The lower deep. It craves not Happiness,   [*Cf. line 94*]
> And there's a mighty step; for that same gift,
> Extended to the greedy cry we lift,
> Tells of some wailful weaker ones bereft.
> [We cannot have it but by *del.*] We have it only by a conscious theft.
> Brave is this Age where long the word will rust   [*Cf. line 97*]
> Which ever as we read it answers lust,   [*Cf. line 98*]
> Till from the warmth of many hearts that beat   [*Cf. line 99*]

100 temperate] measured[?] *del. MS 1*   common] human *MS 1*
101 The] Of *del. MS 2*
103–06 *MS 1:*

> Roars bigger now than in the ages past.
> The shadow of destruction on the vast
> Enlarges with each feeble light upraised.
> The world smokes ominously, itself amazed

108 hot] black *MS 1*
109 Run piling, for one] Are piled, wait but the *MS 1*
112 *MS 1:* Feeling its doom, still, like a sinner's guilt,   the] from *del. MS 2*

Between 112 and 113 MS 1:

> It breeds the furious engines multiplied;
> Shot swifter, like the sinner on his slide.

113 *MS 1:* Yea, daily we may hear it shriek aloud,   *MS 2:* Pules through his godless
enginry shrill loud,
114 If] When *MS 1*   a] each *MS 1*
116 souls] hearts *MS 1*
117–18 *not in MS 1*
119 spur] use *MS 1*
121 men who ply their wits] they who train their young *del.* they who press their wits
MS 1

Between 122 and 123 MS 1:

> —'Tis pity of me bids you read the sign
> That haunts my footsteps, with these eyes of mine;
> Not with my spirit reading all you see

123–26 *MS 1:*

> Distant, well-knowing dire Necessity
> Is mother of our wisdom, & her cries
> Of labour a good omen to the wise,

127 among] amid *MS 1*   which] that *MS 1*
131–34 *not in MS 1*
135–36 *MS 1:*

> And Lucifer's prime agents; but some spur
> Sharp do men need to combat Lucifer!

Between 136 and 137 MS 1:

> The one in his contented oneness curled
> Feels little of the oneness of the world:
> A common peril from an open source
> Mankind require to match their force with force.

138 O'ershadowing men] Assailing them *MS 1*
140 Now must the brother] But in themselves the *MS 1*
142 *MS 1:* Must have at, conquering lest destruction come.
143 men see] they spy *MS 1*
146 Fruitfuller for them when] But when they touch their foe *MS 1*
147 warrior] soldier- *MS 1*
150 *MS 1:* Which bids faith tremble on their strongest rock.
152 Frail men have challenged] Men who have dared *del. MS 1*
153 matched] set *MS 1*
155 control] subdue *MS 1*
156 *MS 1:* What force is of the earth, & under too,
157 granite] strongest *MS 1;* firmest *MS 2;*   now] & *MS 1*
158 the heavens] high heaven *MS 1*

160 Through fear] And thus *del. MS 1*
161 read] see *MS 1*
163 *MS 1 del.:* How shall we waken them that have no bent
167 They have much fear of] Nothing fear they but *MS 1*
168 these they *MS 1*   unnumbered] countless *MS 1*

Between 168 and 169 after space MS 1:—

> —Fain would you prick my nature, sister, fain,
> Swift arrow, would you goad the lumbering wain.

169 and did not faint] if I could fly *del. MS 1*
170 *MS 1 del.* The future I would paint[?] imply
171 will learn to quake] our fight will shake *MS 1*
172 Now] And *MS 1*
173 denser] deader *MS 1*
174 Could I but] If I could *MS 1*

Between 174 and 175 MS 1:

> —The toiler toils as ever: to one end,
> The central, their prime starting-point, they tend:
> And this they sometimes gain because their aim
> Is constant: they've no other: small the blame!
>
> —That language formerly effective rang:
> It has of irony the tenuous twang:
> Such as the hard-yoked sphere the upper casts,
> And strangely with its object it contrasts.
> Why on a mark so prominent discharge
> A shaft so piercing, when it bears no targe?   10
> To hit the shame of [seeking *del.*] hunting daily food,
> Let ridicule be keener or more rude.
>
> —Now have I roused my sister, now I scan
> The special advocate & partizan.

Between 174 and 175 MS 2, NR; corrected NR del.:
> NR:
>
> —Your toilers toil as ever: to one end:
> The central, their prime starting-point, they tend.
>
> —That language formerly effective rang.
> In irony I like more tenuous twang.

176 their] a *del. MS 1*
177 for] to *MS 1*
178 too] that's *MS 1*
179 Yet] But *MS 1*; Yea *MS 2*   defined] discerned *MS 1*
180 *MS 1:* They cast me out, as one unholy spurned,
181 in] with *MS 1*

Between 182 and 183 MS 1:

> That means a novel lightning in the mind
> The question whether heavenly designed
> A fate that frowns to watch the heavens revolve:
> Desire to change it cooling on resolve.

And that means growth: some passion must be spent
To strike the light from dungeon discontent;
Some turmoil of a soil unploughed, unhoed;
But light has reached them and they see the road.
That means the wholesome running of [the *del*.] our blood
Through the world's body: & to know it good,   10
Is the world's wisdom. So the world will feel
The giant which it is from head to heel:
One form, one heart, one brain, all soundly braced;
And not the sprawling dolt we have seen disgraced
For centuries, part courtier, part clown;
Wailing to heaven of [its *del*.] his ill renown;
Assassin now, now penitent in distress
Of conscience glimmering out of drunkenness:
Mainly a dreamer, to propitiate
The merely dreamed of. Shelterless I wait,   20
Dislodged from my old humble cottage-nook,
Where Time had never feature save the clock,
Nor song but of the clock that went its round
And told the end of life [with *del*.] in end of sound.

186 How close the dangers] Of the close danger *MS 1*
188 which folds the] & that is *MS 1*
189 *MS 1:* And love of earth is love of labour, love

Between 190 and 191 MS 1:

    —One must be you, sweet sister, almost more,
      Thus tangled of some issue to feel sure.

    —No lamp of sureness do my feelings trim,
      I have no deeper secret than to swim.
      Because it is my nature on all seas
      To strive to keep my life, I swim on these.

    —But [what *del*.] here's an Age to praise! It blocks my view.
      I have to sleep & dream ere I renew

191 *MS 1:* My vision of a brighter. Faithless, mean,
192 Encased] Wallowing *MS 1*

193–94 *MS 1:*

    Contemptuous of the Good, it swells on Doubt,
    Darkens its eyes to better see without:

Between 194 and 195 MS 2, NR; corrected NR del.:

    NR:

    Is prompt to chase the scut of mad surmise;
    While, [Though *MS 2*] vowed to the [the base *MS 2*] credulity of eyes,
    In mind 'tis furnished with the boring mole's;
    Has windy yearnings, which [that *MS 2*] it calls the soul's.

195 if] do *MS 2*   face] frame *MS 1*; shape *MS 2*
196 my] the *MS 1, MS 2*

197 your] the *del. MS 1*
199 as] for *MS 1*
202 Time's earliest] earth's earlier *MS 1*
203 *MS 1:* Perchance, & only in some spirit of flame
204 At intervals, in proof] Through slime, their sons divine *MS 1*   in proof] to tell
MS 2
208 the] earth's *MS 1*

Instead of 209–12 MS 1:

> O gallant is the Age, I cry again:
> It dares the leap in the abyss of pain
> To heal the wound of quaking ground agape.
> The hero spirit of this Age takes shape
> From its first dawning when that leap he dared.
> The soul of him unto my soul is bared
> Still heading: & no oracle require
> His followers whom devotedness can fire,
> For surety that some wholeness shall result.
>
> —Since dynamite supplants the catapult: 10
> To sit & hatch explosives makes us whole
> By scattering the flesh to free the soul:
> And all should soar rejoicing [with *del.*] as the larks
> To praise the power of atoms armed with sparks.
> Now may Democracy till set of sun
> Laud triumphs of the many o'er the one,
> While anxious earth sees possible her stare
> At one that blows the many into air.
> 'Tis hopeful! And to this we have nigh come.
> The signs are thickening.   20
>
> —No, speak. But own the Age is faithless, rank,
> And dotes for vision on its dense fog-bank.
> Reckless of star above, of rock beneath,
> Through tortuous channels of most rending teeth,
> It drives with press of steam, all unillumed,
> Unpiloted, uncaptained, chartless, doomed.
>
> —Where of the Faithful Ages find you writ
> That they were brighter than half hypocrite?
> The fairest Ages out of dust you rake
> Would greet you with derision or the stake.   30
> But this accepts you, though it listens less
> Than hums your aria for its witchingness.
>
> —Part 'tis a dragon breathing fire for roods,
> And partly 'tis a thing of Nile's mud-broods,
> And wholly a great glutton gorging facts,
> Whose peptic wrenched the maudlin tear exacts.
> More sweet my fitful infant voice of yore,
> Compared with song of mine the moderns roar,
> Provoking all the Manichaean mob
> To discord chorus, growl & jeer & sob.   40

—Let me be silent.
                    —Can you verily hope
Of times when lead the moles, & seërs grope:
These vowed to excavations in the pits,
Those heading by the grace of reckless wits?

Between 208 and 209 MS 2, NR: corrected NR del.:

   NR:

—I see it as a [shape *del. MS 2*] motley form, that plays
God's Jester snared to thread a Pagan maze.
Or, if you will, the limping Momus crowned
With nettle-bells in Christian burial-ground.

—All faces under sun have shadow-sides;
In the full shade more equal hue abides,
A poet says. The thing it is, you sum
When History writes, with all its actors dumb.
Her fairest Age that out of Dust [you *del. MS 2*] we rake,
Would greet you with derision or the stake;   10
But this accepts you, though [it listens *del. MS 2*] men listen less
Than [hums *del. MS 2*] hum your aria for its witchingness;
And [holds *del. MS 2*] hold the admonitions it contains
As inharmonious bass to heavenly strains;
Or of some songful child a vixen nurse,
They hear with languid senses, not perverse.

Between 212 and 213 MS 2, NR; corrected NR del.:

   NR:

The weak are strengthened and the torpid stir.

—Bubbles the mud, and blossoms top the burr!
Now giants are the atoms [Now atomies are giants *MS 2*]
            armed with sparks   [*Cf. MS 1 line 366*]
Aspiring hedgehogs, suicidal larks.
Show us the stale ways quitted for the fresh;
The voluble are lords, [a king is *del.* a tyrant *del. MS 2*]
            hailed King is Flesh.
Specific Doctors drumming in his place,
A banished Devil views with sly grimace;
Spies the grain meagre, plenteous heap the chaff;
Immense machinery rouse the stomach-laugh;   10
Obedient echoes leap to bear reply,
And tainted of their burden whining die.
By gastric ardours goaded past his needs,
The shark for Pleasure shivers while [whilst *MS 2*] he feeds.
Perdition has him in his appetites;
The nostrum-mongers in his recreant frights.
Whate'er his act,—Silenus, scourging friar,—
Instant the secondary hounds the prior.

Between 208 and 209 NR line 3: See Explanatory Notes.
Between 212 and 213 NR line 17: See Explanatory Notes.

He hugs the hair-shirt and he shuns a crease;
Tempts him the starveling, tortures him obese;   20
Insanely a lost sanity pursues;
'Twixt interdict and drug Hygeia woos;
Enjoyment claims as creditor, else thief;
Drinks impious wine, despatches haunted beef!
What conscience the tormented wretch meanwhile
Allies to Life, behold in jets of bile!
But can my thoughtful sister verily hope
Of days when moles are guides and seers [*seërs MS 2*] grope?—

These crooked to excavations in the pits,
Those heading by the grace of eyeless wits:
Around them shades of History cast before
From quills that men must fence or kiss the floor!

—Beneath the surface your ephemerals reave,
Enough for me to feel my people heave.
Heaved they eruptive at volcano-pitch,
Less shamed were earth [Earth *MS 2*] than
       by those wallowing rich!

213 About] Among *MS 1*   Highlands] mountains *MS 1*
214 stream] river *MS 1*   paternal] fruitful *MS 1*
215 *MS 1:* And where august the historic stream he drives
216 An] Some *MS 1*   revives] survives *MS 1*

Instead of 217–18 MS 1:

In grand procession & with priestly calm
He sweeps by Thebes, & mirrors pillar, palm,
On his mild breast, green leaf & ruin-limb:
He is the plenteous crop, the ancient hymn.

219 time] day *MS 1*
222 He is the vast Insensate] He is the flood that wantonly *del.* The vast insensate is he
MS 1

Between 224 and 225 MS 1:

And he is famine, torture, tears & death:
Yet is his overflow his people's breath.

225 *MS 1:* [For *del.*] O they who with barbarian force begin
227 will the current] their progressive *MS 1*
228 Reveal till they know] Reveals, till they have *MS 1*
230 clash] sink *MS 1*

Instead of 231–32 MS 1:

Then seek they with a woe-enkindled soul,
Their God in them, the lighted mind's control.

233 Yet] But *MS 1*
234 up] on *MS 1*
235 he feed] *MS 1, MS 2, NR. corr. errata, de L 1911;* be fed *1901, de L*
236 troublous] tameless *MS 1*

237 *MS 1:*—And so—& it is truth!—your people thrive:
239 erewhile when I gloried] once when I was happy *MS 1*
241 lamp] light *MS 1*
242 prey of its robber] choked dead of vengeful *MS 1*
243 structures built] lights we raise *MS 1*
246 *MS 1:* On their wide flats, & rash or sluggish drift,
247 privations and spilt] their perils & their *MS 1*
248 *MS 1:* Will issue reason armed to bank the flood!
249 release] in peace *MS 1*
250 *MS 1:* The shaping of them in this huge increase!
251 scene] sight *MS 1*
255 *MS 1:* Then fling up heels (no other course remains),
256 Dive down the fumy] And dive down the bright *MS 1*
257 *not in MS 1*
258 They seem: they pass!] The tribe departs *MS 1*

After 258 MS 1:

> —Had I my sister's reading heart as she
> With her blind eyes the spirit of my look!

> —My finger spells you as a blindman's book.   *end of MS 1*

Between 264 and 265 MS 2, NR; corrected NR del.:

> *NR:*

> 'Tis ours to reach, to touch, but is it feigned
> Our own—[within *del. MS 2*] as in our shifty breasts contained—
> Surer than drunken helmsman will at [it *MS 2*] wreck!
> Soured on our firmament we spy a fleck!

271–72 *not in MS 2*
276 their] the *MS 2*

QUEEN ZULEIMA

After line 14 Berg *MS continues:*

> A bride, a bride! a [new-made Queen *del.*] Queen new made,
> *Del.:* Half dazzled by the regal sheen;
> By the crown'd splendour half-betray'd

> But in my glory all forewise
> Tho' keenly edg'd with young surprise:

> Forewise, forewise, and unforewarn'd:—
> Such creatures by the fates are scorn'd.

> And such was I so tracing lines,
> And reading men by mystic signs;

> And in my science overbold,
> And taking often dross for gold;   10

> And spurning gold for very dross;
> Nor mine, nor mine alone, the loss.

But age has skill'd me, and this hand
Is with a deeper insight *or* cunning scann'd.

'Tis well! but that it throbs too much,   [*line 15*]
As if 'twere in [its *del.*] a mother's touch.   [*Cf. line 16*]

Thy mother, tell me! is she far?   [*line 17*]
And art thou, youth, her wandering star?   [*line 18*]

How could she part with thee! how part
From what is more than half her heart!   20

[And *del.*] For thou art fair, and firm of limb,
And much remindest me of him;

Of him, the King, my husband: apt
In blandishment, in war adept.

To see him sit his desert mare,
One would have thought an Angel there.

And in my arms he was no less,
With his [still-thirsting rich *del.*] insatiate caress.

Like him thou seemest, calm above
A world, and a wild woman's love.   30

Thy forehead prompt to beam or frown,
Knits too, as if it dream'd a crown.

I know the dream of such a weight;
It has no sleep, it spurns a *or* has no mate;

It is alone, alone, alone;
Yea, lonelier than this flesh and bone;

This body that so long has leant
Watching the desert from this tent;

And telling wizard truths to those
Who throng'd at daylight's starry close.   40

Thou too, art doing more than dream;
This blood is not a quiet stream.

It may be love—but such a power
Is in thee an unbudded flower.

It may be hate—and yet, methinks,
Thy daily life more nobly drinks:

Drinks from a different morning spring,
And spreads a more majestic wing.

Like yon sole eagle flying thro'
The splendour of the burning blue;   50

And from that dumb, great, friendless height,
Make all subject to his flight;

Del.: The forest haunt, and rustic roofs,
The shady palms, the shining roofs,
The seas, the sands, the crawling hoofs.

If this be so, alack! alack,
Thou dost but follow in my track;

A track that can no quidance lend,
And preach *or* give no warning, but its end.

Ambition soaring over all,
Is human only in its fall: 60

And what a bubbling water-line
I see behind that life of mine!

Yet if thy course can pause *or* learn, and fear,
It is enough thou know'st me here.

O rather, youth, go wed a maid,
A desert [maid *del.*] girl; care not for grade:

Thy beauty, and thy bearing brief,
Will net some daughter of a chief;

Pure, moonlike, modest; like the light
Of almond blossoms; [waxing white *del.*] sweet to sight.   70

Straight as a palm; as tall and fine:
Rich, rich with pastures and with kine.

Dark-eyed, large-eyed, soft-lidded—grave;
In motion like a moonlight wave:

Full of untongued, untaught desires,
Del.: Falls to her cheek in sudden fires
Betrayed in sudden blushing fires

Two spouting wells her breasts—go—go—
She waits thee, flushing bliss and woe.

—No! such is not thy purpose now,
Well I divine by hand and brow: 80

Or is my science overbold?
Do I belie the hand I hold?

Bibliography

ENGLISH EDITIONS OF MEREDITH'S POEMS*

Poems: / By / George Meredith. / [Quotation from "Orion" by R. H. Horne] / London: / John W. Parker and Son, / West Strand. / [1851]
pp. viii + 160.

Modern Love / and / Poems of the English Roadside, / with / Poems and Ballads. / By / George Meredith, / Author of 'The Shaving of Shagpat,' 'The Ordeal of Richard / Feverel,' etc. / London: / Chapman & Hall, 193, Piccadilly. / 1862. /
pp. viii + 216.

Poems and Lyrics / of the Joy of Earth / By / George Meredith / London / Macmillan and Co. / 1883 /
pp. xii + 184.

   Second Edition, 1883.
   Third Edition, 1894.
   Fourth Edition, 1895.

Ballads and Poems / of / Tragic Life / By / George Meredith / London / Macmillan and Co. / and New York / 1887 / *All rights reserved* /
pp. viii + 160.

   Second Edition, 1894.
   Third Edition, 1897.

A Reading of Earth / By / George Meredith / London / Macmillan and Co. / and New York / 1888 / *All rights reserved* /
pp. viii + 138.

   Second Edition, 1895.

Jump to Glory Jane. / By George Meredith. / Edited and Arranged / by Harry Quilter. With Forty- / Four De- / signs in- / vented, / drawn, and Written / By Lawrence Housman. / Swan, / Sonnen- / schein & Co. / Paternoster / Square, London. / 1892 /
pp. 64; full-page illustrations 8.

Modern Love / A Reprint / To which is added / The Sage Enamoured and the /

_____
* For full bibliographical descriptions, see MBF. All volumes octavo in various sizes.

Honest Lady / By / George Meredith / London / Macmillan and Co. / and New York / 1892 / *All rights reserved* /
pp. viii + 108.
Second Edition, 1894, pp. xii + 92.

Poems / The Empty Purse / With Odes to the Comic Spirit / To Youth in Memory / And Verses / By / George Meredith / London / Macmillan and Co. / 1892 /
pp. viii + 136.

Odes / in Contribution / to the Song / of French / History / By / George Meredith / Westminster / Archibald Constable and Co / 2 Whitehall Gardens / 1898 /
pp. viii + 94.

Selected Poems / By / George Meredith / Westminster / Archibald Constable & Co. / 3 Whitehall Gardens / 1897
pp. 245.

"Scattered Poems" in The Works Of / George Meredith / Volume XXXI / Westminster / Archibald Constable and Co. / 2 Whitehall Gardens / 1898 / pp. 267–290. Volume III of *Poems* in the Edition de Luxe.

A Reading of Life / with other Poems / By George Meredith / Westminster / Archibald Constable & Co Ltd / 2 Whitehall Gardens / 1901 /
pp. viii + 128.

The British Academy / The Tercentenary / Of / Milton's Birth / Inaugural Meeting / At the Theatre / Burlington Gardens / Tuesday, December 8, 1908 / (The Eve of the Tercentenary) / Lines By / Mr. George Meredith, O.M., / Written in honour of the occasion /
pp. 4.

Twenty Poems / By / George Meredith / London / 1909 /
pp. viii + 44.
From *Household Words*, [ed. B. W. Matz].

Last Poems / By / George Meredith / London / Constable & Company Ltd. / 10 Orange Street, Leicester Square / 1909 /
pp. 64.
[ed. William Maxse Meredith.]

The Poetical Works / Of / George Meredith / With Some Notes By / G. M. Trevelyan / Author of / 'The Philosophy and Poetry of George Meredith' / London / Constable and Company Ltd / 1912 /
pp. xx + 624.

Index of Titles and First Lines

Poem titles appear in italic type, first lines in roman type. Poems entitled *Song* are listed under their first lines.

Index of Names